ON AWAKENING AND I

On Awakening and Remembering

To Know Is To Be

Mark Perry

Preface by
Huston Smith

FONS VITAE

THE WISDOM FOUNDATION SERIES

Fons Vitae
49 Mockingbird Valley Drive
Louisville, KY 40207-1366
email: Grayh101@aol.com
website: www.fonsvitae.com

Dedicated to

the memory of

Frithjof Schuon

(1907–1998)

in gratitude for

his sacra doctrina

and the shining

example of his life.

Pure Knowledge is the natural form of the Self.

Patanjala Yoga-Sutra

The true lover of knowledge is always striving after being — that is his nature.

Plato

The Heart-Intellect, the Christ in us, is not only light or discernment but also warmth and bliss and thus 'love'; the Light becomes 'warm' to the degree that it becomes our own being.

Frithjof Schuon

The soul is all that it knows.

Aristotle

To be awake is to be alive. I have never yet met a man who was quite awake. How could I have looked him in the face?

Thoreau

Amor intellegere est.

Medieval Sentence

A Sannyasin (a wandering Hindu monk), when walking forwards or backwards, has a perfect comprehension of what he is doing; whether gazing or beholding fixedly (an object), *he understands perfectly what he is doing; whether raising his arm or allowing it to fall, he understands perfectly what he is doing; when carrying his cape, his clothing, or his food bowl, he understands perfectly what he is doing. . . . Whether walking, or remaining seated, while sleeping or waking, while talking or remaining silent, he understands perfectly what he is doing.*

Dighanikaya Sutra

I sleep but my heart waketh.

Song of Solomon 5:2

CONTENTS

PREFACE

THE REASON FOR the crisis in which the world presently finds itself in is lodged in something deeper than the way the world is organized politically and economically. Increasingly as the world westernizes, both the rich and the poorer nations, though still different in many ways, are going through a single, common crisis. To reflect on that crisis should be the starting point of every attempt to think through to a better alternative.

Somewhere there is a basic tension which has produced the spiritual malaise of modern civilization. That malaise is one of loss: the loss of metaphysical certainties regarding higher transcendence, and the accompanying loss of the experience of transcendence. It is strange but ultimately quite logical. As soon as human beings consider themselves the source of the highest meaning in the world and the measure of everything, the world begins to lose its human dimension and gets out of hand.

We are going through a great departure from God which has no parallel in history. If things do not change, we are headed for the first atheistic civilization in history. Any change for the better must start with a change in history's directions, and this can only be accomplished by changing human consciousness. This is where Mark Perry's book enters, for I have encountered few other books that speak more directly and helpfully to the changed outlook that we so desperately need. This is a profound book. Few writings in recent years have done as much to further—in ways that makes life feel different—my understanding of the

11

ultimate nature of things. Perry's thoughts are as advanced as one will find anywhere—this is clearly the higher mathematics of the human spirit.

* * * * *

A LARGE PART of me would like to leave the matter there, but the reader is entitled to a glimpse of why I think well of the book, so I will give one example of the way its author's insights have helped my thinking. No philosophical problem has been more debated than whether truth is absolute or relative, so I was as surprised as I was exhilarated to find the second chapter of this book throwing new light on the issue. Perry's treatment of the issue is abstract, but what he says bears pointedly on one of the liveliest controversies of our day, the liberal/conservative standoff; so I shall cast my short summary in that context. Perry himself gets into the political aspects of the controversy—among other things, this is a book in political philosophy—but I will limit myself to the theological side of the debate.

On the whole, religious conservatives regard the Truth by which they live as absolute and therefore appropriately capitalized, whereas liberals are more tuned to its relativities—the way different points of view splinter the single, all-encompassing Truth into myriad lower case truths. Both positions harbor pitfalls.

The danger that stalks Truth is fanaticism. Because Truth is toweringly important and brooks no alternatives, conservatives are tempted to transgress their neighbors' autonomy and force Truth down their throats. Liberals face the opposite problem, for the danger that haunts relativism is nihilism. Carried to its logical extreme, relativism dead-ends in the view that nothing is better than anything else, which is an unlivable philosophy.

Each side also has its virtues. The virtues of relativism is tolerance—respecting the right of others to live their own lives—while the virtue of Truth is the energy and spiritual wholeness it brings to those who are convinced that the universe is on their side. Liberals are at their worst in not recognizing how much an Absolute of this sort can contribute to life. It can "pull God down" into the human heart and elevate it in the way the "skyhooks" of construction derricks raise steel girders. It gets drunkards out of gutters.

The two preceding paragraphs show liberals as better than conservatives at recognizing the dangers of fanaticism and the virtues of tolerance, and conservatives as better than liberals at seeing the dangers of nihilism and the virtues of certainty. Only one more step needs to be added.

The strength of liberals are horizontal for pertaining to human relationships which are between equals, whereas those of conservatives are vertical in centering on the God/man relationship. From the religious point of view, this makes the issues that conservatives prioritize more important than the ones that liberals are exercised about, for God is more important than human beings, if for no other reason than that he created them. In passing, this difference in ways of prioritizing issues is one of the reasons I class myself as a Traditionalist. To claim that ontological issues are more important than social ones does not lessen the importance of the latter. It is to argue that justice will not be achieved, nor oppression reduced, if their ontological foundations are lost sight of. "Seek ye first the kingdom. . . ."

This condensed reformulation does not begin to do justice to the rich nuances of Perry's treatment of absolutism and relativism, but I hope it persuades the reader that he holds in his hands one of the all-too-rare phenomena today, a genuinely thought-provoking book.

* * * * *

PREFACE

WHEN, IN A gesture that proved to be momentous, an anonymous child handed Saint Augustine an open Bible, all she said was, "Take, read." It risks hyperbole to draw the comparison, but that is all that I really want to say as I hand the reader this extraordinary book.

Huston Smith
Berkeley
January 4th, 1996

14

FOREWORD

To love with the privilege of the immeasurable mind.

Emerson

For Emerson, this American Platonist stranded in the Puritan backwaters of a small New England town, all of life's wager amounted to this: will we or not avail ourselves of the intellectual prerogatives bequeathed to us by virtue of our human birth, will we learn to use our reason to apprehend the Truth, to become conscious of *what is*? For such a mind, nature could be read as a "sublime alphabet," as the sensible trace of Godhead in the world, a perishable reflection of the "ideas" (which are really sacred archetypes) existing in the One Universal Mind: "Nature is but an image or imitation of wisdom," this democratic aristocrat declared. Whereas, in man, the trace of the Divine is best found in Reason, the instrument of the Divine Mind, of which our thoughts are as a glow that can "mix with Deity," becoming one with the all-pervading consciousness of pure Being unpolluted with separateness.

Emerson sought this noetic communion at the "vanishing point of materiality," understanding that "my own mind is the direct revelation which I have from God" and, consequently, that true worship was tantamount to true cognition, to profound awareness, because men themselves, indeed the very dust of worlds speckling the starry void, are but the ever-differentiated contents of Divine Consciousness: God's sublime thinking and dreaming occasion streams of creation that vanish the moment He ceases to "think" them.

If one were to be asked what is the essential quality of being, one would not hesitate to say that it is conscious-ness—the miracle of consciousness—which, for man, is encased, imprisoned, or obscured in a flesh and blood body. And even if, in man or in beast, this consciousness is subservient to sensation, it ceases not thereby to be, in its essential nature, consciousness, namely something lumi-nous, fluid, and free and, because of these, essentially indi-visible very much as light is and which therefore cannot be enclosed.[1] One will note that of all the substances our sens-es can register, light is the only one that cannot be divided without being thereby eliminated.[2]

Material science registers this consciousness in its mode as energy or vibration or resonance, but, for obvious episte-mological reasons, cannot trace its luminous source and therefore is inclined to misunderstand or ignore this igneous essence. And human beings themselves are natu-rally inclined to ignore that they are like luminous sparks spun off from a hidden supernal fire, as the Upanishads teach, or that they are ensouled by a secret light whose glow cannot be extinguished even while it can be darkened by the materiality of existence on earth. Indeed, the impression

---

1. Hence Emerson: "Wisdom consists in keeping the soul fluent, resisting petrifaction." (Recollections taken from an article by Annie Adams Fields, *Mr. Emerson in the Lecture Room*, that first appeared in the *Atlantic Monthly* LI, June 1883, and therefore not necessarily the philoso-pher's exact words.)

2. One could say the same thing about sound with the major differ-ence, however, that unlike light, sound is capable of being modulated from euphony to cacophony. Moreover, it is not self-incipient and, fur-thermore, depends on the nature of the vessel in which it resonates.

16

man on earth has of the cosmos is that of tiny oases of light enshrouded by an endless sea of darkness. In practical terms, it may be difficult to imagine that once the sun has set, all is not just darkness, but that each creature harbors an inner fire—Meister Eckhart's *Fünklein* or "spark"—whose light source, though invisible to the organic eye, is no less bright than the most radiant sun itself. And the trace of this light, invisible in its point of inception, is polarized into consciousness and energy—though, strictly speaking, energy is but an existential echo of what in its origin is pure spirit[3] which, from shadowing to shadowing, from adumbration to adumbration (if we follow the emanationist doctrine of Plotinus) shades itself ultimately into existence as we know it—"Trailing clouds of glory do we come," rhapsodized Wordsworth, "from God, who is our home . . ." (*Intimations of Immortality*).

If the above sequence requires an act of faith on the part of the reader to grasp, in other words if the evidence of what is being proposed is not readily evident, then this may be a testament to how far we as a race have fallen prey to the totalitarian thralldom of matter and of sense experience as opposed to visionary experience which, in some distant golden age—mythical now in its remoteness—must have been the human norm.

In the wake of the foregoing, it must be stated then that this book—or perhaps any book—would not be necessary

---

3. For example, Meister Eckhart holds that the divine essence is *intelligere*, or understanding, a doctrine that supports the intimate connection between soul and divinity, adding that God is *esse*—or being—only secondarily so. The Thomist doctrine, on the other hand, departs from the idea that God's essence is *esse*, a viewpoint that Eckhart rallied to later in his life, which, to our mind indicates the interchangeability of the two terms. In reality, they are indivisibly one in the transcendent quintessence where being is perfect intelligence just as intelligence is perfect being.

were it not for what can only be termed a collective degeneration of consciousness which, incidentally, has in recent times been paralleled by a phenomenal development of scientific inquiry, as well as of literacy: we know more and more, some wit commented, about less and less. But to quote Emerson, "when [we] can read God directly, the hour is too precious to be wasted in other men's transcripts of their readings" (*The American Scholar*). Nonetheless, when compared to unreality, books, like intellectual windows, can provide a preliminary approach to reality and, in many instances, are nowadays the last bastions of ancient wisdom. To lose them would be tantamount to losing our memory and hence our sense of origin and of identity. This is to say that if—in an age where once vibrant ancient traditions are gathering dust in these morgues called museums—books are important, even vital, it is less because of the presumed advantages of literacy[4] over, let us say, primitivism, than because there is no alternative bridge, at least intellectually, for a civilization once its moorings in the eternal have been operatively severed. The human norm which, in the collective sense of the term, is no longer "normal," is to be so bound with its heavenly substance as to be able to dispense with the mental abstraction bookish literacy provides. Put differently, books supervene only once this bond has been cut in some decisive degree and remoteness from origin comes to predominate over direct communion, or once ontological forgetfulness comes, with an ever accelerating downward momentum, to predominate over ontological remembrance. And this is the central advantage that oral traditions have over literary ones,

---

4. The term "lettered" could be substituted for that of "literacy" since to equate literacy merely with the ability to read and write unfairly excludes millennial oral cultures whose literary eloquence is beyond dispute.

namely the preservation of the original word for, strange as it may seem, once words are set down on paper, the reality they connote begs to be forgotten because it loses its practical urgency. More on this in the Chapter "Thought Foul By Thought Made Fair".

As a writer, at this point, we are faced with a dilemma: either we will be seen as cutting the branch we are sitting on by criticizing books in the name of contemplation, whose ultimate effectiveness presupposes dispensing with the mental crutches that books provide, or we will be seen as presuming to be able to write about the truth whose essence, if it can only be grasped contemplatively, must need elude all verbal formulation. The only way to resolve such an antinomy is to recognize the provisory nature of books, somewhat like accepting the need for stepping stones which are forgotten once the goal is reached. In other words, if books cannot embody reality, in the substantial sense of the word, they can nonetheless serve as indispensable pointers and even provide, if they spark vital intuition, a glimpse into or a foretaste of reality. Moreover, in philosophical terms, one would say that Socrates' awareness that he *knows* that he does *not know* requires a preliminary willingness to examine the premises of this ignorance to say nothing of the fact that, as he pointedly reminds us, the unexamined life is not worth living. Inevitably, this examination entails a mental (verbal) effort, whence the necessity of reflection as a prelude to contemplation. In this respect, for us whose substance is spun out of forgetfulness, thinking acquires a paramount importance which books are well suited to serve.

Another, and serious, objection that might be raised is that, as Plato maintains, the one who is *in earnest* will not write, but teach. In other words, if we understand correctly the drift of Plato's words, a man who knows the truth will not want to risk debasing it in print but will step forth and show it by his living example[5] so as to protect it from becoming the toy of rational speculations because, as it happens all too often—and the history of modern philosophy is there to prove it[6]—the truth once it is set in literary form can be divorced from its existential substratum or fall prey to sophists and to casuistry. Our lame response to this is that in a literary age one must fight fire with fire.[7] In other terms, one must avail oneself of the means of the epoch one lives in while endeavoring to turn, in a kind of intellectual judo, the force of the problem back onto itself. All will not be lost if one makes an honest attempt to use language as it was meant to be, that is to say if one uses words to serve reality and not to re-define reality along arbitrary, relativistic, or nihilistic lines.

And this is why we believe that allowing usage (which stems from being while in turn conditioning it) to define language, as is the case in English, instead of language defining being, as is the case in the ancient oral traditions and as was until recently the case in the scriptural traditions, is the surest way to become alienated from one's traditional roots in the deepest, most ontological sense of the term. Therefore, whenever possible, or whenever it is not too outlandish, we will use an older term over a newer one, and we will try to use words according to their etymology hoping, thereby, not to contribute to what we believe is the intellectual free-fall of our civilization—a fall which starts with a betrayal of lan-

---

5. This is what Emerson means when he declares that "character is higher than intellect."

6. Much of latter day philosophy is nothing but renegade cogitation, often premised on little more than metaphysical impotence (Kierkegaard, Kant), dyspepsia (Montaigne), or a full stomach (Hume). In other words, the starting point is not reality but the subject investigating it. And this is a formula for incurable ignorance.

7. Again, Emerson: "Books are the best of things, well used; abused, among the worst."

guage as seen, for instance, in the falsification of the terms "reality" and "idealism" which will be discussed in the "Introduction."[8] And this is why also we choose to use what is called the "royal we" in preference over the more individualistic "I" because our intention, insofar as possible, is not to speak in our name but in that of tradition, much as medieval artists never signed their work because the notion of individualism had no currency before the birth of the Prometheanism re-introduced by the Renaissance. And this is not to contradict Emerson's doctrine of self-reliance when he declares that "Whoso would be a man must be a nonconformist," because the true individual is also the paragon for all the others, and not some eccentric who takes pride in being different—the suicidal cult of difference for difference's sake which has had such a devastating influence on, among other things, the arts. The relationship between the collectivity and the individual will be examined in the Chapter "The Crook and the Flail."[9]

---

8. This can be seen, for instance, in the "chatty" modern translations of the Bible, intended to replace that of the solemnity of the King James' English. In an age of casualness, where names like William become Bill, Lawrence Larry, Robert Bob, it becomes, by contrast, stilted or pretentious to insist on the "thou" of the past. However, if compromise cannot be avoided, on pains of snootiness or incomprehension, it is honorable not to surrender too readily to the tendency towards the trivialization of man—instead of "Lawrence of Arabia," try "Larry of Arabia"—which is characteristic of the so-called "information age," and to preserve a dignity of thought and of deed that reflects the nobility of man's fundamental destiny as *pontifex* or bridge between heaven and earth. This trivialization goes hand in hand with an ever increasing acceleration of work or agitation of life, whereas dignity is consistent with a sense of contemplative slowness. Haste is of the devil, the ancients asserted although, from an altogether different point of view now, one must make haste for the Kingdom of Heaven.

9. In any case, Emerson's doctrine of "self-reliance" is premised on man's reliance on God: "Self-reliance, the height and perfection of man, is reliance on God." So, it is not a question of lawless individualism.

Finally, when writing, one must also be mindful that conceptualization should lead to realization and not to more conceptualization, otherwise words and thoughts become locks and chains. Rumi makes God say in a poem: "What matter words to me? I need an ardent heart; let the hearts become inflamed with love and occupy thyself neither with thoughts nor their expression." That may be the ultimate goal, but this injunction—which is less an indictment of words than a call for sincerity—is not sufficient in itself to guard against subjectivity. The soul, unless it is ripe, requires preliminary intellectual tutoring so as to be led to the very highest, the supreme object its awareness is capable of knowing. Ideally, words and concepts should serve as kindling material for the soul, that is to say, the mind should fuse with being when it is properly awakened—without forgetting, of course, that "in the beginning was the Word."

On the other hand, to be is to know, in the sense that being, when it is noble or all that it should be is the guarantee of the efficacy of knowledge. And this is why nobility of soul, as well as kindness, is a pre-condition of knowledge, at least when it is a question of the truth and of the sacramental nature of reality which if majestic is also unspeakably tender. The divine mysteries, however, do not yield their secrets to idle curiosity: as is stated in the *Puranas*, "Reading, for a man devoid of prior understanding, is like a blind man's looking in the mirror" (*Garuda Purana*, XVI:82). And this understanding—whose essence mingles with the divine intellect—lies in man's immortal substance. To awaken it through the midwifery of words will then be the object of these pages.

Before closing, a couple of quick remarks about this book's style. We use the term "man" in the most generic sense to refer to both man and woman. It is simply impossible to say "man and woman" or "he and she" each and every time; this would clutter the text. As for the new pronoun "he/she", this is a grotesque barbarism which denatures both sexes and is typical of the attempt to deny the positive meaning of cosmic polarities. It is also typical of the incomprehension of the qualitative differentiation between man and woman. Not knowing what their natural role is, they compete on all planes which is an augury—rather late at that—of the disintegration of a civilization. Briefly: man, by his revelational virility, is associated with the pole outwardness (in the best sense of the term) and woman, by her mystery, with inwardness. Thus there can be no intrinsic competition. Moreover, her inwardness and mystery are hardly limitations. Ask the great poets! Unfortunately, in a secular world, and also in a brutally dogmatic religious society, woman as symbol of the celestial is socially eclipsed or even crushed in importance, whence her present-day revolt which also coincides with the end of a cycle of creation since it can only occur as a result of man's forfeiting his role as center and as embodiment of the pole truth—woman representing, in that respect, the pole being. However, the priority accorded "man" in language is meant only in reference to his role as outwardness and therefore does not entail a fundamental superiority.

Finally, to write a book is to address an audience in a given epoch and cultural setting with its own unique problems. In an age of relativism, of psychologism, of individualism, of secularism and the like, indeed, in an age unlike any previous one in history in its modernity and alienation from a human norm premised on means of transport no faster than that of a horse, there are new questions the answers to which might have been taken for granted in other times. If the breakdown of an old-world order opens new pathways to hope and idealism, and a renewal of sorts, it also draws in its generally destructive

23

wake a new skepticism and cynicism which must be taken into account. Hence, this book's attempt to buttress every argument with what may strike some readers as an excess of references.[10] However, different readers have different needs. For those who are convinced of the celestial, this book may belabor the obvious. For those who will challenge every assertion made in these pages, probably no proof will be sufficient. For those who want to believe but are troubled by the social turbulence of our times, there is enough material here to hone their insight and to recall that, despite the folly of men, nothing essential or valuable or beautiful can ever be lost so long as there remains one witness to truth on earth.

---

10. This book is designed to be read from end to end without reference to the copious footnotes. However, if the reader wishes to delve a bit deeper, then the footnotes are there to support and expand the assertions made in the main text. Also, there is an *Index* at the end of the book meant to clarify some of the terminology used.

INTRODUCTION

And ye shall know the truth, and the truth shall make you free.

John 8:32

THE TRUTH IS something sacred. It is not just a concept, a mental construct, an abstraction. Although, for man it usually presents itself first as a notion, something that the mind apprehends, it is far more than an idea: it is reality or being—supreme, unchanging, beautiful, and life-giving. Truth as being, preexists the thinking of it. As a result, it is meant to engage not just our mind but our whole substance, whence Plato can say in his Republic: "The true lover of knowledge is always striving after being—that is his nature." In other words, knowledge for knowledge's sake is not the sincere philosopher's aim.

If one leaves aside, for now, all the various interpretations that the notion of "truth" has conjured over the centuries, one can say simply that truth is pure, unconditioned being, the *esse* of Scholasticism[1] or the *En Sof* of Kabbalism. Dialectically speaking, it is the opposite of nothingness—

---

1. The terminology of Scholasticism, or of medieval philosophy (Anselm, Duns Scotus, Aquinas), will be one of our central points of reference, along with the illuminationist idealism of Neoplatonism (Plato, Plotinus, Proclus, and also, in some essential respects, Meister Eckhart), as well as the summit of metaphysics which the Hindu *Advaita Vedanta* (Gaudapada, Shankara) constitutes.

25

although in fact, since nothingness does not exist, pure being cannot have an opposite given that it is also totality, the pleroma, because nothing can be subtracted from it and therefore nothing can be situated outside of it. The essential attribute of pure being, other than its *esse* or the fact of its "beingness" (*aseitas*), is pure consciousness. In other words, being both "is" and is "self-aware;" it is both object and subject of itself, and both simultaneously—ravishingly so. This is the Godhead or the Supreme Essence or what the *Advaita Vedanta* defines as "being, consciousness, and bliss," *sat-chit-ananda*. In the Neoplatonism of Proclus, the quality of *sat* or "being" becomes "goodness" and that of *ananda* or "bliss" becomes "beauty." To equate "being" with the attribute of "goodness" (or "godness") is simply to recognize that being, because of its totality or wholeness, is necessarily good, for it is in the nature of the whole to reconcile, to unify, to redeem.[2]

If truth is the highest object of intelligence, then it is the only one that can satisfy it to its fullest plenitude, which is as much as to say that truth is the efficient justification for intelligence, its raison d'être. And if truth—*veritas*—is reality, then insofar as we possess a kernel of reality—on pain of non-existence—it must also comprise the substance of our being. The relationship between truth and being could be summarized to say that the essence of knowledge/wisdom is virtue, just as the essence of virtue is wisdom.

To speak of the truth and to speak of being is to admit some kind of distinction between the two. However, aside from the fact that it is the pole being which is the guaran-

---

2. The words "good" and "god" share etymological roots such that "good-bye" derives from "God be with you." The root meaning of the word "good" is derived from the Indo-Aryan root "*ghedh*" which means to unite, join, fit. Thus, strictly speaking, is good that which unites.

tor of truth, the polarization of truth and being can never be substantial in itself since the two are indissociable and, in the essence, indistinguishably fused—though not confused, to borrow a felicitous phrase from Meister Eckhart. Nonetheless, it is this very polarization, illusory at it may be metaphysically, that lies at the core of man's present day exile from his divine origin. Because of this split, in which heart is divorced from mind, man is able to think about the truth without following through existentially, forgetting that the essence of knowledge is worship because awareness of the supreme good—the *agathon* of Plato and the *summum bonum* of medieval philosophy—induces no less than reverence. There is far more to intelligence than the mere capacity of conceptualization. Intelligence, when it is all that it is meant to be, is conception, meditation, concentration, and ultimately an assimilation in which the contemplating subject is assimilated in turn by the nature of the object when this object is the supreme reality. In other words, part of the completeness of recognition of the Supreme involves a re-assimilation into the Supreme. This is why Emerson could speak not only of a correspondence between man and the cosmos, but finally of coalescence, a phenomenon whereby the soul is reabsorbed into its divine universal substance. However, in the bookish, rational, scientific West especially, mental understanding, while often prodigious, has paradoxically become a principal obstacle to the full deployment of intelligence.

Thus man is quite capable of understanding, for instance, the metaphysical basis for the principle of unity, which posits that all of creation is necessarily interdependent, without this knowledge inducing him one whit to love or to mercy which would be the logical existential conclusion of such knowledge. In fact, quite on the contrary, this knowledge may imbue him with a false sense of superiority that can be utterly selfish or, at least, it may lead him to believe that he can grasp reality through a purely mental effort, or he may assume that such knowledge is an end in itself and therefore dispenses him of having to make any other effort such as having to live up, for instance, to its soteriological implications: knowledge of the good or the true that is not salvational or realizational is not knowledge; it is mere cerebration. Contrast this attitude with that of the medieval philosopher Duns Scotus whose concern with knowledge, even of the physical universe, [3] was meant to serve as a support for his growing in supernatural charity. In other words, a material application for his speculative efforts was never the overriding goal. It is scarcely conceivable that science would be subordinated today to an ethical awareness of being, especially given the taboo against consciousness or the subjective component of knowledge which does not lend itself to a battery of measures and calibrations and which, therefore, eludes mathematical verification.

From the vantage point of man, there are two great poles: spirit and matter. For those who are convinced that consciousness is born of matter, this book will prove an exercise in futility.[4] For those, however, who believe that matter is born of the spirit—and this is not an advocacy of

---

3. For instance in his studies on the physical characteristics of intensification and diminution of light and of colors. The study of nature is not just a matter of physics because, as Dante defines it, it is *"l'amor que muove il sole e l'altre stelle,"* ("love which moves the sun and the other stars").

4. In a new twist to putting the cart before the horse, "I myself, like many scientists," comments Nobel laureate Francis Crick—co-discoverer of the double helix spiral or the molecular blueprint at the heart of genetics—"believe that the soul is imaginary and that what we call our minds is simply a way of talking about the functions of our brains" (*Of Molecules and Men*, University of Washington Press, 1966). Perhaps one could revisit the matter in the next world.

creationism[5]—then the stakes become how to live in a way to redeem the spirit from its fleshly bonds or, preferably, how to enable the spirit to shine through these very bonds so that they become revelationally transfigured, a glorious theophany and no longer a sinful tyranny: "The earth, and every common sight / To me did seem / Apparelled in celestial light," writes Wordsworth in his auguries of innocence.

An inductive or ascensional philosophical quest departing from the solid premise of matter and ending with the intuition of metaphysical archetypes would be fruitful provided that one had the requisite contemplativeness—and imagination—to pierce beyond the physical envelope of creation and proceeded from what we know as the visible to the invisible, from the material to the immaterial, or rather from the outside to the inside. This is, roughly speaking, the dialectical premise of Aristotelianism which came to predominate in the West. This approach, when it is all that it can be, does not exclude wonderment which, as Aristotle says, is the beginning of philosophy.[6] But when it is purely rational, or lacking in imagination and especially in intuition, it collapses into skepticism and eventually, into cynicism. The machine age and the brutish world of industrialism, which has all but destroyed the possibility of craftsmanship, was born of just such a collapse.

---

5. To say that the doctrine of creationism is symbolically and not literally true does not, in our minds, invalidate it. However, to believe in it literally is certainly "true enough" and we would never quarrel with that position except that, from a scientific point of view, it becomes difficult then to have a cogent discussion.

6. Just as curiosity is the beginning of science. The difference, of course, is that wonderment is essentially spiritual in its essence, whereas curiosity is amoral and, unless tutored, is apt to be wanton. Wonderment is on the side of union, whereas curiosity is on the side of division.

29

Conversely, a descensional or deductive process leading from the spirit, either through intuition or as grasped
through the abstract logic of first principles—the divine
"ideas"—down to earthly manifestation, has been the preferred course of philosophers who start with the divine
agency of the world.[7] This approach is essentially summarized by the current of Platonism in Western culture,
including some of the Islamic and Jewish intellectual heritage. Of course, intelligence, being what it is, these two
trends have also converged, most notably in the philosophy of a Boethius, an Albertus Magnus, and others in the
Christian West, in the Islamic philosophy of an Avicenna
and an Averroës, or in the Jewish philosophy of a
Maimonides, not forgetting the emanationist teachings of
the Kabbala and the doctrine of the *Sefirot* or "grades of
wisdom" combined with the idea of the perennial eternity
of matter.

One could define the philosophical perspective in this
book as "spiritual realism" if the term "realism" (and that
of "reality") had not become appropriated, more and more
abusively, over the centuries[8] by materialists at the expense

---

7. These two premises have been respectively referred to as *a priori*
knowledge and *a posteriori* knowledge. Though we do not wish to add
to the abstruseness of some of the materials presented by using Latin
terms, it will be necessary to do so from time to time, because there is a
unique precision to the Latin terminology of Scholastics with which
arguments can be mortised and tenoned.

8. A pivotal swing point occurred during the latter Middle Ages
with the debate over the existence of the "universals." Nominalist
philosophers asserted that these universals (such as the generic possibility of birds or flowers, or simply beauty) had no independent reality
from the mind or from nature, but were mere names or, worse, they were
very pejoratively declared to be nothing but a *flatus vocis* or "vocal
breath." This debate helped precipitate the divorce between nature and
spirit as well as between body and mind, existence and principle. Once
the universals were relegated to the domain of mental abstractions (the

of the supra-natural essence of matter; and this is nothing but a capitulation of the mind in front of the overwhelming physicality of the universe as perceived by our animal senses. At all events, reality (*realitas*), for us, is first what distinguishes being from nothingness and, secondly, what distinguishes necessary being from contingent being,[9] or underlying being from the surface space-time modifications which are proper to existence only. Is real what subsists after the perishable or what exists before or what cannot be eliminated. Existence requires being, but being does not require existence in order to be[10]: "I am that I am," God declares to Moses.

In this sense, the notion of reality is synonymous with that of eternity. The difficulty for the sense-bound man results first from the fact that it is impossible to demonstrate to him in material terms (which is the only sense of the concrete he knows) what exactly the notion of eternity is supposed to mean. In fact, to attempt to do so would be to misunderstand the nature of matter which is not real by itself, except in a provisory sense.[11] All that can be said at

---

debate, ironically, marks also the birth of conceptualism), there was nothing to save the notion of reality from being reduced to that of matter. The universals, of course, are attributes of divinity—or, in the case of negative things, sub-divinity—much in the way the American Indians, or shamanistic people in general, see specific animals or natural things as being imbued with a special medicine or power.

9. This subject requires, whenever relevant, the use of philosophical terms such as "necessity" and "contingency," "substance" and "accident," or "absolute" and "relative" which are part of the vocabulary of Scholasticism, itself derived in part from Aristotelianism.

10. "Sometimes I ceased to live," Thoreau mused at the edge of Walden Pond, "and began to be."

11. This in essence is the Mahayana Buddhist philosopher Nagarjuna's position, namely the "teaching of emptiness" (*Shunyavada*) in which he allows for the makeshift nature of empirical truth. Without the notion of *Shunyavada*, without the grace of emptiness or of silence, the world congeals the soul.

31

this point—and this is a logical demonstration only, in the footsteps of St. Anselm—is that were it not for the trace of eternity in man, the very notion of such a concept would never arise in his mind. It is this very dilemma, that of endeavoring to join mutually exclusive dimensions, which points to the difficulty arising from taking matter, instead of the spirit, as a starting point. The yoke of matter, once consented to, imprisons.

One might then prefer to speak of "philosophical ideal-ism" or "objective idealism," the term used by Schelling for describing nature, or creation, as "visible intelligence." However, the term "idealism" itself has become more and more synonymous with abstraction and unreality so that one either lapses into the subjectivism of a Bishop Berkeley, who denies the reality of matter, or falls for the intellectual impotence of a Kant who denies that man can know the supra-sensual absolute.[12] Moreover, idealism has often been the hazy bastion of spiritualists who denigrate the earth in a thin-blooded attempt to redeem the spirit. Such a position is ultimately alienating because, on the one hand, it is not possible to transcend existence as such—the issue being to transcend oneself or, actually, one's limitations because the self cannot transcend the self—and, on the other, it amounts to ignoring the bonds between divine agency and earthly result; it is to orphan creation. Spurned, rejected, spiritually anathematized, creation avenges itself by scourging the spirit. Moralism—not morality, of course—begets depravity. However, idealism, as the belief in the marvelous, is the antidote to cynicism and all despairing defeatisms. It is to believe that in the vale of tears of this earthly life, there is a better world. As such, it

---

12. Kant's error is not to say that reason (*ratio*) cannot know the real, but to reduce man's intelligence to reason alone, that is to say to leave out the intellect without which reason can only grope.

is a salvational instinct that is a close brethren of faith—the capacity to believe before one sees. Thus, if, in the name of reality, one must choose between idealism and a realism that is in actuality but a materialism, then one must prefer the former which does not deaden the notion of truth by limiting it to a sense-perceivable universe. In its strictest sense, idealism is belief in the supremacy of the ideational universe as the key to reality. Thus, it has nothing to do intrinsically with vague sentiments of the good or the better, but rather with a vertically intellective sense of the perfect and the incorruptibly true.

The dilemma posed from having to choose between realism and idealism comes from the difficulty of reconciling existence on earth with existence as such, of reconciling the idea of the perishable with that of the eternal. As previously mentioned, the temptation is to dissociate the two, to despise the earthly so as to safeguard the incomparability of the ideal and this trend has led to endless mischief. In the history of Christianity, one could cite the example of Docetism, rightly adjudged a heresy—although hardly a sacrilegious one—a doctrine which, in an attempt to preserve the heavenly nature of Christ from any fleshly stain, proposed that he had only a shadow body and that he only appeared to die on the cross. The same has been said of the Buddha, but in a perilously different way, by proposing that he is but a myth and never existed historically, nor needed to exist to be real which is an absurdity, because one then might as well propose that creation never happened or that it is unreal.

The Docetist tendency reappears under many guises. One such instance is that of a scholarship zealously bent on denying the existence of an earthly Beatrice, claiming that Dante and the other *Fideli d'Amor* were in the habit of personifying *Sophia* under the conceit of a beautiful maiden, which may well have been the case in principle but not sys-

33

tematically so because this idea does not exclude the possibility of a human support. Notwithstanding Dante's own insistence that Beatrice existed—he tells us of his astonishment that such a pure creature could exist in the flesh which is but dust (*Vita Nova*)—to reject the existence of such a person carries a number of philosophical risks in its wake, not least of which that of dehumanizing the Divine. We could also reverse this to say that to depreciate the earthly for the sake of the ideal amounts to not understanding the ideal. The crux of the issue is this: there is nothing in fact that needs to be transcended, but rather something that needs to be realized; this is the meaning of holy transfiguration, when the alchemist's lead is turned into gold. It is precisely because the creature can be a symbol of an archetype that it is deserving of worshipful respect. With regard to this, there are two pitfalls that need to be avoided: that of an opaque and sentimental idolatry, which deifies the relative, and that of a mental and sublimizing abstractionism which desacralizes creation. Even though the two are often confused, transfiguration is at the very antipodes of idolatry.

To give everything its untainted due is not to introduce an abyss, as artificial as it is impassable, between Creator and creation, or between the archetype and its earthly reflection, or between the symbol and the object which exemplifies it. Whatever benefits may accrue from this, for example a religious opportunism that sees in the world nothing but a charnel house, come at a major cost and carry the risk of spiritual suicide. The central risk is that the rejection of the creature, or simply its underestimation (which amounts practically to the same), places the human ego in a position of not owing accountability to a concrete God, because if man is nothing what then is God? Eckhart, in a daring ellipsis paradoxically meant to provoke faith and not to goad temerity, addressed this mutuality between

God and man to say that God is nothing without man. In other words, greatness is incumbent upon man, because he is, as Emerson says, "a god in ruins;" he does not have the leisure of throwing his life away.

The solution to these opposite perspectives[13] is not to choose one over the other but, as in the symbolism of the mythological strait of the "clashing rocks," the Symplegades,[14] it is to thread a middle course through the two, to find the necessary point of coincidence between the contraries, to understand, in Hindu terms that, since an absolute gap is inconceivable, *Samsara* is *Nirvana*, namely that the creation cannot be other, in its essence, than paradise. This is the same as to say that the root of being is bliss. Traditional symbolism explains how the *Janua Coeli* or the gate of heaven has two leaves or sides of an "Active Door" by which, as they "clash," the entrant may be crushed. What saves him is knowledge or truth. And what is knowledge—true knowledge—if not liberation from fratricidal pairs?

If existence is, in its essence and in its fountainhead, paradisiacal, then knowledge must lead to spirituality, or to a sense of the sacred, because, as the German Alchemist and Rosicrucian, Henry Madathanas, says, "an intelligence lacking in spirituality is only a false and borrowed light." The touchstone of knowledge will be virtue which is existential intelligence. The conjugation of knowledge and virtue will be wisdom and it is wisdom alone that can save man from the divisiveness of partisan ideologies, no matter

---

13. This is not to say that either Aristotle or Plato stood exclusively at one end of these possibilities. It is a question of point of departure both of which are legitimate, even though religion may prefer that of idealism. The problem comes from making an absolute of what can only be a premise. Neither Aristotle nor Plato can be held responsible for the abuses others have subjected their philosophies to.

14. Cf. Ananda Coomaraswamy's essay "Symplegades".

how much they stake their claim in the divine. In its true meaning, the word philosophy means "love of wisdom." There is probably no notion that has been subject to more abuse than this word, for it has come to be taken as a license to construct a system of knowledge which can be profane or speculatively sterile—and, indeed, has become increasingly so over time. It has also become associated with the idea of a purely rational system of knowledge divorced from its intellective roots in the spirit and hence ignorant of the influx of inspiration and of grace. This is why it has been the object of the most savage censure by theologians (to wit Ashari's, and even Ghazzali's, condemnation of Avicenna) in spite of efforts by an Aquinas to codify it within the framework of religion.[15] Ironically, it is philosophy's very disinterestedness, coming from the nature of its object, namely the truth, that opens it both to attack and to abuse. Because philosophy, by its intrinsic nature, cannot have a dogmatic agenda—being premised on detachment and not on passion, on knowledge or evidence rather than on faith—its adherents can seem cold-bloodedly cerebral to the point of indifference or to the point of a mundane speculation that pretends to know without necessarily engaging itself ethically.[16] But that is not the fault

---

15. Which did not prevent him from misunderstanding Avicenna, which may prove the impossibility of reconciling philosophy with theology as he attempted to do.

16. Descartes, while not quite ruining the notion of philosophy—he was after all a masterful logician (which makes his exercise even less forgivable)—compromised its premise of certitude by advocating a methodology based on initial skepticism. Even if this skepticism was meant to lead to an absolute, it nonetheless fissured certitude and allowed for the birth of the corrosive disease of relativism. Today one speaks of radical anti-Platonism whose adherents (none deserving of mention by name) think that they have a duty to break the mold of philosophy itself. Descartes, by his thorough exposition of rational tools, offered latter-day philosophers the noose by which to hang themselves.

of philosophy as such. False philosophy should not be used as a reference to inveigh against true philosophy (this is a tautology). It is truth, and nothing else, that is the necessary justification for philosophy, not religion, not a given historical and cultural setting, not the ruling prejudices of the vulgar masses. What validates philosophy cannot be the opinion of such and such a rationalist, but the nature of the object which it is meant to contemplate.

In a stricter sense, a philosophy that does not have the truth, or the nature of reality, as its object should not properly be called philosophy. This would be an abuse of language. Nonetheless, one is entitled to define philosophy as the capacity to pursue an independent and purely rational inquiry into truth, with all the potential this entails of speculative wandering, whereas religion starts from the foundation of divine revelation. So it does not have a charter, or an obligation, to explain the truth, only to formulate it. Hermeneutics, or the interpretation of scriptural texts, is adventitious and, in any case, will not stray outside of certain dogmatically pre-established parameters; therefore it begs the question. As for philosophy, probably the greatest trap for its practitioners is the assumption that truth will yield its prize if they are clever enough to put together the right combination of thoughts. What is forgotten, however, is that truth, being sacred in its essence, belongs to a dimension that transcends thinking as cogitation and which therefore requires, so as to become fully three dimensional, the intervention of a supra-rational factor of grace or, at least, of inspiration. In other words, it requires the intervention of a transpersonal agency. It is not enough to gather the material, to have the tinder and the flint: the spark erupts as the result of an act combined with a pre-existent substance.

One might reproach us for stating that truth and the divine are one and the same thing, claiming that to assume that the essence of truth is divine is a presupposition that requires an act of faith and not the verification of an evidence, which is the proper realm of philosophy while the former belongs to the domain of religion. First of all, one would like to say that philosophy and religion should be natural allies[17] by virtue of their common object, the nature of the Real which, according to Proclus, is truth, beauty, and the good. However, philosophy has the capacity to deny itself—and to do so "philosophically," even if illogically so—which religion does not have[18] and this is why it has earned religion's censure because, misused, it can destroy faith which is the life blood of religion. This is to say that religion is concerned less with knowledge as such than with salvation, or with knowledge inasmuch as it is conducive to salvation. It operates through dogmas and not certitudes as such—though dogmas are meant to serve as practical certitudes. Moreover, even if religion claims certitude for its dogmas, understanding is not required by the adherents for these to be operative, only belief. And whatever threatens faith is brusquely rejected, irrespective of its intellectual worth. Now to respond to the objection, one will have to say that, unless one believes that the essence of reality is purely material, the truth and the divine must necessarily coincide, and this at every level of manifestation where there is a positive quality. Enough said. The chapters that follow will attempt to prove this in a variety of ways.

---

17. Eckhart called Plato "that great priest," which indicates that philosophy and religion are not intrinsically incompatible. And John Scotus Erigena could state with perfect logic that: "True philosophy is true religion and conversely true religion is true philosophy."

18. Of course, religion has the possibility of heresy. But this is something that religion has the capacity, precisely, to censure. Philosophy has no such recognized body of orthodoxy to refer to.

In the meantime, it is not artificial to distinguish between philosophy, theology, gnosis, and metaphysics.[19] Even if they overlap and blend, and providentially so because integral knowledge is one, they do have purviews that are distinct enough to merit differentiation. Since those of religion and philosophy have just been dealt with, we will only mention that gnosis essentializes religious practice, it is esoterism, whereas metaphysics deals with first principles in a non-dogmatic manner.[20] One might also say that gnosis is the mystical or operative application of metaphysics—and in fact a metaphysics which is not gnosis is not really metaphysics but philosophy.[21]

To open a brief parenthesis, it should be noted that part of the reason philosophy has been so severely censured by religion—which believes that supreme knowledge is impossible without the double concourse of faith and of grace—is the confusion that has reigned about which faculty in man is properly that of knowledge. We are talking about the confusion between intelligence understood as reason and intellection. Following Plato, we will say that

---

19. To the list, one could add cosmology, which is really the science of symbolism.

20. We particularly like Avicenna's distinction between physics which is concerned with physical things "inasmuch as they move," and this is properly the realm of science, and metaphysics which is concerned with the existent "inasmuch as it exists." This brings us back to being, the *esse*.

21. To clarify these nuances, one could say that Aristotle was a philosopher first and a metaphysician second, whereas Plato was integrally a metaphysician, a gnostic, and a philosopher, but not a theologian. Aquinas a theologian/philosopher first and a metaphysician a distant second; Eckhart a pure gnostic/metaphysician; Avicenna a philosopher and a metaphysician (not excluding its gnostic finalization); and Shankara a pure metaphysician/gnostic but not a philosopher—although if one is a pure metaphysician it is not necessary to be a philosopher.

reason's purview is the realm of opinion, which is clouded or indirect knowledge, whereas the purview of the intellect is truth or the domain of certitude, that of direct knowledge, with which it in fact is ontologically identified. The intellect, or *nous*, which as Eckhart says is *"increatus et increabile"* (uncreated and uncreatable), is the trace of the Absolute or of God's divine being in the soul. Since it is the soul's quintessential root in the divine, from which it can never be completely severed, it is one with the spirit or the Logos. Most men, even though unaware for the most part of the ontological possibilities of this faculty inherent to their being, have some preliminary access to it by way of the faculty of conscience which, if developed or allowed to shine, can in principle lead to spiritual realization because conscience is the trace of divine certitude in our consciousness by which we can infallibly ascertain the difference between right and wrong, at least as regards the correctness of our intention if not to the facts of the situation itself.

In the light of the above definitions, and controversies, what should our intellectual point of reference properly be termed? To avoid the ambiguities generated by the term philosophy alone, we would like instead to call our premise that of the *"sophia perennis"* or the perennial wisdom, a term already consecrated by use, and one which includes the freedom philosophy has to speak of truth outside of a strictly religious framework, while at the same time being a term which excludes the profane license of philosophy to roam into the wasteland of barren speculation. Moreover, the attribute of "perennial" is necessary to emphasize that this *sophia* is not progressive in the sense of an evolutionary knowledge, but that it derives its authority from its reference to a timeless center which transcends traditions, cultures, and credos. While it is easy to forget it or even to reject it in the name of reigning ideologies, it can never be

40

out of fashion since its nature is one with "the Spirit that bloweth where it listeth."

In view of its ever recurrent actuality which shines through the forest of doctrinal forms, it is like the light which lends colors their hue without being stained by its participation in them. It can never cease to exist since knowledge as such is one, no matter how subordinated it may be to a prevailing set of beliefs, or prejudices, which seek, for different reasons to arrogate to themselves the certainty that can only belong by definition to truth alone. And just as it can never be permanently eclipsed without thereby removing the noetic heart of existence as such, likewise its witnesses can never be entirely absent from the midst of men—never mind how anonymous or uncelebrated.[22] These witnesses have what, in Christian terms is known as the baptism of desire or the baptism of the spirit. The Holy Ghost knows its own and can guide them even outside, if need be, the usual framework of a given religion. By "outside" is meant that these people's kindred religionists would not recognize them as one of theirs[23] which brings up the controversial point that religion, while rooted in divine revelation, may be not only anti-intellectual—which is comprehensible (although not justifiable) inasmuch as there can be a real conflict between reason and faith as we have seen—but also it can be surprisingly anti-mystical, not intentionally of course, yet as a

---

22. The recent re-discovery of a Marguerite Porete, a medieval mystic whose name all but disappeared, or the hitherto unknown Lilian Staveley, an English mystic at the turn of the 20th century, are but two of what we must assume are many examples, even if few and far between, of silent witnesses to God's grace.

23. Marguerite Porete, on the Church's orders, was burnt at the stake. In a different sense, Hypatia, the last official Neoplatonist of the Alexandrian School, was killed by an angry Christian mob. Eckhart was under critical investigation by the Church when he died.

matter of practical fact.[24] Part of the reason lies in the mandate religion has of offering salvation, with the minimum necessary means of grace, to the widest possible body of men. In so doing, it is obliged to take into account, not a mystically gifted elite, but the broadest common denominator of a human collectivity which, in the main, is either barbarically passionate and willful, or stupidly lethargic and mindful of peace and comfort, and, in both cases, prone to forget the divine. As a result, religion must not only reject what is contrary to faith in the sense of heresy while channeling heavenward the energy of this mass, but it feels itself compelled to reject also what may appear— from above now—as contrary to faith or as too daringly individualistic.[25] A good example would be Meister Eckhart's teachings about the birth of Christ in the soul— premised on the virgin ground of its essential substance— which, while immaculate, could compromise the whole

---

24. No less an authority than Gregory the Great, who was also the founder of the medieval papacy, strongly affirmed that the Church, in this life, is no better than a *corpus permixtum* or a mixture of good and bad. This will surprise those who believe that all of religion is somehow wonderful and who forget that God, when attempting to rope man in, is a realist first and an idealist second.

25. This rejection may occur even at a very high level of spirituality such as in the famous case of a Junayd, himself a Sufi mystic of a very high rank, condemning a Hallaj for enunciating publicly doctrines that were meant to be kept secret. However, in this case, the censure is only public, though it cost the life of Hallaj, but not intrinsic. In other words, Junayd, in his implicit role as a guardian of public morality could not grant the former the license to speak recklessly, even though he might privately concur with the teachings. Society has its rights and religion's first duty is to preserve the viability of social needs within a context where they can somehow harmonize with Heaven's requirements or, at least, where they do not become antagonistic to these. In the case of Meister Eckhart, the Church was not wrong in questioning him—it had no choice but to do so—all the more so as some of his formulations, those on the nature of evil for instance, were objectively problematical.

idea of obedience and of dependence on an outside authority, which is the foundation of exoteric religion, and give foolhardy individuals the impression that they need answer only to themselves. Religion will not allow scandal to come, even if it be only apparent.

Because of this concern, namely of addressing the needs not of the best of men but of all of men, religion is, strange to say, far from offering a perfect example of spirituality. Thus the Iranian Sufi, Abu Yazid Bistami, known for his renunciation of renunciation, could declare: "The people most separated from God are the ascetics by their asceticism, the devotees by their devotion, and the knowers by their knowledge." Moreover, the servility of humilitarianism, for example—statements such as "I am the worst of sinners"—conflicts with the possibility of the soul's kingly essence, and indeed, when carried to an extreme, prevents its fulfillment by maintaining it forcibly, and against its immortal nature, in a state of semi-abject dependence in which it forfeits its intelligence since it must defer in all matters to ecclesiastical authority. In this perspective the faithful are taught that the highest virtue is obedience because this is the state most proportioned to the greatness and unfathomable nature of the divine mystery. To think becomes tantamount to doubt and to question means to defy; both reflexes are stigmatized as stemming from pride or from ingratitude. Trust in the appointed guardians of the Church's teachings is promoted as being infinitely meritorious.[26] If that is fundamentally the case, then one might well wonder why man was created with the faculty of intelligence—as well as that of imagination—because to obey without discerning is not humility but stupidity, even if morally forgivable or even if morally laud-

---

26. Even though the above comments are couched in Christian terms, this phenomenon is typically found in all religions.

able inasmuch as the sufficient reason for blind obedience is God which ennobles the intention. Be that as it may, such a merit still does not allow one to present obedience as an absolute superiority. It does nothing to explain why it would be said that man is created in the image of God if the highest state he is entitled to is that of groveling servitude. And the Church then wonders at the burst of free-thinking that came in the so-called "Enlightenment" period? But where was an intelligent human being, in other words someone with a profound sense of causality, to find guidance when catechized to believe that thinking was a form of sin? If God created man in noble pride—"thou art all fair my love"—and to carry the Law within himself, then one can understand why some want to hold priests responsible for having taught him guilt and shame.[27]

This summary, simplistic as it is, touches on the problem of a perspective that emphasizes man's unworthiness and castigates his independence while claiming to offer him the keys to everlasting happiness by bribing him, under the shadow of hellish threats, with a paradise that only a fool could love perfectly. To be a child of God should not be confused with childishness. And this is precisely the problem that a dogmatic authoritarianism cloaked in the trappings of ecclesiasticism fails to grasp—perhaps in spite of itself and perhaps also out of overcompensation for man's tireless tendency towards heedlessness when not frank revolt.[28]

---

27. Eckhart carries the issue one step further by fervently exhorting his congregation to be free even of God—although he asks them to do this through God: "Therefore let us pray to God that we may be free of God that we may gain the truth and enjoy it eternally."

28. The Catholic Church forced the relieving alternative of Evangelicalism, coming as a safety valve, when it denied all right to knowledge and power of decision to the congregation, arrogating these exclusively for the clergy. Martin Luther wanted the Bible translated into

If one looks at the situation from the perspective of
spiritual homeostasis, the soul, deprived of its capacity of
full intelligence and autonomy, can seek to replace the
absence of the sense of intellective certitude with an excess
of devotional zeal which also compensates for the exaggeration of negative qualities such as those of sinfulness,
unworthiness, weakness, helplessness, dependence, meekness and all that promotes a kind of mystique of fear of a
creature racked by scruples currying favor in the sight of a
stern overlord, grudging in his favors.[29] It is as if the soul
now could derive a sense of opaque certitude by the sheer
intensity of its fervor and efforts. Such a path may be quite
heroic, to say nothing of the fact that it does correspond to
the very real fact of man's vulnerability or to his insignificance in the cosmos. Thus it would be arrogance to criticize
the numberless martyrs who, following this path of merit,
laid their lives down for the greatness of a God they loved
and feared. But this is not the point. What is relevant here

---

the vernacular so that any man or woman could read it and interpret it
for himself or for herself without the meddling interference of priests.
Later, the Baptists developed the idea of "soul competency" (or "soul
liberty") in which the individual assumes spiritual responsibility for
himself. Such a decentralization of authority carries with it the risk of
democratic relativism, but it cannot be avoided. The idea of "soul competency" is fundamental to a perspective that wants to keep open the
direct channel of communication between the soul and God, while preserving the integral moral worth of a free will able to be nobly self-
accountable. And if it fosters individualism, this is more a factor of the
collectivist problems resulting from a world in which demographic
forces are out of control than an issue of inappropriateness per se.

29. It is this kind of a "loser's" mentality, culturally institutionalized
and blended with mercantile values, which earned the withering scorn
of a Nietzsche which of coursed won him an antichrist's status in the
Church's eyes when in fact, as Ananda Coomaraswamy, among others,
has pointed out, his "superman" (it is really an "Überman" or "over-
man" that he had in mind) is an intuition for what is known in
Hinduism as a *jivanmukta* or liberated being.

is to detail some of the effects of a perspective which forfeits knowledge.

The essence of religion, its intellective core, is gnosis or direct knowledge of the truth for without it, religion loses the kernel of its consciousness as well as its doctrinal raison d'être, though not necessarily its vitality, for awhile at least. However, faith, or a dialectical path erected on faith alone, cannot carry the banner far into the battle; no amount of dogmatic intensity, of piety, of devotionalism can replace the loss of gnosis. While it is true that sacraments, when maintained and performed correctly, can vehicle the divine presence and thus sustain the efficacy of the religious path, they cannot replace doctrine. Thus, ineluctably, once the truth becomes a mystery rather than an evidence, religion's doctrinal body is likely to be taken over in the course of time by zealots and Pharisees. The doctrinal element will be gradually supplanted by an intensification of meticulous prescriptions and the original spirit of a religion will be smothered by a deadening multiplication of rules and supererogatory practices which are meant to capture the believer in a kind of religious net in which every circumstance of his daily life is accounted for by "do's and don'ts." Two large examples of this are Judaism and the epoch of Brahmanism in India whose suffocative hold needed to be aired out, so to speak, by the arrival respectively of the figures of Christ and of the Buddha.

It may be appropriate at this point to define in more detail what is meant by intelligence and by knowledge. Intelligence, in its most technical sense, can be defined as the capacity to be logical, be it with ideas, with human situations, or simply with material things. More broadly, it is the capacity to be objective, first in regard to oneself and then in regard to others. However, these definitions do not take into account the fullness of the singular miracle of consciousness whose scope vastly transcends the social imperative of getting along with other people and the utilitarian imperative of ensuring one's material survival. Therefore, it can be said that the gift of intelligence is far from finding its ultimate justification in merely putting two and two together, however vital this skill may otherwise be.

Rather, if intelligence in man is the faculty that allows him to know, or at least to intuit, that there is such a thing as the Absolute and consequently that with respect to this Absolute everything else—absolutely everything else, including his own self—is relative to one degree or another, then it can be said that such a faculty is the instrument whereby he can establish a distinction between what is Real and what is unreal, or less real. And this initial discernment, at whatever level, can become the point of departure for a transcendent trajectory, for an entire process of ontological reminiscence that can lead man to return back to his root in Godhead, source of all reality, while at the same time help him become, as he grows in spiritual grace, a living witness to the trace of this Godhead in creation. Thus it is tempting to say that intelligence, inasmuch as it is the faculty of complete adequation to what is eternally Real, is wasted if it is not employed for a spiritually realizational purpose whose end must be no less than the Divine Object itself, since this is the supreme value it can perceive. In other words, it is not overly sublime to state that intelligence—human intelligence—is not fully itself if not invested in its ultimate capacity which is to know the Real. To discern between right and wrong, simple as this may sound, between good and bad, beautiful and ugly is the start which, leading from correct choice to correct choice, will restore consciousness back to its primordial nature as surely as a dirty mirror when cleaned will be able to reflect the brilliance of light. In its essential nature, "intelligence has only one nature, namely luminosity," the Germano/Swiss metaphysician Frithjof Schuon

47

teaches in *Spiritual Perspectives and Human Facts*. And its content, knowledge, "only saves us on condition that it engages all that we are: only when it constitutes a way which works and transforms, and which wounds our nature as the plough wounds the soil."

Moreover, intelligence's instrument, the mind, may in a certain sense be likened to a hoe that prepares the ground so that the proverbial seed of the Christic parable—which is really each man's heart—can be planted in the right soil, that of Truth and Goodness, to bring forth its bounty of fruit in God's time, ideally within the span of a human lifetime. Through intelligence, then, man must not only prepare the soil but first of all must choose the most propitious ground. And this choice, in its ultimate consequences, is that between life and death, or between what is life-giving and what is life-removing. And, having made the choice, intelligence will then be proper concentration—heart, mind, and will—on the best. On the basis of these criteria, schematic as they may seem, the measure of a man's intelligence will lie in his ability first to set his eyes on the one thing that matters, or that matters ultimately, and then to pursue it tirelessly to his dying breath. And this ability is less a matter of intellectual brilliance than one of fundamental willingness to do what is right. This is why knowledge, when integral, is always realizational and hence salvational.[30] One must add here that the mind is not capable of containing the truth; it can conceive of it but the truth, in that it is a living thing, can only be contained by the heart. "Neither heaven nor earth can contain me," God tells the prophet of Islam in a famous *hadith* (saying of Muhammad), "but the heart of my believing servant does."

---

30. Thus St. Bernard: "But where charity accompanies understanding and devotion accompanies knowledge, any being of this sort will fly—it will fly without end, because it flies into eternity."

If intelligence is man's preeminent faculty, then it can be said that to be man is to know—*homo sapiens.* Conversely, not to know is in a sense not to be fully man. Knowledge, be it only potential, has its prerogatives and corresponding sanctions: because man can know the Absolute, he cannot as a result escape the penalty incurred through its rejection or the avoidance of this knowledge, for not to avail himself of it, and all that it entails morally, amounts in the last analysis to rejecting nothing other than himself, that is to say his root identity in God without whom he is but a shadow on the verge of becoming nothing at all. Schuon, has remarked that "man is condemned to the Absolute." Finally, there is no choice: even if man is fully free to reject the Absolute, he can only do so by way of suicide.

Every creature has its natural habitat, whether it be the sky for the birds, the forest for the deer, or water for the fish. In man's case, his habitat is knowledge,[31] because man, as his consciousness capable of total objectivity proves,[32] is above all a creature of the spirit meant for the spirit. In the deeper sense of knowledge, one will add that man's natural habitat is spirituality,[33] because prayer is the natural result of his understanding when it is operatively

---

31. "The first thing created by God," Muhammad says, "was the Intellect."

32. Objectivity presupposes detachment and detachment presupposes a fundamental identity that transcends the phenomenological realm of accidents—wherefore the celebrated Vedantic injunction "*Neti, neti*" ("not this, not that") or simply renunciation, for the root cause of ignorance is mistaken identity which, in turn, produces mistaken attachment. Eckhart insists on the necessity of renunciation and detachment or impassivity (*Abgeschiedenheit* or *Gelassenheit*) as the primordial foundation for the spiritual path.

33. "The human person was created to contemplate the Creator so that he might always seek his beauty and dwell in the solemnity of his love," Gregory the Great tells us in his *Moralia on Job.*

49

total. In other words, recognition of the Real, which is pure holiness—or "wholeness"—elicits prayer, or adoration, just as prayer, in its turn, leads to the Real.

The salvific or redemptive quality of knowledge[34] can only be overlooked at our own peril, because knowledge misused or simply pursued for its own sake, that is to say without an eye to ultimate Truth and moral transfiguration, can veer from remedy to poison. Moreover, if Truth is the reason for being of man, then he does not have a funda-mental "right" to error: he does not have a right to be wrong. The popular saying that everyone is entitled to their opinion is a recipe for chaos.[35]

One cannot wholly agree with St. Augustine when he holds that full knowledge of Truth, or of Godhead, is impossible for man this side of the grave,[36] because knowledge by definition cannot in itself be limited, if for no other reason than that its organ, the intellect, is uncre-

---

34. Of the seven gifts of the Holy Spirit, mentioned in Isaiah 11:2, (wisdom, understanding, counsel, fortitude, knowledge, piety, and the fear of the Lord) it is interesting to note that at least four—or a majori-ty—of these gifts have to do with knowledge in some form. These gifts, called *dona septiformi gratiae* by Gregory the Great, formed, if we follow Bernard McGinn's explanation in his book *The Growth of Mysticism*, the bedrock of latter Western theological tradition.

35. One will hasten to add, however, that in a secular society where there is no proper body of authority, no one instance has a right to set itself up as absolute arbiter of right and wrong, because that would risk political tyranny, as is seen in fascism, for instance.

36. It is important to note, however, that Augustine's reservations may be implicitly aimed less at the limitations of knowledge as such than at the intellectual impotence of cerebration typical of all systems of philosophy that wish to operate specifically outside the framework of Revelation—which is the only foundation for certitude—and, in gener-al, outside of divine grace. He was anticipating, *avant la lettre*, those cre-dos advocating the "pure religion of reason" such as we find in a Spinoza or a Kant. Nonetheless, it is a position that an Erigena, for exam-ple, did not hold as absolutely to.

ate (Eckhart) and therefore eternal; thus it is bound neither by spatial localization nor by temporal experience,
nor even by physical conditioning. In other words, the
"organ" by which man can assess the formal world and
the relative cannot itself be formal and relative; only the
Absolute—and, in the human microcosm, its instrument
the intellect—can know the relative. Man was created to
know God, and the proof of this is gnosis and the phenomenon of the pneumatic, a human being who is the
embodiment of intellective wisdom, someone whose
soul's tendency is naturally ascensional, who gravitates
upwards, towards light, without the cudgel of moral
sanctions. However, one must subscribe entirely to
Augustine's view when he stresses the impossibility of
full knowledge outside of ethics, that is to say outside of
virtue which is the reflection of sacred being, because
knowledge, when it is all that it is meant to be, is not just
objective perception but fundamentally—and felicitously—union involving the essence of the subject which
shares a common identity with what it knows. Indeed, it
is identity, however veiled, that constitutes the basis of all
knowledge and therefore the sufficient impetus for love:
we love what resembles us or, rather, what we resemble
ideally. This is what Augustine wishes to convey when he
says that love is the goal of knowledge, a thought echoed
by Aquinas when he states that "love takes up where
knowledge leaves off." But this sequence can also be
reversed to say, in the words of a Sufi adage, "Falling in
love thou shalt see," which, with Gregory becomes
"amando comprehendere."

Thus love is also knowledge because love, in essence, is
but enhanced consciousness or ecstatic knowledge. In
other words, it is the very consciousness of the qualities of
the beloved that serves to heighten love. One likes to say
that love is blind, but the truth is that love has a transfig-

51

uring or even a eucharistic virtue which instead of reducing a person to what is most perishable in himself or herself transmutes that person back into something of his or her immortal best, and that is hardly a lie even if the object of such love does not live up to the quality of the sentiment bestowed. At any rate, one cannot argue logically for the possibility of love without awareness. If anything, it is supra-awareness, even when misled, because the capacity to love is, when the cup is drained, the capacity to be for it is the capacity to transcend death and that is not an illusion. And this is why also if a person dies of love, he or she is considered to be a martyr. Love is sanctifying, whence the gravity of its abuse.

Finally, however, knowledge in man cannot but be, in the last analysis, anything other than the knowledge that God has of Himself. In that respect, it is transindividual in its essence and need not therefore involve the emotion of love in the more sentimental acceptance of the term, that is to say insofar as the definition of love suggests a lingering, and still limitative, duality between human subject and divine object. Indeed, knowledge, in its ontological depth of depths, is transpersonal in that it presupposes that duality is transcended or never has been: "No one is my God," Eckhart boldly declared, "and I am no one's soul." In this manner the individual subject knows only inasmuch as his individuality is reabsorbed into the object of his contemplation or only inasmuch as his individuality (or the *principium individuationis*) no longer interferes with this vision—a vision which is at once a participation and a communion, the merging of the river with the ocean. Once again, the foundation of all real knowledge is identity and, on the basis of that identity, duality is then understood at its proper level.

To say with St. Bonaventura that contemplation can be perfected only in the next life[37] is to say two things: one, that contemplation, being in its prototype an act of full participation with Godhead, cannot be consummated while man is confined to the flesh (*homo carnalis*) or, rather, so long as he makes, for all practical purposes, of his carnal existence—as opposed to that of the spirit—his primary or concrete pole of reference. But, to say this, is also, in good logic it seems to us, to ascribe too great a supremacy to this tyranny of the flesh—or rather to its passional agency, because, in itself, the flesh is innocent and even susceptible of being restored incorrupt, as the phenomenon of the Resurrection and that of the Ascension prove. And it is also to forget that the flesh can be fully transcended, via consciousness and with the necessary help of divine grace, while here on earth, to say nothing of the fact that the body, in that it is also a divine symbol, can serve as a theophany of the spirit, or a temple to house it, and therefore can be a practical support for intellective consciousness as the doctrine of Hatha Yoga demonstrates. The doctrine of Tantrism, likewise, rests on this analogy.

To unconditionally assert that existence in the flesh prevents full knowledge amounts finally to robbing man of the intellective prerogatives that are inherent to his nature as *imago Dei*. Furthermore, it is to place inordinate emphasis on the individual, because man, when engaged in an act of pure and sacred, hence unitive, contemplation,[38] transcends the radicalness of the subject-object polarity. He is

---

37. Actually this is a Pauline doctrine.
38. Gregory the Great affirms that contemplation of the divine was the original Adamic state. According to this Church father, the Fall was the loss of contemplation because it was a turning away from inwardness—which is union—to outwardness or the sense of separateness from which the possibility of sin was born.

then no longer just a man, but God-man through communion and inasmuch as his knowledge of the True can convey a blessing, just as a mirror, as has been previously mentioned, infallibly attracts light. Illuminated by the vision of the Real, man becomes oblivious to the infirmities of the human condition. He steps outside of time and then is no longer just of this world, but already of the next—or of the real world. He is no longer just here but everywhere. More on this can be found in the Chapter "Thy Center Is Everywhere".

Paraphrasing Schuon, we will say that if God is pure spirit, then man cannot be fully joined to Him outside of intelligence which is the essence of consciousness. Until man has met the Truth, he is like a sleepwalker who moves about without knowing who he is or what life is for. He cannot be himself until he knows who he is, not just intellectually, but also existentially for his behavior is the touchstone of his knowledge. For man, to know is to be. Only like can be known by like, as it is mentioned in the teachings of Hermes. This means that if God is pure spirit, then the purpose of this book will be to demonstrate that man too is in his essence pure spirit. And pure spirit itself, insofar as it is disincarnate, or not of a fleshly or material art, is nothing other than pure consciousness, and consequently bliss by way of the freedom that infinite awareness procures. To know is to be. Man must relinquish all at the threshold of the grave except one thing, which he can never dissociate himself from, nor elude, and which he will carry into the next world: that one thing is his "I" consciousness—be it in its theomorphic depths or be it as mere egoity—and with a character to match.

One cannot conclude a chapter on knowledge without bringing up the fact that to approach the divine via intelligence involves also a process of unknowing. For all of the knowledge one can assemble about Reality, one cannot for-

54

get that Reality transcends all that can be said about it. And, as Plato said, God alone is wise. Thus, Aquinas terms his knowledge as no more than a *docta ignorancia*, a "learned ignorance." In Christianity, as in Buddhism and also Taoism, there is a long apophatic tradition, one that emphasizes the approach to God via a negative under-standing,[39] if one may say, and which presupposes a will-ingness to establish the soul initially in a shrine of fertile darkness. In Buddhism, one speaks of the Void because anything positive that can be said about the ultimate ground of Reality is only a veil. The silence of Sri Ramana Maharshi was meant to convey this teaching in a direct existential mode. Socrates claimed only to know that he did not know. Man must learn to think with his heart, which implies the extinction of the mind, the moon rejoining the sun: "I sleep but my heart waketh."

---

39. "We cannot know what God is, but rather what He is not." (Aquinas) And from the *Tao-Te Ching*: "The *Tao* that can be expressed in words is not the eternal *Tao*." Should we therefore cease to think since Truth cannot be grasped by thought alone? To say that It transcends for-mulation does not mean that it is inconceivable or that it cannot be grasped in any way. Schuon's doctrine of the relative absolute is the solution to this dilemma.

55

1. THE EIGHTH CARDINAL SIN

Our Lord Jesus said: It was not impossible for
me to raise the dead, but it was impossible for me
to cure the stupid.

Hadith of Muhammad

THAT INTELLIGENCE IS, essentially, a virtue—a virtue equal
to kindness, charity, or humility—is a notion that may
come as a surprise to some. Indeed, in the rational West at
least, one is accustomed to equate intelligence with purely
mental attributes, defining it as the dry faculty of reasoning,[1] to see it as an abstract eye, wholly deprived of feeling,
able to gaze with mathematical imperviousness on the play
of phenomena.

What this restrictive notion fails to take into account,
however, is that reason is but one faculty among others,
namely that it is an instrument or means, albeit privileged
in that it allows intelligence to deploy itself operatively,
but hardly its only mode of perception or of expression.
But reason itself is neither the source nor the substance of

---

1. For example, the abusively named "Intelligence Quotient" measurements which exclude, among many other things, contemplative
genius, the sense of goodness, or the wisdom found in traditional crafts.
One speaks now, in recognition of the manifold nature of intelligence, of
an "Emotional Quotient" which measures the ability to handle human
situations.

intelligence. The fact that it can operate with virtuosic obtuseness when not illuminated by an intelligent motive or by a worthy objective, should suffice to prove its subordinate role as a faculty, a rank that it shares, though not equally to be sure, with all the other faculties such as intuition, memory, sentiment, instinct, and even sensation,[2] all of which are used by intelligence. Before proceeding further, one ought to mention that reason is not absolutely synonymous with mind because the mind, when defined as spirit or as Emerson's "oversoul," is inherently synthetic or unitive,[3] whereas reason is inherently discursive. Reason is stilled—but not extinct—once consciousness is absorbed in the divine.

If reason is a central faculty in that it winnows the perceptions harvested and stored by the other faculties, it is not for all that the agent of knowledge, even though it is

---

2. Reason is superior to sensation in that sensation is a peripheral faculty meant to inform reason. Also, reason is not strictly dependent on sensation, contrary to what materialist philosophers like Hume and finally even a Kant assert, because it still has recourse to logic and can receive data supra-sensually or directly from the spirit via the soul—though this can be largely atrophied in our mental culture of machines and computers. Moreover, in spirituality, the senses can be systematically put to sleep in view of favoring inward knowledge. That said, sensation, in that it can feel for example the warmth of love by rebound, which reason cannot, can be said to be related to the heart. Therefore, its subaltern role has its compensatory qualities owing to the principle which has that extremes meet. Now, that sensation, or the senses, can clog reason in the unregenerate man—which is why ascetic mysticism tries to deaden it—is no prediction of its role in the sage. Suffice it to say here that sensation need not be contrary to sense: it has no power of its own either to veil or to reveal.

3. This does not protect it from becoming the prey of multiplicity, however, nor from the depredation of desire and agitation. Moreover, mind is often defined in opposition to heart when in fact the two faculties prolong each other, the former in objective mode, the latter in subjective mode.

unique to man thus setting him decisively above all other creatures which neither know what they are nor have any need to. Man is the only creature that knows he is mortal.[4] An animal, on the other hand, has no notion of self-relativization: it is what it is and nothing more,[5] whereas man can be almost anything, including an animal.

Knowledge in the full sense, if it is not to be the mere gathering of information, is rooted in being, as has been previously explained. To know is to be, just as to be is to know, because no man can know more than he is. In other words, before man can know something, he must first of all be something. Augustine gives us the prototype of this principle when he states that "in God, to be is the same as to be wise." Conversely, ignorance, for man, is a form of non-being or, at most, a form of peripheral being involving perforce a preponderant measure of mindlessness, or lack of awareness. The fact that knowledge can be divorced from being, however provisorily, does not detract from this fundamental axiom.[6]

Having said this, we are not unaware that one of the strangest paradoxes of "fallen man"—that is to say man

---

4. In a completely different sense, animals do have a sense of their impending death. But this does not mean that they have the capacity to speculate about their own end.

5. One of the proofs of the falsehood of the theory of evolution is that animals incarnate attributes and therefore are part of the cosmos' store of riches. There is no need for them to evolve, except in the most relative of senses, because they are perfect in themselves. The notion of improvement is senseless because it would be as if the part sought to become the whole. Moreover, a butterfly does not need to become a bird to be perfect, or more perfect. A universe in which each species had "evolved" to become the one supreme specie is unimaginable, unnecessary, and thus absurd and impossible. Otherwise all fish would be birds and all birds would be cats, and so on and so forth.

6. In the Vedanta, one distinguishes between *aparavidya*, the "lower wisdom," which involves mental learning, and the non-dual *vijnana*, "plenitude of knowledge."

ON AWAKENING AND REMEMBERING

separated from his theomorphic substance[7]—is that, on a certain plane or in certain limited respects, he can know more than he is. For instance, he can know the truth in his mind while espousing error in his being. Or understanding in the mind can preclude understanding in the heart. This is the post-Edenic schism between mind and heart, the cause of some bizarre and sometimes even monstrous possibilities, which religion is come to mend. At first sight, this aberration would seem to refute the premise of the indissociability of knowledge and being. But in this case one is invariably dealing with a knowledge that can be merely partial or external, and therefore one that does not constitute—to borrow from mysticism—knowledge in the heart, the only one that matters in the end because the only one to survive the grave.

All knowledge, when integral, is knowledge in the heart because knowledge at its core operates on the basis of identity and only subsequently, or externally, on that of alterity or via otherness, whence the use in spirituality of the term "eye of the heart." The knower and the known must share some basis of filiation[8] without which there would be no basis of contact. With animals, the filiation is only partial in that they represent only one particular archetype, whereas man is the synthesis of the cosmos and this is the basis of his knowledge of it, whence the doctrine of identity.[9] Reason is to the heart what the moon is to the sun, a mirror; in each

---

7. Scholasticism: in created things essence and existence are different, but they are one in God.

8. "Let me know myself, Lord, and I shall know Thee," St. Augustine prays. Meister Eckhart brazenly states that "the soul is not *like* God: she is identical with him."

9. Conversely, release from the bondage in manifestation requires, in the doctrine of Theravada Buddhism, that the individual soul realize the truth of *anatman* (literally "no soul"). This is less the way of extinction than that of non-selfishness, for as long as the soul considers itself to be individual, it cannot free itself from the otherwise endless round of

pair, the former borrows its light—identity—from the latter.[10] It is this principle of identity, be it ever so veiled or
ever so remote, that allows for certainty in understanding.
To use a bold ellipsis: man could not know anything at all
were he not capable of knowing everything. Plato supports
this when affirming that if the soul is immortal and rational, then it knows everything that can be known; this is the
very basis of Socratic midwifery—maieutics or bringing to
birth ideas innate to the soul.

Moreover, without this principle of identity, man could
not, for instance, love a rose nor know it in any way were
it not that he mysteriously carried the archetype of the
rose—which is ultimately the archetype of beauty—in his
substance.[11] Whereas the bee can only "know" the rose as
nectar, man can love it for itself or see in it a message from

---

rebirths. Free from all particular identities, the soul is restored to its root
identity in the One Self. In the *Bardo Thodöl* or *The Tibetan Book of the
Dead*, the soul of the deceased is immediately confronted with appari-
tions of wrathful and beneficent deities. If the soul is able to perceive the
identity between its own innate luminosity and the great light of reality,
then liberation is achieved. But to do so, the soul must shun the temptation of identity with a host of beings that will confront it, and which,
finally, are but the projections of its own soul substance.

10. Schuon defines reason, in his landmark *Logic and Transcendence*,
as "the faculty to know indirectly in the absence of a direct vision and
with the help of points of reference" (Ch. "Evidence and Mystery"). In
other words, unlike the intellect which knows actively, the reason cannot know anything by itself. On the other hand, for Plato, reason is practically speaking synonymous with Schuon's notion of the intellect.

11. Here an objection could be raised, that to know evil or anything
ugly, foul, or vile need not imply identity as a necessary preliminary.
Very true, but in this case it is a question not of intimate affinity, but of
intimate revulsion predicated on the very positiveness of a prior archetype. Only a luminous essence can disavow darkness. It is a matter of
the real refuting its counterfeit or opposite, of health rejecting disease.
What is axiomatic is that only a positive can recognize a negative, not
vice versa. Only the absolute can situate the relative.

paradise. Or he has recourse to the poetic power of metaphor which allows him, in virtue of the unity of beauty, to see in a rose a symbol of a beloved maiden. To affirm this is but one small way to illustrate the doctrine of the "unity of the real" (the *wahdat al wujud* or the "unity of existence" of the Sufis to which we will return), a doctrine whose principle of operation Eckhart summarized in his famous saying: "The eye with which I see God is the very eye with which God sees me," whereby knower, knowing, and known are conjoined as one. Hence knowledge, in its essence, entails an act of deep communion[12]—in Plotinian terms the journey of the one to the One. This brings us back to Hermes' only like can know like: "If you cannot equate yourself with God, you cannot know Him." Wherefore Christ's injunction, "Be ye perfect as your Father in Heaven is perfect," which would be meaningless if man were not linked in his heart first to his Maker and then, by kindred extension to all of His creation. No relationship can be established between things, or beings, and myself without underlying kinship: "*Mitakuye oyasin*," a Sioux Indian greeting says, "We are all relatives."

IF ONE AGREES that knowledge, and especially gnosis, is the paramount quality that differentiates man from the animals, it follows then that it must also be his reason for being,[13] otherwise his faculty of thought, and the whole capacity for cosmic awareness it entails, would be absurdly gratuitous, indeed impossible since a faculty is always a signpost of being. In other words, without knowledge, man

---

12. It is not by accident that the Bible uses the verb "to know" to describe conjugal union.

13. Hence Leibniz: "It is the knowledge of necessary and eternal truths that distinguishes us from mere animals and gives us Reason and the sciences, raising us to the knowledge of ourselves and of God" (*Monadology* 28-30).

is not fully man,[14] a want that opens wide the gates to every subhuman tendency imaginable, as is all too dismally evident if one looks at history. And knowledge, in its turn, is meaningless without Reality. Thus intelligence where man is concerned[15] could be defined as his capacity to know Reality. Or again, man is intelligent to the degree that he understands—or wishes to understand—Reality, and of course all that this entails both morally and eschatologically.

The supereminent role of knowledge may become more apparent if one starts from the premise that the universe is, in its essence, pure consciousness (*chitta*) mani-

---

14. Proof positive of this, were it necessary, can be obtained by reflecting that man, were he deprived of the capacity to think, would be a kind of brutish creature bent on replenishing itself and propagating itself. Concurrently, one could ask what reason would be without Truth. Inconceivable as this is, reason would then be a faculty of fantastic or diabolical cunning totally dedicated to obtaining one's self-advantage. And that this is, in fact, its use in irreligious men does not account for its purpose. Incidentally, too much is made in pseudo-Zen circles of recovering the primacy of spontaneity at the expense of reason: to break the mold of mental categories does not mean that one need resort to irrationality. Nor is a "liberated" instinctuality the same as mindfulness; nor—for those who confuse sincerity with vulgarity—is crudeness the proof of naturalness or of concreteness. One of the strangest, and finally perverse, psychological paradoxes is the example of intellectuals who develop a complex about their intellectuality, the spell of which they seek to exorcise by debasing themselves in a misbegotten attempt to return to the primacy of pure being.

15. We leave the door intentionally open because different beings have different kinds of intelligence. For example, angels, who cannot sin, have an intelligence that does not parallel exactly that of man who alone among all created beings is capable of that depth of ignorance which, schematically speaking, matches the height of knowledge his nature is heir to. Regarding the moral impeccability of angels, there is reason to believe that the term "fallen angel"—as it applies to Lucifer— is a contradiction in terms given that angels are creatures of light and therefore have no shadow.

fested as being;[16] in Vedantic terms, *Maya* (the cosmic illusion of manifestation) is the dream of *Atma* (the supreme being). And, "In the beginning was the Word,"[17] which accounts for the fact that phenomena are really but coagulated modes of consciousness. If the body is known to be the unfolding of the heart projected as creaturely form,[18] then, macrocosmically, the universe would be the unfolding of the Creator's heart, which explains how the universe was created out of divine love.

With respect to the foregoing, we can say that intelligence in man is a question, not of mental ability,[19] as we have mentioned already, but of awareness, and in its arche-

---

16. "The Divine Mother revealed to me in the Kali temple that it was She who had become everything," Ramakrishna, the celebrated Indian *bhaktic* mystic, told his disciples. "She showed me that everything was full of Consciousness. The Image was Consciousness, the altar was Consciousness, the water-vessels were Consciousness, the doorsill was Consciousness, the marble floor was Consciousness—all was Consciousness, I found everything inside the room soaked, as it were, in Bliss" (*The Gospel of Shri Ramakrishna*). And, by analogy, this is why the American Indians venerate the earth as Mother Earth and consider, therefore, that nothing produced by her is inanimate, not even stones.

17. When, in the opening lines of his *Faust*, Goethe proposes to substitute "action" for the divine Verb or Word—"In the beginning was the Deed"—he is in fact attempting to substitute the effect for the cause, because cosmologically speaking action results from knowledge, not inversely. God is one before He is two. Thus action, which is knowledge applied, entails duality, namely an agent plus a deed.

18. Schuon comments that the human body is a formal manifestation or image of intelligence. And to paraphrase this, one could say that man's body is an image of truth and of strength, whereas woman's body is that of love and beauty, though as *anthropos*, both share common characteristics which precede their differences. Following this, man's body would be truth as principle and woman's truth as being.

19. It is well known that there are intellectually deficient human beings who nonetheless have phenomenal mental skills, for example the quantitatively exhaustive memory of certain autistic types.

typal essence, pure awareness—*vijnana* or the state of *atman* (the individual soul) as identified with the spirit. Thoreau described this as the auroral capacity in man to have a permanent dawn in his consciousness.[20] And awareness rises proportionately with detachment from self (*anatman*), something that implies both the virtues of total humility and of charity. In other words, without humility and without its active extension as charity, no real awareness. Conversely, to work now from without within, charity deepens with humility which, in its turn, fosters awareness—humility being here emptiness for God and availability to His will expressed through "thy neighbor."

Hence, to be intelligent is not to know this or that, but to know— intellectively—real from illusory, or what is of essential value from what is dispensable, and then, morally, to know right from wrong. The stupid person is the one who does not make use of this innate sense of right and wrong—or of good and evil—inherent in the very definition of man who, unlike animals that are horizontal (or horizontally active and vertically passive), is a vertical creature as evinced by his erect stature.[21]

---

20. "We must learn to reawaken and keep ourselves awake, not by mechanical aids, but by an infinite expectation of the dawn, which does not forsake us in our soundest sleep" (*Walden*).

21. That birds are the only other creatures whose head is placed above the shoulders does not infirm the symbolism of man's erectness. First of all, of the birds only the owl can assume a perfectly vertical posture when perched, the others being more or less oblique; however, in flight, he can only proceed in a horizontal mode. The main reason for what must really be termed the semi-erectness of birds probably has something to do with the symbolism of their realm, that of air, which is associated with the ideas of altitude, of light, of freedom from inertia, and thus by association with verticality. Thus the morphology of a bird— which is the form of its type of "intelligence"—results from an existential affinity with the nature of its realm. Incidentally, the association between the owl, the bird of Athena, and wisdom is far from fortuitous.

Given that the stakes ultimately involve man's redemption or that the right choices will finally trace a path back to God, it becomes apparent that stupidity—which could be defined here as the propensity to make the wrong choices over and over again or, by dint of comfortable habit, to prefer sleep over wakefulness, or ignorance over knowledge— entails far more than a harmless notion of dullness or befuddlement, but rather, in its radical intent, so often disguised by chummy conviviality, a willful avoidance or even a rejection of truth.

Let us understand this well: intelligence, at its root, is a tropism or a kind of deep ontological instinct, engraved in the heart,[22] that compels man to migrate back towards the light whence he originates. This is his celestial birthright. In this respect, intelligence cannot be divorced from conscience, St. Jerome's *scintilla conscientiae* or the trace of light which constitutes man's intellect, the seal of the Divine in man's heart without which he could not live even for an instant and which in the end determines that, in Boehme's words, "every soul is its own judgment."[23]

TO RETURN TO the premise of this chapter, if virtue is a form of luminous or *sattvic*[24] being and being a form of consciousness, then virtue is intelligence, no longer merely

---

22. Sai Baba, famed Indian saint at the beginning of the 20th Century, venerated by Hindus and Moslems alike: "It is all within you. Try to listen inwardly and follow the direction you get."

23. And again, Boehme: "God casts no soul away, unless it cast itself away."

24. In the ancient Hindu Sankhya school of philosophy, creation is divided into three *gunas* or basic cosmic qualities: *sattva*, or the ascending, static, and luminous quality, *rajas* or the expanding, dynamic, and fiery quality, and *tamas* or the descending, dark, and heavy quality. The coined adjective *"sattvic"* is derived thus from the Sanskrit term *sattva*.

conceptual, but existentially operative and consequential.[25] Formulated differently, one might say that intelligence is preeminently a function of awareness. And awareness, in its turn , is not only a factor of capacity—or scope of character, existential breadth of being—but also, and above all, a factor of receptivity or of mindfulness. And what is receptivity if not foremost a matter of attitude and therefore of virtue? Furthermore, if we can understand that the Truth, or Reality, is sacred,[26] then we can understand how knowledge involves virtue, "For to know thee is perfect righteousness" (Wis. 15:3). Starkly put, truth remains a sealed book to the impious, for what is sacred can only be known through holiness of being. For Plato virtue not only presupposes knowledge, but virtue *is* knowledge.

And if intelligence—understood here as a whole attitude in reference to Reality—may be said to be a fundamental virtue, then its converse, stupidity, may be said to be, and ineluctably so, a form of sin against the Holy Ghost.[27] As Ramana Maharshi bluntly puts it: "You can be

---

25. Hence Schuon can say in *To Have a Center*: "It is important to understand that in spirituality more than in any other domain the character of a person is part of his intelligence" (Ch. "Intelligence and Character").

26. Nothing is more deadening to the soul's faculty of idealism than to make a virtue out of ordinariness, in other words to reduce the Real to the commonplace and to make of the plain, the earthbound, and the prosaic a measure of spiritual humility. Examples of this abound in spirituality, for instance of claiming that the Blessed Virgin was a simple village girl—she who was a direct descendent of the royal house of David. If, on the one hand the rustic and the simple, along with folk wisdom possesses a charm and vigor that is part of the magic of naturalness, one must not forget, on the other hand, that spirituality is synonymous with the patrician qualities of nobility and distinction that lie at the antipodes of what finally is a proletarian attempt to keep man sod-bound.

27. Be this term understood here in its meaning of *mahat* or the universal, macrocosmic intellect (*buddhi*).

said to commit the murder of Brahma by not realizing that you are Brahma."

Indeed, one could expand this to say that God as surely lives in a righteous deed as He may be said to "die" in an iniquitous one; in Christian terms, this amounts to crucifying Christ again. Sentimental tears cannot dilute the fact that the karmic consequences of stupidity can be disastrous, to say nothing of the agony of the eruption of consciousness resulting at the end, because no man can escape his conscience forever. The web of *Maya*, to be sure, offers myriad attenuating circumstances for a man to plead ignorance, at least with respect to relatively minor faults, the venial sins. And mishap is part of the learning process. Furthermore, men cannot be held to an absolute standard of knowledge, otherwise there would be no manifestation which, by cosmological definition, entails ignorance. But they are held—in principle at least—to an absolute standard of morality which, be it said in passing, can be adhered to in the absence of this knowledge, for virtue starts with obedience according to this saying that "fear is the beginning of wisdom."[28]

It may now be apposite to make a distinction between a horizontal ignorance, which is merely a question of a lack

---

28. Also, and very obviously, the direct moral responsibility of the carnal (or hylic) type, who is by nature compulsively concupiscent, cannot be equal to that of a purely spiritual (or pneumatic) type. In other words, Heaven is less forgiving of those who "know better." The pneumatic type is identified with the *guna* of *sattva* (the ascending or luminous tendency in the cosmos). In a descending mode, the psychic type is identified with the *guna* of *rajas* (the expansive, fiery, and, in man, passional tendency). Finally, the hylic type is identified with the *guna* of *tamas* (the descending or darkening tendency). As for the three human types, they correspond respectively to the tripartite division known in antiquity of spirit, soul, and body.

of information, and which is therefore morally neutral, and a vertical ignorance which involves a principial blindness—the *avidya* or nescience of the Vedanta—and which therefore cannot be morally neutral since it implies ignorance first of oneself, which is not forgivable, and then, by spiritual inference, ignorance, if not directly of the Self, at least of Its delegate human projections on earth according to the principle that "he that receiveth whomsoever I send receiveth me."

Thus if ignorance should not hastily be equated with stupidity,[29] it should nevertheless be apparent that when protracted, in other words when either systematically or complacently adhered to over time, it loses whatever initially mitigating quality of unawareness or inconscience it could plead, for after awhile it can no longer claim the status of ignorance, precisely. Conversely, the heedlessness of youth cannot be judged by the same moral parameters as that of an elder. An individual destiny, when seen from above in the eternal simultaneity of space, is the actualization of a fundamental tendency of soul: "For as he thinketh in his heart, so is he" (Prov. 23:7). What we are saying is that the waste of such a sacred faculty as intelligence must have some correspondence with sin, in the sense of an ontological transgression whereby an individual betrays his fundamental vocation, his God-given raison d'être as a man. And, for want perhaps of a better term, we will call this sin that of stupidity.

---

29. For instance, not knowing one's multiplication tables is not necessarily a matter of stupidity. An example, apocryphal perhaps but wholly plausible, is that of a Sufi saint who never learned more than the first two letters of the Arabic alphabet—the lightning-like vertical *alif* and the womb-like horizontal *ba* ("a" and "b"), because having grasped their meaning, which is the joining of the principle to the soul (analogous to the Hindu coupling of the bolt of lightning and the lotus), he attained spiritual realization. The contemplative man, who has a natural sense for essentials, has little appetite for discursivity.

IT IS OFTEN stated, in the democratic Western cultures, that people are entitled to their opinion and this without regard to the possible merits of that opinion. Now it is one thing to concede that, in a society deprived of effective doctrinal authority,[30] no man can lightly stand as judge over another without risking to unleash the arbitrary forces of tyranny. But one cannot overlook, however, the cumulatively detrimental effect that enough errant opinions will exercise over individuals in a given collectivity; there is a principle of deterioration in nature that applies to societies as well. The ancient adage *vox populi vox dei* [31]presupposes, for the most part, a "normal"[32] social order—if this predicate can have any meaning in an age ruled by habits rather than customs—not one in which moral institutions are in full-scale collapse and in which the only check on wanton license is the length of time the shock of novelty needs to be dulled in a civilization which is fast loosing its sense of shame. Freedom of thought should not mean freedom of error, because error is contrary to freedom, just as lameness is contrary to efficiency: a house divided cannot stand.

If it is not always easy to establish the criteria by which right and wrong are to be adjudicated, this does not mean that right and wrong do not exist or that they are but arbitrary distinctions. Man—every man and woman—carries

---

30. Traditionally, that is to say in all ancient cultures, education was normally the province of a priestly class or of the Church, and this for what should be critically obvious reasons.

31. The foil to this adage, of course, is that error, like misery, loves company. And, unlike knowledge, it cannot exist alone.

32. The term "normal" has become outlandish in a society that becomes more and more heterogeneous by the day. "Normal" comes from "norm," and this cannot be simply a matter of popular convenience because societies degenerate and therefore can deviate from the Norm which is originally, in the time of the guardian spirit ancestors, identical with archetypal reality.

THE EIGHTH CARDINAL SIN

within him the original law, the law which even the stars must heed, and this law can never be violated with impunity. In a society where an intellectual and moral elite is no longer established, wrong thinking and error spread ineluctably until they usurp what should be the natural order of things, becoming the overwhelming and crushing "norm." Animals, whose instincts are a form of natural intelligence and of "certitude," are spared these debates for they cannot have opinions, so they cannot err. Now, the realm of opinions, as Plato comments in his *Republic*, is not of the same elevated or uncontaminated˙ order as that of knowledge whose purview is the realm of certainty. Therefore, opinion can err according to the degree of an individual's subjectivity. As a matter of fact, opinion always involves a greater or lesser measure of uncertainty barring which it would not be opinion. This measure is of course perfectly tolerable provided it does not trespass into extra-individual domains where the collectivity's spiritual welfare is at stake. Moreover, opinion, even when dim, can be a speculative prelude to knowledge. But it is a fantasy to grant opinion a status which belongs by right only to certitude, because opinion, to prevail or to rule, needs force, be it plebiscitary or military; it does not carry this force within itself.

To resume with the main argument, the relationship between thought and being is that between light and substance, or spirit and soul. As the Bhagavad Gita enunciates, whatsoever a man thinketh, that he becometh.[33] In other words, there is a direct equation between right thinking

---

33. "Whatever occupies the mind at the time of death determines the destination of the dying; always they will tend toward that state of being" (Ch. VIII, v. 6). "Thinking" has, of course, a generic meaning here and it involves not so much the particular thought at the time of death, or just the mind as such, but the soul's fundamental nexus of preoccupations, both conscious and subconscious.

and an individual's well-being. Just as truth has a luminous agency on a person's soul and, by extension, on his physical health, so likewise error can undermine this person's well-being, to say nothing of his becoming in the afterlife which is a crystallization of his earthly course. Only intelligence can reverse the decaying or even corrupting influence of stupidity.

As Parmenides of Elea declared: "Thinking is identical with being." If this is so, then the salutary hygiene that correct or true thinking imparts to the body/soul complex[34] has been either seriously underestimated or wholly overlooked in the Christian West where reason has never succeeded in freeing itself, on the one hand, from the stigma of unbelief associated with it ever since the Christly redress of the spirit which the Pharisaical letter had suffocated and, on the other, from the morally disengaged pyrotechnics of Greek sophistry which boasted that it could use logic to make evil seem just as appealing as virtue. This taint was only intensified, in spite of Augustinian scholasticism,[35] with the advent of so-called humanism which is radically inhuman since it divorces man from his divine origin thereby making of him a *de facto* god. Christian theology has historically tended to treat reason as a pagan intruder in the temple of faith, denouncing it as the enemy of the heart, whence an irreconcilable break that has unwittingly not

---

34. The spirit is not included in this complex since, by definition, it cannot err being that it is supra-individual. Nor is it susceptible to growth and decay. What wrong thinking does is to effect its exclusion from consciousness. Also, if *mens sana in corpore sano* is true enough in principle, with some restrictions of which ailing saints offer compelling examples, the reverse can be said to be far truer owing to the decisive superiority of the mind over the physical body, which, as alluded to earlier, is really a materialization of mind.

35. But even the logic of this scholasticism, just as with Duns Scotus and Aquinas later, granted reason only a subaltern role to love.

only widened the post-Edenic divide between mind and heart, but has also unintentionally prepared the terrain for atheistic rationalism since, by refusing to provide explanations that respond to certain legitimate needs of the intelligence, it has forfeited the high terrain of logic, leaving it unprotected from the depredations of free-thinkers. Even Aquinas in his attempt to reconcile reason and faith ultimately surrenders the fortress by declaring knowledge's impotence to know supernatural reality: "We cannot know what God is, but only what He is not" (*Summa Theologica* I, i , 3; i, 30). Or the self-canceling affirmation: "The highest knowledge we can have of God in this life is to know that He is above all that we can think concerning Him" (*De veritate* ii, 10), because if this is so then wherefore the divine gift of intelligence? Aquinas even berates man for daring to push the inquiry further: "Why should infinitesimal minds expect to know more about the Infinite?" Therefore, in questions of ultimate importance, his *Summa* begs the question and has recourse to the classical apophatic expedient of Christian fideism when confronted with too pressing an interrogation from the Hellenistic *ratio*: "It is a great mystery!" We can hear the sniggering of Voltaire across the ages. Yet, Aquinas is right in protecting the articles of Christian faith from a cynical questioning which can only repel divine grace. And he is right if he makes intelligence synonymous merely with reason which, without the concourse of the intellect, cannot understand what is supra-rational. However to say that God is ineffable should not mean that He is incomprehensible to adequate reason or to intelligence born of virtue. Leibniz's *Theodicy* suffers from the same lameness, though purportedly a defense of God as its title indicates. Indeed, since the advent of the Renaissance especially, Christian apologetics has floundered because it has been unable to address cosmological problems such as evil or free will with any measure of rational success.

73

Yet the Delphic injunction, "Know thyself," cannot in reality be said to be of less vital significance than the Biblical injunction to know God, to say the least. In fact, the one goes necessarily with the other. And, as indeed must be the case owing to man's ontological rootedness in God, this mandate has been re-echoed by Christian luminaries such as St. Augustine—"Let me know myself, Lord, and I shall know Thee"—or Meister Eckhart[36]—"No man knows God who knows not himself first"—to mention but two notable examples. Hence, it follows that the same faculty of reason, because of its fulcrum role at the dividing line between outwardness and inwardness—or between worldliness and spirituality—can, when separated from metaphysical principle, "collude"[37] with passion to bring about man's ultimate alienation just as it can, when informed by Truth, collaborate with intellectual intuition to return the soul back to God, in a great reflux of consciousness, more effectively than were it to work by faith alone.

And, needless to say, it is not a question—as some modern pseudo-spirituality supposes—for man to "think" himself back to God, though this is not impossible with a pure contemplative such as Ramana Maharshi who was naturally penetrated with the sense of the Divine Presence, but rather a question of not leaving out any part of his faculties in this conversion: "Thou shallt love the Lord thy God with all thy mind," Christ commands, not just with "all thy heart" and "all thy soul." And "with all thy mind" means that obedience to be obedience need not be blind; indeed, as has

----

36. Frithjof Schuon once wrote that "Eckhart was a manifestation of St. John," the Evangelist who is considered to be the prototype of Christian gnosis (*Considérations générales sur les fonctions spirituelles*, *Etudes Traditionnelles*, Paris, Novembre-Décembre 1939).

37. Properly speaking, reason cannot "collude" or "will" anything since it is only an instrument, the seat of desire being the heart. However, it can be suborned to cooperate with falsehood.

been stated before, one must know why and to whom and to what one is obedient; otherwise one is just influenceable, not obedient. But this is not to diminish St. Anselm's *credo ut intelligam*, "I believe that I may understand," for faith is a necessary preliminary for man whose starting point is always a greater or lesser measure of ignorance.

THE BIAS AGAINST intelligence, or knowledge, in favor of faith—however expedient it may otherwise be in certain religious traditions[38]—inevitably inflected the medieval doctrine of the *peccata capitalia*[39] to set moral priorities on man's volitive and affective duties at the expense of his intellective prerogatives. These sins were indirectly opposed to seven cardinal virtues: four "natural" or pagan virtues because extolled already by Pythagoras and Plato (wisdom, courage, justice, and temperance) and three "theological" virtues (faith, hope, and charity). Now, it is interesting to note that the first of the so-called "pagan" virtues, namely wisdom, was somehow dropped by the wayside by a pietist Christianity anxious to keep man humble and on the "straight and narrow;" and yet it was the first named. Moreover, if pride can be inversely equated with wisdom in a certain sense, it is rather humility that it excludes—although wisdom is the supreme remedy to the ultimate sin which pride is. As for humility, it is not directly synonymous with wisdom, though surely no one can have wisdom and not be humble. But the fact that the notion of wisdom carried a philosophical connotation ren-

---

38. It may also be a question of spiritual opportuneness for given individuals, as a precaution, for instance, against the excesses of cerebralism or, what is far graver, against the temptation to know everything with the mind alone.

39. These cardinal sins are: pride (*superbia*), sloth (*accidia*), envy (*invidia*), lechery (*luxuria*), anger (*ira*), gluttony (*gula*), and avarice (*avaritia*).

dered it awkward to integrate as a virtue proper if not making it frankly inassimilable in a moral context that stressed the paramount merit of devotion while treating intelligence with suspicion when not with the hostility of anathemas. Nonetheless, it is worth retaining that Christianity began this list with wisdom at the top, even though by neglecting it later, it left this "virtue" for the humanism of the Renaissance and the Enlightenment to appropriate, however abusively.

Thus the "seven deadly sins", as they are also known, are ordered around the notion that love is the greatest virtue. If stupidity—which parallels the *avidya* of the Vedanta, but without exact synonymy—is omitted whereas sins like gluttony or avarice are not, it is partly because intelligence, at least in a fideal climate extolling the moral supremacy of total obedience for the individual who is "the worst of sinners," is thought to be almost exclusively a divine attribute which it would be presumption and folly for a mortal to lay claim to. Yet when the Bible says that "man does not live by bread alone, but by every word that proceedeth out of the mouth of God," this presupposes a faculty in man for which these "words" must be fully intelligible if they are to have more meaning than the mere exhortations of a mule driver to his train.

At this point, it is necessary to say that, in enumerating an eighth deadly sin, we do not presume to improve on the providential symbolism of the traditional septenary which harmonizes with many others.[40] We mention it simply because it has some essential relevance to the total alchemical economy of the soul's spiritual work, to say nothing of the fact that not only is it the contrary of wisdom, the first

---

40. Such as that of the seven days of Creation, the seven days of the week, the seven sacraments of the Church, the seven visible planets—to name but a few.

of the cardinal virtues mentioned, but that in another cosmological context it might have been included instead of,
let us say, the sin of avarice or that of lechery or anger.[41]
Indeed, it is a question here less of symbolism or of numerical symmetries than of the fundamental nature of things.

Now, one might want to point out that stupidity is not
a sin but rather a state of mind, or simply obtuseness, that
is consubstantial to sin as such and therefore not worth
singling out. However, if intelligence can be perceived as
a distinct quality, then it seems logical that its converse,
stupidity—understood here not as mere vacuity or asinin-
ity but as culpable ignorance[42]—can likewise be said to
operate as a distinct state of consciousness or, if one

---

41. For instance, in Buddhism, nescience (which is related to stupidity) is listed, along with suffering, lust, and ill-will (which is close to
malice—a sin against the Holy Ghost), as one of the impediments in the
doctrine of the "Four Noble Truths", and whose defilement of the soul
stands as one of the main obstacles to enlightenment. Indeed, defilement, in its generality, contributes to *avidya* (ignorance), requiring a
"cleansing away" (*vyavadana*) that restores the radiance of the jewel (the
heart). In the *Yoga-Sutras* of the Sankhya metaphysics of Hinduism,
nescience is listed as the first of the five great impairments (*klesa*).
Nonetheless, Christianity, being a divine revelation, does not wholly
overlook this, to say the least. Thus Aquinas takes a step, or a half step,
in the direction of listing nescience as a sin by mentioning "uncaring
ignorance" as one of the cardinal sins—the accent, though, being on the
emotional pole, or on the lack of moral charity or on the insensitivity, but
without pardoning the component of ignorance.

42. Instead of stupidity, one could have spoken, like in the Far-
Eastern philosophies, merely of ignorance (*avidya*). But this latter term,
in Western culture at any rate, is both too vague and too inclusive. Its
main connotation, that of simply not knowing, is wholly neutral, morally speaking, and certainly need not connote stupidity. Whereas stupidity, not only connotes ignorance, but an actively indulged state of ignorance that is, to a greater or lesser degree, and more or less consciously,
willed. It presupposes on the part of the subject an intimate identity with
ignorance and an affinity with denseness or, as the Hindus would say,
with something *tamasic*.

prefers, lack thereof, but a lack that is willfully maintained, or consented to, for whatever reason on the part of the subject. It is certainly an initial condition that serves as a catalyst, or as a fertile terrain, for the other moral blindnesses. At any rate, it is altogether possible to observe stupidity as a general attitude in the formal absence of one or another of the specific cardinal sins. For instance, a person might demonstrate a foolhardy obtuseness in the face of repeated remonstrance without necessarily being either greedy or envious or avaricious, at least not in the crudely specific sense of these terms. Or, he may display a sentimental attachment to a failing and cling to it no matter how silly or absurd it is, and he may do so even at the price of public ridicule, perhaps out of an irrational need for self-preservation whereby he protects his individualism. Or he may choose a destructive course of action out of depression, fully aware of the consequences but unwilling to amend his behavior, perhaps out of a cynicism which stems always from a lack of faith. Of course, this lack of faith, which is another of the sins against the Holy Ghost, results from a hardening of the heart which is a form of denseness. And this proves that different faults usually share a common substratum and, as a result, can become interchangeable just as when acquiring one virtue, one acquires the others, at least potentially. But the issue here is to differentiate virtues and their corresponding inversion.

The difficulty of defining stupidity as a sin on a par with the other deadly sins results directly from the fact that the virtue it disfigures, namely intelligence, essentially transcends individuality proper and, as such, is situated outside of time. Therefore, it is not in itself limited to the hide-and-go-seek play of causality between agent and object found in the realm of *nama rupa* (name and form) inherent to manifestation. In other words, intelligence could be said to be, in some respect, a more central virtue[43] than even humility or charity, and certainly than either temperance or prudence. In this respect, it is comparable only to love in its importance. The other virtues, in their practical or utilitarian import, are more specifically attributes of post-Edenic man,[44] one might say—without forgetting that man as such is dust in regard to the Absolute who alone is good, as Christ reminds us—whereas intelligence belongs wholly to God and only to the individual insofar as he is potentially theomorphic. Moreover, stupidity, for its part, does not always involve passion the way the other cardinal sins do, though they, in turn, cannot exist without a preliminary stupidity since all starts with consciousness, or the darkening thereof.

NOT TO BELABOR the point, but sentimentality being ever ready to forgive attitudes or types of behavior that do not threaten our profane comfort, it may be worth restating several aspects of this issue. On the face of it, stupidity would seem to be a rather innocuous bumbling, the perhaps innocent result of simply not knowing better. Again, while this may be true as regards horizontal matters, it cannot be so as regards vertical issues, because to be man is to know better; it is, by definition, to be aware of reality, if only intuitively.

Thus, if one is to say that stupidity is more than a mere lack of intelligence, namely a tendency of the soul to be reckoned equally with all the vices with which it colludes, while being at the same time distinct in its own right, how

---

43. Virtue should be understood in its most radical extension as a vital or necessary state of being and not in its occasional meaning of good deed.

44. Of course, each virtue has its celestial archetype, humility and temperance referring respectively to divine simplicity—or oneness—and to divine purity, charity to divine communion, and so forth.

could one define it? One might say that one of its essential features is a lack of a desire to transcend oneself which is combined with a stale self-complacency and a corresponding obtuseness in regard to the mediocrity of one's unregenerate self. Hence, the first attribute of stupidity is inertia, not just in the sense of the sin of sloth (*accidia*), but much more in the sense of the cosmic tendency towards massive obscurity which, as has been mentioned earlier, corresponds to *tamas*.[45] In other words, it is first of all an indifference to light, or a refusal, whether passive or active, to heed the call of the luminous and ascending tendency (*sattva*) in divine manifestation.[46]

Secondly, and in the wake of the former, stupidity is characterized by a lack of a sense of proportions whereby the lesser or imperfect or impure is preferred to the greater, the perfect, and the pure. In a word, the stupid man prefers himself to God. And he does not see that the huge universe with its lofty snow-clad mountains and "multitudinous seas," its sheltering valleys and mysterious forests, its sentinel stars and roaming winds is vastly more important than he himself can ever possibly be. In fact, this creature finds little or nothing wrong in just being himself and may even wax presumptuous enough to advocate a doctrine of "sincerism" (*sincérisme*) whereby he is foolishly apt to equate whatever he happens to be—in the random occurrence of his perishable accidentality—with a species of naturalness or even assumes that this is a human norm of sorts, never mind how objectively trivial, mediocre, or

---

45. *Tamas* as a necessary cosmic tendency (*guna*) is not evil so much in its inception as in its conclusion, since without it the universe could never exist except as a potentiality in the divine mind.

46. One might say that, soteriologically speaking, a substance must become transfigured into light before it can be properly redeemed. "*Nadevo devam arcayet*," it is said in the *Gandharva Tantra*: "No one who is not himself divine may (successfully) worship the divinity."

base. Concretely, his personal self appears to him vastly
more real or infinitely worthier of concern than not only
that of his fellow man, but of the entire cosmos, let alone its
divine Cause. Or it may be that he will project his own subjectivity onto the rest of humanity, judging it by the same
cubbyhole standards he uses for himself.[47] This man has no
notion of hierarchical values and he has no inkling that he
is the puppet of a dream pierced by urgent fleshly prompt-
ings. By long self-indulged reflex, he is loath to surpass
himself, suspecting that such an effort is artificial or frankly
unnecessary. And he is wary of any injunction to self-
restraint, which he deems unnatural. Another assumption
of his is to take the behavior of the vulgar masses as some
kind of norm and to find in their sheer quantity of numbers
a comfort for his own banality.

This indifference to self-transcendence often goes along
with a rejection of idealism, though it is disguised as "realism." It takes matter and not the spirit, or light, as the criterion of Reality, overlooking the fact that matter does not
have its origin in itself.[48] In other words, the stupid person
prefers to vegetate in what is really a state of semi-
consciousness[49] since no one who is closed to the divine
can claim full wakefulness. Thus he will think only insofar
as it is practically necessary to in order to ensure the satis-
faction of his desires or only insofar as inconvenience
goads him to. But, as Socrates reminds us, the unexamined

---

47. A perfect description of this type of individual can be found in
Plato's metaphor of the cave in *The Republic*.

48. The idea of the eternity of creation, borrowed from the Greeks
and propounded by Avicenna and Averroës, and which was strenuously rejected by Aquinas and others, is not exactly synonymous with the
perennity of matter qua matter, because matter can be resorbed into the
subtle state which does not interrupt the permanence of creation, only
its modality in a given moment.

49. "Stupid" comes from "stupor".

life is not worth living. That is to say, the extraordinary gift of intelligence could never have been bestowed upon man were its purpose to work merely as a kind of cunning whereby he could obtain a material advantage over animals or other human beings while protecting his ego from the mortifying awareness of its nothingness before God.

Moreover, thinking is not a dispensable luxury, something that can be postponed or forfeited without consequence.[50] It is a vital necessity if man is to "shuffle off this mortal coil" of illusion. Not to think is to sleep or, worse, to dream. To know is to be awake and hence, potentially, immortal. "Meditation," says Aristotle, "is the occupation of the Gods."

Because man is aware of the Absolute, he cannot excuse his relativity.[51] Because, unlike animals, he can know that there is something greater than himself, something marvelous, he cannot with impunity bask in the lesser.[52] His intelligence, capable of conceiving the Truth, determines it so. Man's reason for being is not to build great cities or to analyze doubt; it is to know God and, by extension, to recognize and revere all in manifestation that reflects His Truth, Beauty, and Goodness. To ignore that vocation is the crassest and most impardonable of stupidities.

A WORD SHOULD be said here concerning an affiliate dimension of the problem discussed. If one starts with the idea that God is Truth and Beauty or at once pure transcendence and pure immanence, or pure intelligence and pure being, then stupidity would be to truth what ugliness is to beauty.

---

50. Cf. for instance Richard M. Weaver's *Ideas Have Consequences* (The University of Chicago Press).

51. Schuon has emphatically stated: "Man is condemned to the Absolute."

52. Julian of Norwich, a 14th century English prioress, sums it up thus: "Our Soul may never have rest in things that are beneath itself."

Moreover, since every point of view or disposition of the soul must have an existential counterpart according to the mind/existence division outlined, which retraces in microcosmic mode the principal polarization of spirit and being that runs through all of creation as warp and woof, then one can say that the gauge of real intelligence is beauty of soul.[53] In other words, an awareness of Truth absolute is mirrored in holiness of being, that is to say in virtue. If intelligence is to be not merely speculative and disengaged or sterile, but concrete, living, and operative then it will find embodiment in a type of behavior that mirrors its vision. Conversely, beauty of behavior—and we have in mind above all dignity[54] which is the spousal complement to man's erectness of stature—can serve in its turn as preparation for the awareness of Truth:[55] "Worship the Lord in the beauty of holiness" (Psalm 29:2).

Now, if the conscious foundation of dignity is awareness of the sacred, then it is no exaggeration to say that ugliness, or vulgarity for that matter, can correspond to the foremost sin against beauty,[56] which has been defined

---

53. Aquinas affirms that "beauty relates to the cognitive faculty" (*Sum. Theol.*, I, 5, 4).

54. Whether of posture, gesture, speech, or dress.

55. Dignity of attitude at all times is an existential form of consciousness of the divine, a kind of existential *mantra* (invocatory formula). Indeed, there is no mantra without *yantra* (a sacred diagram and, implicitly, any visual symbol), no word without image, and no *japa* (invocation or repetitive prayer) without *mantra* and *yantra*. Subtract the image and the existential support, and prayer risks being merely cerebral.

56. It is a question of beauty as such and not of comeliness which in itself is not a moral attribute just as homeliness is in no way a vice, although both have their karmic significance. In the words of Plotinus: "We ourselves possess Beauty when we are true to our own being; ugliness is in going over to another order; knowing ourselves, we are beautiful; in self-ignorance, we are ugly."

as "the splendor of the real."[57] If these assessments strike a layman—who may be unaware of the symbolism of attributes and their existential supports in behavior—as unduly severe, one might answer that for the sincere lover of Truth nothing man does or beholds can be unimportant since he perceives in earthly phenomena the trace of their archetypes or, as the case may be, of their deformation. Need one be reminded that man, unlike animals, is nothing without education and tutoring? Or that, in the absence of these he can, again unlike animals which are totally what they are, become almost anything on the sliding scale of the vertical axis which ranges from divinity to demon? Moreover, the nature of the world—society—is to fall, to disintegrate, and to degenerate. Thus, it requires on the part of man an incessant effort to overturn this downward pull and to rise, or at least not to fall, for which he needs to enroll all of his modalities of being from the intellectual to the existential, including those pertaining to his surroundings and decorations.

TO RETURN TO the main topic, it is man's innate intelligence, or the fact that every human being has a conscience at his core, or that he is linked to God by an intellective ray—it is this faculty, whether man wishes it or not, which, once all is said and done, stands as judgment over him.[58] That is to say, man's intelligence enables him to be fully objective in regard to himself and this objectivity

---

57. We are unsure of the origin of that phrase, which seems to belong to the Neo-Platonic current in Christianity.

58. In Christian theology a distinction is made between *synteresis*, which is the function in man's conscience that serves as a guide to his conduct, and of *syneidesis*, whose function it is to pass judgment on acts already performed. In other words, conscience has both a prospective and a retrospective function even though it is, in itself, timeless.

84

THE EIGHTH CARDINAL SIN

entails a measure of sacrifice and even of death to the ego[59] just as one's final death involves a return, however brief, to consciousness or to full intelligence of who one is.[60] At that momentous juncture, man is at it were placed on a prominence that overlooks the maze his earthly sojourn had been. He sees in one instant, in the simultaneity of pure space, all the ways and byways he took[61] and which, then, seemed to unfold through a sequence of blinkered time. At that moment, the individual sees in the light of his substance, or archetype, who he really is and how he either fulfilled or betrayed his possibility.

He becomes thus his own immanent judge because his substance-being which, having now awakened,[62] perhaps only for a flash, recognizes and situates in one glance his accident-being. If the latter is in harmony with the former, then there is resorption into the archetype whereby the individual is crystallized in heavenly conso-

---

59. Be it said in passing, this is also the definition of nobility: the noble man or woman is the one who consents to this death over and over because he or she is not bent on self-gratification, and is ever-ready to sacrifice his or her self-interest for the sake of a greater good.

60. This is not in contradiction with the notion of the posthumous sleep of the deceased, alluded to in the monotheistic scriptures, awaiting resurrection on the Day of Judgment, because this sleep corresponds to a waiting period before a new crystallization. The sequence after death might be described as a momentary awakening, then a transitional falling to sleep , before a final awakening. In the case of the great souls, or those who are spiritually prepared, we assume there is no sleep since they have fulfilled their *dharma*.

61. This is partly why survivors of near-death experiences can claim to have seen all of their life unfold in one recapitulative instant. Also those who are about to die can have this experience. A description of a similar experience can be found in Tolstoy's depiction of Prince Andrei on his death bed in *War and Peace*.

62. It would be more accurate to say that the individual awakens to his substance because his substance-being is never "asleep" since it partakes of the eternal wakefulness of the One Being.

nance of identity with his immortal self, and the duality, which occasioned so much misunderstanding and suffering, is salvifically extinguished or redeemed. If, however, his accident-being is at variance with his substance-being, then immediately his center of egoic gravity works centrifugally to cast him back into the wheel of existence—or round of ignorance—known in the Hindu-Buddhist cosmologies as the *Samsara*. Words surely cannot do justice to this mystery in such a schematic outline[63] as this which is meant, finally, less to fathom posthumous becoming than to highlight the central role intelligence holds in this settlement. In the verdict above, it is as if the center rejects the periphery, but not so, of course, for the man who has realized the center—or who has fully intended to—while here in his earthly sojourn. This restoration of full intelligence, at least in regard to himself, is as permanent for the saintly as it is bitterly fleeting for the impious, namely those who preferred themselves to God, as well as to their fellow men, because in choosing themselves, paradoxically, they rejected themselves. This is one of the meanings of the Parable of the Sower.

Another way to address this rather complex issue would be to say that when the individual's center, upon death, passes judgment on itself, this is the same as to say that his potential stands in judgment over what he did with

---

63. It is only by means of geometry or of numbers that man can intuit other states of existence. Notions such as center and periphery, of verticals and horizontals, or notions such as unity, duality, triplicity and the like, can render intelligible to the intellect dimensions of creation that remain sealed to one's existential imagination which relies on sensations and images—whence the importance of Pythagorean mathematics. However, imagination can, in turn, round out these schemes, restoring them to their two-dimensional nature, while the heart can then supply the third dimension of living evidence.

THE EIGHTH CARDINAL SIN

it.[64] And this potential in the case of man is divine by virtue of his theomorphism. To be more specific, one should probably add that it is man's intellect, whose root lies in Godhead, that witnesses his deeds, a witnessing which, by the same act, is at once an assessment.[65] Simply put, it is the greater, or the best, in man which passes judgment over the lesser, or worst—the prince that judges the frog. The abyss, as the case may be, between what he is in his essential self and what he happens to be is the exact measure of the rebuke:[66] the greater the divide the sharper the reproof, wherein its implacability because it is above all an effect of nature—poetic justice, if one wills—or one in which the sentimentality of subjective preferences can have no part.

Perhaps these clarifications can help dispel, were it possible, some of the resentment man may feel at the notion of a "punishing God".[67]

---

64. Aquinas says that when the soul departs from this world it immediately recognizes, on the one hand, the grandeur and holiness of God and, on the other, its own absolute unworthiness. And this realization is the source of unbelievable suffering (Rev. Matthias Premm's *Dogmatic Theology for the Laity*). It will be clear that in this case those who have little or no egoism will suffer little or not at all. Again, consciousness alone is the catalyst for this restoration of the self.

65. Although it is really God who judges via his delegate intellect refracted in man, in practical terms man borrows this authority from God and therefore can be said to stand in judgment over himself.

66. "I was now suddenly overwhelmed by a most horrible, unbearable, inexplicable pain of remorse for my vileness: for I seemed suddenly to be aware of Him standing there in His marvelous purity and looking at me—not with any reproach, but with the sweetness of a wonderful Invitation upon His face." Thus writes Lilian Staveley about one of her visions of Christ in *The Golden Fountain*.

67. "Nothing burneth in hell but self-will," we read in the *Theologica Germanica*. But lest we be accused of robbing God of His kingly prerogative as final arbiter, we hasten to add that it is His seal that lends the personal intellect its power. In fact, this faculty belongs to God; or it is the parcel of divinity in us without which we would have no reality at all.

"*ATMANAM VIDDHI*," "KNOW thyself!" This is the unwritten injunction that seals birth in the human state. The essence of *Jnana Yoga*, the path of wisdom, is to follow the line of ontological inquiry—guaranteed only by correct ritual—that starts with the "Who am I?" which, from self-dispossession to self-dispossession, leads back to God and hence back to one-Self . This is certainly not the only way but, in that it involves the consciousness of man's root identity, the most central. Consequently, no penance, however otherwise necessary, can atone as completely and as directly for the sin of stupidity , or ignorance, as knowledge whereby man is "purified by the austerity of wisdom" (Bhagavad Gita).[68]

This is not at all to say that salvation can be a result of correct thinking in which religion can be dispensed with, but rather that prayer needs to be validated by intention before it can be consecrated by grace.[69] And intention is nothing if not consciousness. And consciousness itself, if it is to be sincere, must be intelligent. This is why all prayer is molded by words and not grunts.

In its essence, intelligence involves a eucharistic act in the deepest and most universal sense of the term, whereby the knowledge gained operates through the extinction of the selfish ego: "Knowledge as a sacrifice is greater than any material sacrifice" (Bhagavad Gita). Ultimately, as it is emphasized in *Advaita Vedanta*, only knowledge (*vidya*) can effect a lasting release (*moksha*) from the

---

68. Also, "Verily a man may be counted among the people of Prayer, Almsgiving, Pilgrimage, and Holy War, until he is counted among those apportioned the Good (of Paradise); and yet he will not be rewarded on the Day of Resurrection except to the degree of his intelligence" (Muhammad).

69. "Not every one that saith unto me, Lord, Lord, shall enter into the kingdom of heaven" (*Matt.* 7:21).

sheathes (*koshas*) of bondage in nescience. It is "the fire of wisdom that turns all to ashes" (Bhagavad Gita) and restores earthly substance to celestial luminescence, which transfigures coal back to its diamond essence.

2. THE TWIN PITFALLS OF FANATICISM AND RELATIVISM

MAN, when left to his own subjectivity, tends to gravi-tate temperamentally to one of two opposite poles of intellectual blindness: either to fanaticism, which is pas-sional absolutism, or to relativism. For the pure relativist there is no such thing as absolute truth, whereas for the fanatic, a relative truth becomes an absolute truth. Where fanaticism would say: "What I believe is the only possible truth," relativism would counter: "Since many affirm this, in as many different ways, then nobody is right," or "Everybody is right in his own way and," therefore, "deserves to be heard;" or "Everybody is entitled to his or her opinion,"—and other such inane formulations, inane because, if one thinks about it, no one has the "right" to be wrong, except by accident.[1]

But extremes meet: these two poles, radical though they be, are in many ways opposite more in appearance than in substance, for their espousal[2] entails in both instances an abdication of the intelligence in the face of a

---

1. One might want to bear in mind, however, that a man has a tem-porary right to be ignorant, and a permanent right not to know every-thing. This is only too obvious.

2. We are arguing in the abstract, that is to say, irrespective of the intellectual content of these positions, which can be left aside for the time being.

reality that it cannot adequately grasp.[3] And both parody
objectivity in the sense that, with fanaticism, the advocate
takes personal assurance from his deference to an exclusive
dogma or set of beliefs that he will affirm with a vehe-
mence that is indirectly proportional to his willingness to
examine them whereas, in the case of relativism, the advocate's ostensible deference works through a species of
reductio ad absurdum in which he seeks to discount not only
his but, by "sympathetic" extension, any man's ability to
know the Truth. So it is that both positions entail a kind of
false—and therefore self-righteous—humility (if this be the
term to describe what amounts to a forfeiting of critical
intelligence). Both, moreover, are equally self-interested,
because that is the nature of error. And both involve a fundamental betrayal of man's essential vocation which, in
virtue of his God-given intelligence, is to know the Truth.
Finally, both, albeit each very differently, make an absolute
of the relative—fanaticism by dramatizing the letter of the
law and relativism by sentimentally divinizing the peripheral or the non-essential, as we will see.

All things being equal, the polarizing difference
between the two positions is more a question of psychological style or of means than of substance, to say nothing
of the fact that any fanatical absolutism is perforce relative
in direct measure to its exclusivism, just as, conversely, any
relativism eventually verges on an absolutism in that it
erects ignorance as the only possible constant of human
experience. But when seen from a psychological point of
view, they are distinct enough to merit separate treatment.
Temperamentally, fanaticism—which is really a misguided
or misapplied absolutism—corresponds to nature's

---

3. For instance, for relativism, Bergson's insufferable *fallacia conse-
quentis*: "Intelligence is characterized by a natural incomprehension of
life" (*Creative Evolution*).

processes of hardening and psychologically to a stiffening or to a kind of sclerosis of consciousness which can be dictated by fear or by arrogance, or both, whereas relativism conspires with nature's processes governing slackness and dissolution, and psychologically with weakness or with moral dissipation. And it, on the contrary, results quite presumptuously from a lack of fear and from a kind of false modesty—though this will require some explaining.[4]

As with all error, both extremes are traceable, in their instinctive tropisms, to fundamental dimensions of Reality which have been misunderstood. Reality in its divine totality, can be described metaphysically as being both absolute and infinite, or geometrically as being both vertical and horizontal or, from the point of view of consciousness, as comprising an intellectual dimension and an existential one, spirit and being, masculine and feminine. In this respect, fanaticism would correspond, as regards its practical application, to an excess—or to a misapplication—of the sense of the Absolute, at the expense of the liberating mercy of the Infinite, just as relativism would result, again as regards its practical application, to an overwhelming or over-diluted sense of the Infinite, without the bracing strength and protective vigor of the Absolute.

If we may open a brief parenthesis here, we would say that we would have preferred, from a semantic point of view, to have paired the term "absolutism"—instead of that of fanaticism—with that of relativism, in the sense of a left-right polarization. However, relativism proper is not the horizontal complement of absolutism, but its vertical opposite, and hence, negator. Therefore, absolutism carries a positive connotation that relativism can never share. As

---

4. Relativism is not, however, immune to a disguised form of arrogance since to refuse any objective body of authority except the dictates of one's own mind can be insolent and overweening.

we see it, to be an absolutist is to believe in God, just as to be a relativist is to believe in the world, or in nothing. Or, to be an absolutist, is to believe in the Truth, just as to be a relativist is to believe in anything.[5] However, not to put too fine a point on it, it must be allowed that relativism, as expressed by such or such an individual, may be inter-mingled with some degree of religious faith, although only a lukewarm faith, at best. As for the absolutist, in the true sense of the word, he combines, in some mode or another, the dimensions of both the Absolute and the Infinite in the sense that insofar as he believes sincerely in God, he will both fear Him and love Him. It is all too easy to confuse absolutism with fanaticism—the relativist (very conve-niently) does not see any difference at all—when in fact fanaticism is an ugly parody of absolutism. The hero who is ready to die for his suzerain lord or for his lady, out of an absolute sense of sacred honor, is perfectly capable of being magnanimous with his enemies and chivalrous with the weak. To be ready to die for the sake of a noble cause is not fanaticism.[6] That being said, this chapter intends to address more particularly the issue of a false absolutism, namely fanaticism, and that of a false "infinitism," name-ly relativism.

---

5. This is why relativism is preponderantly a "fin d'époque" dis-ease, obtaining universal currency only in the final phase of a society in the throes of decomposition.

6. The case of the *kamikaze* Japanese pilots going to battle for the emperor with the certainty of death is not necessarily fanaticism, although once a cause becomes political, it forfeits its right to absolutism and can easily veer into fanaticism—something that demagogues exploit all too well. Only the true or the right deserves absolute alle-giance. Also, one will want to distinguish between the individual, whose motive may be integrally noble, as is the case with many if not most of the *kamikaze* mentioned, and the political puppeteers.

93

TO UNDERSTAND WHAT the root of these twin errors is, one needs to know what it is that is being distorted. Metaphysically, Reality is one or it is nothing for, logically, there cannot be two absolutes. At the heart of metaphysics lies the notion of the monad which, as single, is the Absolute and which, as including the multiple or the infinite, is the divine pleroma.[7] Multiplicity is then but the Absolute refracted through the prism of All-Possibility and this is what the Vedanta states, reversing the equation, when it says that *Samsara* is *Nirvana*, namely that all multiplicity is ultimately reducible to unity and cannot, therefore, exist outside of unity, that is to say separately,[8] except in an illusory mode much like ripples in a pond which for all their undulation never cease to be water. But that is not to say, as a false immanentism would have it, that *Samsara* as such is co-essential with *Nirvana* as such or, in a similar train of thought, that beauty must be seen in ugliness, good in evil,[9] as proof of depth of contemplative

---

7. Cf. Nicholas of Cusa's "absolute maximum" and "relative maximum." Or Plotinus: "One principle must make the universe a single complex living creature, one from all." Sufism makes a distinction between the *Ahadiyah* (the One as Unique) and the *Wahidiyah* (the One as unified in its variety).

8. "There is no difference in It whatsoever. He who sees difference in It, reaps death after death" (*Brihad Aranyaka Upanishad*, IV, 4, 19).

9. Or, as one modern re-hasher of Kashmir Shaivism formulates it: "And see in everything, no matter how horrific or terrifying, the same gracious force that lies within." While it is true that eventually "everything returns to God" and that evil works in the end for the good—because unreality cannot overcome reality—it is just as true that, wherever and so long as duality rules, evil is evil. When Ramakrishna says that he saw in a wicked man "the Power of the Divine Mother vibrating," he is describing, in our opinion, more a result of his love-intoxicated vision—in which the universe is continuously transfigured back into its radiant essence—rather than an intention. Or, what he sees is the fact that evil must borrow its energy from the good. At any rate, discernment has its rights: it is illogical to claim, on the one hand, as *bhaktism* (the

94

insight, or that God is "especially present" in the least part of His Creation.[10]

Hindu path of love) is wont to do, that everything is divine while, on the other hand, rejecting ultimate identity, *mutatis mutandis*, between the *atman* (the individual soul) and *Atma* or *Brahma* (the divinity), a position which is the cornerstone of the metaphysical perspective of *Advaita Vedanta*; one cannot have it both ways. Unfortunately, this same indifferentiation of outlook led even a mystic of Ramakrishna's exceptional stature to be far more tolerant of an ambiguous—if not frankly heretical—movement such as the Brahmo Samaj than the facts warranted.

10. The Taoist doctrine of holy lowliness is at an infinite remove from what is finally a perverse kind of humilitarianism whose love of the despised amounts in fact to an implicit indictment of God's majesty and beauty. Unfortunately, Christianity, by hurling anathemas at material creation, paved the road for this reflex compensation. Thomas Merton, to take but one recent example, strains the truth when he writes that "Each particular being, in its individuality, its concrete nature and entity, with all its own characteristics and its private qualities and its own inviolable identity, gives glory to God by being precisely what He wants it to be here and now, in the circumstances ordained for it by His love and His infinite Art" (*Seeds of Contemplation*). Nonetheless, Merton is touching upon the Zen-Shintoist notion of *wabi* or the "esthetic flaw" that marks the pure spontaneity of God's Self-creating and the simple uniqueness of each moment of His being (Cf. Clara Ines Perry's *Cup of Immortality* in "Studies in Comparative Religion", vol. 17). What Merton is not making allowance for, however, is the sheer randomness that occurs with growing intensity as one moves out towards the periphery of creation—a randomness that strives to reach, without ever achieving it totally, a point of absolute chaos. More importantly, in Scholastic terms, if the accident can reveal the substance, it can also mar it. In that God's creation manifests His being, it lauds His perfection. But in that it is also other than He, it is imperfect and therefore also God-denying and, as such, just as much in need of redemption as man's own soul. To praise it in these conditions is to forfeit discernment and can furthermore amount to sacrilege. One loves God because of the best in creation, not the worst. Nettles are not roses. However, a Christian might respond that this perspective rejoins Augustine's: "Even our sins are necessary to the universal perfection which God established." (Words, then, lose their useful meaning!) No, the real motive for such contorted reasoning is the attempt to reconcile the possibility of imperfection with the notion of an all-perfect Creator.

That Reality is experienced by such or such a man as being "many," as refracted through the prism of his particular ego or existential possibility and circumstances, obviously does nothing to impugn the intrinsic "unity of existence," the *Wahdat al Wujud* of Sufism,[11] because even if phenomena, when beheld from the outside, appear as bewilderingly varied or mutually destructive or absurdly disparate, they cannot be, when fathomed from within, wholly independent or unrelated—as the transmutation cycle, for instance, of the four primal elements demonstrates: earth dries up and is transmuted into fire, fire is changed to air which, when cooled, comes down as water, and so on and so forth. Life is unceasing transfiguration. The entire chain of beings, indeed each creature, partakes symbiotically in the common or primal ground (*Urgrund* in Eckhart's terminology) of existence, no matter how divisive or "absolutely" different its modalities—as seen, to take one striking example, in the relationship between predator and prey, a relationship that affirms in its savage way the one Being's deathless self-sufficiency in which no part of it can, as it were, forever elude the others, nor for that matter survive without them. This is God—as the Vedic Agni[12]—feasting on Himself and with Himself, ever self-consuming and ever self-reviving in a universal communion of sacrifice and redemption.[13]

---

11. Hence Thoreau's facetiously profound observation: "I don't see how I can kill time without injuring Eternity."

12. For the ancient Hindus, Agni was the god of fire and of the hearth or sacred altar and, as such, the direct mediator (or transmuter) between heaven and earth. The hearth ritual, found in all pagan people, celebrates the symbolism of the life-giving and also life-transmuting nature of the divine heart. The sacred pipe ritual of the American Plains Indians belongs to the same cosmological culture.

13. This terminology, of course, is only applicable to God as "Purushic" manifestation. Cf. in the *Rigveda* the original sacrifice of

In this way, were a man to have full access to the powers of his imagination—and what is imagination, ideally, if no the capacity for ontological reminiscence?—the notion of God could be grasped through a rapturously inductive ascension[14] that could start from literally any point in creation,[15] for nothing exists, in the eye of the contemplative poet, except as a link in a processional pageantry of the divine Whole.

In this manner, a spark testifies to the sun or a flower to paradise or, metaphorically, to love and to bliss, the accident or the creature always suggesting the substance or the archetype, or at least a promise of the divine substance, although not necessarily directly so—to wit the privative, or more or less hideous, phenomena found in manifestation whose

---

Purusha from whose dismembered body creation is fashioned. The same symbolism applies to the myth of Osiris and we will recall the sacrifice of Christ: "This is my body." Also, the Vedic rite of *Agnihotra*, the fire sacrifice, or in the *Taittiriya Upanishad* the idea of Brahma worshipped as food (II:2), or: "Oh, wonderful! Oh, wonderful! Oh, wonderful! / I am food! I am food! I am food! / I am a food-eater! I am a food-eater! I am a food-eater!" (III:10). Or: "I, who am food, eat the eater of food!" When the individual dies, it is Agni who consumes him on the funeral pyre, not just flames. Compare the above with a Christian formulation of the same metaphor as expressed by St. Ignatius of Antioch before his martyrdom: "I am God's wheat, and I am ground by the teeth of wild beasts, that I may be found Christ's pure bread." These formulations illustrate the transubstantiating essence all creation shares in virtue of the essential oneness of the Creator's being. This is why Eckhart could say that it was possible to have God-realization while eating, which is really a form of communion as some of the ancient Germans, who ate in silence, understood.

14. Reversing Proclus' declination of the One into increasing plurality. Thus to remember would be to pray and to pray would be to soar, to take wing back to the sacred Infinite become depth of Oneness.

15. Hence, again, Thoreau: "Such is beauty ever—neither here nor there, now nor then. . . . If I seek her elsewhere because I do not find her at home, my search will prove a fruitless one."

97

"processional status" is existentially center-fleeing (instead of center-finding), or basically light-denying and love-denying, being more separative than unitive by dint of their preponderant tendency (or function) in the cosmic economy of things. Vultures cannot soar like hawks.

IN VIEW OF the divine pleroma that the universe manifests in awe-inspiring abundance, atheism—of which agnosticism is but a lukewarm variant, despite its pretensions of humility—is merely a confession of abysmal ignorance[16] or a declaration of impotence, of a dreadfully small mind, for the Absolute, the Infinite, the Eternal, the Paradisiacal, and Truth can be demonstrated both rationally and empirically.[17] Indeed, to be for man is potentially to be everything, because "man," as *pontifex* or bridge-maker between heaven and earth, "is the measure of all things," as Protagoras said, but by virtue of his intelligence (not by his subjectivity—as the Sophists suppose) which is the objective synthesis of universal consciousness (the *buddhi* of the Vedanta). Were it not so, the Eternals would be utterly inconceivable.

Not to belabor the point, but it should be manifest that the nothingness which a nihilism professes or, more specif-

---

16. "I say, that of all idiocies, that is the most stupid, most vile, and most damnable which holds that after this life there is none other" (Dante, *Il Convito*).

17. One proof is the indestructibility of matter and its purity: earth, in itself, is perfectly clean. Another is the idea of the good and that of unity as forming the constitutive core of existence because an intimate fissure is just as inconceivable as is the possibility of an absolute flaw; if that were the case, nothing could hold together. There are obviously many, many more proofs, endless proofs, and grander proofs. But not every proof, no matter how perfect, works for every mind; in that case, however, the deficiency is not on the proof's side. Not every man possesses what Thoreau referred to as the gift of auroral consciousness (cf. previous chapter).

ically, the nothingness into which a creature supposedly disappears at death, cannot exist as a positive reality, for nothingness—it hardly needs to be said—is literally nothing:[18] it does not exist anywhere at all or in any shape or fashion. Therefore, something that is, that exists, proves by this very fact an archetype and, with respect to that essence, can never become nothing, for even though such and such an entity "disappears," its form abides firstly and principially[19] as such—or as the genus if one wills—then, secondarily, and temporarily as actualization in the ceaseless surge of new variants bearing witness to it.[20]

And more to the point for this book, consciousness whether as sentience in the lesser creatures (or entities) or as intelligence in man, is not just happenstance awareness, this or that person's incidental experience, but potentially everything. In the lesser entities, such as small animals and, as one moves down the scale to reptiles, fishes, insects, and plants, consciousness is less and less individualized and more and more generic of the particular attribute that a

---

18. Some uncompromising materialists in the mold of a Lucretius might prefer to say that death is but a realignment of molecules to which consciousness is subordinated. In other words, without the right combination of molecules, no consciousness. But such intellectual acrobatics simply postpone the inevitable hour of reckoning.

19. Not to be pedantic but out of a scruple for clarity, one should clarify, from time to time, the use of different metaphysical terms which are not part of one's everyday vocabulary. "Principially" is derived from the idea of "principle" which is the original cause of something as well as its ruling agent. For example, the sun, like the sparks from fire, derives its light from a principle of light, just as man derives his being from a principle of being or an original being.

20. This view of reality is at the heart of the nomadic-hunter cultures who in hunting an individual animal such as a gazelle are mindful of praying for its soul so that its prototype will continue to send the individual hunter more of the same. Whence the remarkable idea of what is termed the "grateful prey."

whole specie represents[21] instead of being intelligently comprehensive as in the case of man.[22] Or one could say, they function as attributes of God's omniscience, of His universal Self-awareness. More generally, the life of any single creature, man or animal, proves—and can only prove—the One Eternal Being which is its sustaining force as seen in the fact that the creature must borrow every breath of its life. And the breath, no sooner taken, must be forthwith returned.[23]

Likewise, it should be self-evident that none of the negative attributes of human consciousness such as hate, envy, malice—which are divisive and hence destructive—can have any permanent reality, because their plane of application can only be relative, otherwise the cosmos would be rent down the middle and pulverized before it could ever

---

21. "[The sun dancers] also put rabbit skins on their arms and legs, for the rabbit represents humility, because he is quiet and soft and not self-asserting—a quality which we must all possess when we go to the center of the world," Black Elk recounts in *The Sacred Pipe* (Joseph Epes Brown).

22. One could say that an animal compensates his intellectual inferiority to man with a kind of existential superiority. In other words, if man is by essence intelligence, an animal would have existential qualities that would be qualitative counterparts to this gift. For instance, man's swiftness of intellect would be qualitatively matched by an animal's fleetness which man cannot equal. Or one could say that a hawk does not have man's sense of transcendence, but he can soar heavenward, whereas man is physically earthbound. However, such polarities are merely extrinsic and operate only in material manifestation, namely in the realm of the physical body. But they do not operate on the archetypal level since pure intelligence coincides there with pure being which is a manifestation of consciousness—and not vice-versa. This, incidentally, is why in Genesis, the Lord God is said to have brought "every beast of the field, every fowl of the air" unto Adam to have them named, which is to say to receive their catalyzing identity.

23. The Sufi doctrine of the "Renewal of Creation with each breath" (*tajdid al-khalq bil-anfas*) is related to this.

100

be fashioned—for "Evil destroys even itself, and if it is complete becomes unbearable" (Aristotle).[24] It is the positive attributes of human consciousness such as love, gratitude, and forgiveness that, being unitive, and hence restorative, bespeak the fundamental unicity of existence[25] which is whole before—and after—it is fragmented: "The whole is of necessity prior to the part" (Aristotle). If Reality is whole because it is one, then as consciousness it is love. And as being reposing in its infinite oneness, it is peace. As love and peace it is beauty. And as one or unique, it is majesty. Finally, as reality—or enduring *Urgrund*—it is truth. This knowledge is inherent to those who have not lost their Edenic innocence and capacity for wonderment, which is why Christ said that only children can enter the kingdom of heaven.

To COMPLETE THIS brushstroke summary of the metaphysical backdrop for this chapter's main theme one could say that Reality could be defined as Oneness manifold, Absolute-Infinite. It is these two dimensions, which we have said, lie at the origin of the terms absolutism (in its connotation for this chapter as fanaticism) and relativism, which we propose to define but not necessarily according to their accepted philosophical use, because we are not concerned here with the schools of thought[26] that have appropriated them, but first of all, in the essential notions they convey and, secondly, in their psychological manifes-

---

24. Negative qualities depend on positive ones for their existence, just as death depends on life.

25. As we have mentioned before, Dante's "the Love that moves the sun and the other stars."

26. For instance, the political doctrines of absolutism or the scientific theory of relativity, or the economic school of relativistic pragmatism, the *laissez-faire* of the bourgeois liberalism that spawned modern individualism for both good and bad.

tation because this will have an important bearing on how an individual approaches reality.

Indeed, the notions of absolutism and relativism—or rather "infinitism"— carry an intrinsic meaning directly related to the metaphysical concepts of necessity and freedom which are interwoven in the very fabric of manifestation, be it in the rhythmic relationship of contraction and dilation, or in the attributes of hardness and softness, of cold and heat, or be it in the divine qualities of Rigor and Mercy,[27] or be it in the moral alternatives of obligation and choice, or in the physical attitudes of erectness and grace. These twin cosmic qualities pervade all realms where duality rules and hence all phenomena find their origin in them or in some combination thereof, expressed through innumerable modes and degrees. Moreover, these twin polarities can operate either vertically, as in the case of divine rigor and divine mercy, justice and redemption, or horizontally, as in the case of cold and heat—the vertical vectors entailing a moral or eschatological dimension that does not apply to the horizontal ones which, all things being equal, are neutral because it depends on how they are applied by man rather than on what they are in themselves.

Thus, to return to the original dichotomy, one can say that fanaticism has, quite indirectly and in spite of itself, a positive prototype which is that of the Absolute, albeit disfigured in passional dialectics wherein a narrowly defined objective takes operative precedence over all other alternative considerations, just as relativism refers, again quite indirectly or even inversely, to the pole of the Infinite in the sense of *vanitas vanitatum*. In this case, the awareness of the

---

27. As illustrated in the Pharaoh god-man holding the harvester's flail, symbol of discernment and kingly justice, and the shepherd's crook, symbol of contemplative goodness and priestly mercy—emblems of his two sovereign functions which we will explore in depth in our Chapter "The Crook and the Flail".

transient nature and basic voidness of all phenomena conditions a sense that nothing manifest can have any durably
determinative value, that "it is better to go to the house of
mourning, than to go to the house of feasting" (Eccl. 7:32),
dust unto dust. Therefore, it is not worth (the relativist
believes) attributing any absolute value to things that can
only change and disappear. However, there is a world of
difference between detaching oneself contemplatively from
the illusoriness of existence (the *anitya* or doctrine of
"impermanence" of Theravada Buddhism) in view of the
Real and inferring, as the relativist does, from the illusory
nature of manifestation the nothingness of being.[28]

NOW, WHAT THE relativist fails to see is the difference
between a legitimate absolutism[29] and an irrational fanaticism. While it is true that all fanaticism is perforce abso-
lutistic, absolutism need not be fanatical, because a decisive
recognition of the immutable as opposed to the ephemeral,
of the real as opposed to the dream, or of the central as distinct from the peripheral[30]—in short, a sense for the essential over the accidental constitutes without a doubt the single most important reflex in human existence if a man is to
wake up permanently so as to escape the endless cycle of
births and deaths engendered by ignorance (the *avidya* of

---

28. This, in broad outline, is Schopenhauer's nihilistic conclusion
which served as the leaven for the angst of modern relativism.

29. If there is a legitimate absolutism, the question arises if there is
equally a legitimate relativism? The answer is yes and no, but basically
no. All civilizations begin in absolutism and end in relativism. Yet discernment between the essential and the relative—which is the doctrinal
foundation of any spiritual path—does entail an intelligent sense of relativity. However, since this is premised on a clear sense of the Absolute,
this is not relativism proper, which, on the contrary, rejects the idea of an
absolute. One has to stand for something; one cannot stand for nothing.

30. Emerson: "Philosophy, Infinite and Finite; Relative and
Absolute; Apparent and Real."

the Vedanta) which orchestrates the endless to-and-fro of manifestation. Certitude is not fanaticism.

When Christ says: "Let your communication be Yea, yea; Nay, nay: for whatsoever is more than these cometh of evil," he is referring, among other things, to the dissolving centrifugality of existence which seeks to achieve, from fragmentation to fragmentation, an ultimate nothingness. In the process, as it whirls out into chaos, it attempts to abolish—or melt—the distinctness of all created forms.[31] And this distinctness, the exclusive identity which sets one thing off from another, is the stamp of the Absolute. That is why man's affirmation of That Which Is—by contradistinction of that which is not—ultimately spells the difference between happiness and misery. This is the deeper meaning of the proverb, "He who hesitates is lost." In short, affirmativeness is the bedrock of character.[32] Its opposite is ambiguity, spinelessness, or the lukewarmness of the relativist who dwells in an unwholesomely penumbral realm of ever-shifting half-truths,[33] oblivious to the fact that the cosmos will "spue him out" at the hour of Judgment, that is to say, when Reality reasserts Itself, when God's "I am" reaffirms "That I am" (Exod. 3:14).

Moreover, an awareness of the vital urgency of "pleasing the Lord"—"*Messire Dieu premier servi*" as Joan of Arc liked to say ("My Lord God comes first")—can, depending on a believer's degree of sincerity, set a soul ablaze with an all-consuming fervor that scorns semantic exactitudes or

---

31. In man, this tendency becomes what in French psychology is referred to as *l'amour de la boue*, which could be bluntly translated as "love of muck."

32. Santayana grasped this very well when he said: "Character is the basis of happiness and happiness the sanction of character" (*Reason in Common Sense*).

33. In painting, the mixing of too many colors results in muddiness.

maudlin nuances which, as is drearily the case with mundane literati, dilute to insipidity or even deaden into narcissistic indifference whatever core heavenward thrust they might have. In this case, salvational expediency, such as that in affective mysticism,[34] takes operative precedence over metaphysical adequacy of exposition.

This remark brings us to an important point: it is crucial to distinguish between a so-called "fanaticism" that is ultimately legitimated by the transcendent value of its object (or objective)—beauty, after all, is worth dying for—such as that of the first Muslims rushing to martyrdom on the battlefield to reap Paradise, and a fanaticism which is blindly hysterical and ultimately base, such as that of modern-day Muslim fundamentalists—to wit "suicide squads" or cannon-fodder infantrymen—whose arrogation of mystical dialectics for purely political ends is not only fraudulent, but, in that it can subvert the meaning of religion, even satanic, if only because one cannot use the lever of the Name of God to mobilize men for objectives that are inherently secular:[35] "Thou shalt not take the name of the Lord

---

34. For example, Savonarola's ruthless bonfire of the vanities or Martin Luther's violent repudiation of Rome. There is of course a line that cannot be crossed and that is the one separating right from wrong. An excess is not necessarily a wrong—for instance the periodic iconoclastic bursts that rent religions. But when Calvin declares that the "elect" consists only in a handful of souls that will be saved whereas the damned will be teeming in throngs, and that moreover all of this has been decided once by God and for all of eternity, he is setting perfectly arbitrary limits on divine mercy—a position which Calvinism subsequently softened. Likewise, Zwingli's rejection of the true presence in the Eucharistic species set him in opposition not only to Catholic dogma, but to other Evangelical reformers, beginning with Luther himself.

35. The Spanish Inquisition (which was more specifically political in its aim than the mandate Pope Gregory IX had in mind) exceeded the scope of its rights—if it ever had any—when it became an instrument of state policy, namely when nationalistic hegemony was pursued through the means of religious persecution. The rights it might have had would

thy God in vain." It is also a question not only of the value of the objective, but also of the intention, since an end which is noble in itself can be compromised by iniquity in its pursuit. Moreover, on a minor scale, there is the question of self-righteousness, the hypocrisy of which is to perfume one's moral stench with the pretense of impeccability. Now, a truly pious man will bestrew himself with ashes and dust before he will subtract for himself any of God's perfection: "What callest thou me good," Christ asked.

To sum up the foregoing, a passional intensity of commitment can be ignited either by a noble purpose, in which case the passionate element is leavened by sanctifying heroism, or it can be set in motion by a petty purpose, in which case the passion is rendered more densely obtuse by the very meanness of the objective. Stated differently, the fanatic's basic transgression is to arrogate a position that, by virtue of its content of eternity, can only belong by right to the absolutist. And it is truth—not opinion—that makes the *de jure* absolutist. However, zeal for the House of the Lord can render many an excess forgivable[36] so long as the agent is not acting on the behalf of his own selfish interest, for a relative injustice can always be compensated by the greater good promoted thereby—to say nothing of the fact "if thy right eye offend thee, pluck it out, and cast it from thee: for it is profitable for thee that one of thy members perish, and not that thy whole body should be cast into

---

consist in defending the articles of faith, provided that this did not become an expedient for secular power. Likewise, the Catholic Church's trafficking in indulgences was an arrant abuse of religion for a material end that was one of the immediate causes of the Reformation.

36. For example, the practice in certain penitential orders of referring to man's corporeal body as "Brother Ass" which, on its narrow plane of application, can be spiritually opportune. Nonetheless, on the plane of normative primordiality, of the Edenic wonder of "man created in God's image," such a designation borders on sacrilege.

hell." (Matt. 5:29) Radical ends sometimes require radical means.

Also, and more importantly, what is allowable in the eyes of Heaven for the man of God, may not be so for this or that individual, except and only insofar he is impersonally mandated by a legitimate social function such as that, to take an extreme example, of a public executioner.

And there is always the problem, notorious with religious fundamentalists of whatever persuasion, of taking one aspect of the Truth and divorcing it from its legitimizing context, to the point that it becomes distorted and obsessively—and perhaps destructively—determining in the consciousness of an adherent.[37] In that case, the chances that the doctrinal truth may still carry a theurgically transformative value dwindle in proportion to the individualism of the recipient. To spuriously appropriate a truth, or more exactly its dogmatic formulation, is to use it not *ad majorem Dei gloriam* but *ad majorem mei gloriam*. And, needless to say, the "recipient" can consist of one individual or of a whole collectivity.[38]

In any case, the ideological intemperance of fanaticism always involves first a suspension of the agent's critical fac-

---

37. This, of course, is the basis of heresy, as in the famous example of the Manichean dualism of the Cathars who, seeing only evil in matter and above all in the flesh, could not admit the theophanic nature of the universe and therefore rejected the Eucharist. Whatever truth "this pestilential error"—as Pope Innocent III termed it—could contain, such as that "flesh and blood cannot inherit the kingdom of God" (I Cor. 15:50), was nullified by the Cathars' rejection of Christ as man. And, be it said in passing, their denunciation of Rome's lucre, however otherwise justified, was simply the Trojan Horse used to penetrate the citadel of credibility. It is a favorite technique of falsehood everywhere to attack a greater but perhaps less immediately obvious truth by vociferously promoting a lesser but far more sensational one.

38. Communism misappropriated the idea of the brotherhood of man to destroy the principle of the elite.

107

ulties, which would otherwise threaten to relativize or refute the one-sidedness of his bias, and secondly a need to convert others to his viewpoint for error cannot live without company. In other words, since a prejudice is by definition indefensible, it can then only be vindicated—quite illusorily so—through the numerical advocacy of others in the sense that might makes right. Common sense is literally crowded out, or made to feel guilty. And anyone who disagrees is immediately deemed a heretic, a corrupting relativist, or summarily dismissed as being spineless. Fanaticism is the rule of thugs: the loudest, the strongest, the most arbitrary and unfair wins.

However, it bears repeating again and again, especially in an age of relativism, that it is important to differentiate an abusive zealotry from a legitimate absolutism.[39] What is overlooked is that man as delegated by Heaven, or simply when objective, no longer speaks merely in his own name.

ONE CANNOT CLOSE this particular topic without addressing a particularly specious objection leveled, by "freethinkers"[40] especially, against absolutism in any form, namely that absolutists, by virtue of their claim to repre-

---

39. The abrogation of feudalism which is sacerdotal in essence (or sacerdotally monarchic) by Renaissance humanism is one such example of a legitimate absolutism being tagged with the stigma of excess. Yes, there were abuses, but an abuse is not the same as an intrinsic falseness. In fact, an abuse is an indirect proof of the validity of a perspective or a system, otherwise one could not speak of an abuse, precisely. In any case, if an abuse amounts to a disqualification, then nothing could stand, for who would dare throw the first stone?

40. Someone needs to explain to us why an individualist, who is a slave of his subjective impressions, deserves the laudatory appellation of "free"-thinker! Rather, we suspect this term conceals a whole program for remorseless iconoclasm.

sent some kind authority, engage in forcible indoctrination of others, even to the degree of mind-control. Now, while it is altogether true, that in the case of fanaticism, passion tyrannically displaces intelligence and that collective zeal tends to abolish, or trample, pluralism of opinion, and while it is true that faith and reason collide antinomically, notably in passional mysticism, it does not necessarily follow that intensity of belief should entail mindlessness or, reciprocally, that objectivity should entail emotional disengagement: too many moral cowards are all too eager to pawn off their indifference as being a virtue—a dignified objectivity or an impartiality befitting, they aver, a civilized man. As a matter of fact, it can be exactly the reverse, namely that fullness of awareness will dictate intensity of conviction,[41] which intensity may indeed appear abusive to the lukewarm.[42] To be dazzled by the Truth or deeply moved by beauty is not an indication of subjectivity. The problem, then, lies not on the side of truth proper, but on that of man. Mind-control, in the negative and manipulative sense of the term, namely what is referred to colloquially as "brainwashing,"[43]

---

41. To be dazzled by the Truth or moved by beauty is not an indication of subjectivity.

42. It might be worth specifying here that mystical fervor and physical frailty are far from being mutually exclusive. Simone Weil concentrated with fierce intensity on God to free herself from the awareness of her frightful headaches. Bernadette of Lourdes used extreme physical suffering in her last years as a lever for God consciousness and love.

43. Free-thinkers, or libertarians, in order to safeguard the primacy of untutored opinion, indiscriminately lump under this generic term thought reform, ideological molding, catechism, the learning by rote of the Vedas or the Koran, the rites of passage in primitive societies, political demagoguery, codes of allegiance in fraternal orders, cultism, etc., with no regard to crucial qualitative differences. Even parents are attacked now for attempting to mold their children—instead, we suppose,

109

involves not truth but error for "only error can be transmitted," as Taoism remarks.[44]

Therefore, before one can speak of mind-control, one must first ask what it is that is "controlling" the mind, truth or error? In other words, the stigma incurred involves not so much the method, but the validity of the contents of the indoctrination. Indeed, by definition, Truth per se,[45] which is illuminating, cannot obfuscate. Nor can it be inflicted, as such, upon someone blindly because Truth, if it is to convince, presupposes understanding, be it merely intuitive, on the part of the respondent—in which case, the very premise upon which "brainwashing" is posited is nullified. Whereas error, to be communicated, always involves, not understanding quite logically, but self-interest—be it merely that of someone fearing for his life who accepts error to save himself from persecution.

Now if the fact of having one's mind "controlled" by Truth, or by a true doctrine, excludes the possibility of "brainwashing"[46] in the vulgar sense of the term, this does not disallow the possibility of legitimate indoctrination,[47] to which catechistic practices the world over attest. What

---

of letting them just drift passively and be "molded" by a media which, in a democracy, is nothing but a fancy whore serving the highest paying customer. Who then, if not parents, will teach children right from wrong?

44. Truth is part of the core of our being, just as the Vedic *Rta* or "cosmic order," and therefore it cannot be instilled but actualized. Error, on the other hand, is something acquired because it is fundamentally extrinsic—or parasitic—to our human substance.

45. This is an important *distinguo* because it is not a question here of truth as translated by man.

46. Which, let it be emphasized again, can only take hold following the extinction of understanding.

47. St. Bernard of Clairvaux's *fides suadenda, non imponenda,* "faith must be the result of conviction and not be imposed by force," should not be taken to mean tolerance of heresy.

free-thinkers forget—in what amounts finally to a repudiation of the very notion of authority—is that man is born an anarchist. Just as the vine cannot yield its best fruit without a stake, so a soul needs an axis if it is not to be warped by the random growth worldly opportunity offers and, it might be added, a mold or a frame if it is to grow to its fullness of strength. Without a chrysalis, no butterfly, Chuang-Tzu could well have said. No freedom without necessity. Or, without the Absolute, no Infinite. What is the strength of the infant soul if not a traditional religious framework? Again, what matters here finally is less the means or, surprisingly, even the intelligibility,[48] but the intrinsic correctness of the mold, or teaching, because a dogma that is doctrinally or spiritually correct carries with it a mysteriously transfigurative or theurgic virtue which, accordingly, benefits the recipient whether he consciously understands it or not.[49] In any case, full understanding—namely realization of the Absolute—can only come at the term of the Way, never at the beginning.[50] This is partly what the Buddha meant when he said that attainment of Buddhahood brings about the remembrance of one's former lives.

---

48. We say "intelligibility," not "cogency," because Truth is rarely understood at first given man's natural ignorance.

49. This is how Plato's mimesis can spark, via the particular, vital reminiscence of the universal. The only pre-condition is that the mimesis be formally correct—as in the case of orthodox ritual or in that of sacred *mantras* (invocatory/incantational formulas). Although we are naturally loath to try to explain the causality of sacred phenomena which elude scientific inquiry, the topic obliges us to say that this mimesis could be said to operate by way of rhythmic echo which, from reverberation to reverberation, gradually awakens ontological remembrance and brings about self-restoration through the dissolution of the recipient's habitual state of existential amnesia. Incidentally, it is crucial to note that, in this case, mimesis is the opposite of mimicry. All told, mimesis is the foundation of Tradition.

50. The Cherokees speak of death as being the threshold of "The Understanding."

Be that as it may, even the most clouded understanding[51] confers by echoing analogy a foretaste of illumination for, as Ali, Mohammed's son-in-law said: "The fear of God makes one secure."[52] And, to start with, this is nothing other than having a healthy sense of proportions.

At any rate, man's outward baseness of substance requires kneading, the *mortificatio* of the alchemists, for the sugar cane will not yield its sweetness till it be crushed: "As many as I love, I rebuke and chasten." (Rev. 3:19) God, in virtue of His Absoluteness, punishes; and, in virtue of His Infinitude, redeems.

A PERFIDIOUS HABIT of the relativist is to accuse anyone who takes an affirmative stand on a principle, or on an issue, of being by that fact intolerant or even a fanatic. He does not ask "What is the merit of the position?" but "Why is he so extreme?" as if intensity of conviction constituted an automatic disqualification—unless that intensity is directed to allowing everyone to think just as they please. Again, one will have to see in this the relativist's insistence that everything is merely a matter of opinion, never of knowledge and absolutely never of certainty (the doctrine of fallibil-

---

51. One must not overlook the fact that every man has access to his conscience, at least as long as it is not irretrievably repressed or before it atrophies, for instance as a result of too many unconscionable acts or false attitudes. In other words, there is always that spark of divine consciousness in him without which he would not only not be able to judge, but he would cease to exist since his existence is a factor of God's "remembrance" of him. In practice, this means that every man always has at his disposal sufficient criteria upon which he can rely, not necessarily to make the correct choice at the outset, but certainly to avoid the morally reprehensible—be it only of persevering in an incorrect choice. "O my heart, rise not as a witness against me," we hear from Ancient Egypt in an inscription on a scarab placed on the chest of a deceased.

52. Hence King David: "The fear of the Lord is the beginning of wisdom."

ism). On that basis, he denies others the right to decisive contradiction. In fact, if peremptorily contradicted, as he may well deserve to be, the relativist is readier to make *ad hominem* imputations about his interlocutor's character, for instance, than to examine the premises of his own position. (One sees in this how much intellectual laziness there can be in such an axiomatic position.) He "begs to differ" as a matter "principle," for he is less interested in the truth than in having a personal opinion all of his own. At the same time, he rejects out of hand the notion that there are truths or realities that can have nothing to do with conjecture, were it only that they pre-date man, because man is issued from Reality and not vice-versa.

And in rejecting the possibility of objective truth—which, incidentally, is an absolute position—the relativist does not want to see that he is thereby protecting his license to be as subjective as he pleases, though he would be the last to admit this because, in keeping with the speciousness of his reasoning, he claims—with true Pyrrhonian sophistry—that skepticism is the only reasonable recourse allowed a man given his natural limitations, and that therefore the first duty of objectivity is to recognize man's ignorance.[53] And, it might be added, in rejecting the possibility of absolute truth, he makes short shrift of kings, heroes, saints, and all great men, or anyone whose loftiness of values threatens his scrupulous mediocrity.

---

53. Hence Montaigne: "To philosophize is to doubt." For those who would object that we are quoting the valetudinarian philosopher out of context, we will say that the goal of this failed stoic was not for man to know the truth—an impossible enterprise in his eyes—but first of all to learn that we do not know, so as somehow to avoid needless error (a point that Kant was later to develop in exacting detail), and secondly to make our peace with ignorance, because this is all that lies within man's reach. This is defeatism disguised as wisdom and has nothing to do with Socrates' recognition of his ignorance.

113

Now, if it is indubitably true that diversity of opinion in a human collectivity can recapitulate, in its own quantitative way, the diversity inherent in Reality, whose complexities cannot normally be summed up by any one individual, one must at the same time take care to situate the level on which this diversity can be legitimately suffered. And this level is, precisely, the plane of relativity which accounts for the innumerable variety contained in the metaphysical principle of All-Possibility. However, a society's common weal, lest it unravel, must have both a weft and a warp, because diversity without unity—or at the expense of unifying principles—can only lead, over time, to chaos,[54] the interim being filled, as is well known, with the ever more leveling tyranny of the lowest common denominator.

Where the idea of transcendent Truth is denied, in other words, where the notion of the Absolute is practically speaking rejected—along with its human counterpart, authority[55]—the unifying principle is left to the chance expediency of prevailing social circumstances, custom, and the consensus of majority rule, if not arbitrary dictatorship. But then sanction is no longer a matter of truth or of eternal values or simply of quality, but of quantity or brute force—which amounts to the same thing. Both the pluralism of the masses and of mob rule are heedless of the fact that one truth should prevail over a thousand errors.[56]

---

54. Jefferson overrates the good sense of the masses when he asks: "Were it left to me to decide whether we should have government without newspapers, or newspapers without a government, I should not hesitate a moment to prefer the latter." Had he known the possibility of a truly enlightened ruler, he might have thought differently. However, in plurality rule, newspapers are a safeguard against tyranny.

55. The relationship between truth, knowledge, and authority will be fully developed in a later chapter: "The Crook and the Flail".

56. We will remember Thoreau's "I am a majority of one."

TO RETURN TO our initial point, relativism is ever ready to extol its intellectual vagrancy as a legitimate exercise of unprescribable freedom forgetting that, from the point of view of the *Sanatana Dharma*—the Eternal Law which rules the movements of the stars and their human flocks—all beings will be ineluctably held to account: a creature can sooner escape death than he can escape this Law for Reality always reasserts itself ontologically in the fullness of time.[57] This is why any transgression ultimately is a transgression against oneself.

And because he rejects immutables and binding commitments, a relativist delights in obliquities of reasoning, in clever rationalizations, quibbling niceties, and the like, sometimes giving lofty currency to his psychic profligacy with terms such as "stream of consciousness," the better to safeguard the primacy of blindest impulse. In this way, he revels in multiplicity—forgetting that "My name is Legion"—oblivious to the fact that he is, in the last analysis, but succumbing to a species of psychic entropy, namely to a degradation of impressions—much like modern art's—that ultimately spells the dissolution of his senseless theatrics and ridiculous claims to "personal meaningfulness." In the meantime, he has an answer—or rather an excuse—for everything, seeks to explain everything away, and wantonly fornicates with all manner of errors, which, he would contend, have factual respectability. Luther aptly described unregenerate reason as the "Devil's whore" for it sports obscenely with truth or, to be exact, with trickily interchangeable pieces of truth. This is the nature of decomposition: remove the absolute and collapse is unavoidable.

---

57. As seen, for instance, in the Tibetan art of the *tangka* paintings where time (or the round of existence) is depicted as partying briefly before the open maw of Eternity.

More importantly, what is easily lost sight of is that skepticism's specious profession of humility and tolerance is but a sophist's subterfuge to bow out from ultimate accountability. In other words, this evasiveness is an artifice that allows, quite fictitiously, the relativist to postpone self-reckoning with his own remissness, because to judge—insofar as it is not only legitimate but vital to do so—is to judge oneself. Therefore, one would not be wrong to see in relativism merely a disguise for moral cowardice, no matter all the bluster and posturing to the contrary.

To situate these comments in proper perspective, one must remember that a relativist's point of departure is always himself, that is to say his strictly personal experience of reality, whether partially valid or absurd. In practice, he sees himself as being concrete and his personal needs as being the only empirically real. It is not that he denies the reality of others, but existence recedes in realness in direct measure that it eludes the immediate grasp of his senses. Having no absolutes—except himself—he condemns the rest of the universe to relativity. Likewise, he fails to see that his idealism—insofar as he makes any claim thereto—is merely a lethal sublimism that flatters his sense of personal uniqueness.[58] Other people are, by that token, esteemed only in that they can provide a supporting cast to his individualistic pretensions, meriting consideration or

---

58. This inflated sense of self is also shared by the fanatic, which goes to prove that all character vices share a common substrate of egomania and have, therefore, little to do with reality. It might be worth remarking, at this point, that our use of the term "Reality" is not the same as the so-called "reality principle" of psychoanalysis which is, all told, mostly material and therefore of little import when assessing what is relevant to man's final ends which are supra-material. We are not saying, however, that material reality is unimportant, but simply that it cannot have decisive eschatological bearing, otherwise asceticism, and the *contemptus mundi* of which it is the empirical support, would be mere hysteria.

116

love only insofar as they can be enrolled as accomplices to his sentimental fancies. But let someone deny him his claim to subjective omnipotence and that person's motives will be forthwith open to question; we have said this. And were this not to suffice, but that person will also become an expendable commodity which can be betrayed with tranquil impunity.

What is more, the relativist operates with a sense of moral immunity, born from his unimpeachable sense of self-righteousness, even if more or less unconscious. And this self-righteousness—which the fanatic shares in reverse mode—results from an assumption he has of his intrinsic merits[59]—again a trait that he shares with the fanatic[60]—are equal, he deems, to those of any man. His grandiose humanism would accept no less. At worst, he justifies failure, if he must, in the fact that he shares the same imperfections of all mortals. As a result, whatever he does of wrong can never really be his personal fault, except perhaps superficially so, since he is entitled from the very

---

59. We say "intrinsic" merits, because he is always willing to berate himself about incidentals by way of a sop to Cerberus, which allows him to camouflage his underlying motives and so to remain, at bottom, unassailably self-satisfied.

60. If the fanatic had any honest sense of his relativity as a person, he would not be so vociferously willing to assert his opinion. That said, the fanatic is often vaguely aware of a lack in himself, a gnawing fear that perhaps he is not, after all, the navel of the universe, or that his convictions might be less than sound—in short, he does, after all, have an inkling of relativity. But, far from investigating this, he suppresses it and redoubles his zeal because what matters, finally, is not the truth but being right, absolutely and crushingly right about something, be it his professed or implied superiority. In contrast, the relativist is rather smug about himself and therefore feels no urgency to commit himself to any kind of exclusive position. The egocentrism of both attitudes, however, in spite of the spectacular difference in style, is, at bottom, pathetically the same.

117

ON AWAKENING AND REMEMBERING

outset to be ignorant given that no man can lay claim, he thinks, to any decisive knowledge.

In fact, the "moral" core (if one is permitted to misuse this term) of relativism consists in a refusal to accept any final responsibility for one's beliefs and, above all, for one's actions. And, concurrently, with often beguiling candor, the relativist is ever prone to blame circumstances for his deeper shortcomings, all the more so when he is imbued with sincerism (from the French *sincérisme*, namely "sincereness" erected as a philosophy). Not least, this attitude is fully in keeping with one of relativism's most unshakable tenets, namely that good and evil can only have expedient, never fundamental, import. Evil, for the relativist, is much more an issue of civil impropriety or a violation of humanistic idealism, reformable if given the right opportunity, than a question of *vade retro Satanas*. At the same time—and never mind the frequently maddening inconsistency of his behavior—the relativist will declare that he is always "true to himself," irrespective of whoever that "himself" happens to be at any given moment—as if one could be true to something that is forever shifting. Not surprisingly, he pays scant attention to the relativity of this "himself" which, as the case may be, can be almost anything: apparently good, perfectly mediocre, or bad—it does not matter. In his inability to transcend himself, he paradoxically rejoins the absolutist he despises by making of himself, or of his personal experience, the only effective absolute of his life.

IF WE HAVE spent more time detailing the relativist than the fanatic it is mainly because relativism is intrinsically indefensible in a way that absolutism—even the most fanatic—is not. To be an absolute relativist is to be nothing at all, whereas to be an absolutist may or may not work depending on what one is absolutist about. Moreover, the absolute

118

and the concrete coincide, therefore absolutism, by standing for something, rejoins at the very least something of the reality of existence, whereas relativism, when complete, dissolves into nothingness.

However, in agreement with our opening salvo, we do need to compare both of them a bit longer. For one, it may be worth contrasting the relativist's and the fanatical absolutist's attitude towards the failings of their fellow men. The relativist, in his need to forgive himself, seeks moral consolation, as mentioned above, in the fact that all men are fallible. In so doing, he conveniently rejects the notion of perfection, forbidding thereby any man to be better than himself or to sit in judgment over him. In tandem with this, he often exercises a kind of indiscriminate charity which is often but the cover for a resentfully self-pitying humanism that, in its attempt to divinize the world, is really a rejection of self-transcendence. Conversely, the absolutist—or, more precisely, the fanatic—holds others to impossible standards whereby, if they disappoint his prohibitive expectation, he is vindictively quick to hang them. But the net result of both these positions, however opposite their approach, is to preclude accountability to one's fellow men—the one through a kind of tolerance or sentimental solidarity with the plight of man, especially wayward man, that, in blurring all distinction of moral hierarchy, is finally sub-human in its denial of man's possibility of theomorphic greatness[61]—superiority is a possibility he resents—and the other, on the contrary, through an intolerance that is selfishly inhuman and thereby dismissive of contradiction which, of course, narrows the great universe to himself and robs him of the possibility of learning from others. Neither excess is conducive to discriminative intelligence, to say

---

61. This indiscriminate solidarity with the "weak" implicitly resents God as a tyrant.

the least, although the relativist usually has more imagination than the narrow-minded fanatic.

By way of a parallel, and finally of a perverse attempt at self-preservation, the relativist is ever ready to vaunt, usually only in the abstract, the merits of all other human beings by affirming, for example, that every man has an automatic and quasi sacred right to life, whether he be a savior or a criminal, because, on the one hand and as has already been pointed out, no man has the right, he believes ardently, to stand in absolute judgment over another— above all not over him—and, on the other hand, no crime and therefore no sanction can be commensurate with the unconditional value he ascribes to life.[62] He does not see that in this blanket dismissal of judgment, he jeopardizes the welfare of an entire collectivity.[63] But this disproportion between means and ends is entirely consistent with his own lack of self-relativization, to say nothing of the fact

---

62. It would be easy to argue that either human life is indeed sacred, as the relativist maintains, and must then be protected, unconditionally it would seem, in which case a murderer, by depriving his victim absolutely, forfeits by that very fact absolutely all rights; or else to argue that human life is not unconditionally sacred, in which case there can be no irreparable stigma in an execution. In both instances capital punishment is logically warranted as the only penalty commensurate with the crime of murder. One cannot hold both positions at the same time, though it is possible to say that while life is sacred in itself, the individual bearer can forfeit this immunity. And to those who affirm that in executing a murderer, a civilization stoops barbarically to the level of the criminal, we would respond that it is just the reverse, namely that by not executing him, a civilization colludes with him. It is in this sense that a Joseph de Maistre's vindication of the public executioner as the guardian of the social order must be understood. This, of course, presupposes true justice. Nor can we forget that, above the executioner, is God the owner of life and of death.

63. Whence Pythagoras: "Those who do not punish bad men, wish that good men may be injured."

that, as we keep on repeating, it leaves the door wide open for all manner of self-acquittal and self-justification.

And in connection with this, we alluded above to the fact that another aspect of the relativist's core intolerance of the Absolute is his espousal of the cause of the victim or the loser, or people and creatures he perceives to be such. The cause of the loser, we say, or that of the "underdog," because in actual fact the relativist does not keep company with "the meek that shall inherit the earth,"[64] given that his apparent charity is but a revolt in disguise. Therefore, he despises the truly humble who efface themselves before legitimate authority or reverence a superior. Indeed, in tune with his philosophical minimalism, he resents hierarchy or any order that discriminates between a greater and a lesser—an "injustice" that rankly offends his ever-blameless sense of "fairness." Consequently, he will take vigorous exception to anyone who dares affirm that, let us suggest by way of meaningful symbolism, a lion is a superior creature to a hyena. Or, he does not see why a rose—though he may love it passionately—should be considered "superior" to a nettle. We will see in these examples that it is the notion of superiority[65] which he finds both abhorrent and intimately threatening. Also, owing to his non-discriminating sentimentalism,[66] he is afraid that to establish a qualitative distinction between

---

64. Or, he will support them so long as they are not manifestly the Lord's anointed and so long as they do not "inherit the earth," because, as one must continue to insist, his love of flawed things betrays his refusal, yea, his unconfessable resentment of holy perfection.

65. Although he often secretly craves recognition and high standing.

66. "Non discriminating" because, according to his logic, "discrimination" amounts to discriminatory prejudice. One must remember, he prides himself on his fairness, and to be fair, he believes, he must refrain from all value judgments. A typical position is to believe that God created all creatures out of His goodness and that therefore even the most obnoxious creature is deserving of our love. Curiously, the fanatic may adopt a similar position by way of compensation, perhaps, for his

121

two things—however noble the one and loathsome the other—is to praise one at the necessarily belittling and consequently "cruel" expense of the other.[67]

No creature, not even a fly—and that is as revealingly specific as we care to be—is too abject to merit an inspired rush of sympathy on his part. He does not perceive that, as has been so rightly remarked, he who does not know how to despise does not know how to revere. Stated differently, "No man can serve two masters": to extol the inferior—or simply to place it on par with the superior—amounts to misprizing the superior, no less. And again, to repeat, this leveling—fundamentally unscrupulous in its philosophical premises—is always an attempt, albeit cloaked in apparent kindness, to justify oneself, especially one's shortcomings, because it removes the normal vantage points intelligence needs to operate effectively. To reject the notion of the superior is to reject both discernment and transcendence.

One should also make clear note of the fact that this leveling, which is individualistic (because it safeguards arbitrariness) and finally profane if not bizarrely Promethean, should not be confused with the Hindu and Buddhist ethical code of *Ahimsa* (the non-harming, that is to say, respect for all sentient beings) of which examples can be found in all traditions, whether Christian or, most notably, American Indian,[68] the moral basis for which is that man, who cannot create anything living—who cannot "coin the similitude

---

general intolerance—the example of a monster of Neronian scale who takes pity on mice while coldly putting to death thousands of men— which goes again to show that extremes meet, though of error in this case.

67. These comments may be too much of a generalization, but we are talking about extreme types or, at least, outlining the overall tendency.

68. The Great Spirit may send the vision-quester a messenger "even one as small and as seemingly insignificant as a little ant," Black Elk mentions in *The Sacred Pipe*. And, in an altogether different religious hemisphere, the Koran gives speech to an ant and also mentions that God "inspired the bee."

even of a gnat" (to cite the Koran)—and who himself was
made from a "lump of clay," should not harm or destroy
any creature.[69] It is a respect born from man's sense of his
own utter nothingness in the face of the Absolute, a respect
that he owes to all creation, first of all out of humility, then
because all four-legged and winged creatures are his brothers, and finally because, by his intelligence, he is God's
appointed caretaker on earth.

The notion of respect, however, even that of a compassionate respect that wants to be all-embracing in its love
and extended to include the remotest reaches of manifestation even until the last of sentient beings has entered (or re-
entered) *Nirvana*,[70] far from excluding discrimination quite
on the contrary entails that if the lesser is deserving of consideration, then the greater will be vastly more so; that is
the key. In fact, it is in view of the greater, precisely, that
this consideration must not be scanted the lesser. The lesser is then seen as being a component or a trace of the
greater in the sense that "inasmuch as ye did it not to one

---

69. We say "harm" not "kill," for it is a question here of gratuitous
destruction, not of legitimate use of God's providence such as is the case
with the great hunting cultures of the nomads.

70. Inevitably, and although sincerely pious, this sense of universal
compassion is open to certain quantitative abuses given man's individual limitations. For instance, in volitive mysticism where effort, and corresponding merit, is everything, devotional efficacy can entail sacrific-
ing some intellectual discrimination—as is the case of certain Buddhist
monks who allow lice to feed on them. In this instance, personal
hygiene, namely the idea that cleanliness is next to godliness, is subordinated to a compassion that, to be perfect, must overcome all "self-
interested"—hence "egotistical"—sense of personal discomfort. Also,
and more essentially, the meditating monk identifies himself intuitively
with the cosmic Purusha of which his physical body then becomes a
symbolic support. The sheer heroism of this merit compensates (morally but not intellectually) whatever inadequacies this perspective otherwise contains. And, in any case, there can be no question here of humanistic hypocrisy.

123

of the least of these, ye did it not to me" (Mat. 25:45). For he who cannot respect the lesser can in no wise respect the greater.

The consideration, now, the relativist pays the lesser is altogether of a different order, for his love, we will remember, involves a rejection of the transcendent in that owing to his sentimental worship of the literal or the material—and to his inability to understand archetypes— he divorces the effect from its cause and thus may, for instance, loudly bemoan the death of any single creature, which is not the same as legitimate grief. To paraphrase Islamic dialectics, his position is really that of an idolater guilty of the sin of associationism (*shirk*), namely of granting the periphery— the creature in this case—prerogatives that can only belong, metaphysically speaking, to the center. Or, it is to absolutize the relative while, *ipso facto*, relativizing the Absolute.

In contradistinction, true compassion is rooted in reverence for the divine cause: "Whosoever shall receive me, receiveth not me, but him that sent me." This concrete recognition of the divine cause is nowhere better illustrated than in the myths of the great hunting cultures the world over. The example of the ritual of the returned blood shows that the infinite bounty of the celestial realm can never be depleted by the slaying of the hunted animals provided symbolic restitution of the borrowed creature be made to the Creator.[71] It is worth noting, however, that the provident source will just as surely dry up if the animal be

---

71. "It takes powerful magic to spill blood and not to be overtaken by the blood-revenge," writes Leo Froebinus in *Volksmärchen der Kabylen*. Compare also, in this context, the Cree Indian "thanksgiving" ritual of *Mukushan* ("peace"), acknowledging the Great Spirit's gift of the caribou. For "primitive" people know that one cannot mistreat nature without dire personal consequences. It is interesting to note that when the hunter has treated the animal with proper respect and gratitude, for example by using only a beautiful and clean weapon, future animals will come to him to be slain, it is said.

wantonly slain as if it be wantonly worshipped, for God is not only proud but also jealous: His grace will be just as readily withdrawn if His gift is scorned or if it is loved to distraction. Contempt and idolatry are not so far apart.

BECAUSE PSYCHOLOGICAL RELATIVISM coincides with the Infinite's endlessness of possibility or with the power of illusion—namely *Maya* when divorced from *Atma*—there are simply too many modalities to cover in one chapter. And also, given its subjectivism, it conspires with the absurd, namely with "the possibility of the impossibility," as Schuon termed it. Therefore, care must be taken not get ensnared in its labyrinthine meanders when attempting to define it. It will suffice to contrast it with its opposite vice, fanaticism.

In a word, one could say rather roughly that fanaticism results when passion usurps the place of intelligence and relativism when sentiment does so. In other words, relativism is really a kind of sentimentalism[72] in that, metaphysically stated, it cherishes accidents at the expense of the substance, weeping over futilities while overlooking scandals, or straining at gnats while swallowing camels, or jeopardizing tradition to save an eccentric.[73] In the case of fanaticism, it is not so much a question of sentimentalism[74]

---

72. One will distinguish between sentimentality proper, which is simply the capacity for affectivity, and sentimentalism which is to let intelligence be determined by sentiments instead of intelligence guiding the sentiments.

73. Of course, if the individual is really a "majority of one," then it is the tradition that may need to be reformed, because no individual who is a moral exemplar can be treated as a detail. However, his merit is no more than the value—which is by definition trans-individual—that he represents or embodies. And there is always the exception that confirms the rule.

74. It is difficult to be axiomatically precise when discussing categories of subjectivity which is a fluid and highly plastic realm.

as of intemperate emotionalism.[75] It is easy to see that passion, which is in essence egotistical, is always fundamentally intolerant when left to operate alone or, in other words, when it leads instead of being led by intelligence, which can channel it, or at least by an ideal[76] that can redeem its excesses which otherwise, like a fire, can be ravaging when not directed. Sentiment, on the other hand, tends by nature to be allocentric (the opposite of egocentric) in that its essence is love.[77]

In making these distinctions, it not a question of censuring either sentiment or passion, both of which have their indispensable role to play in the economy of the human psyche. Rather, it is a question of addressing an imbalance that results when either of these tendencies overflows, as it were, its appointed boundaries and swamps consciousness. Thus, passion tends to be divisive where sentiment is unitive. For instance, in the case of religious belief, where fanaticism (or passion) will stress God's rigor and justice, relativism (or sentimentalism) will stress His mercy and forgiveness—abusively in both cases because it will always be a question of an excessive emphasis of the one or the other.[78] Where passion is unkind,

---

75. Emotion could be said to be the human side of passion and passion the animal side of emotion.

76. Idealism is a form of existential intelligence in that it corresponds to an intuition of higher reality.

77. We are talking about passion and sentiment in themselves and are therefore entitled, it seems, to say that passion as such is exclusive because it is a form of concentration, just as sentiment as such is inclusive because it is diffuse. That being said, it is entirely possible that the object of a passion, when noble, can lead a person to overcome egocentrism and become generous, just as the object of a sentiment can make a person selfish. Again, the problem is not passion per se, but the exclusivity of passion.

78. An excellent example of objective balance between the sense of the Absolute and that of the Infinite—if such it may be termed—is St.

sentimentality is indulgent: where passion, in its discriminative fury calls doves snakes, sentimentality, in opaque
permissiveness, calls snakes doves. Objectivity, however,
sees doves as doves and snakes as snakes, for it does not
have a vested personal interest in sweetening poison or in
poisoning sweetness.

While it is not surprising that fanaticism is by basic temperament irrational and consequently that it operates
through compulsive monomania (*idée fixe*), stubborn invec-
tive, and the absurd juxtaposition of disconnected slogans,
that, in short, it violates intelligence, it may, at first sight,
seem surprising to see that sentimentalism resorts to intense
reasoning, because reason and sentiment tend to become
enemies when not subordinated to intelligence's guiding
agency. Upon closer examination, however, there is a homeostasis of the psyche, a system of spontaneous checks and
balances, whereby one excess is compensated by another in
order to maintain a semblance of equilibrium. In the case of
relativism, excess wetness of sentimentalizing is lopsidedly
compensated by excess dryness of ratiocination. Indeed, reason, when cut off from its intellective root, becomes a sterile
mentalism and the pawn of subjectivism which uses it to
arrogate to itself some semblance of credibility.

Theresa of Lisieux's fervent prayers for a criminal sentenced to death:
she never prayed that the verdict be overturned but that the murderer
be converted. Her prayers were answered, quite miraculously it would
seem, when Pranzini, a hardened criminal inured to scruple, and
already on the scaffold, unexpectedly beseeched the priest for absolution of his sins and went to his death after thrice kissing a crucifix.
Contrast her intercession with that of the modern-day Church appealing
to parole boards the world over to commute the sentence of death-row
inmates—and this with no consideration for their catechistic obligations.
Having said this, it would not be surprising if some "deconstructionist"
historian will say that the Little Flower of Lisieux was "behind her
times" or that she was bound by the narrow moral conventions of her
milieu. The devil never rests.

127

Both fanaticism and relativism, however, are, in the last analysis, equally inhuman—the former in its gratuitous harshness[79] that cannot take account of Reality's inherent complexity, and the latter too, though quite paradoxically, because of its declared humanism which makes of man a god and, in so doing, excludes the divine without which man, as *imago Dei*, ceases to be man.

IN FINE, MAN, on pain of erring, cannot dispense with balance. It is balance—and it is not a question here of either reasonableness or neutrality, those pseudo-virtues masquerading as objectivity and conspiring with mediocrity— that is the true measure of a man's virtue and hence of his honesty. It has often been stated that there can be no charity without justice, for kindness without due rigor is but weakness, just as rigor without due kindness is but cruelty. Only the strong can be generous. In other words, the sense of the Absolute, which entails not only sacrifice and courage but above all discernment and, as a result, reverence,[80] must be graced with the sense of the Infinite, which entails not only charity and love and gratitude, but also holy devotion. The Infinite is the bliss of the Absolute.

Indeed, for the man who is awake, the universe is resplendent with signs of God's Absolute/Infinite Being. For instance, taking support in millennia of Egyptian worship of Ra, or in Vedic rituals, or in Shintoism, or in the timeless infinitude of all nomadic primordialism all of which venerated the sun, one could say the whole mystery of existence is summed up in the daily epiphanies of

---

79. Fanaticism will over-emphasize the possibility of hell (Calvin) whereas relativism will deny it.

80. Because to know the Real from the unreal entails forthwith an affective reaction of reverence for the True and simultaneously immediate recoil from the false. To know the Real is to behold the sacred.

sunrise and sunset:[81] at dawn, the sun's light gives life to all creatures and manifests God's infinite diversity of possibility, testifying to the inexhaustible plentifulness of His "words." At twilight, the sun's extinction marks the return of all created things to the darkened void from whence they issued; the world is restored to original Oneness.

However, as each dimension is mirrored in the other—God, being Whole, is never exclusive—sunrise also manifests the Absolute's radiant fullness of presence, whereas sunset reveals, in its turn, the universe's glimmering infinitude—and relativity—of multiple possibilities set in their starry archetype.

---

81. "In the alternation of night and day, and what God has created in the heavens and the earth—surely there are signs for a god-fearing people" (Koran 10:6).

3. THE VEIL OF SUFFERING

Ad astra per aspera [1]

FROM AN ESSENTIAL perspective, creation results from God's Self-awareness[2] or a state of non-dual duality in which to be is to know and to know is to be. The world, on the other hand, exists as outwardness or separateness only to the measure in which the Self is free, at a certain level, to ignore Itself as Self. And this ignorance of the Self—or inasmuch as the Self can be veiled—is in turn sustained by man so long as he does not know—or does not wish to know— what his true nature is, the essence of which is plenitude of knowledge. Were a thief to know that in his ontological heart of hearts his consciousness merged with that of the One Self, he would become a saint. But he does not care to. Therefore the world exists, because to exist—that is to say to be distinct in its own right—it needs to "deny" Reality— total Reality— in some fashion and to a greater or lesser extent. This over-simplification of the basic issue has the merit of highlighting what is at stake in being born in the human state which is defined by the consciousness of the Absolute.

Before proceeding further, one should probably make a distinction between creation and the world, because the

---

1. "To the stars through effort."
2. Avicenna: "The world results from God's self-knowledge."

130

occurrence of suffering is not the immediate by-product of separation *in divinis*. Suffering occurs as a kind of ultimate repercussion at the outermost fringes of manifestation of what is at first a blissful differentiation in which the wealth of divine possibility unfolds in blooming abundance. The awareness the Self has of Itself coincides with the quickening spark or impulse it gives each latent possibility which opens up in firework bursts of joyful exuberance.[3] Thus, contrary to our human experience, in which hardship is a law of existence, the overwhelming majority of manifestation belongs to paradisiacal realms. If one cannot sense this empirically, one can know it according to the metaphysical principle of the rule of quality which determines that reality and eternity coincide with the true, the good, and the beautiful.[4]

Creation operates on the basis of a cosmic principle of division which at first is fructifying and abundant, but, when left to complete its projection into the void, is eventually narrowing and terminating. The origin of suffering arises from the ultimately dolorous consequences of this original division. But this fact is probably too abstract for most people to grasp in meaningful terms, and thus may be more or less inoperative for he or she who is caught in the clutches of the cosmic illusion which earthly existence represents. Instead, it may be more profitable for him or for her to begin their inquiry from the direct, unavoidable, and painful experience of suffering itself. Wherefore suffering

---

3. This is why one finds so many references to *jubilatio* or jubilation—the hosannas—in Christian mysticism as a key factor in the awareness of the divine presence.

4. Likewise in manifestation, according to the Hindu doctrine of the four ages, the *Kali Yuga* or "dark age," which is characterized by forgetfulness of the divine and by transgression, is but a fraction of the length of the three preceding ages.

and how to escape it? This is Buddhism's great dialectical premise.[5]

That suffering and sorrow are the ineluctable ransom of existence, no man can deny. Whatever illusion he may otherwise have of the world or of himself, he is fated sooner or later to drink the cup of life down to its mortal dregs, for all life ends in death: "This is the noble truth of sorrow. Birth is sorrow, age is sorrow, disease is sorrow, death is sorrow . . . in short, all the five components of individuality (*skandhas*)[6] are sorrow," Buddhism asserts (*Samyutta-nikaya*).

Concurrently, man's happiness hinges on his acceptance or refusal of this "noble truth," irrespective of whether he understands it or not. In other words, faced with the absolute inevitability of pain, suffering, and death, man has in essence but two choices, upon which his destiny will be made or destroyed: resignation or revolt. One might remark that there is in fact no choice since revolt is folly. This is quite true. However, from man's subjective point of view there is an alternative and that is proven by the fact that man can end up in a state of revolt, be it only unconsciously so. One might also want to add a third alternative, that of despair. But despair, insofar as it is a negative judgment concerning God's goodness—and an implicit rejection thereof—is at root a kind of passive revolt.

---

5. Each of the great revelations addresses a central fact of human existence. For Buddhism it is man's suffering; for Christianity, man's sinfulness; for Judaism, man's transgression; for Islam, man's hypocrisy. The case of Hinduism is more complex since this religion englobes a number of different *margas* or paths. The path of *jnana* or knowledge, for instance, starts from the premise of man's ignorance.

6. These *skandhas* (or "heaps" of aggregates constituting a person) are the form or bodily shape, sensation, perception, volition, and thought. They are considered to be disassociated at death, although this is probably only true in the lower beings—both animals and baser human beings—since in the case of sanctified persons, there is a crystallization of the personality which has rejoined an archetype.

132

From a purely individual point of view, that of a man who feels that he has been flung into existence without seemingly any choice or personal responsibility in the matter, suffering, and all its attendant tribulations, can appear as a grievously unjust lot. And when he is summarily told that God is the author of his trials and God will test his faith—for example, that "The Lord trieth the righteous" (Ps. 11:5)—he may be tempted to see in God's sovereignty a tyrannical omnipotence before which he can only grovel, while hoping somehow to placate this Lord's wrath or ill humor and to secure His mercy, the dispensation of which seems unaccountably arbitrary and dishearteningly unpredictable. And, in his misery, man may be prone to hold God somehow responsible for whatever torment endured—no less!

This dramatically human notion of merit and reward, and of transgression and punishment, is one of the possible—and unfortunate—consequences of depicting God in purely anthropomorphic terms. In psychology, this phenomenon is termed "projection," namely the tendency of attributing to someone else one's own attitudes or traits. Although God must of necessity don a human countenance when addressing man, one must not forget that, as Eckhart reminds us, "Before creatures were, God was not 'God'."[7]

Still, if one is to speak of God at all, one cannot avoid human terminology lest one make of Him a speculative abstraction that men, who for the most are emotive and not intellective, could no longer grasp or relate to in personal terms. In any case, God is not just essential Absolute (*Parabrahma* or *Brahma nirguna*, "non-qualified") but also Being and Creator (*Ishwara* or *Brahma saguna*, "qualified"). Thus, to address in the Lord's Prayer God as "Our Father"

---

7. Something Nietzsche distantly sensed in spite of his dialectical evolutionism.

is not only legitimate and hence metaphysically correct, but it entails a whole relationship which is concretely human as well as divine.

To return to the specific complications ensuing from a purely anthropomorphic depiction of God, or of God's relationship with man, it is understandable—though not pardonable—that man may see God ostensibly as a despotic sovereign who threatens and cajoles him with the eschatological desserts of hell and heaven, who punishes him severely should he be found wanting or, if one looks at things from the vantage point of individualism and potential revolt, of a God who might take some kind of sadistic delight in sporting with man, subjecting him, gratuitously it would seem, to dread difficulties.[8] Why, asks the senti-

---

8. As depicted in the themes of Greek tragedy, for instance the plays of Aeschylus where the universal issues of hubris and nemesis—insolent pride and celestial revenge—are settled through often gruesome tribulations that involve reckless passion, murder, somber terror, exile, and inexpiable guilt whose grim *karmic* reverberations can never be allayed so long as man is man: "The shed drop doth crave new blood" (*Libation Bearers*). If we mention the author of *Prometheus Unbound*—and one should include Euripides: "To none is given / To know the coming nor the end of woe; / So dark is God, and to great darkness go / His paths, by blind chance mazed from our ken" (*Iphigenia in Tauris*) and Sophocles: "We are blameless but confess / That the gods are pitiless" (*Trachinian Women*)—if we mention Aeschylus it is because this author has been specifically appropriated by Promethean cynics of every age— a Shelley, a Freud, or a Sartre being but the most recent exponents. For such an outlook, human existence is a cruel joke, because—to paraphrase from Sophocles' *Oedipus at Colonus*—that man is most blessed who was never born, and next happiest him who dies in infancy (cf. Joachim Du Bellay's "*La complainte du désespéré*"). One is also reminded here, but in the context now of religious faith, of Job's cry of agony: "Let the day perish wherein I was born" or of Christ on the cross: "My God, my God, why hast thou forsaken me?"

mentalist, does God inflict pain on me if He is ever-merciful and lovingkind?[9]

Stated more soberly, we would say the problem is that of reconciling suffering, which is the lot of all human beings, with happiness, which is their most fundamental aspiration and, potentially, in view of their theomorphic identity, their birthright. Indeed, given the universality of suffering, man may wonder whether happiness is but the precursor of grief, a poisoned gift, delicious in the tasting but excruciating in the voidance.[10] To this one might say— and by way of bitter irony, perhaps, for the man in the grip of woe or to the survivor of a natural disaster—that suffering proves happiness, and not the other way round. In other words, if man suffers it is because he is made for happiness. Expressed differently, if happiness were not his essence, he would not suffer. In the same vein, health does not prove disease, nor life death.[11] Quite on the contrary. To think otherwise is fundamentally errant, because that would amount to thinking that creation is in its essence flawed or evil.

But, to repeat, why does a bounteously perfect God allow suffering or seem even to inflict it? And why—to play along with this script—does He subject man to trials? A general answer would be to say that this issue is directly related to the age-old metaphysical problem of good and

---

9. It is clear that not every reader will relate with these kinds of attitudes. However, just as with the question of relativism dealt with in the previous chapter, these are basic tendencies encountered in societies where individualism has become rampant.

10. No wonder, then, that one may find apparently absurd a recommendation in the Mahabharata (meant in fact to induce disillusion with all things earthly, not bitterness with God) as the following: "Hope is the greatest torture there is and despair the greatest happiness" (text quoted by the 18th Century commentator Mahadeva Vedantin).

11. "The world does not leak because death is not a crack," Rabindranath Tagore said in one of his poems.

evil, and that hence, where there is evil there is of necessity—for the believer at least—temptation, trial, and struggle. If the reason of being for man is to manifest God, or the divine, even in the remotest reaches of the cosmos, then, from a voluntarist point of view at least, his love of God is "nothing" until it has been proven through suffering, because it is easy to be "good" when all is going well. But such an answer does not really address the concrete human experience of the problem. Therefore, if we are to grapple with the psychological specifics of this issue, we would say first of all that whoever asks such a question is implicitly assuming that he is somehow deserving of ease. Or that it is unfair for him to have to suffer since, again he assumes, he is "good"—or "good enough"—not to merit pain. Part of the cause for this personalization of the issue results from the secularism of a society that fosters individualism while limiting if not abolishing man's innate sense of eschatological realities which, under normal circumstances, would set man's position in its proper cosmological context. Thus one of the consequences of individualism is that it makes a person feel, whether naively or arrogantly, that he is in principle entitled to anything he wants and consequently indebted to God for nothing. In other words, one is dealing here with a basically modern phenomenon of psychology which is never encountered in a fully traditional world premised on the sacred,[12] namely a world in which it is God, and by extension the cosmos and its immutable order, and not man, who is accorded priority of importance—unless man lives in accordance with the golden law of heavenly *dharma*. And one where life and its attendant comforts is not taken for granted as an inalien-

---

12. In his *Candide*, Voltaire's acerbic mockery of Leibniz's "best of all worlds" would have been unthinkable in an integrally traditional society where religion is the divinely appointed guardian of social criteria.

able right, but is regarded as something that must be earned even while it can be lost at any moment, for it is not the fact of biological existence that is important, but the quality of being. That fact alone should, in principle, suffice to situate the limits of the above attitude's admissibility. Mere existence is a state that is shared with any marsh and is, when taken alone, irrelevant.

These remarks, however, are likely to remain a dead letter for the humanist vulnerable to what is in fact a debilitating disposition, because his resentment at having to suffer masks a self-indulgence which, in the last analysis, prevents self-transcendence. And instead of taking stock of his weakness and acting to change and thus to become a master of his own destiny, he yields to the temptation of facility and berates Heaven,[13] be it only implicitly, for not rescuing him from a misery which may be, all told, nothing finally save the fruit of his own laziness or remissness. Curiously, in an inverse way, a pious man may share a similar kind of passivity with the humanist when he says that such and such a trial, such and such a defect, or such and such a misery is "God's will," which, properly speaking, is absurd. What he really means to say is that he accepts such and such a tribulation as part of his destiny which is willed by God. However—apart from the fact that God may tolerate a trial but does not "will" one—there is a kind of fatalism in such a formulation which discourages the use of gifts such as intelligence or perspicacity and the active use of one's free will which are from God and are therefore also "willed" by God, and preeminently so, to be used. The gifts allow man both to discern and to choose, and to choose is to will. Otherwise man is but a sheep.

If one makes abstraction of the particular predicament that existence on this "dull earth" entails, one could read-

---

13. But, "Whoever blames God, despises his mercy" (Boehme).

ily imagine Elysian realms where men would have souls like flowers, would find their entire sustenance in light, and need no longer roam nor toil, a land of blissful ease where death would be but a gentle sleep and a prelude to new happiness. But such a realm, to say nothing of the constellated spheres of Paradise which do not concern us here, could never account for the full range of possibilities entailed by divine manifestation, or the *Samsara*. Schematically stated, the phenomenon of creation involves first differentiation, which is qualitative, then, in the wake of this motion, separation whose centrifugal impetus aspires to a point of absolute negation, or of total otherness (alterity), that can never be reached literally since nothing can exist outside of God's own self-subsistent infinitude.[14] We say can never be reached "literally," but not symbolically or even empirically because from the point of view of man's experience, which is our present focus, these gradations, whether operated through a transition from the subtle to the ever denser layers of grossness or whether experienced through the fragmenting principle of individuation (*ahamkara* in *Sankhya* philosophy), result in degrees of separation—or otherness—that for all practical purposes are relatively absolute. Consequently, if bliss is the experience of unity, then the experience of separateness involves to some extent or other, suffering.[15] Remove suffering and one abolishes the *Samsara*. Likewise, to abolish trials—

---

14. For, as Erigena in his *On the Division of Nature* specifies, Divine Nature can be said to be "neither creative nor created since, being infinite, it cannot produce anything which can be outside itself."

15. Separateness as such need not entail suffering, except possibly in a subliminal way, because love is premised in part on otherness. Also, separation is the necessary prelude to a union, a union which, temporarily unavailable, induces one to rediscover it and, if possible, on a higher or profounder level. Separation, moreover, is a proof of union for what is the grief of separation if not the need for union lost.

which are the human experience of this suffering—is to abolish man, or at least man after the *Krita Yuga* or original Golden Age. Otherness from God, to be terminally consummated, must therefore involve suffering.[16] In fact, the entire nobleness of man's existence in this vale of tears consists in his capacity to suffer and to love God at one and the very same time. One could even say that a noble suffering is a way of knowing God, because base men, whose conscience is callused, cannot suffer in depth.[17] In other words, man would not suffer were he not divine in his essence.

At the same time that God projects Himself into the cosmic void, as it were forgetting Himself in the darkening reaches of His radiation, He is also ever remembering Himself, for He can never fully part with Himself, whence man's ontological nostalgia which, in its essence, is no less than the veiled trace of God's self-recollection.[18] In this sense, all suffering, all sorrow, all broken-heartedness are, in their root, echoes of man's intuitive need to recover that original unity *in divinis*. And this brings us to the first meaning of God's "allowing" man to suffer, for could man but see it, his pain is really in its heart, or ontological depth, nothing other than God's secret call for him to return. And this call, insofar as it is resisted[19] or not heeded to its fullest

---

16. As Schuon writes in *Understanding Islam,* Ch. "The Koran": "Man's sufferings testify to the mysteries of his distance and separation, and they cannot not be, the world not being God."

17. This does not mean that they cannot suffer acutely, to the point even of committing suicide. However, the suffering of souls in hell is said to be commensurate with their awareness of God, Whom they have ignored or rejected while on earth. Thus, deep suffering always involves knowledge.

18. This is why, as Bernard McGinn has highlighted (*The Presence of God*), the mystic's awareness of the absence of God is a form of awareness of the divine presence.

19. The tale of Jonah is instructive in this respect.

consequences of mystical union, will involve ever renewed varieties of suffering—at least so long as an individual does not forfeit his faith for one of the more bizarre consequences of nihilism is the serenity it can procure, albeit a very superficial one, to be sure. Insouciance—always insolent underneath—might be a better term to describe what is in fact a flattening of consciousness.

When it is said that God tests man's faith, one might more accurately say that He is in fact summoning him, by letting him taste the nothingness of earthly consolations. This "call," however, which in fact amounts to a blessing in disguise, does not concern miscreants, nor that part in man which corresponds to disbelief. In this case, the frustration of desire is merely the sanction nature metes out to intemperance.

Indeed, not all trials can be said to be blessings in disguise; far from it. For one cannot forget that the very relativity of all terrestrial phenomena means that they are marked by imperfection, corruption, and impermanence. Therefore, to the degree that a man invests his vital substance and his happiness in them, or to the degree that he clings to them, he will axiomatically meet with sore disappointment. In this respect, man, who by nature possesses the capacity for total objectivity, has but his own passional stupidity to blame for this suffering. Immanent justice is the penalty for ontological transgression. In any case, birth in the human state implies for all but the pneumatic type— who naturally ascends heavenwards, by dint of celestial gravity one might say[20]—progenitive desire whose appetitive impulse ceaselessly perpetuates the Wheel of Existence's motion (the *Samsara*).[21] The world is born of the

---

20. Schuon once said that man must learn to fall heavenwards.

21. Whence the comment of the Buddha: "From lust creatures run into distress, they are tormented in the six states of existence and people

urge towards multiplicity and perpetuated by the illusion of separate selfhood, whereas death is the resurgence of the underlying unity of the One Self which, to follow a Sufi metaphor, "inherits the reeds out of the mat." Man can ignore this only at his peril.

IF THE ACT of Creation entails separation and suffering, does it thereby entail abandonment for man? To say that God creates is to say that He projects Himself into the void. And since He is simultaneously both the Subject and Object of this cosmic act, He can therefore never be wholly absent from His creation, for it is His awareness or His being, however indirect as regards the periphery of manifestation, that sustains the worlds. His awareness of Himself is their animating principle.[22] And were He to forget them, be it for the merest spark of an instant, they would forthwith cease to be. The whole doctrine of immanence rests on this principle of Divine Presence and, in turn, this principle should be of immense consolation for a contemplative person. Concurrently, God continuously projects His Mercy even into the remotest reaches of the *Samsara*—as the sacrifice of the Bodhisattva reminds us, a celestial being who comes on earth for the sake of the redemption of men, postponing his final re-entry into Paradise to save souls.

---

the cemetery again and again" (*Saddharma-pundarika* or "Lotus of the True Law"), which in turn recalls Christ's admonition to those who sow according to the flesh.

22. God is not "personally" present in flowers, for instance. But in that they are a manifestation of His celestial nature, one could say He is present in them as beauty. One might even add that they are manifestations of His love and of His joy, for everything in nature has a spiritual, or at least, a psychic origin of which the object is, as it were, a condensate. And lastly, flowers prove the essential goodness of creation which finally no misery can refute or even compromise.

ON AWAKENING AND REMEMBERING

Dharmakara's vow[23] not to enter *Nirvana* until the last of sentient beings is saved means, among other things, that no part of the *Samsara* will ever be forsaken by God.

Thus it is that the process of manifestation entails a process of progressive separation, estrangement, and ultimate exile in which "the children of the kingdom shall be cast out into outer darkness" where "there shall be weeping and gnashing of teeth," (Mat. 8:12) and at the same time a parallel motion of return, redemption, reconciliation, and ultimate (re-)union in which God reclaims Himself, as it were, in view of His fundamental unity of being which can never in fact be sundered *ab intra*. To wish it were otherwise, in other words to wish that the cosmogonic unfolding outside of God could be operated solely by joy, in joy, and for joy alone is simply utopian.[24] Creation myths the world over attest to the fact that the passage from potentiality to actuality, from essence to entelechy,[25] or, *mutatis mutandis*, from immortality to mortality, involves sacrifice and terrible suffering: mythic tales depict a tangled web of betrayal, desertion, intrigue, perjury, trickery, abduction, rape, deceit, incest, repudiation, murder, parricide, castration, poisoning, strangling, disease, famine, genocide,

---

23. Which in its fulfillment belongs to Amitabha Buddha, as Schuon explains (cf. *Logic and Transcendence*, Ch. "Dharmakara's Vow").

24. One will bear in mind, however, that, more intrinsically, as the *Chandogya Upanishad* says: "Where there is joy, there is creation." It is important to differentiate between creation as act, which results from an overflow of divine love, joy, and bounteousness, and creation as consequence—a duality which retraces, on its plane, the distinction between Brahma as *karana* or cause and Brahma as *karya* or effect.

25. We are using this term in a material sense, though in its deeper meaning of passage from possibility to fulfillment one could speak of sanctity as being the "entelechic" fruit of prayer. If, to paraphrase a famous Patristic saying, *Nirvana* became *Samsara* so that *Samsara* could become *Nirvana*, then one is entitled to speak not only of a "descentional" process of entelechy but also of an "ascentional" one which, in fact, the former prepares.

THE VEIL OF SUFFERING

and myriad natural disasters following in the wake of man's establishment on earth.[26] What is crucially important to note is that before this veil of suffering unfolds God admonishes man not to eat from the "tree of good and evil," the consequences of which introduce separative consciousness[27] and thus, in the course of things, the beginning of the play of mistaken identities which is one of the sources of man's subsequent tribulations.[28]

---

26. Mention can be made, at random, of the myths for example of Isis and Osiris, Izanagi and Izanami, Orpheus and Eurydice, or of the harrowing tribulations of Inana, the combat between Marduk and Tiamat or that between Indra and Namuci, the abduction of Sita, the numerous "extramarital" loves of Zeus—the list is endless. It is important, however, to understand that these myths transcend the narrow moral interpretations in that they concern cosmic phenomena. In other words, incest and murder between gods does not necessarily carry the same spiritual consequences as that between mortals, which is not to lessen their gravity, cosmically speaking. Moreover, the terminology used is man's and, therefore, does not do justice to the nature of the phenomenon. For instance, the term "incest" is a very approximate one because it is probably difficult to explain with another verb the intimacy between gods who, as the progenitors of all beings, are still too close not to be unrelated; the ancestors of all men are of necessity "brothers" and "sisters." Finally, the more gruesome of the creation myths probably must be situated at a much latter stage of creation, one closer to the *Kali Yuga* if not one directly ushering it. And, also, creation itself does not necessarily follow a literal time-line, but operates in phases between which there are isthmuses each of which is as a return to a beatific center followed, each time, by an increasingly temporal and hence ever more brutal deployment where birth occurs in pain. Creation, as explained in the Book of Genesis, is highly synthetic and schematic, which is typical of all the monotheistic traditions which do not elaborate on realms outside of the immediate province of the *Kali Yuga*.

27. Or a kind of *tamasic* objectivity, namely one in which form will predominate ever more exclusively over substance.

28. One finds the same forewarning as a central motif in fairy tales and legends, where the prince or the princess begs his or her earthly paramour to refrain from one critical deed or question, whose commission provokes a curse that banishes him or her from the realm of innocence.

Hence man's estrangement and indifference, though it kindles God's wrath outwardly—for His majesty does not allow for the affront of man's heedlessness—aggrieves Him inwardly.[29] This is why the Koran says that God "prescribes for Himself Mercy," for God, Who is so completely unity in every single mode and modality of His nature, cannot possibly "want" separation as such. That man deserts Him happens in spite of Him, if one can put it so boldly. In other words, man's Fall is a consequence of his God-given freedom. But this freedom was meant for knowledge and love, not sin even though it is one of its potential consequences—"potential," not necessary, but one without which this freedom would not be free, precisely. Separation—separation as suffering—is the ransom, not the *raison d'être*, of man's God-given objectivity.

NO DISCUSSION OF man's trials and suffering would be intelligible without understanding something of the predicament man finds himself in as a result of his dual nature—at once divine and human. The root of the Arabic word for man (*nas*) means "to forget".[30] To be born man, then, is to be born in a

---

29. It may be objected that when discussing cosmology we resort too easily to human imagery. In defense of this dialectical liberty, we might quote Erigena: "When we hear that God wishes, loves, chooses, sees, hears. . . we should think nothing else than that His ineffable essence and power are being expressed by meanings co-natural with us lest the true and pious Christian be silenced concerning the Creator, and dare say nothing of Him" (*On the Division of Nature*). Also, sacred literature of all traditions lends a human voice and understanding to God which is simply a way of recognizing that God is pure consciousness in all of its modes, whether of understanding, perception, or love.

30. Arabic, like all ancient languages, possesses a semantic homogeneity that gives it a didactic genius not found in modern languages which are largely determined by the vagaries of usage—as opposed to tradition which emphasizes preservation not change—and which can therefore express meanings that end up being arbitrary because often at

state of forgetfulness, wherefore the Platonic doctrine of reminiscence which is premised on the fact of integral original knowledge—and, also, wherefore religion: without religion,[31] man has utterly no hope of escaping the mesh of *Maya* and, in fact, cannot become integrally human.[32] Left to himself, namely to his "narrow-verged life in the flesh," man feeds on illusion just as he himself is the food of illusion. He is a shadow whose "life is wind" and who, in *Samsaric* terms, wanders from existence to existence driven by, as we have seen, ever-renewed lust. However, the meaning of being born a man, and not some lesser creature, is the capacity to return to God and thus, by symbolic extension, to restore creation, of which he is the intelligent synthesis, back to God. In this sense, to be born a man is to be born at the intersection of two mighty cosmic tendencies, the one God-denying in its ultimate centrifugalism and the other God-affirming in its ultimate centripetal force. Suffering would then be the inevitable price of this cosmic divergence, perforce ever-contending, whose battlefield is finally the heart of man.

---

variance with the etymology of words. It is difficult, if not impossible, to think error in an ancient language without either creating new words or violating the rules grammar as well as the etymology of established words. Thus, the word for revelation in Arabic, *tanzil*, means a descent (from Heaven). No one would dare to use this word in any other sense without risking the worst of associationism (*shirk*)—the ultimate sacrilege in Islam.

31. Intellective reminiscence can, in principle, dispense with rites and dogmas. But this is not the issue here, quite apart from the fact that intellective knowledge is not actualizable for most men without the concourse of religion. However, religion is often a double-edged sword because it can also block access to this knowledge when its ritual means and psychic ambiance become an end instead of the womb it was meant to be. When Schiller was asked which religion he followed, he answered: "None of those that you've mentioned. And why? Because of Religion."

32. "There is no doubt that the man who does not worship Shiva is an animal and remains endlessly wandering in the cycle of existence" (*Yoga Shikha Upanishad*).

This being said, and we have already touched on this, it is entirely possible that a given individual can drift from propensity to deluded propensity without experiencing any real suffering while in the flesh because, in this case, he does not fight the impetus of gravity that is leading him away from himself, that is to say, away from his fullest possibility as a being created in the image of God. That he can reap success and joy in abandoning himself to the free course of his passions may seem paradoxical at first sight, that is if one falls short of examining the eschatological consequences such unconscionable a behavior entails: "Wherefore doth the way of the wicked prosper? Wherefore are all they happy that deal very treacherously?" (Jer. 12:1) What we have here is an illustration of the law of inverse analogy ruling manifestation, the one which, on the one hand, determines that "The first shall be last" and, on the other, "They that sow in tears shall reap in joy." In other words, to the "prince of this world" is given the dominion of the kingdoms of the earth for the "brief" duration of the latter stages of a *manvantara* (the Sanskrit *Puranas'* cycle of four *Yugas* or time periods) before the Prince of Peace casts him out. The devil has but this earthly life, and the posthumous states that are its psychic prolongations, in which to work his mischief; without his agency, which is the principle of cosmic separation, the world could not stand "outside" of God. Correspondingly, success in worldly ambition is readily obtainable if man, in a Faustian pact, stakes his immortal soul in the bargain. In the same way, sensual intemperance, especially when combined with the heedless energy of youth or when freed from the constraints of moral scruples, can provide seemingly endless ecstasy initially, that is to say before the law of karma reclaims its dues, for every man reaps what he has sown.

But for the man of God, whose happiness can never really be of this world, being born entails suffering for he

146

must struggle to reverse the downward tendency of the cosmogonic projection, the inertia and ceaseless pulling and tugging of which relentlessly seeks to drag him down and away from the happiness of his celestial origin. Religious tradition is unanimous in saying that it is "the righteous" that are tried, the children of light whom God desires to retrieve from darkness. In the meantime, the weaning from the world involves such sacrifice and mortification as profane men[33] can have little or no notion of. In this decisive respect, a trial can be understood to be the mark of God's favor,[34] whereby He seeks to retrieve a soul, through painful disillusionment perhaps, from manifestation's oblivial drowning waters. Sufi tradition relates that those whom God tries the most are His prophets; next, are His saints; then the believers. As for the disbelievers, He lets them be. Apart from the fact that a prophet is by profoundest nature the most estranged of beings on this now darkened earth, owing to his wholly celestial substance, it also follows that he is the one who can bear the harshest suffering because he is morally incorruptible. Therefore, he must assume the burden of sacrifice for the sake of others. And more: his life as such is already a living sacrifice meant to fulfill not just the scope of his sacred possibility which "darkness comprehendeth not," but the full scope of his redemptive mission among men. Since his very existence

---

33. The term "profane", while specific to non-religious individuals, could also apply to anyone who lives as he pleases, according to his talents perhaps, even with discipline, but in a self-satisfied way, that is to say without ever seeking to question who he is and what his life means. To be profane, or worldly, is finally to lack a sense of self-transcendence.

34. This reminds us of Gregory the Great's admonition to the sick to see their affliction as a mark of providence. It is not that injury or illness should be seen as a stigmata of divine election—although it might be—but that injury or illness, instead of being the crutch of the profane, can be the wings of the believer to transcend the imperfect realm of outwardness.

147

constitutes a negation of the world as illusion, it unleashes
the forces of ignorance which cannot but oppose him in a
vain effort to assert the truth of their lie. At the same time,
he is fated to act as a lightning rod that, by channeling the
world's fury, spares men from destruction. In this respect,
Christ's agony and crucifixion need not be elaborated
upon. And by extension, saints and then believers, in their
way or, in Hindu terms, through sympathetic reverberation
with Purusha's original sacrifice, participate in this
redemptive gift of self. As for disbelievers, they live "in
peace," oblivious to the cosmic wager that existence
entails. Their habitual moral stupor insulates them, perhaps not from anguish, but certainly from the fear of God:
"For herein is the evil of ignorance," Plato has Diotima say
in his *Symposium*, "that he who is neither good nor wise is
nevertheless satisfied with himself: he has no desire for
that of which he feels no want."

And the trial, when appropriately heeded, that is to say
accepted with "beautiful patience," as is enjoined in the
Koran, serves then as a mode of preparation whereby the
vessel of man's heart is readied to receive the overpower-
ing influx of grace. This perhaps harsh preparation follows
the same law of existence that makes it necessary for the
pot to be baked in the kiln lest it lose its shape and be dissolved back into its primal substance as clay.[35] Similarly,
this has been the goal of Hatha-Yoga one of whose practical purposes was originally to strengthen the *sadhaka's*
body so that it could withstand the otherwise shattering
impact of spiritual realization.[36]

---

35. "No substance can be rendered perfect without long suffering,"
advises the German alchemist, Henry Madathanas. "Great is the error of
those who imagine that the philosopher's stone can be hardened without first having been dissolved; their time and their work are lost." And
nothing but sincerity can endure this heat.

36. By mentioning this example, we do not mean to imply that spiritual readiness is a matter of physical endurance, because in these

To be born man, as already stated, is to be born ignorant, weak, and errable—over and over again. But just as
adversity, when not overwhelming, serves to strengthen,
so God, to enable man to come to Him fully, tries him
because strength and knowledge cannot be imparted without tribulation—"None can be crowned without a struggle" (2 Tim. 2:5)—at least not on this earth or in the phase
of the cosmic cycles wherein duality predominates materially over unity, density over transparence, and gravity over
levity; or, in human terms, passion over intelligence. And
were God to do the work for man, as many a fool might
wish, man might as well cease to be. The fact is that man's
body—and by extension the framework of his temporal
existence here below—can be likened to the alchemist's
athanor, that vessel in which the soul is readied much in
the fashion of the elixir of immortality.[37] And, in certain
respects at least, the greater the trial, the deeper the

---

questions virtue and contemplation are what matter foremost.
Nonetheless, in its own order of importance, the body, which is *devata* or
the visible form of Brahma manifested as *jiva* (i.e. the Self when contained in the vessel of both the subtle and gross body), cannot be excluded in integral spiritual adequation with the Real. Quite the contrary.
Thus if a certain spiritual perspective, owing to the corruptibility of all
created things, places the accent on the necessity of shedding the body—
that "inflated bladder of skin" (*Agni-Purana*)—the more essentially normative or primordial point of view is to recognize it as a projection of the
spirit in matter and consequently as an intrinsically sacred support for
knowledge: "Among the 840,000 types of embodied beings, the knowledge of Reality cannot be acquired except through a human body"
(*Kularnava-Tantra*, 1:14). The choice of perspectives depends on whether
one chooses to place emphasis on the body as material substance (bone,
skin, sinew, blood, etc.) or the body as form and symbol, and hence as
temple of the spirit.

37. As where the Bible says that God will bring the elect "through
the fire, and will refine them as silver is refined, and will try them as
gold is tried: they shall call my name, and I will hear them: I will say, It
is my people" (Zech. 13:8-9).

149

realizational process: "God left him to try him, that he might know all that was in his heart" (2 Chron. 32:31). We say "in certain respects" because we are not advocating a *karma-marga* of mortification and effort. All we mean to point out is that just as "necessity is the mother of invention," so a life of ease is not conducive to self-transcendence. Or, as a folk saying reminds us, "spare the boy, destroy the man." Without hardship, man, who is born asleep, cannot awaken. It is difficulty—much as the irritation of the grain of sand provokes the oyster to produce a pearl—which introduces the providential interruptions in man's habitual complacency and goads him to reach beyond himself.

And it is difficulty that fosters salutary self-examination,[38] because without it, the great bow of the will cannot be drawn to loose the arrow of the intent. A slack life is an aimless life; the moment effort ceases, decay supersedes. And man, who is directly situated on the vertical axis, as evidenced by his erect stature, cannot withdraw felicitously from the imperatives to which his divine essence obligates him. Therefore, he cannot find any durable repose in horizontality: if he is not ascending, he is declining.[39] A tribulation that rescues him from horizontality, whose stupor can inure him to the damage of surreptitious degeneration, can be marvelously providential. But only a sincerely spiritual man, someone capable of sweet resignation, could understand how deprivation can prepare the way for

---

38. And so Beatrice tells Dante who, after his beatific intuition of her, has gone astray, lured by multiple worldly affairs, that "If I refuse my salvation to you it is to make you reflect." (Quoted from Louis Paul Guigues' Introduction to the *Vita Nova*.)

39. The medieval mystic Walter Hilton formulates it thus: "For a soul may not stand still always in one state while that it is in the flesh; for it is either profiting in grace, or impairing in sin" (*The Scale of Perfection*).

heavenly harvest or how, to quote the Confucian sage Mencius, "Grief and perturbation bring life, whereas prosperity and pleasure bring death." This consideration alone should situate the limits of a kind of sentimental charity that wishes to swaddle a distressed man in soporific comfort.[40] Indeed, man is not temperamentally prone to fathom what a curse joy can be to the untried soul. God may salutarily withhold it until the ripeness of His time.

IF GOD TRIES man it is not—perish the thought!—out of cruelty. Yet, this truth needs recalling given the Luciferian revolt, be it only latent, that pits fallen man against his Creator. If God tries man, it is out of love and mercy, as unbelievable as this may appear to a soul in the grips of bitter suffering. To believe this requires the faith of a King David who sets the example in his supplication: "Examine me, O Lord, and prove me; try my reins and my heart. For thy lovingkindness is before mine eyes" (Ps. 26:2-3). Were it not so, were a soul not tried to its fullest capacity, the risk is that the seed of grace might not take deep enough root to bear its fruit; it would be at the mercy of any and all the contending forces that drive the world to distraction and to destruction. Or there would be for man the capital risk of hypocrisy, that he pay mere lip service to God while he persevere in iniquity,[41] for man does not know himself and is therefore easily the dupe of his professed intentions. Indeed, the devil has no compunction to ride the mount of man's idealism, for he well knows how to usurp man's virtue or to cloak himself in man's piety—so long, that is, as man harbors some vestige of ambition which, when intelligence fails, only repeated mortification can counter-

---

40. This is the essential meaning of Nietzsche's contempt of pity.
41. "Thou art near in their mouth, and far from their reins" (Jer. 12:2).

act and annul: "The heart is deceitful above all things, and desperately wicked: who can know it?" (Jer. 17:9)

And, of course, the more man wages this "unseen warfare," which "must be constant and never ceasing,"[42] the more he will provoke by way of backlash the disruptive force of passions and set himself, first against the full brunt of worldly inertia and, next, against the hurling tide of centrifugal fate—to say nothing of arousing evil which forever stalks the unwary. The more man tries to transcend himself, the greater the trial or the steeper the challenge; this is a law of existence that God cannot amend[43] without, as already remarked upon, terminating the possibility of creation. But for man not to accept the wager of holiness, which is his for the realizing, *Deo juvante*, mediocrity and oblivion will be his lot, if not Hell.[44] Whence Christ's words: "I came not to send peace, but a sword." This is why a man, to avail himself fully of the heavenly privileges of his birthright cannot shun the path of heroism. And indeed, evil will then league itself strenuously against him the moment he attempts to disengage himself from the opiate of heedlessness.

At the same time, the challenge is perfectly tempered to each person's individual possibilities, because it involves finally nothing other than the aspirant's own capacity for

42. As is stated in *Unseen Warfare* (1:15), a classic work of Hesychast spirituality.

43. Assuming God could contradict Himself in such a manner which, of course, is impossible.

44. "The lasting elimination of our miseries depends on our conformity to the Divine nature, or on our fixation on the 'kingdom of God which is within.' As long as men have not realized sanctifying 'inwardness,' the abolition of earthly trials is not only impossible, it is not even desirable; for the sinner—the 'exteriorized' man—needs suffering to expiate his faults and to tear himself from sin, or to escape from the 'outwardness' from which sin derives" (Frithjof Schuon, *Esoterism as Principle and Way*, Ch. "The True Remedy").

152

perfectibility. Therefore, as it is said in a famous verse of the Koran which Muslims recite as a prayer: "God tasketh not a soul beyond its scope" (*The Cow*, v. 286).[45] In the process, however, it may be necessary for the soul to be tried beyond what it considers bearable in order that it learn to jump over its own shadow: "The Lord chastened me sore," David says, "but He hath not given me over unto death" (Ps. 118:18). And if it be objected that tribulation can continue in spite of the sanctity of an individual, one could respond that the suffering is then borne sacrificially for the sake of others, because the stronger the support the more weight it will be given to bear, it seems. This is the plain reality of the situation outside the spheres of Paradise. Moreover, nature leaves nothing unused.

There are countless examples of saints bearing, with superhuman fortitude, unspeakable suffering for the sake of saving souls or of alleviating the fate of those in Purgatory. However, what matters finally is not the possible agony endured, but the redemption, individual or otherwise, it can bring in its wake, for God is constantly amending with mercy the catastrophes following in the wake of the outermost act of creation. One might further say that God fully assumes upon Himself—in the hearts of His saints and of His believers—the ransom of woe and affliction entailed in this cosmic separation,[46] for, in the normal course of things, He can help man only through man. Similarly, owing to the limitations inherent in the *Samsara*, He will rescue a soul from error only through suffering: "As many as I love, I rebuke and chasten" (Rev.

---

45. Likewise the Bible: "God is faithful, who will not suffer you to be tempted above that ye are able." (1 Cor. 10:13)

46. Likewise: "My children, from the day I destroyed My house below (the Temple in Jerusalem), I have not gone up to dwell in My house on high, but have dwelled in the open in the dew and the rain." (Quoted from a Jewish holy writing, the *Seder Eliyatu Zuta*.)

3:19). Thus it is that given man's proclivity to inertia, if God is to be truly compassionate, He need first appear to be ruthless.

For the rest, and much more prosaically stated, the proximity of danger spurs an alertness that frees man from fatal sloth. Much of the providence of warfare among nomadic people finds its moral or opportune justification in this fact.

THE CONSIDERATIONS ABOVE bring us now to a subsidiary topic, that of suffering freely espoused by man as a means of spiritual liberation, namely the question of the practice of austerities. It may be worthwhile to remark that when making mention of the sanctifying merits of suffering, we have essentially in mind the inevitability of suffering in a world where conflict, disease, deprivation, death, and evil operate, and not the *via negativa* of Christian passional mysticism, the austerities (*tapas*) of the *sadhus*, or the "way of blame" (*malamatiyah*) in Islam, all of which involve particular circumstances and a special calling, and consequently which can hardly be said to be normative on a large scale, whatever their usefulness may otherwise be in the spiritual economy of a human collectivity. The point is that while it is one thing to suffer, it is quite another to cultivate it vocationally, and in fact perilous to do so without a divine warrant, for it is important that man not impose his conditions on Heaven or assume that Heaven's help is conditional upon the heroism of his individual effort which It has no need of, to say the least. Demons can practice *tapas*.[47] What God wants is man's heart, not his efforts.[48]

---

47. In the Bhagavad Gita the *tapas* are classified as virtuous (*sattva*), ambitious (*rajas*), and perverted (*tamas*).

48. "I require only a burning heart," Rumi has God say.

The "Path of Smoke" (*Pitri Yana* or "Way of the Ancestors"), which is transmigratory—as opposed to the deliverance offered by the "Path of Light" (*Deva Yana* or "Way of the Gods")[49]—is thronged with former ascetics who overlooked the fact that objectivity towards oneself is the greatest of all mortifications. Suffice it to say that the practice of austerities is meaningless in itself, a mere technical virtuosity, unless the adherent has the sufficient spiritual substance and uses the exercises as a support for the practice of virtues and as a means of intensifying the sincerity of prayer and reliance on God.[50] Its prototype is the idea of sacrifice whose motive force is that of love and not willpower as such. Unless these means are used judiciously—and sparingly at that—they may serve only to heighten egoity when in fact they had been intended to deaden the "old Adam".[51] That the performer of austerities may, in the process, stumble into ephemeral experiences of bliss (a species of still "dualistic union" or what in Hinduism is known as *samprajnata samadhi*) is all too obvious.[52] But far from constituting a guarantee of spiritual progress, they may prove the most delusive of snares.[53] The problem is

---

49. Cf. Bhagavad Gita (8:23-6) and Chandogya Upanishad (5:3-10).

50. Ideally, *sadhus* who make a vow of standing perpetually, that is to say without sitting or lying down for years on end, are seeking by such superhuman means to force the soul to find rest in God alone.

51. The fact that the austerities of *sadhus* can increase the *tapas* or the inner energies (which, at root, are those of divine creation) exponentially makes their practice as perilous as the riding of the tiger—that favorite metaphor of Chinese alchemical imagery.

52. William James described some of this in his classic work *The Varieties of Religious Experience*—a treatise which in its absorbing documentation of the empirical completely misses the spiritual.

53. So we learn from Ibn Ata 'Illah that: "More fearing are the gnostics in a state of spiritual expansion (*bast*) than they are in contraction (*qabd*), for few are those in the state of expansion who stay within the confines of spiritual propriety (*adab*)."

not, of course, the bliss itself—which, in itself, is a grace—but its intermingling with the recipient's passion or self-interest, or simply with his psychism. And the damage the possibility of premature bliss can wreak, as mentioned earlier, is something that a frustrated soul may not take sufficient account of. Indeed, it can prove in time—and this is the great paradox—a greater suffering for the unready than the raw experience of suffering itself. And this is another possible reason God may withhold His Grace from an aspirant for, in these matters, spiritual ripeness is everything. And God knows best.

The shroud of materiality that encloses man's waking state can be partially rent through forcible asceticism, leading to the inflow, not necessarily of bliss, but far more often of supra-sensory experiences[54] which are merely psychic—such as the visualization of auras—and therefore purely sensational, not spiritual,[55] because finally, being that they are not supra-formal, they do not transcend the realm of individuality.[56] Again, what is important to bear

---

54. It is well known that starving the body, for example, can produce varieties of euphoric light-mindedness.

55. Thus, no less an authority than Gautama Buddha condemned the practice of austerities. However, that this method can be a legitimate *marga*, or path, under certain conditions and in certain spiritual climates, goes without saying. The history of Christian martyrs, the asceticism of the Desert Fathers, and the countless examples of Christians desirous of participating in the sufferings of their Savior are heroic testimony to this possibility. The austerities of 4th Century ascetics such as a St. Jerome, a St. Senoch, a Macarius, or of the "pillar hermits" such as the monk Wulfilaich who, winter and summer, lived for years perched on a column at Trier, constitute perhaps extreme manifestations of volitive *contemptus mundi* that serves to remind men of both the difficulty for the soul to transcend the flesh as well as the fact that the flesh is, after all, conquerable.

56. And it is precisely this point that makes of the practice of austerities a double-edged sword, for they can lead to the acquiring of quasi

in mind is that the prototype, and hence whole purpose of suffering, is the principle of sacrifice which, as Schuon said in some of his unpublished writings, "Must compensate . . . the 'existential transgression' or the 'cosmic sin', that is to say our very manifestation in that it seems to usurp or contradict, in a way that is somehow titanic or Luciferian, divine Life."

It is one thing to bear with humble stoicism the arrows of adversity which the mere fact of existence on earth looses against one in the due course of a full life, and quite another to "Strive always to choose, not that which is easiest, but that which is difficult," St. John of the Cross exhorts in his *Ascent of Mount Carmel*. To systematically seek, as the Spanish mystic tirelessly did, poverty, hunger, lowliness, wretchedness, humiliation, sadness, narrowness, dryness, obscurity, censure, pain, and even to cultivate despair as a habitual state of soul can prove more psychologically problematical than spiritually fruitful, because such mortification can be said to be, in its ultimate literal consequence, God-denying—not in intention, surely, but in form—for if God is Light, Beauty, and Mercy, then excess penitence amounts at some point to a form of operative doubt in these qualities which, all things being equal, should inspire beauty, not shame.[57] Or, at the very

---

miraculous powers (*siddhis*) which are usually more magical than spiritual and therefore can tempt the individual to dispense or even to "compete" with God. This phenomenon is far from being infrequent in a society still bathed in spirituality.

57. Nonetheless, it is also true that awareness of the celestial beauty of those very qualities is what has shamed many a mystic into this kind of mortification because of the contrast of our human unworthiness; it is a question of where one places the emphasis, whether in man or in God. Moreover, as Luther might have remarked, the individual soul must be wary lest it take anything for granted as regards Heaven, even—or especially—divine mercy, and become as a result remiss.

least, one might venture that such methods could be fault-ed for their crudeness.[58] Now if exceptions do confirm the rule, they nonetheless are also legitimate possibilities. That the author of such profound a work of mystical poetry as *The Dark Night* was a saint proves the spiritual validity of such a vocation which, to be fully understood, must be seen in the context of the sumptuous foppery, gilded hypocrisy, and worldly extravagance which Renaissance Spain represented at the height of its imperial greatness as it bestrode the edges of the universe. His life of silent hero-ism was a singular refutation of this type of secular ideal or, at least, its necessary safety valve: without humility, there can be no glory.

Moreover, the emphasis on suffering and, in general, on the negative experience of existence on earth is entered upon only as a preliminary phase, much like the phase of calcination in the *mortificatio* and *nigrido* (blackening) of the alchemists, and therefore is not meant to be a perma-nent stage along the heavenly ascent.[59] In Theravada Buddhism, following teachings in the *Mahasatipatthana*

Therefore, when taking exception to the excess—and it is really the excess that is at issue here—of such methods, one is thinking less of the individual merit of a given aspirant than the suitability of the means when compared to the universal norm of man as *imago Dei*—which also deserves to be taken account of through a *via positiva*.

58. This is why the noted Afghani saint Hujwiri could say: "Repletion with contemplation is better than hunger combined with mortification, because contemplation is the battle-field of men, whereas mortification is the playground of children" (The *Kash Al-Mahjub* or "The Lifting of the Veil").

59. Yet, for many a mystic, it is their *marga*. Thus a San Pedro Claver lived in the Spanish colonial town of Cartagena—the "Golden Gate" to the New World—a life of extreme penance. And this is the legacy he left men as attested by his skeletal remains on unsettling dis-play beneath the main altar of the church bearing his name in Cartagena today.

Sutta, monks meditate in the shadow of skeletons hanging from rafters as an aid to focus on the transience of the flesh body. This, however, is but one of four methodical stages. Once mastered, or once proper bodily awareness is reached through this shock technique,[60] the monks move on to ego consciousness and finally to consciousness of the One Self. The idea is to become perfectly objective about one's body, one's mind, one's feelings, and so on, until complete detachment is attained. Or, full wakefulness.

To summarize the preceding comments, one might say that if misery can foster renunciation and self-transcendence in a pious soul and if unavoidable suffering, borne with the equanimity and calm fortitude for instance of a Pius Antoninus or a Marcus Aurelius, presents itself as a full spiritual path, in some degree or another, to all human beings, avoidable suffering, for its part, namely suffering that is personally espoused and not "imposed" by God— or, rather, destiny—entails a very real risk of morbid individualism, depending on the case.[61] The "accumulation of merit" that spiritual mortification in principle garners can be unwittingly compromised by a possibly concurrent accumulation of self-emphasis. Voluntarism is too close to willfulness.

To RETURN TO the main topic, when a St. Theresa of the Child Jesus thanks God "For all the graces you have granted me: in particular for having made me pass through the crucible of suffering," it is not, as some cynics have suggested, out of a neurotically selfish masochism—it troubles

---

60. There are also meditation techniques that are practiced in cemeteries. A Christian equivalent of this are the heaps of skulls one finds in some monasteries, or simply the skull that some monks keep by their bedside in their cells as a permanent reminder of life's illusoriness.

61. Self-depreciation or self-loathing is often not without a strong undertone of narcissism.

us to even acknowledge such criticism—but because without this suffering she, who was not a gnostic contemplative, could have neither detached herself sufficiently from existence—as she herself claims, at any rate—nor, above all, received the chance from Heaven to prove the fullest extent of her total love for Christ.[62] The suffering was the untransferable ransom of her love for her Lord and her aspiration to be betrothed to Him. Indeed, from the perspective of affective mysticism, as well as for man in his "otherness from God, full sincerity allows no other alternative. "How I thank Heaven for having let me find only bitterness in earthly friendships!" the Little Flower of Lisieux writes in her autobiography (*Histoire d'une âme*), because "I know, O my God, that the more you wish to give, the more you make us yearn." In this affirmation, Theresa touches upon one of the essential reasons for God's trying man's faith, namely generosity: "I was a hidden treasure, and wanted to be known," as Sufism expresses it.[63] But since man, by fleshly propensity, is not naturally detached from earthly consolations, and since, by dint of his theomorphic vocation, he is at the same time made for Heaven, the conversion from the world to God entails usually forcible and repeated wrenchings away from the stuporous illusion material delights offer. Figuratively speaking, it may be that God cannot replenish man without first allowing him to starve.

But more to the point, God wants to be found—as the Sufi quote above tells us—even in, or in spite of, the great-

---

62. The deeper meaning of suffering's element of providence can be assessed from these words taken from the book of Wisdom (Douay Bible): "Because God hath tried them, and found them worthy of himself" (3:5).

63. Similarly, Augustine opens his *Confessions* with these lines: "Thou has created us for Thyself, and our hearts know no rest until they repose in Thee."

est darkness, for there can be no trial or suffering that can compare with the beauty of His grace. Thus, to paraphrase *bhaktic* mysticism, He, as the Beloved, is there for the embracing even—or especially—in the dreadest tribulation.[64] In fact, in His desire to assure Himself of the seeker's genuineness and depth of love, commitment, and sincerity, He may well lead him through the byways of sorrow and humiliation and disillusion, for it is these tribulations that will not only help the recipient slough off the world like an outworn layer, but form him to receive the gift whose preciousness passes all reckoning. In this manner, trials can provide for the soul a unique mode of spiritual maturing for which no substitute exists, lest earthly man not be man, nor the world the world. This is why Theresa could say, without the slightest shade of ill-feeling, that "My consolation is to have none on earth."[65]

In a certain sense, the *bhaktic* mystic is never completely sure of the absolute sincerity of his love for God—a doubt which can make him agonize with scruples—until he has been tested by the extremes of wretchedness existence can occasion. Worldly people have literally no idea of such scruples, which are born of the holiest integrity.[66] This is why Theresa can ask: "Is there a greater joy than that of suffering for your love?" It is in the moments of the most desolate darkness and abandonment, which are

---

64. In the words of one famous mystical Persian poet: "Those to whom Love draws nigh," Attar wrote, "are the most severely proven."

65. If we are fond of repeatedly quoting St. Theresa of Lisieux here, it is not that we intend to set her forth as a paragon of what spirituality should be, but because she—and her "Little Way"—is a model for what we would call the *marga* of love and suffering, a path which, incidentally, she did not properly choose, although she welcomed it with the sweet resignation typical of true humility.

66. Hence Dante: "O noble conscience and clear, how sharp a sting is a little fault to thee!" (*Purgatorio* III)

inseparable components of the human state, that the mystic soul can declare the absoluteness of his trust and faith in God. The trial consecrates the mystic's purity of resolve: "The kingdom of God is only for the thoroughly dead," as Meister Eckhart remarks.[67]

Many personal problems concerning the notion of Heaven-allowed trials and suffering should vanish if one considers that the essential purpose of man's existence is sanctification and the corresponding annihilation—through conversion—of the *moi haïssable* (the hateful self). Having said this, one does not mean to imply either that all men should try to become saints—that is not the objective of salvational theology—or, by extension, that all men are capable of sanctity. Such an expectation would be perfectly unrealistic, at least within the confines of the *Kali Yuga* where the overwhelming mass of mankind is not ascending and cannot be so, by cosmic definition. However, if this cyclical predicament—whose cosmic briefness escapes the puny measures of our mortality—must of necessity affect the enormous bulk of the human collectivity, it obviously cannot decisively restrict the "salt of the earth" were it not for whom mankind would have no more reason for being.

If God created man in His own image, it was not to have him wallow in sensuality and idleness, or to fritter his life away in chit-chat, or to compete with Him in Promethean creation. It is the saint and the hero, and also, but in a humbler mode the artisan, who are the sufficient reason, and redeeming justification, for that miraculous possibility, not of men, but of man as such. And sanctity, except perhaps in the most intellective (or pneumatic) of

---

67. A Hindu holy woman was asked when one could be certain of safety on the spiritual path; she sent back, for answer, a little plate of ashes. (From Whitall N. Perry's *Treasury of Traditional Wisdom*—the most remarkable compendium, we believe, of traditional knowledge ever assembled.)

THE VEIL OF SUFFERING

men, can only be as it were chiseled out of man through
deprivation or tribulation.[68] But even for the "divine man"
on earth, the *jivanmukta* ("released while living"), or for the
Bodhisattva, or for the Avatara, suffering is unavoidable as
long as he is subject to the categories that constitute terrestrial existence, especially in the *Kali Yuga*.[69] However, it
becomes in this case the means through which their providential destiny is shaped for the living benefit of the
world.[70] To repeat: suffering is the ransom of cosmic separation without which the world would not be the world. It
was the ignorance of this law that allowed revilers to taunt
Jesus on the cross to save himself: "If thou be the Son of
God, come down from the cross (and) we will believe." But
. . . "My kingdom is not of this world."

To exist involves a series of equilibriums that ultimately have to be broken. The soul, when left to itself, is always
seeking to establish itself concretely—and as comfortably
as circumstances allow—within whatever set of proximate
reference points, be they material, sensual, or egoic, that are
available to it or that constitute the bearings of its immediate psycho-corporeal experience. That is why mystics
speak of the leap of faith that is necessary if the soul is to
break free from and transcend the confines of habits and

---

68. "God tests by removing, man proves by renouncing," Schuon
once remarked.

69. These categories, according to Schuon, are essentially five in
number. They are: space, time, form, number, and matter. (Cf. Schuon
From the Divine to the Human, Ch. "Structure and Universality of the
Conditions of Existence".)

70. In the light of so many maudlin controversies about the nature
and fate of suffering, it is worth reflecting on Eckhart's penetrating
observation that "In none of Christ's sufferings did his Godhead come
to the help of his manhood." Moreover, the fundamental reason for
being of the Avatara, or human incarnation of the divine, is an imperfect
world, precisely. In Christ's words, "They that be whole need not a
physician, but they that are sick" (Mat. 9:12).

customs: "Blessed are they that have not seen, and yet have believed." And, usually, it is trials and suffering that provide the necessary goad for this leap which may otherwise never be taken. Some men have become saints as a result of being suspended over a yawning abyss, wherein no comfortable alternative was allowed them by Heaven save to rise so as not to fall. In this sense, a misery that no earthly consolation can stave off may serve as the providential catalyst that sparks a liberating need to transcend oneself so as not to be crushed by despair. Christ tells Sister Consolata: "My heart is conquered more by your miseries than by your virtues."[71]

While one recognizes the inevitability of suffering in the *Samsara*, and while one ought not to lose sight of the possible providence always potentially at work in earthly trials, it is nonetheless important not to concede inordinate scope to tribulation, forgetting in the process that suffering can only be a factor—as well as a penalty—of outwardness, for "Thy existence is a sin with which none can be compared," the Sufi woman saint, Rabia Al-'Adawiya, remarked. In other words, suffering is a phenomenon premised on outwardness or on remoteness from the immovable Center which, in virtue of its divine quiddity, is bliss. Suffering can only reach man from without—whence the term "veil of suffering"—and therefore becomes complete only insofar as he commits his personal center, namely his heart, to the periphery, for his innermost center, as ipseity (or selfhood), belongs to God. The heart of *Samsara* is *Nirvana*.

TO CHOOSE GOD entails for man a rupture of his profane equilibrium, a breaking out of the chrysalis of habits and

---

71. Also, David: "The Lord is nigh unto them that are of a broken heart" (Ps. 34:18).

daydreams, an awakening which usually involves a stir-
ring up of a soul's myriad potentialities. So long as man
remains in a state of sleep, his deeper possibilities—and
perhaps his core defects (*sanchita-karma*) as well—remain
dormant. But let a crisis supervene,[72] and the little cocoon
the ego has venally spun for itself unravels and the cheat-
ing or the lie or the hypocrisy or the shallowness of an
individual's petty existence is then exposed forcing him to
avail himself of resources he never dreamt he possessed.[73]
In the process, however, the "Old Adam" will not readily
relinquish his hold on life, and the contrast between a
man's possible greatness and effective meanness can set
off a chain of antagonistic reflexes. This is the point of
departure of spiritual warfare, for when a soul is thus
awakened its different faculties and tendencies which,
until directed or re-directed, raven after appearances, will
vie for supremacy in claiming man's heart: "Know ye not
that they which run in a race run all, but one receiveth the
prize? So run, that ye may obtain" (1 Cor. 9:24). And this
race or combat, before victory is secured, must of necessity involve defeat—many defeats, perhaps gallingly bitter.
Indeed, the subjugation of the senses (*indriya-jaya*) is usually not obtained without humbling setbacks: the sincerity of he who seeks to taste of the honey of Brahma must

---

72. Suffering and love are the two biggest catalysts for self-transcendence—or self-destruction—a man can experience. And love, of
course, when deep, involves suffering for in it a man is made to taste the
utterness of his destitution. His poverty is revealed by the wealth of the
beloved's beauty or qualities which, in last analysis, are intimations of
the paradise he has been exiled from and for which he longs—did he but
know. Conversely, suffering can, through its relentless frustration of selfish desires, open up into love, or at least into universal sympathy, unless
bitterness is allowed the spoils.

73. As Goethe perspicaciously remarked: "It is in limitation that the
master first shows himself." And Emerson: "Drudgery, calamity, exas-
peration, want, are instructors in eloquence and wisdom."

be put (severely) to the test because, unless he be wholly pure, this victual will be as poison to him. Renunciation in view of the objectless ecstasy (*nirvikalpa-samadhi*) requires integral poverty[74] as indispensable prerequisite. The passage from complication—which is the debt of the Fall—to simplicity, from agitation to serenity, from division to wholeness—which is holiness—involves as many deaths as there are attachments. Thus, in India, when an aspirant was ready to undertake the legendary flight from the self to the Self, he approached the spiritual master "with fuel in hand" which symbolized his willingness to submit to the spiritual path which is universally likened to a purificatory fire. And, invariably, by undertaking to ascend the steeps of Verticality, the stakes are increased by an exponential multiple, for the *sadhaka* (the spiritual traveler) now treads the "razor's edge": the merest slip can have lethal consequences for him who has wagered his immortality.

The "nothingness" of earthly phenomena, at any event, cannot just be believed by the aspirant, but must be experienced in the flesh before the spell of worldly *Maya* is dissolved, for man—insofar as he is but man—is an inveterate disbeliever.[75] It takes a piercing discernment, and complete equanimity, to penetrate through the murk

---

74. "Only the thread of our existence is suitable for the eye of the needle" (Rumi).

75. Thus, it is related in the Koran, when former disbelievers are arraigned before God, they beg for a reprieve of their sentence, to return to earth one more time that "I may do right in that which I have left behind (23:100 and 6:27-8). But the Koran has God say that, were they granted this chance, they would only revert to disbelief owing to the obduracy of their hearts which "were hardened and became as rocks, or worse than rocks for hardness. For indeed there are rocks. . .which split asunder so that water floweth from them. . . . Which fall down for the fear of God" (2:74).

of phenomena. And to repudiate their sorcery requires a heroic effort of the will which must now consent to whatever suffering necessary[76] to find that priceless pearl of wisdom. Moreover, there can be a certain latent foulness, or propensity towards transgression and evil, that cannot be decisively extirpated from man except through mortification,[77] whether this be opportunely self-imposed or whether it result naturally from the contrast between angel and beast that forms the feuding alloy of our fallen nature: *duo sunt in homine*.

Also man, in that he, unlike every other animal, is a microcosm, symbolically recapitulates in his being the whole of manifestation[78] and therefore, be it only potentially, the entire struggle between good and evil, for man's

---

76. Owing to the terrible and possibly brutally harsh implications of this realizational process, it might be worth specifying here that, as Schuon has noted in some of his unpublished writings, "Women should not seek this state; it completely contradicts their inner structure; their way is another. I do not say that they cannot experience such a thing, for they are human beings like men; God knows best what suits each soul; what I do say is that they should not seek such a death. In man there is much that is violent which in woman ripens slowly." Indeed man—insofar as he is obviously different from woman—is by fundamental character related to the axis of the Absolute, the unique, the single, and is therefore judging; whereas woman is, also by fundamental character, intimately identified with the Infinite, the complete, the whole, and is therefore unitive. Man discerns and abolishes so as to affirm; woman unifies and forgives so as to redeem. What man can obtain by noble force, woman obtains by noble patience; what is his for the seizing is hers for the receiving. As their respective morphologies suggest—the one angular and muscular, the other rounded and bountiful—man is predominantly exclusive, woman inclusive. But, insofar as both are *anthropos*, and of this before they are sexually distinct, these normally polar attributes may overlap more or less extensively depending on the individual.

77. "This kind can come forth by nothing but by prayer and fasting" (Mark 9:19-29).

78. "Within this body dwells the mountain of Meru (the center of the universe) . . . and all the stars and planets. . . . In this body wander the

167

free will renders him capable of both Heaven or Hell. Thus, if he embarks on the quest for the Absolute, he may experience, in some degree or another, something of the titanic struggle that pits them against each other. One must remember that man, by virtue of his theomorphic identity, stands at the timelessly immutable center and, by virtue of his outwardness, he also stands at the very edge of the cosmic endlessness of All-Possibility. And it is through him, through his transubstantiating remembrance of God, that creation can be spiritually converted and restored to its divine origin. It is against such a cosmic background that all privation and suffering are to be properly situated.

ALSO, AND BY no means least, there is the subjective dimension of trials, for, incontestably, a tribulation that for a profane person may amount to a bitter experience may prove sweetness to a believer owing to his fear of God[79] that determines first his humility, then his loving trust. Thus, what for a profane person may amount to fruitless misery may, for a believer, prove a grace carrying in its wake inestimable blessings. Patience is here both the proof of humility and the one virtue that answers the mortification of time and converts it into joy incorrupt. This is why it is said that haste is of the devil. Also, crystallization—which is sudden—cannot supervene before slow gestation and decantation have run their course. Time is the necessary concomitant of creation. And, seen now from the point of view of man, time is midwife to Eternity.

---

sun and the moon—the cause of creation and destruction. . .. All the creatures that exist in the three worlds (heaven, earth, and hell) are also in this very body" (*Shiva-Samhita*—one of the great seminal texts on Yoga).

79. The fear of God is reverential respect in its devotional essence, not the arbitrary cringing of a self-interested soul threatened by anything mightier than itself.

It must not, moreover, be forgotten that meekness and lowliness—expressed here as sweet resignation to the inevitable—are what ensure that "My yoke is easy, and my burden light." Indeed, man's measures are not God's: the vertical and intemporal axis (the projection of truth), whose luminous "center is everywhere and circumference nowhere" (to paraphrase Nicholas of Cusa), bisects the horizontal axis at every point of earthly becoming. In this sense, man has at all moments potential—if not effective—access to divine grace which may, if not virtually rescue him instantly from his stumbling peregrination through the *Samsara*, at least enable that his toil and labor on earth are not endured in vain when the closing chapter of his life steals on him. There is no commensurate relationship between these two dimensions: the vertical one can of a sudden annul the horizontal's karmic ineluctability or transfigure into bliss what had been woe. Patience in the Name of God is all;[80] for the seed cannot bear its fruit in the ripeness of God's time before it die. All maturing begins in the womb of darkness or in the anonymity so despised by the ambitious. Death, whose absoluteness no man can elude, constitutes either the final destruction of a life whose birthright was wasted pursuing vanity or the final liberating consecration of a life of patiently persevering virtue. The whole purpose of earthly life is, then, a preparation for death which operates as a crystallization.[81]

In this context, effort—which the egotist, in his self-serving laziness, bemoans—is, as previously remarked, the

80. Hence, in Ecclesiasticus (Douay Catholic Bible) we find: "But trust in God, and stay in thy place. For it is easy in the eyes of God on a sudden to make the poor man rich. The blessing of God maketh haste to reward the just, and in a swift hour his blessing beareth fruit" (11: 22-24).

81. "True philosophers," as Plato said, "are always occupied in the practice of dying." (*Phaedo*, 67 D) It is not a coincidence that, in the *Katha Upanishad*, it is Yama, the god of death, who reveals supreme knowledge

necessary human concomitant of trials. Without effort, no knowledge. Hence effort—the willingness to exert oneself—as *karma-yoga* is really a gauge of one's sincerity, as well as a means for the development of character, for what is gained lightly is lightly dismissed; time is the anchor of value. In the Hindu spiritual treatises,[82] knowledge (*jnana*) and action (*karma*) are likened to the two wings of a bird which cannot fly without both. This is why God may have a merciful interest in letting a soul struggle for, as St. Teresa of Avila confides, God once let her understand "not to consider myself forgotten, for He would never abandon me, but that I must do everything in my power to help myself."[83] One sees in this that, when grappling with tribulations, the absence of a response from Heaven may be anything but a mark of disfavor, as the stories of St. Francis' companions likewise illustrate.

If "everyone shall be salted by fire" (Mark 9:49), then attitude is of paramount importance in determining not only how tribulation is to be borne, but especially how it is to end. In this sense, suffering can work much in the same

---

to the young brahman, Nachiketas. Objectivity entails a form of death, not for subjectivity, but for deluded subjectivity.

82. The *Yoga Vasishta*, for instance.

83. That this *karma-yoga*, requiring the combination of willpower and effort, is a universal and indispensable feature of human existence is shown in the life of the celebrated Indian Chief Plenty Coups of the Crow who, "in is first mountaintop vision was told by a certain Dwarf-Chief that he could give him nothing. That he already possessed the power to become great if he would but use it; then he would go far. 'The difference between men,' this spirit being said, 'grows out of the use, or non-use, of what was given them by the Divine Being in the first place.' Because of this, he would be given nothing special, not even the usual medicine bundle. All men have a natural power, the Dwarf-Chief further explained, to deal with life's demands within them. Plenty Coups had a will, and he must learn to use it; to make it work for him." (Quoted from Thomas Mails, *The Mystic Warriors of the Plains*.) "God helps those who help themselves," we find in Proverbs.

way as a medieval trial by ordeal whose outcome reflected a divine judgment; it is a cosmic means of sifting the wheat from the chaff, the sincere from the pretenders, truth from error. If properly accepted, it can prove an extraordinary means to self-transcendence, operating, *Deo juvante*, even in a relatively short time,[84] a transfiguration of character that perhaps years of effort and prayer could not by themselves achieve.[85] Conversely, such a catalyst can prove a fateful means of worsening if man is embittered; wherefore the meaning of the Bible's—and the Koran's—repeated allusions to God's "hardening the hearts" of the wicked. What fire does not purify it destroys.

ALTHOUGH WE DO not intend to be exhaustive in this treatment of such a topic, there is another aspect to trials and suffering that can be easily overlooked but which deserves mention. Owing to the law of inverse analogy ruling manifestation, it happens that gifts or assets, such as a musical talent, physical beauty, or a certain charisma—which, in themselves, are blessings or the fruits of good karma—can prove a bane to the recipient depending on the use—or rather misuse—he makes of them. Physical beauty, for instance, can easily be the occasional cause for the sin of narcissism and blind its bearer not only to the real origin of this gift, but to his own existential relativity, namely to the fact that he, like any man, will ineluctably age, wrinkle, and die. On the other hand, a physical blemish or a painful failing can, for a humble man, prove a spur to a saving self-transcendence, perhaps not otherwise achievable had he

---

84. Assessing duration is a question of a sense of proportions. As Schiller says in the last lines of his play *Joan of Arc*, "Pain is short, and joy is eternal."

85. We have read somewhere that Sufis say that a moment of suffering, if offered unconditionally to God, can abridge the work of years of prayer.

been born with more socially appealing personal assets. The relative ostracism his failings or blemishes may condemn him to can impart a salutary gravity to his character, rescuing him from frivolity. God's guiding providence in these matters can rarely be literally ascertained, for in the economy of different human possibilities and destinies, "one man's meat may be another's poison." In any case, our measures are not God's: and because "My kingdom is not of this world," our tribulations have decisive importance not for this world but for the world to come, unjust as this may strike our human shortsightedness.[86]

There can be no real, or permanently effective, understanding without virtue. And virtue, to become incorrupt, must usually be forged under the blows of adversity, negation, privation, mortification: this is the price of Eternity— or the price for confusing the temporal with the intemporal, of treating the ephemeral as if it were meant to be permanent. In the meantime, man will be taught by parables so that those whose "heart is waxed gross" cannot understand. The seemingly lucky may prove unlucky, the unfortunate blessed for "the last shall be first." And those who cannot pierce the veil of appearances will be condemned to wander. In this sense, trials and sufferings can be seen as parables whose meaning will yield their secret only to the pure of heart. There is absolutely no logical reason why an egotist should attain to understanding and no possible way for him to learn except through suffering. Truth and vice are mutually incompatible just as truth is the reward of virtue.

IN THE FOREGOING considerations, we have dealt with suffering as a kind of "Passion Play" that presupposes darkness

---

86. The encounter, depicted in the Koran (18 : 65-82), between Moses and the mysterious figure of Al-Khidr, is instructive in this regard.

and ignorance resulting from the great divide sundering man from his divine origin. And in so doing, we have purposefully omitted the intellective dimension which, insofar as a man has access to it, can if not annul tragedy, at least delimit its relative scope without which it might prove unendurable.[87] Of course, virtue can serve as an antidote to the poison of frustration and thus can retrace, in an existential mode, what intellective understanding might dissolve through direct knowledge (*pratyaksha*).[88]

Now, it may seem highly paradoxical for the passional man to be told that suffering is but joy obstructed or a poverty in view of richness. However, it is important to keep in mind that suffering, on pain of non-existence, collaborates in the promotion of a greater good, just as evil works for the good, and is therefore ultimately self-defeating and brought to naught. Suffering as suffering is meaningless and can therefore never be an end or a positive reality on its own. Suffering is the crucible of beatitude or it is nothing. Stated differently, it is the immortal in man that suffers to be mortal. Thus, for the contemplative no suffering can equal that of beholding that he exists, namely to see that his life as ego-centric personality constitutes, in the last analysis, the single most daunting obstacle to being. And it is this very distress, this agony, which constitutes his fore-

---

87. To appease the anxiety of his devotees over his suffering, Ramana Maharshi, when in the last throes of his fatal and very painful illness, quoted a verse from the *Yoga Vashista*: "The *jnani* who has found himself as formless pure Awareness is unaffected though the body be cleft with a sword. Sugarcandy does not lose its sweetness though broken or crushed."

88. Thus Schuon: "Metaphysical consciousness . . . carries its dimensions within itself: the detachment it implies is not really distinct from it, and that is why it is indispensable, not insofar as it can be a suffering or a sacrifice, but uniquely insofar as it is an 'emptiness,' a 'poverty,' or an 'extinction' in view of the plenitude of the Self" (*Gnosis: Divine Wisdom*, Ch. "Love of God, Consciousness of the Real").

most qualification for joy. This "ableness," as the author of *The Cloud of Unknowing* expresses it, "is nought else but a strong and deep ghostly sorrow . . . and well were him that might win to this sorrow. All men have matter of sorrow; but most specially he feeleth matter of sorrow, that wotteth and feeleth that he is. . . . And whoso never felt this sorrow, he may make sorrow: for why, he never yet felt perfect sorrow. This sorrow, when it is had . . . maketh a soul able to receive that joy, the which reeveth from a man all witting and feeling of his being" (Ch. 44).

Also, and perhaps most importantly, given that fallen man is by birth a natural hypocrite, as Islam emphasizes, all of his attitudes or states, however meritorious, tend to be tainted with self-interest except suffering, whose pain forges honesty. So it is that one might say that wherever pain is deep it can never be unjust, alchemically speaking, though its occasional cause may be terribly unjust. But the wise never suffer in vain.

ONE CANNOT CLOSE this chapter without addressing the idea expounded in the *Sankhya* philosophy that all suffering is simply a by-product of deluded perception, of a confusion between the principle of pure consciousness or *Purusha* and the existentiating principle of created being or *Prakriti*.[89] So too, in the Upanishads, suffering is defined as resulting from the individual self's (*atman*) ignorance of its true nature's root in the all-pervading

---

89. This polarity corresponds very roughly with that of spirit and matter, or—by transposition—with that of soul and body though, in certain decisive respects, what Western philosophy knows as "soul" can be empirically situated on the side of *Prakriti*, at least until it has been redeemed. On another level, this polarity corresponds to the masculine-feminine complementarity. More exactly, it corresponds to the active and passive agencies in nature, or what Scholasticism terms the *natura naturans* (nature as cause or the creative force) and the *natura naturata* (nature

Supreme Being or Brahma. The cycle of rebirths (or rather, as in the earliest of the Veda texts, as "redeaths" or *punarmrtyu*)[90] endures so long as this individual self continues to be identified with the principle of egoic separateness (*ahamkara*) as personal mind, personal perception, personal sensation, and personal desire. Illumination would then be the rediscovery of underlying unity and liberation from the alienation of separateness.

Formulated differently, suffering is defined as the arrogation by *Prakriti* to itself of the one consciousness, immanent to all beings and belonging, in fact, only *de jure* to *Purusha* in its entirety. The ultimate consequence of this is for the individual to assume a near godlike self-importance which, at the right time, can only be crushed by Heaven. The wager then, according to this perspective, is for the individual soul to remember the One Self into which he is subsumed. Were that it were so simple, or so obviously difficult.

The elliptical density of these Vedantic formulations seems to imply that illumination, or the realization of Truth, should coincide with the cessation of suffering and that, conversely, suffering is exclusively the penalty of said ignorance. Now while the general principle is absolutely correct, because suffering, in its psycho-physical dimension belongs exclusively to the realm of mortality (*Samsara*), and also because there can be no division in the Supreme Self which is Pure Consciousness, what this principle—or rather its formulation—overlooks is the possibility of suffering occurring precisely because of illumination or, at least, from the

---

as effect). However, some claim that the pole *Prakriti* contains both the active and passive modalities within itself, while *Purusha* remains wholly disengaged. How one allocates their purviews depends on where one draws the line between spirit and manifestation.

90. A term which kills the aura of adventurous "romance" that so many Westerners see in the possibility of transmigration.

potential for illumination. For instance, the Virgin Mary as *mater dolorosa* certainly did not suffer as a result of deluded ego consciousness. The same can obviously be said of all the saints, although one might want, in this case, to make certain distinctions between the nature of their knowledge since some are much more *bhaktic* than *jnanic* which is to say that they are ruled more by the pole of love, which, for man on earth, works through obscurity,[91] than the pole of knowledge which is, by nature, immune to the polarities of light and darkness. Many of the difficulties of situating the boundaries of suffering are resolved if one takes into account the distinction between Brahma *nirguna* (unqualified) and Brahma *saguna* (qualified), namely that of God as Beyond-Being or Supreme Principle (*Parabrahma*), neither male nor female, and God as Being with His Human Countenance. Thus one may even make so bold as to say that God, in His dimension of Mercy, suffers, just as the saints in Paradise who remain intercessors for souls can suffer for these souls.[92] Indeed, the idea of divine compassion loses all meaning without suffering; the Bodhisattva or divine being suffers, not because he is ignorant of the essential oneness of *Purusha* and *Prakriti*, but because he partakes of the agony of creation which, on its plane, is an objective fact.

Conversely, if one can speak of a God who loves and who suffers, one is entitled, in a similar way, to speak of a God who can wax wroth, who can punish, who can destroy and thus be the cause of pain, although in this case, the terrible attributes of divinity are explainable in terms of justice which, itself, is a function of divine mercy. In other

---

91. This is why a St. Bernard believes that man cannot know God while on earth but only love Him.

92. Thus one finds in the Bible: "Likewise the Spirit also helpeth our infirmities: for we know not what we should pray for as we ought: but the Spirit itself maketh intercession for us with groanings which cannot be uttered" (Rom. 8:26).

words, the harsh aspects of God are subordinate to His benevolent essence and are set into motion only once equilibrium has been ruptured and therefore are triggered to restore this equilibrium.[93]

IN CONCLUSION, THE fundamental reason for this chapter is to lift a corner of the veil concerning the enigma of suffering so as to absolve God of the charge skeptics or miscreants level against Him, namely to hold Him responsible, to some degree or another, for human misery.

The fact is that God, Who is unity and therefore love or wholeness, has utterly no part in division as such, nor all the more so in the pain ensuing therefrom. Though it is true that owing to His majesty, He repudiates baseness and therefore "avenges" duality, as it were, this purification is a subsidiary and therefore incidental effect of His radiance. Moreover, did He not Himself undertake to bear man's suffering in His own being,[94] to sustain the burden of duality, creation could not last a single instant. It would be crushed or pulverized at the first hint of separation.

---

93. In the Ninety-nine names Islam attributes to God, one finds some like "The Distresser" (*Ad-Darr*), "The Avenger" (*Al-Muntaqim*), "The Preventer" (*Al-Mani*), "The Dishonorer" (*Al-Muzill*), "The Constrictor" (*Al-Qabid*), and others which take account of the "Face of God" which is turned towards the divided portion of His Creation. "But My Mercy precedeth My Wrath," as the Koran teaches.

94. For, when all said and done, nothing finally can take place outside of God: "All you have been, and seen, and done, and thought, / Not *You* but *I*, have seen and been and wrought," wrote the Persian mystic, Attar, in his paean to divine unity, ". . .Pilgrim, Pilgrimage, and Road, / Was but Myself toward Myself; and Your / Arrival but *Myself* at my own Door; Who in your Fraction of Myself behold / Myself within the Mirror Myself hold / To see Myself in, and each part of Me / That sees himself, though drown'd, shall ever see. / Come you lost Atoms to your Centre draw, / And *be* the Eternal Mirror that you saw: / Rays that have wander'd into Darkness wide / Return, and back into your Sun subside" (*The Parliament of Birds*, transl. Edward Fitzgerald).

177

What needs to be borne in mind is that either man is created in the image of God—in which case he is free and must pay the price of this privilege, be it only to expiate the collective ransom stemming from the historical transgression of his forebears—or else he is merely a sentient creature without intelligence or will, a mere atom, somehow conscious, cast adrift, moving and colliding helplessly to and fro, hither and yon, as modern existentialism would have us believe. But were this so, he would not even be aware that he could suffer for, to paraphrase what was said earlier, only the eternal in man suffers from being temporal. And it is only temporality that can, as it were, suffer, for Eternity itself is synonymous with beatitude.

All sacred traditions attest to the unique preciousness of being born a man: "Blessed is human birth; even the dwellers in heaven desire this birth: for true wisdom and pure love may be attained only by man" (*Srimad Bhagavatam*).[95] In other words, to be created in the image of God means that man has an intelligence capable of knowing the Real, which means it is made for the Truth. With intelligence comes freedom; with freedom choice; with choice, responsibility, and with responsibility, sanction. Were man not man "a god in ruins," as Emerson remarked with his usual profundity of insight, he would not suffer, except physically, nor would he need to struggle morally. However, it is his intelligence—and its existential counterpart (and proof) freedom—that exposes man to the vicissitudes of fortune and, all told, renders him deeply responsible for his ultimate well-being. It is this truth that Boehme had in mind when he affirmed that: "Every soul is its own judgment." Consequently, a noble man blames no one else and nothing, no set of circumstances, for whatever plight

---

95. Whence in the Koran (2:34) God's command to the angels to prostrate themselves before Adam.

he may endure. He is self-reliant and therefore self-accountable. Of the four types of spiritual aspirants described in the *Shiva Samhita*, the best is characterized by, among other things, his ability to keep his struggle to himself and to be a refuge for all people. "So help me God!"

4. THOUGHT FOUL BY THOUGHT MADE FAIR

Knowing ourselves, we are beautiful; in self-ignorance, we are ugly.

Plotinus

WHY PRACTISE A *mantra*? Why not just "feel" God or "feel" worshipful, instead of thinking about it? Is not thought the enemy of contemplation, or the mind the enemy of the heart? If one is to answer these questions, the reader will have to consent to think for a moment. The sufficient empirical reason for the practice of a *mantra*, namely the conscious and methodical repetition of the name of God or, which amounts to the same, of a sacred formula, is that man is a thinking being (*homo sapiens*). And, as such, he cannot not think and therefore cannot will or undertake anything without reflection. In fact, he cannot be without thinking; even when not reflecting, his mind is in a state of ceaseless ideational activity, and this includes his sleeping state except that, then, this activity is mostly non-rational because thought patterns here are disjointed and normally subordinated to the sense impressions which produce them in collusion with one's desire nature.

We say "sufficient empirical reason" because the objective justification for this method of prayer is, of course, the excellence of the Divine Object itself. This

180

distinguo between justifications is worth noting simply because the Divine Object could be invoked, one assumes, through means other than verbal prayer, but not by man for whom thought is the only available medium, at least to start with or insofar as he belongs to earthly manifestation which, in that it involves duality, entails the polarization between mind and heart, principle and being, truth and realization. In other words, access to the heart, or to pure being—Ruysbroeck's "Pure Nature"—must, for man, pass first through the mind insofar as this faculty operates as the instrument or bridge of his "outwardness." Where duality predominates over union, it is the mind and not the heart—understood as the seat of intellective consciousness, and not just the harbor of sentiments—which takes practical precedence so that instead of the mind working as a reflection of the heart—as it does in the case of spiritual union—it is the heart which reflects the mind according to the inversion of poles that marks the Fall.

For man, governing his thoughts is hardly easier a task than controlling mirages: they elude almost all attempts at direction, if not in the moment when the mind can be actively focused around a task or point to be made, certainly for the overwhelming span of a human existence. The question for the individual then arises to what, or to whom, he will surrender his consciousness, because surrender it he must. Or, what, or who, is to have determinant sway over it because, contrary to certain pseudo-Zen techniques of *vacare Deo*, man cannot live in a vacuum. And it can be all too easily lost sight of that a human being becomes whatever he thinks. That is to say, the predominant train of his thoughts over an entire lifespan—or maybe simply the one compelling thought, concern, or ideational complex uppermost at the moment when death seizes him—carries with it a realizational power that crystallizes his substance, affecting his "rebirth"[1] into a realm that will be the macrocosmic replicate of his basic existential state or fundamental inclination. If an individual can understand this, that is to say if he can grasp the eschatological import of his thought processes, then it becomes a matter of vital urgency for him to ensure that his soul not fall hostage to a thought, or to a line of thinking, that he would have posthumous reason to regret. Knowing that "whatever a man soweth, that shall he reap," he will take care not to let his thoughts dilapidate his immortal substance in a waste of trivial concerns, let alone of destructive musings. He will learn to think things and not to be thought by things. This issue is the entire crux of the Eastern doctrine of karma, for all attitudes and, with even more reason, all deeds are the proximate offspring of intentions which first manifest as thoughts. Always, in the fields of time, the seed precedes the crop.[2] Thus one can say,

---

1. Caution must be exercised when borrowing from the terminology of transmigration so as not to lapse into the kind of simplistic literalism that plagues reincarnationists of all stripes. We mean to use the notion of transmigration only by way of analogy, namely as a symbolic prop that allows us to account for the multiplicity of extra-human possibilities without presuming to predict their specifities which, as such, we assume, lie outside the scope of human investigation.

2. In this oak and acorn debate, one might object that thoughts mirror intentions. But, metaphysically, the world is the actualization (or objectification), of the Platonic *ideos*. This, however, involves the polarization between Being and Beyond-Being or between Brahma and Ishvara. Strictly speaking, nothing can start outside of original unity; thus, *mutatis mutandis*, all desire and volition begin in the heart. But if it is the heart's general predisposition which, in principle, decides the mind's receptivity, one can say that in practice the mind itself, when in the realm of duality, operates in its turn as a point of inception that catalyzes the heart's latent inclinations. Obviously, one must make a distinction between the heart as such and the heart usurped by the ego in its passionate egocentrism.

technically speaking at least,[3] that everything man wishes or does is traceable to a thought or to a nexus of thoughts. In other words, for man, who is himself the issue of divine thought,[4] all sequential processes of karmic engendering begin with thoughts and need never occur were thoughts not first to come forth. Wherefore Patanjali asserts in his *Aphorisms* that the essence of Yoga is "restraining the mind-stuff (*chitta*) from taking various forms (*vrittis*)."[5] The emergence of thoughts is already an utterance, silent though it be, which may or may not find verbal expression for, as the Gospels tell us, "out of the abundance of the heart [understood here as the seat of consciousness, as well as of desire] the mouth speaketh," so that "every idle word that men shall speak, they shall give account thereof in the day of judgment."[6] Of course, a sound sense of proportions must be maintained here lest an individual be tempted to engage in an excruciating examination of his conscience—though this has its methodological utility in certain monastic disciplines—because one must not lose sight of the fact that one supreme thought can extinguish a thousand importunities. Where the hawk swoops, the sparrows scatter.

---

3. We are not interested here in examining psychoanalytic causalities which finally do nothing to elucidate vertical priorities, because the former belong to the horizontal realm of individuality, whereas the latter belong to the spirit which is the ultimate determiner of being.

4. For example, "He hath chosen us in Him before the foundation of the world" (Eph. 1:4).

5. *"Yogah chitta vritti nirodhah"* (*Pada* I, *Sutra* 2).

6. To elaborate: utterance is not necessary for the commission of the thought. When the Gospels emphasize speech, they do not necessarily mean the literal voicing of thought, which is merely a difference in degree and not in kind—critical as this may however be—because adultery, as Christ admonishes, is committed already in the heart. In other words, the sin is less in the execution than in the intention.

What matters here finally is to know that if words or thoughts carry with them a conjuring magic, then this principle works with all the more reason for sacred formulas which can, when applied methodologically, reverse and consequently redeem the inherently centrifugal and dispersing power of thought, as well as of speech which is its effective means of expression.

The metaphysical prototype of the word-being complex discussed above is to be found in Biblical formulations such as "the word was with God, and the word was God," or references that equate Christ with the Word or, as one finds in the Psalms, "Quicken thou me according to thy word."

MAN IS SURROUNDED by phenomena, both outward and inward. Now, one may ask, how can an individual be surrounded by "inward" phenomena? The answer is that for the sage, namely the truly objective man, all phenomena occur outside of who he in his immortal self, even the apparently subjective affinities and aversions that determine other men's priorities and that appear to emanate from within. For the sage, even his ego is seen as something outside of himself. And both kinds of phenomena—both the world circumstances and happenings and correlatively the inner impressions and impulses—are not, moreover, concretely real except in the measure of man's experience of them because, in the last analysis, it is his awareness of them that invests them with a measure of empirical reality.[7] To say, however, that they are not "real" unless consented to, through man's subjective participation, is not at all the same as to say, à la Hume and all later existentialists, that these phenomena are

––––––––––––

7. Thus one reads in the *Shiva Samhita* (2:45) that "All things grow out of Maya-captivated mind."

184

devoid of objective reality. Positive things such as the warmth of the sun or the warmth of love, the song of birds, a harvest banquet, a maiden's beautiful dance, a waterfall, or even painful things such as cold, suffering, or death are fully real independently of a given individual's personal perception of them—as is attested by all men's universally consistent experience of them.[8] What can be said, though, is that the allocations of priorities or the subjective degree of intensity these phenomena assume in a given individual's consciousness can be vastly different, even opposite to another individual's; this is plain common sense.

FOR THE INDIVIDUAL, from his earthly vantage point, there is first the world or the socio-historic milieu in which he happens to be placed—according to his karma, one will add. Then, more broadly, there is nature or the universe. The first dimension is temporal, whereas the other is fundamentally spatial. And lastly, there is manifestation as such, which is what it is—separative but also unitive, depriving but also restorative, both veiling and revealing, painful and healing. And then parallel to this set of objective conditions, there is a given individual with his personal tendencies, concerns, aspirations, desires, and frustrations; also, his abilities, which in fact constitute the objective factor in the subjectivity of his personality. And finally, there is the mixing or cross-pollination of these two sets of dimensions whose interplay produces, so to speak, a third dimension, that of the personal destiny whereby a same, nominally objective phenomenon can be

8. This is the level of consciousness designated in the Vedanta as *vaishvanara*, namely "common-to-all-man"; its field is the waking state where the consciousness is outward-turned via the gates of the five senses.

experienced either as a positive or as a negative depending on this given individual's outlook.[39]

When Shakespeare has Hamlet—who is the prototype of everyman at grips with the *Samsara*—say that "there is nothing either good or bad, but thinking makes it so,"[10] he was certainly not advocating an existentialist's nihilistic credo which posits that a thought or deed can be divorced from an objective scale of values. What he meant is firstly that, in a general sense, "one man's meat can be another man's poison," and secondly, and more essentially, as regards intrinsic morality,[11] that a given attitude or action—irrespective finally of the ethics of a given milieu, which of course can never be entirely disregarded—is, in the eyes of God, only as good as its intention. Shakespeare's words could be further interpreted to mean that a given phenomenon or situation can be well or ill received depending on one's state of mind.[12] Be that as it may, it should be quite evident to a director of conscience that an individual's subjective experience of something plays a decisive role in that something's meaning and hence in its reality for him.[13]

---

9. One could also designate these three dimensions, microcosmically, as those of *dharma, karma,* and *jiva,* the last being that of the individual self with his personal character. Law, destiny, individuality.

12. Which is almost an exact paraphrase of the quotation from the *Shiva Samhita* cited above.

11. By intrinsic morality we mean not the social canons of right and wrong, crucial though these may be, but the nature of things.

12. "O God," Hamlet further expounds, "I could be bounded in a nutshell and count myself a king of infinite space, were it not that I have bad dreams."

13. We have encountered somewhere in Hindu scriptures, the scene of a recently deceased lady of great beauty. Before her body is shrouded, a dog chances by and thinks "What a good morsel I might steal." Then a *chandala* (an outcast) comes by and thinks "Too bad she's dead! What a torrid night we could have shared together." Later, a prince appears on

Since man cannot initially evade multiplicity, which is inherent to duality, and since, being subjected to it, he cannot not think—thought being the necessary correlate of duality or the necessary bridge of consciousness between duality and unity—the question arises then, how can man free himself from the seemingly random play of phenomena, especially as actualized in his consciousness in the form of bustling ideas all vying for his attention[14]—turn by turn uplifting then depressing, pleasurable and painful, fascinating or trivial? And how can he, instead of being determined by these phenomena to a lesser or greater extent, how can he himself actively determine them or, more realistically, determine that they do not determine him? For unless a person can present to them a superior force of presence—of centeredness, of realizational force, or simply of holy innocence—that can neutralize or even convert their ceaseless onslaught, he is bound, as Hinduism and Buddhism teach, to be consumed by them in seemingly never-ending cycles of deaths and rebirths.[15] And for man,

---

the scene and sighs: "Alas, such beauty and to have died so young! Would that I could have wooed her." Lastly, an itinerant ascetic wanders on the scene and, rapt by her beauty, promptly falls into *samadhi*, praising the Name of the Lord. So each being according to his nature.

14. Animals are not consciously subject to the polar multiplicities of duality since they are morally unambiguous. However, in their own way, they can of course be just as subject as a man to the engrossing absoluteness of momentary happenings, and even more so given their relative naïveté. And, on the "moral" plane, they can become vectors of different psychic influences, either benefic or even malefic. But this fact does not entail an element of will power or of conscious identity, entailing responsibility, which is precisely what differentiates man from animals—although their inclinations towards the good or the bad are real enough to merit a designation as an instinctual predisposition to what in man becomes free will.

15. It is surprising (and dismaying) to note that when, as has already been mentioned, a typical Westerner learns about the doctrine of

this eddying of phenomena plays itself out first and foremost on the mental plane: the battlefield of Kuru in the *Bhagavad Gita* starts in the mind and resolves itself therein—attendant outward circumstances and events being, finally, but the occasional stage props that enable the illusion a measure of reality.

In other words, what needs to be emphasized is the extraordinary conjuring power of thoughts, their "magical" potential to produce flesh-and-bone actualizations,[16]

---

transmigration, instead of recoiling, as do Easterners, with dread at the Dantean prospect of having to journey through what might be eons upon eons of new existences all of which end in death, his curiosity and imagination are aroused at the prospect of experiencing new states of being (or is it the same being?) oblivious to the parentheses of pain that will usher him in and out, again and again. Moreover, in their escapist fantasies, they forget that they will not experience these "new" states as the same ego participating in a play on stage, for instance, but as an empirical absolute with no "before" and "after." Perhaps this is why the monotheistic traditions maintain an official silence about these posthumous states, for religion, if it is to effectively engage man's attention and, above all, his sincerest effort, must be both opportunely elliptical and threateningly dogmatic. Westerners, owing to the mixture of analysis and passion that characterize them, unlike Easterners who tend to be more impersonal, have an individualistic bent that predisposes them, for good or for ill, to adventurism.

16. This fact accounts for both the deliberately sparse speech of nomads and their love of eloquence. In daily usage, they choose their words carefully because they believe that uttering a word can conjure the possibility it refers to and that, therefore, unless the word is suited to the realities of the situation, which thereby protectively circumscribes its scope of effect while at the same time exhausting its magical potential, it is best left unspoken. For instance, to evoke such possibilities as "treason," "illness," or "death" gratuitously—namely in the absence of their actual occurrence—is considered bad luck. And, conversely, they are diffident about describing their good fortune for fear of exhausting its possibility or of attracting the attention of the "evil eye." This attitude of awe before words strikes the citified men, who are wont to squander speech in streams of chatter, as mere superstition. For the nomad, however,

because as a man thinketh, so he becometh. Furthermore, according to a Spanish proverb, habits are at first cobwebs then chains. The same can be said about thoughts, and with all the more force given that they seize the soul from within until nothing short of an exorcism of sorts will expunge their hold. But if "thought" is the illness, so can it be the cure, wherefore the necessity of prayer in general, which is really sacred thought, and of the jaculatory prayer[17] of the heart in particular, whose repetition substitutes the healing Oneness of the Name of God for the disjointing multiplicity of the world: "In the same way that a swimmer perishes if he ceases to move," Schuon writes, "so a man perishes if he no longer prays: if he no longer pronounces the Name of God and thus ceases to manifest Reality in the world of illusion."[18]

MAN LIVES IN a universe where everything revolves around, or tends towards, a center of gravity. In metaphysics, one would say that the pole Absolute is every-

---

who lives right next to the origin of things, words hold a formulaic power which is lost once these words stray from their etymology, once their meaning is diluted or cheapened by idle use which holds nothing sacred. Incidentally, words are meant to mold men, as is the case with sacred language, not men words, as is the case when usage (and no longer meaning) becomes the norm as is seen in modern societies. Having said this, there is a genius of culture that cannot flower except in the sheltering confines of an urban civilization, allowing for word plays, derived meanings, shades and nuances, and so on, and which correspond to a wealth that lies in the human soul and which cannot be developed in the brutally harsh environment of nomadic survival. But a derived meaning too often becomes the premise later for flattery, trickery, and mendacity. Keeping one's word is not as important for city men, whereas it is a matter of life and death for nomads.

17. "Jaculatory" prayer or one that is "darted up" or "hurled" to God.

18. Private writings.

where present in the pole Infinite. Concentric hierarchies hold everything in nature in rows of serial organization that do not allow deviation,[19] each possibility being, once manifested, what it is once and for all according to set immutabilities—Buddhists would say according to their *dharma*—that forbids trans-specie metamorphosis. Variety, even in its most riotously exuberant, has its limits—not necessarily in number, but in form according to the pole Absolute. Thus no creature, or thing, can "jump out" of its genus (*natura non facit saltus*), an extravagance which only the theory of evolution considers plausible.[20] The expression "neither fish nor fowl" does not apply to animals which are perfectly what they are. No grass-grazer will ever become a predator, or vice-versa. To expect this would

---

19. "It is not for the sun to overtake the moon, nor doth the night outstrip the day. They float each in an orbit" (Koran, 36:40). Likewise, the male/female polarization is absolute as regards the respective fathering-mothering functions of the sexes though there are "yin-yang" exceptions that confirm the rule. Thus, in the animal realm, one finds the exception of the male seahorse which has a womb-like pouch in which the babies are hatched. But such a possibility, as that of hermaphroditism in some invertebrates, occurs only at the periphery of manifestation, although, since opposites meet, it might also reflect something of the center's hermaphroditism, that of the Spirit, as well as, *mutatis mutandis*, that of spirituality.

20. Had Darwin spoken of the plasticity of divine All-Possibility, whose polymorphous nature gives rise to the endless variety of species, all would have been well. There are no gaps in *Purusha*, who gave his body in sacrifice to creation. Thus, nature and all its beings, when seen from the inside, forms a continuous whole of interrelated parts which complete each other (something the Roman poet Ovid understood well); there are no absolute scissions between the different realms of animals which gives us birds which swim and even dive and swim underwater, and fish which fly, or amphibians which are able to live equally on land and in the water. There are plantlike animals and plants which are carnivorous. And there are insects, such as butterflies, which are almost like flowers.

be tantamount to eliminating nature's polarities of hard and soft, and all the others. However, if each specie is immutably crystallized, this does not mean that an individual animal, a single tree, or even a piece of stalactite be the exact duplicate of each single member of its kind, because there is a relatively wide latitude here for differences in degree or in quality as allowed by the variations in the perfection of each being or object, variations in health, and, for beings, variations in disposition—to say nothing of possible hybridization (although this can only work as a re-arrangement of a pre-ordained and specifically limited set of variables).[21] The pole of the Infinite is not just present in variety as such—the variety of species—but within each specific set of species as well; this is the "breathing room" in manifestation.

Because of their formal immutability, good and evil are not choices available to the animal, vegetal, and mineral spheres, nor to man, it should be added, insofar as he partakes unavoidably of animality or can be said (in a very limited sense) to be a "rational animal"—an expression fraught with philosophical ambiguities, but technically correct. This is why the body of man, which clearly belongs to the animal sphere—not specifically in its form which is a projection of the vertical intellect, but as regards its physical needs—cannot be said to be the source of evil as the sometimes excessive zeal of certain religious moralities would have it.[22] In fact, evil is never

---

21. If one takes the canine possibility, for example, which presents an absolutely astonishing number of mutations, at no moment can one breed, be it the biggest or smallest dog, stray outside of its "lupus" prototype. From the point of view of the formal distinctness that makes a dog a dog, there is something unique which separates it absolutely from the feline species, for example.

22. Though flagellants are really attempting to scourge the ego when they punish the flesh, it may be morally advantageous for them to scapegoat the body as evil.

possible in the substance as such (*Prakriti*), nor therefore in matter which is the projection of the pole substance, or its ultimate condensation.[23] Evil originates in duality insofar as it leads to a scission in the consciousness of unity or, more precisely, to a divisive scission in this consciousness—because duality, is not in and of itself a premise for evil as is attested by the "hide-and-go-seek" mystery of love.[24] Once duality is established, though, the potential is laid for, as would be said in Scholastics, the "accident" to arrogate the prerogatives that can only belong to the Absolute in virtue of Its unity. The most flagrant example of this is the illusion of selfhood that individuals assume, each person—or ego—laying claim to a uniqueness of personal identity which, when extreme, ultimately pits the "accident" against the "substance," the person against the One Self.

This is the reason that man who, by ontological definition, is born at the intersection of the vertical (truth/spirit) and horizontal (being/soul) vertices of All-Possibility—or who appears at the junction of the centrifugal/centripetal spokes of manifestation (the Neoplatonist procession/

---

23. Nor is the corruptibility of matter itself an evil. According to Jacques Maritain's felicitous expression, evil is a wound in being. By that token, being itself is sound.

24. This is why we cannot follow Erigena when, straying from his Neoplatonist sources and distancing himself also from the earlier Latin Christian understanding of man as the *imago Dei*, he explains sexual differentiation as being a consequence of the Fall, as if the paradisiacal ideal would be to regain a kind of lost androgyny—a state that does not exist in an individually specified mode (which would be something of a monstrous anomaly), but is only a symbolic way of describing the divine essence which is both masculine and feminine. The blessedness of the Virgin's celestial state—Mercy be!—does not consist in her regaining a lost masculine part, just as Christ does not cease being masculine in Heaven. The Holy Spirit, however, is androgynous, in the sense of transcending sexual polarities.

return) and their concentric hoops or realms—is capable of undergoing every type of metamorphosis possible, as the legendary encounter between Ulysses and the Enchantress Circe illustrates in its own way—from the best to the worst, the sublime to the heinous. For those who would dismiss such mythological allusions as "old wives tales," it may be worth pointing out that the "ancients," in their tales, taught by way of symbolism and analogy—contrary to modern literary devices such as the novel whose focus is first literal or material verisimilitude and secondly psychological plausibility, though this second criterion of "reality," by its ignorance of supra-individual archetypes, usually flounders in the most transiently accidental and therefore discardable aspects of human experience.[25] The scientific objectivity of Flaubertian "realism" or the impressionistic subjectivism of a Proust, by their emphasis of the personal or the accidental to the detriment of the truly universal, trap the reader in a maze of peripherals (over-ripe with specious meanings) and leave him the unprotected prey of his Minotaur instincts—all the more ravening when

---

25. True, the idea of "archetypes" has become fashionable in modern parlors. However, we are no longer dealing with intellective archetypes as attributes of divinity, but generic leitmotifs which, even if noble in their idea (subjects such as the *magna mater*, of Diana the huntress, of the warrior, the father etc.) are almost invariably expressed—à la Jung— through rather ordinary, trivial, if not downright vulgar or even diabolic, exemplars. This is hardly surprising in an epoch nurtured, for instance, by an Aldous Huxley (*The Doors of Perception*) to discover a cosmos in the creases of one's blue-jeans or taught by a Krishnamurti that any word—even the name of a popular consumer brand—can serve as a *mantra*. One is embarrassed to have to make such a point. The thing most lacking in a modern culture—in which the floodgates of the infrahuman have been blown wide open—is what defined a traditional culture such as the Christian Middle Ages: a sense of the sacred which is marked by a sense of grandeur and a corresponding sense for the noble of which dignity of speech and of behavior bears witness.

193

unchecked by the light of reason. Man's natural imagination, locked in the stifling confines of such literalism, whether of the objective (or semi-objective) or of the subjective kind, begged for an outlet which, instead of being transcendent, led to infra-realism, such as the irrationally cryptic meanderings of a Joyce, which is always devoid of nobility because seditiously seeking grandeur in the trivial and the most banally quotidian, or to the phantasmagoria of a Gabriel García Marquez which, instead of freeing imagination upwards, ends by enslaving it in the chthonic grossness that underlies all such forays into the absurd. Even the so-called symbolist poets (Mallarmé, Maeterlinck) and their literary offspring (Valéry, Yeats, Breton) mar whatever archetypal imagery they stumble upon because they prefer to approach truth via the subjective or even the irrational, without proper regard to the logical absurdity of such an endeavor—to say nothing of the fact that the Holy Spirit will not assist them in what is, all told, a sacrilegious endeavor to violate the sacred mysteries or, failing that, to make a pastiche of them.

Whereas if for the ancients the individual is paradoxically important only in the measure of his impersonality (or transpersonality)—because it is this effacement of the noisy and forgettable ego which allows the universals to shine through his substance—for the moderns the individual is important in direct measure to his rejection (be it active or merely acquiesced to) of these very same universals—for instance the rejection encouraged in psychoanalysis of the father prototype.[26] In other words, the moderns

----

26. It might be objected the religious equivalent of this Oedipal rite of passage could be found in the teachings of some Buddhists that they must "burn" the Buddha if they find his image or even "kill" him should they encounter him. What is left out is that such teachings—which nonetheless are ill-sounding—are set in an intensely religious context in which the fundamental meaning should be transparent. What the spiritual aspirant must do, in fact, is rid himself of artificial notions of the

194

measure man's singularity by his accidentality and by what is most eccentrically peculiar to him, which is to say that his prestige is measured by what is least immortal in him, by what Eternity is most apt to pulverize once he is ripped out of his fleshly sheath. What is (suicidally) forgotten is that, singularity can only belong properly to the Single, to what is One, the Unique and that, in consequence, an individual can only be important in an absolute sense to the degree he can manifest—or serve as a vehicle—of the One Self.

Because of his freedom, man alone, of all creatures, can tend towards any of an endless number of different centers of gravity that range from the blessed to the accursed.[27] And whether he wishes to or not, each man is born a satellite of a center of gravity,[28] or perhaps even of conflicting centers of gravity. The decisive difference between him and an animal is that he can choose which center of gravity he will be an orbiting part of.[29] And this choice comes down to two basic alternatives: the world or God; there is no other. More importantly, though, man's intelligence, which is characterized by its capacity to discern between the real and the illusory, enables him to identify with the Center and thus, in principle, to transcend—not as ego but as consciousness—the endless play of vicissitudes that characterizes the orbit-

---

Buddha and this is done through the sacrifice of individuality, precisely, not its enhancement. There is a damning world of difference between revolt and effacement.

27. Koran: "Surely We created man of the best stature / Then we reduced him to the lowest of the low" (Ch. 95).

28. Augustine describes his own center of gravity in his *Confessions* as: "My weight is my love; by it am I carried wheresoever I am carried" (XII : 9, 10).

29. An example of this analogy is that of the whirling dervishes, in imitation of heavenly bodies circling the sun, seek to circle the truth or God. And this is why, too, most traditional dances and ceremonies follow a circular pattern.

ing periphery. "When I go back into the ground, into the depths," Eckhart says, "into the well-spring of the Godhead, no one will ask me whence I came or whither I went."

TO RETURN BACK to ideas, and to the words that connote them, it is worth remarking that unless a person has an operative center of consciousness which secures him from drifting through the *Samsara,* or which immunizes him from stray thoughts—the image of Ulysses lashed to the mast (the vertical axis) comes to mind here—his consciousness is a fertile seeding ground for an incessant stream of usually loosely connected and often disparate musings, preoccupations, or reveries that feed and multiply, parasite-like, on his vital substance. The saying that the devil finds work for idle hands is most apt here, because if a man is not improving in grace—to paraphrase the English alchemist Thomas Norton—he is by that very fact impairing in waste.[30]

If man, unprotected by grace, were freed from the lock of the five senses[31] and could behold the universe, not as a broken substance transiently solidified in mutually exclusive phenomena, but as the ever-flowing continuum

---

30. Man's identity with the vertical axis does not allow him to rest, as do animals, on a given level: he is either rising or descending. To play with this imagery, the ascent or descent can, of course, be more or less oblique depending on the individual's degree of natural virtue.

31. The five senses have, of course, their normative significance and therefore can be gates to understanding and not just a barrier. For instance, the polarization of vision and hearing corresponds generally to the polarization between the objective and the subjective (respectively, knowledge and being), while repeating this polarization each within its own sphere—the right and left eyes, for example, corresponding respectively to the objective and subjective but within the general realm of the objective. Again, touch and taste correspond respectively to the objective and the subjective—touch being related to the pole form and taste to the pole substance—although one cannot be dogmatically exclusive about

196

of consciousness that it is—of which dense matter would be merely the falling-off point or congealed echo—then he might see a kind of rushing, whirling particle maelstrom of infinitesimal multitudes or a multicolored tonal ocean of interwoven light and darkness no sooner forming than dissolving to reform forthwith,[32] simultaneously appearing and disappearing.[33] This reality (or experience) has both a macrocosmic or external significance and a microcosmic or internal one according to the law of like outside, like inside—the inside being here the universe of man's subjective consciousness[34] in which myriad particle ideas, when not stilled or reconciled by truth—the light of which establishes the normative proportion of things *sub specie aeternitatis*—rush and eddy in a tumult of semi-chaotic confusion—as the experience of dreams proves (the *taijasa* of Vedanta), for dreams dissolve the temporary partitions erected between the solids as validated by the waking state of bodily experience (the *vaishvanara* of Vedanta). Now this realm of swirling flux applies only to centrifugal *Maya* and all that it entails of progressive loss of light, order, and bliss (the entropy of the physicists); this is the domain of the galactic reaches of manifestation, the outer edge of which is made up, metaphorically speaking, of chilled cosmic

---

such allocations. And finally, the sense of smell—whose prototype is the "love of perfumes"—could be said to correspond to the marriage of polarities found in the Divine Substance. Practically speaking, however, the five senses reflect the fate of intelligence inserted into matter and therefore multiple or discursive or separative rather than single and unitive, analytical rather than synthetic.

32. Goethe's *Hexeneinmaleins* or *Prakriti*'s multiplying witchery.

33. Astronomers and physicists now have the physical means of verifying some of this through their telescopes.

34. Of course, to speak of an "inside" is relative because man's subjectivity, when seen from the point of view of the divine substance which sustains it, is really an objective outside. Man is in fact inside God—though, when profane, he can be said to be subjectively "outside."

debris. However, it goes without saying that the universe is not just dissolving flux: in its essence, it is unifying bliss.[35] Moreover, given that each universe is intrinsically a homogeneous unit—a macrocosmic reflection of the original being, Purusha/Osiris—its parts are interdependent and therefore preserve proportional relationships. Harmony is always static in its essence (though it can also be dynamic in its manifestation), the expression of eternal equilibrium. What individual human beings are not conscious of is that the order they see is partly the result of a concatenation of social contacts and of habits which exclude the soul's potential relationship with a wholly new order of reality which opens up at the hour of death. At death, this chainwork is dismantled and, unless the soul is centered spiritually, the fragility and illusoriness of these links is made devastatingly apparent.[36] The world and the life that had once appeared so solid and permanent is disassembled and folded away like a circus tent.

Maya is really *Atma*'s dream; as *Atma* dreams or as *Atma* thinks, so the worlds arise. *Maya* is coherent in that it reflects *Atma*'s homogeneity of Self; but since only *Atma* can be real—or really real—the world cannot be real except by echo and evanescently so, and therefore it is in itself no more than an image-making substance. In this sense, all the empirically real objects in manifestation, such as creatures, mountains, trees, or flowers, are but the projections of

---

35. Thus, in Tagore's hymnal words: "The light of thy music illumines the world. The life-breath of thy music runs from sky to sky. The holy streams of thy music breaks through all stony obstacles and rushes on" (*Gitanjali*).

36. The Dutch mystic Hadewijch, as she looks at the vortex which is the reality of her experience of union with God: "And in the middle under the disc [the seat of God] was a whirlpool turning so fearfully that heaven and earth might wonder at it and be afraid... the deep whirlpool that is so fearfully dark that is divine union in its hidden storms" (*Vision 1*).

Platonic ideas, namely something that *Atma* can "think," or imagine. And *Atma* is not lacking in imagination! Man's experience of them, refracted through the arresting confines of his corporeal-temporal entity (the body-time prism), freezes, as it were, what is in fact an ever-cascading flux of fugitive forms—perfect stillness existing only outside of the realm of what is referred to in the Vedanta as the realm of *nama rupa* (name-form). But unless one conclude, with the relativists, that all is but flux and change, it is worth repeating that the Immutable is reflected in the perfection of form. Indeed, it is crucial to distinguish here between Form and Substance, because if it is clear that individual objects cannot endure in their material form: their genus' singularity—in that it can re-manifest itself again and again, albeit in new bodies—proves the permanence of the archetypical "ideas" which offers the contemplative the display of the One ever newly refracted in the multiple. Therefore man need not despair: what is true, beautiful, and good is never lost provided he not seek to cling to its material shadowing. The Islamic sin of associationism (*shirk*) is to idolize the accident at the expense of the substance. And it is really the substance man loves when he is drawn by the external object.[37]

Against this backdrop of a reality that is a dynamic surface everywhere punctuated with seemingly static forms, the whole reflecting the play of the Infinite and the Absolute, man is at once a disengaged witness, thanks to his intelligence, and both an engaged object, owing to his materiality, and an engaged subject owing to his personal consciousness. The problem for him becomes then, is he to be merely a mote amongst motes, "the chaff which the wind driveth away," as the Psalmist says, a fleeting shad-

---

37. "It is not for the spouse that the love of the spouse is dear, but for the love of *Atma*," one finds in the *Upanishads*.

ow buffeted or preyed upon by other commingling shadows, or is he to enter into a covenant with the Eternal that
will shelter him and "dash his enemies"? Is he to exist
husk-like with no real substance, the bastard by-product of
other people's dreams, his derelict-being the feeding-
ground of stray thoughts come as carrion-crows to feed on
his spiritual vitals,[38] profaning the virginal substratum of
his immortal being? Or is man to repel the fever of multiplicity and become truly one again in the Name of the One
by steadfastly thinking on the One again—as the Bhagavad
Gita enjoins? In other words, thought can only be—initially—cured by thought. By thinking on the Real, through
discernment between the permanent and the illusory, the
mental substance of consciousness—though unstable and
forever shifting—can be converted into a profound and
undisturbed awareness of the True, the Good, and the
Beautiful. And as the consciousness of these grows in the
soul, then their reality absorbs the substance of consciousness, transforming it and redeeming it. Prayer, whose quintessence, is repetition of a *mantra* of a divine name, if not
the very name of God, is revealed as sacred thought. "Fix
thy mind on Me," God, in the form of Krishna, tells the

---

38. Because one must not lose sight of the fact that thoughts have no
life of their own till, by allowance—in this case, of the passions—they
breed and multiply on subjective consciousness, and which, unless they
are either repelled or converted, they will slowly deplete to death. In this
manner, hundreds of little "throwaway" moments can function as fledg-
ling anticipations of future possibilities that will karmically reappear
(the *samskaras*, "latent impressions" or residual staining of the primally
pristine mind-stuff that combine with the *vasanas*, the "latent tendencies" originating in egoic illusion) in new guises along the Wheel of the
Samsara. Yet one must bear in mind that one supreme moment—of heroism for instance, or one good deed, especially when spontaneous (what
Hindhus call *satyagraha*, an "act of truth")—can instantly atone for a
hundred mistakes or even erase perhaps eons of karma. The good is
gold to evil's dross.

warrior prince Arjuna in the Bhagavad Gita (9:34). And this "fixing of the mind" is operated best through jaculatory prayer.

It has been remarked that this kind of prayer—which in its essence is really prayer of the heart and not of the mind—is at the very opposite of thinking. While this is true of profane thought, or of unregenerate thought which is wildly restless, it cannot be true of thought as such inasmuch as the substance of thought is consciousness. Moreover, God is known at first through His Name, for as the modern-day Hindu saint Ananda Moyi said, "It is with His Name and His Form that this world has come into existence, and it also ends with His Name." Now, a name is not something that is meant to be grasped by any other faculty except thought. To say "name" is the same as to say "word" and the idea of "word" implies consciousness—be it of the heart or of the mind[39]—not just being. Now, one might say that, in the higher mystical states of rapture, thought is extinguished. But what is in fact really alluded to here is discursive thought or the idea of thought in its dualistic function of seeing the world in terms of schismatic subject and object, not to thought as consciousness. In mystical rapture, there is a fusing of mind and heart, but not an extinction of thought as such—unless by "thought" one means only the outer mind. Moreover, inner union with God does not exclude outer awareness, as the possibility of sober ecstasy shows us. A prejudice one finds among many devotionalist mystics (*bhaktas*) is to assume that "loss of (*outer*) consciousness" when experiencing divine rapture constitutes some kind of de facto superiority over a God-awareness in which the world—or consciousness of the

---

39. Again and again, in the Bible, one finds allusions to the "thoughts" of the heart. For instance, "The word of God. . . is a discerner of the thoughts and intents of the heart" (Heb. 4:12).

world—persists. It is the same prejudice which wants to minimize the role of logic and reasoning, or even to assume that these are somehow inimical to spirituality, and which seeks in intensity of fervor and emotionalism[40] a sign of union, or at least of sincerity. In fact, it is the reverse that is true: perfect spirituality entails perfect consciousness of the true. And perfect consciousness is perfect objectivity which entails perfect logic and reasoning (*recta ratio*).[41] This is not to say that love of God should be emotionless to be more perfect, but that love of God need not entail loss of consciousness or the forfeiting of intelligence (and reasoning), which would be irrational apart from the risk of depreciating the one faculty by which we are most God-like. The point is that thought in its origin, just as in its substance, is really pure consciousness of the Real.[42] When in duality, it mirrors the fragmentation of reality, but it is not multiple in and of itself. Thus it becomes multiple first when the discriminative intelligence of the ego is turned towards the outer world which is made of duality and, secondly, insofar as the ego is more or less the dupe of this duality—or is more aware of duality than of underlying unity. In Yoga, a distinction is made between two types of concentration (*samadhi*): one is termed "concentration with consciousness" (*samprajnata samadhi*) and the other is termed "concentration without consciousness" (*asamprajnata samadhi*)

---

40. This is the method of sects such as the Holy Rollers, the Shakers, the Quakers, of Revivalists, of the new Pentacostalists, and many more.

41. Saints are characterized by their sound reasoning, or at least their good sense, even when their knowledge is partial owing to the fact that they often represent one perspective and not knowledge as such. Though Joan of Arc was an illiterate peasant girl, ignorant of the ways and wiles of the world, her disarming logic trumped the cleverness of the lawyers at her trial.

42. Thus Dante had no doubt that "the first speaker said first and before anything else 'God'" (*De Vulg. Eloquentia*, I, 4:30).

which, in its literal translation, is a contradiction, unless one understands that "without consciousness" means "without discursivity," namely the trance-like state of a being who has transcended his ego-body individuality, because in fact it is a question here of a kind of supra-consciousness: "I sleep but my heart waketh."[43]

The first type of *samadhi* has often been described as "impure" because it is considered that so long as there remains a trace of thought there remains the seeds of mortality,[44] namely of renewed transmigration. Again, the issue, as we see it, is not thought per se, but egoic desire of which thought becomes the medium, because the mind is passive and therefore reflects the nature of the subject. At any rate, to seek to eliminate or to transcend thought is absurd. Where would one start? Nor is thought, or thinking, the culprit because thoughts can be either pure or impure. True, the mind-stuff is susceptible of being contaminated, even in the case of saints because "dirt" is the inevitable by-product of earthly existence; but, in this case, the sullying can only be superficial and obviously does not engage the substance of consciousness. The truth of the matter is that if the mind reflects the heart, then cleansing the heart will wipe the mirror of the mind which then can reflect reality in its original brilliance. As the Zen patriarch Dogen enjoined: "Think the not-thought." He did not say "Do not think."

---

43. St. Bernard—whom Dante designated as his supreme guide in The Divine Comedy—refers to this elevated state of the soul (in his *Sermons on the Song of Songs*) as being "snatched from itself by a holy and vehement thought (*cogitatio*) . . . so that it surpasses the common use and custom of thinking." And also he mentions that "it is truly a sleep that does not dull the interior sense but leads it away (*abducat*)."

44. Conversely this is why *asamprajnata samadhi* is also referred to as "seedless *samadhi*."

WHEN KING DAVID says, "I am purposed my mouth shall not transgress," one could say that he is alluding implicitly to the power words have of creating reality,[45] or of opening, by their utterance,[46] a channel for the soul into the reality of which they are the referents. For "mouth" he might have substituted "mind"[47] except that the span between thought and speech is symbolically the same as that between intention and deed—wherefore the vow of silence,[48] and its practical support abstinence, found in the methodology of all monastic disciplines. Indeed, if thoughts never find utterance, they inexorably lose their grip and recede, and, deprived of effective sustenance, ultimately vanish[49] leaving place for the underlying primal Void in which the voice of God eternally resounds. Eckhart: "God is the Word which pronounces itself."

But the interiorizing virtue of silence requires the active or manifesting virtue of speech to balance it, without which

---

45. "He spoke, and they were made" (Ps. 148:5, in the Douai Bible). And the Koran: "God says 'Be'! and it is." Creation springs from the utterance of divine thought, a process that is illustrated in the mythological allusion to Pallas Athena springing fully armed from the forehead of Zeus. So, too, in the Hindu scriptures: "Utterance brought forth all the Universe" (*Satapatha-Brahmana*). This is why it behooves one to be mindful of one's speech.

46. Therefore the Koran says: "And We shall inherit from him what whereof he spake, and he will come to us alone" (19:80).

47. Or "heart" because it is known in physiognomy, that the shape of a person's mouth—which utters "words" and which fashions "kisses"—reflects the nature of his heart. Thus the symbol of the human mouth includes the twin functions of knowledge (words) and love (kisses), further proof that the two are not to be artificially separated.

48. One is reminded here of the sealed vessel in the alchemical *calcificatio*, which is the preliminary stage of the whole process.

49. It is not that silence can still one insistent thought, but that by sealing the floodgates of speech, it reflexively stills the soul's urge towards multiplicity. In Hobbes' words, *ratio est oratio*, "thought is speech."

204

it might induce too much passivity, just as speech in turn requires silence so as not to fritter away into agitation. *Oratio et jejunum*: "prayer," which is the prototype and hence sufficient reason for the unique gift of speech, and "fasting," namely the withdrawal from the appetitive world, are the right and left hands of any integral spiritual path. The pilgrim can only be self-effacing in view of an affirmation: he prepares by means of silence, namely the stilling of the thought processes, the *vacare Deo* whereby God can reveal Himself.

Prayer is the active anticipation of this grace, for by his affirmation of God instead of his ego, man can then become—*Deo juvante* (God helping)—the mouthpiece of God. If thought and speech can prove the ruin of man—of man without a center that transcends the inherent sterility of his egoity—so thought and speech, once ritualized by means of prayer, can operate his redemption.

In speech, the soul marches out through the portals of the mouth and declares either its majesty or its triviality, either its wisdom, beauty, and kindness, or its shallowness, either its nobility or its baseness. And the words, once uttered, carry in their wake a reverberating influence. As an African proverb says, "of the words in thy mouth, thou art the master; once spoken, thou art their slave."

If thought can be said to be the conscious beginning of multiplicity, so one supreme thought (St. Bernard's "*vehemente cogitatione*"), particularly as synthesized in a divine formula, can, by reversing the centrifugal diffusion of consciousness, rescue man from the agency of diversity—always potentially divisive for the unregenerate will—and restore him to the original unity lying at the heart of existence.[50] And of all thoughts, the Name of God is the verbal

---

50. An "ecstasy" which Bernard "calls a death, because," as Bernard McGinn comments, "it removes the soul from life's cares" (*The Growth of Mysticism*).

symbol of Reality. Thus, to pronounce this Name is to affirm Reality which is Truth, Beauty, and Goodness. Thought is made to apprehend the Truth whose transubstantiating essence is rendered operative through speech which is meant to declare it. And since man lives in time, or since time is the necessary correlate of his distance from God, or since time is the ransom of duality, he can convert the multiplicity of moments back to primordial oneness through the repetition of the One who converts time's fragmenting—and ultimately destructive—impetus.[51]

One could argue that man could likewise be saved by the means of a sacred image, or maybe a sacred sound, a heavenly melody or a heavenly fragrance, or for that matter, even by taste, for all sensible supports that are good remind a spiritual person of paradise[52] and can therefore produce a kind of restorative communion with the *Summum Bonum* of the Neoplatonists, assuming a proper human context.[53] But these, to be theurgically operative in the fullest sense—that is to say salvational—would entail a

---

51. Chronos (or Saturn), the grim reaper, is traditionally depicted with a scythe. We can do no better here, in summarizing the above, than to quote from Whitall N. Perry's Chapter on "Invocation" in his *Treasury of Traditional Wisdom*: "The invoker reconstructs the heavenly *Sacrifice* implicit in creation by converting what has been a macrocosmic 'descent' into what is now a microcosmic 'ascent', wherein his multifarious and fragmented being is recollected, reintegrated and finally resolved through the theurgy of the Divine Name into the undifferentiated and primordial unity of the Supreme Principle, with which this Name is essentially identified."

52. One is reminded of Buddha's "Flower Sermon" where, without uttering a word, he lifted a flower and, of all the disciples, only one smiled in comprehension. This gesture marks the origin of Zen.

53. In the absence of pure contemplativity (of the likes of a Tagore), which is dispassionate by definition, these "sensible consolations," as they have been termed, normally require a ritual or even a religious cultural framework in order to neutralize their potentially siren-like

preliminary stilling of the mind-stuff and of the senses which feed it. In other words, without a naturally pneumatic predisposition, which beholds the metaphysical transparency of phenomena, they are merely pleasurable. Nonetheless, even assuming the pneumatic's capacity for pure contemplation, man is not just a watery surface, passively reflective—though this analogy has its place in spiritual symbolism, for example in the alchemy of humility. And even if these "sensory" means can operate parthenogenetically[54] for a given individual—rare as this possibility may be in the age of passion (*Kali Yuga*), they work only to release consciousness—by way of Platonic anamnesis—from its post-Edenic slumber, or dullness, or serve as catalysts for an intuition of heaven. But given that man is a thinking creature, these "means" require the active centering or focusing of a *mantra* or, at least, of prayer. It is not enough to feel good, one must learn to be good. And this requires reflection and meditation. In uttering the Name of God, man, who cannot be good ("whole" or "god") by himself, assimilates something of the being of God Who lends him wisdom and goodness, or restores him to the wisdom and goodness whereby he was created.

The sufficient reason for man's existence, as we have said repeatedly, is to know God and all that this entails by way of devotional virtue and of love and respect for His creation, otherwise he would not have been created a rational being, but an animal.[55] And to know God is first to know His Name and then to call on it with all of one's faculties. But the second action is sparked from the first: knowledge fires action, truth directs being.

---

allurement which can lock the soul in a narcissistic embrace, or dissipate it, instead of freeing it heavenward.

54. From the Greek *parthenos*, "virgin" and *genesis*, "engendering."

55. We are following here Aristotle's explicit distinction in this vital point.

207

MODERN LANGUAGE (OR should one say parlance?) has become more and more connotative of the "accident" owing to its reliance on usage[56]—as we have remarked—and not on etymology, as is the case in fully traditional cultures. And with the complicity of relativism and democracy, it has sur-

---

56. Usage, of course, has certain relative rights as can be seen by the hundreds of dialectical varieties that underscore the rich diversity of ethnic patrimonies born of man's associations with distinct geographical settings, for these can engender a colorful lifestyle unique to the seascape, woodlands, plains, or mountains that nurture it. But these "rights" can be no greater than the validity of ethnic customs themselves whose father-to-son, mother-to-daughter legacies of folk wisdom and customs protect against wayward individualism, while hearkening back to the archetypal (and God entrusted) patrimony of the ancestors which they are meant to preserve. Also, there are vernaculars, tied to time-consecrated traditions of native tasks that possess vastly more soul and reality and aristocratic simplicity than Parisian salon niceties that emasculate words of their elemental power. In making these remarks, one must remember that a language too rich in synonyms is often poor in virtue. In other words, when the attribute takes precedence over either the substantive or the verb (depending on the particular language's main strength or point of structural emphasis—in German, for example, it is the noun, in Arabic the verb) then the dream eclipses reality, impressions (opinions) rule over certitudes, the subjective over the objective. Too many shadings of meaning dissipate the force and therefore integrity of original words, opening the way for all kinds of artificialities and conceits which serve as a fertile ground for dissembling, prevarication, hypocrisy, and, in short, to dissolution, because, as Eckhart states, "words derive their power from the original Word." This is why language can never evolve in any meaningfully absolute way; it can only degenerate.

However, we have examples where the vernacular "earns" pride of place over an archaic language which cannot "adjust" to the flowering of customs. Dante's use of vernacular Italian to write his *Divine Comedy* is one of the most spectacular examples of this. Latin's intellectualism ill-suited it to the lyrical beauty of the Italian soul's need for song and poetry, for its spontaneity, its love of wine and women, of dance and merriment born from the particular magic of its sun-dappled countryside of rolling hills and curling shorelines.

rendered to the secular which, by definition, follows the shifts of fashion[57] and economic priorities.[58] In such manner, language loses, over time, its magic to conjure reality while substituting in its place an artificial or even an inferior, or vulgar, or false "reality." Thus, for a people accustomed to using language trivially and carelessly, more and more ignorant of the elemental meaning of rhythm and phonetics, it may seem absurd to believe that words can be anything more than a convenient, opportune, and near fortuitous abstract of the things or feelings they are meant to convey. It may be hard to believe that they are more than just connotative signs, but can actually convey an existential or magical influence that is valid in itself and therefore, if so, need to be handled with the greatest care.[59] Leaving aside the elaborate numerological science of letters and sounds found in ancient languages, let us simply recall that reality is not there for the

---

57. All things, not just material organisms, are subject to the law of entropy. Wherefore the insistent stress—in Vedic Hinduism for instance, but also in all liturgical practices—on correct pronunciation and grammar.

58. The "cyber-speak" or "techno-babble" of 3rd millennium people is but the latest example of this subordination of language to function and behavior. Rock, rap, and the psychedelic experience have also infiltrated the language of a downstream culture powerless not to absorb whatever is dumped into it or which has become porous to the infra-real.

59. From another point of view, it might be said that language, when she loses her modesty, is a whore who adopts the mannerisms of her customers. Of course, the reverse is even truer, namely language, owing to the principle of analogy, when noble and correct, can elevate. Thus: "thanks to the principle of analogy, such verbal coitus works no less salubriously in its magic than actual ritual intercourse, or indeed sexual intercourse of any kind" (J. J. Meyer: *Trilogie altindischer Mächte und Feste der Vegetation*). The key operative principle here is the idea of communion with the reality words connote and without which they would be meaningless. On a negative plane, the verbal force of blasphemy derives from the nature of the reality reviled. Likewise, a curse is more than just a convention of vowels and consonants.

209

words but the words for the reality;[60] that is to say, a word derives its meaning, effect, and validity from the reality it connotes and is thereby its phonetic—and noetic—equivalent, sharing in its root an identity of essence according to the law of proportions and of signatures holding the worlds together.[61] All of sacred scripture is founded upon this truth, wherefore the strictness of retaining the Vedas and Koran exactly as originally transmitted.[62] Conversely, the cult of the new-fangled, so prevalent today, always colludes with the destruction of a civilization.

---

60. That words, in turn, can create a new reality of their own, as alluded to above, is a result mostly (but not entirely) of their misuse, because their function should be first of all evocative and not provocative. And that usage is not, in principle, a reliable benchmark can be seen in the fate of a word such as "myth," which was meant to describe a story about reality, has become synonymous with unreality, namely its diametrical contrary. There is also the case of new words being coined to reflect a shift in customs and these words then acquire a conditioning influence of their own. For instance, the slang word "guy"—innocuous though it may sound—is actually antithetical to the notion of man as *pontifex*. No mere "guy" can ever become a saint, or even a hero: it is a question of "man" who, we will remember, was meant to be a citadel of the Lord. And a civilization composed of "guys" is a civilization which has lost its raison d'être because it is a civilization which excludes grandeur. The average man of the *Krita Yuga* would stand like a superman next to men of today: his virility, beauty, nobility and luminous poise would be difficult to behold.

61. However, from yet another point of view, a word can even be said to be superior to the material thing connoted just as, in Platonic terms, Ideas are superior to their created projections, insofar, at least, as the archetype is always superior to the accident. But this presumably does not apply to perfect creation and to perfect creatures, because in this case there is no conflict between the principle and the effect because there is no meaningful separation, but a perfect crystallization.

62. And likewise, in its way, the superiority of the King James version of the Bible which preserves the majesty of the original Word to such a degree as to merit the designation of an inspired writing in its own right and certainly to a degree that can only be defiled by modern

THOUGH REASON IS a faculty of duality, it can discern the One. And though the heart is a faculty of unity, it can mistake itself for the One, and therefore be two—both real man and impostor. For the unregenerate heart, the restoration of unity starts in the mind with the knowledge—or remembrance—of the One which, when methodically assimilated through prayer, alone can cure the rift in the heart and dissipate the illusion, not of individuality per se, but of separate or autonomous individuality.

Thus for man besieged and invaded by the hubbub of myriad mental impressions,[63] or simply for man afflicted with the atomizing fever of thought, the sovereign cure is the Name of God whose utterance puts the world to flight. The Name of God, being the name of Truth—or being the Name of What Is—dispels illusion, centers the soul,[64] freeing it from disassembling multiplicity, and has the power to miraculously transfigure it back into its celestial prototype according to the magic of analogy which lies at the heart of all language. For the soul which feeds on multiplicity, this Name will perforce be experienced as a "narrow gate" because it abolishes discursivity though, unbeknownst to the untested soul, it opens onto the infinite: where there once was irreconcilable diversity, there is now harmonious breadth and liberating vastness: "I am black but beautiful," we find in *The Song of Songs*.

---

recastings which—despite the remote possibility of occasional technical improvements—take no account of society's gradual secularization over time and its concurrent loss of the sense of the sacred. For instance, the dignity of the King James' "thou" and "thee" account better for man as a divine creation than the prosaic "you" of the so-called "up-to-date" versions.

63. It is no mere coincidence that references to demonic possibilities frequently mention a terrifying babble of sounds accompanying them: "Thy name is legion."

64. Koran: "God makes firm those who believe by the firm Word" (*Sura Ibrahim*, 27).

From a certain point of view, it is possible to see everything in terms of speech—according to the notion of the *Logos Spermatikos* of the Stoics, for instance—because speech is in its essence noetic rhythm, and this is the texture of reality.[65] If God speaks in light then, by analogy, the sky utters the sun and the sun in turn spells nature[66] which, symbolically, recapitulates, in its own mode, all of manifestation, both the heavenly and the earthly *Maya*, as well as the infernal one. Language, together with his upright stance, is what distinguishes man from the entire animal kingdom, because it is the tool of his intelligence which is fashioned to know Truth. Without language, man is no longer human. And, conversely, he is human only to the degree that his language is adequate to the realization of his theomorphic essence. If it is true that, as a Zen master phrased it, "You need only open your mouth and you already succumb to ten thousand delusions," then it is just as true to add that by substituting the Name of the One for the many, one can overturn the tyranny of multiplicity's hold on the soul or convert its dissociative impetus.[67] It is important to understand here how language is par excellence the vehicle of intellective (and intellectual) communion and remembrance; and all communion—as also remembrance—involves, finally, a fundamental act of transubstantiation, whether for good or for evil.

---

65. "Utterance (*vak*) brought forth all the Universe. He (*Prajapati*) pronounced '*Bhu*' (Earth) and the Earth was born" (*Satapatha-Brahmana*). Likewise, the Vedas are considered to be antecedent to creation because they contain these primogenitive, eternal syllables whence the gods and the rest of created beings and things issued.

66. "The monogrammatic syllable 'Om'," says Ananda Coomaraswamy, "is the totality of all sounds and the music of the spheres chanted by the resonant sun" (*Hinduism and Buddhism*).

67. As Schuon explains it, "the invocation is a determining response to the discourse of the world which wants to determine us."

212

If a man feels that he is nothing, that he is consumed by fruitless preoccupations, may he find consolation in the fact that God is something. And may he find further solace in the fact that he can know this with absolute certitude. That he can know this through the Name of God, which carries the divine presence Itself. And that in pronouncing it[68] he can not be nothing because this Name is the symbol of Reality, of all that is, and of all that he is in his immortal consciousness reflected intellectually in his mind and intellectively in his heart.

---

68. Within the proper ritual and initiatic context, of course, barring which the soul becomes its own master and, therefore, its own slave.

5. ON DIVINE NESCIENCE

*And it repented the Lord that he had made man
on the earth.*

Gen. 6:6

A MORAL DILEMMA that is of some psychological consequence for man is the notion of God's omniscience, the
idea that God knows everything, even that which, from
man's empirical standpoint, has not yet happened. Defined
in this fundamentalist sense, divine omniscience would
seem to rob man of his free will, for what freedom is there
in a choice that proves to be merely the actualization of a
pre-determined course?

As we shall explore, the theological impasse entailed in
this approach results from a tendency in monotheistic religions to overemphasize the metaphysical notion of the
Absolute at the "expense" of that of the Infinite,[1] whence
their number of apparently antinomical formulations.

To illustrate the possible paradoxes attendant on this
emphasis, we shall refer extensively to one central example
taken from the Old Testament. The passage wherein God
comes to the prophet Samuel declaring: "It repenteth me
that I have set up Saul to be king . . ." (I Sam. 15:11) would

---

1. A necessary emphasis, perhaps, in the *Kali Yuga* where man's passional individualism does not predispose him to perceive what Schuon
called the "metaphysical transparency" of phenomena.

214

seem to contradict the principle of divine omniscience. The reader may indeed wonder how God did not foresee the future transgressions of a Saul when He anointed him to be the first king of Israel, blessed him, and entrusted him with the guardianship of his Chosen People: "And Samuel said to all the people, See ye him whom the Lord hath chosen, that there is none like him among the people?" (I Sam. 10:24)

Later, Samuel is charged to inform Saul that "the Lord hath rejected thee from being king over Israel" (I Sam. 15:26). And: "The Lord hath rent the kingdom of Israel from thee this day, and hath given it to a neighbour of thine, that is better than thou" (I Sam. 15:28). These, and other such formulations in the Bible, introduce the idea of a God who appears to be ignorant both of the quality of His elect and of the possible consequences of His decisions. One could object that such statements merely reflect the Bible's anthropomorphic style of dialectics. Yet, although undeniably true, such an objection does not really address the question, for we have in Saul the instance of a man who is solemnly invested with divine grace only to be later divested of this grace. These two incontrovertible facts are not subject to dialectical interpretation. Therefore, unless one concludes that God is capricious, impulsive, or fallibly human in any of a myriad ways[2] —in which case the idea of God loses all cogency of meaning—one is left to consider only the impossible notion of a divine "mistake".[3]

---

2. As depicted, for instance in the poetic conceits of a Homer (for which he was reproached by a Plato) or in the humanized drama of the Icelandic *Eddas*—although even these characterizations have symbolic justification, however perilous this may be for their exegesis by mere mortals.

3. Strictly speaking, of course, a mistake cannot be divine in any way; that would be an absolute contradiction in terms. However, if one agrees that God's creation cannot be perfect—or perfect to the same degree its Creator is—then the idea of a "mistake" is merely synonymous for the idea of imperfection, or of "lesser perfection."

In this light, it is logically difficult to reconcile the above statements with the latter affirmation where God tells Samuel that "the Lord seeth not as man seeth; for man looketh on the outward appearance, but the Lord looketh on the heart" (I Sam. 16:7), a statement that restores the notion of divine omniscience. The Bible, and sacred scripture in general, abounds with other such seemingly contradictory ellipses[4] where the purpose is to enunciate different and often mutually exclusive truths which no single statement can adequately summarize given the fathomless complexity of the divine mystery, on the one hand, and, on the other, the limitations inherent to creation.[5]

However, the issue that concerns us here is the seeming fallibility of God and, consequently, that also of his Prophet, Samuel, whose authority rests on his certitude in spiritual matters. How could an omniscient God be so grievously mistaken about the chosen vessel of His grace, especially in the light of His claim to see into the hearts of

---

4. Cf. in the Koran (*Sura* "The Daybreak"): "Say: I seek refuge in the Lord of the Daybreak / *From the evil of that which He hath created*" [italics ours], an audacious ellipsis that abruptly attempts to preserve the notion of divine omnipotence. (The synthetic pithiness of the original Arabic does not come across in English.) Similarly, when the Bible states in the case of Saul that "an evil spirit from the Lord troubled him" (I Sam. 16:14), it is referring to the All-Encompassing nature of God, a notion which, by implying that nothing can take place outside of God, seeks to further emphasize man's complete dependence on Him.

5. Contraries which in God are harmonious (*diversa sed non adversa*), and therefore are not contraries, become antagonistic in creation, or at least, in the latter cycles of a creation when form becomes increasingly hardened and thereby negates—or excludes—substance as well as negating other forms. Thus the complements of heat and cold, which in God's intellective essence work prototypically as love and intelligence, or as life and purity, battle on earth as fire and ice. Likewise, one can imagine an archetype for winter in paradise, but it would be one in which creatures are not subject to freezing and one in which the possibility of purity is manifested without its correlative harshness.

216

His servants? And what faith then can Israel have in His choice of Prophet whose duty it is to represent God's will to the people? This paradox is resolvable only if a distinction in rank (hypostasis) be made between God as Godhead and God as Creator.[6] In other words, to borrow from the Vedanta, Ishvara cannot participate fully in the omniscience inherent to Brahma alone since to create is first to separate and thus to differentiate. And differentiation involves an element of cosmic ignorance in that separate levels of reality or separate components of manifestation can only exist on the basis of a degree of reciprocal "ignorance"—or unawareness—of each other without which they would be indistinguishably fused.[7] In this sense, creation proceeds as a kind of destitution in view of an ultimate restitution[8] in which God provisorily forfeits, as it were, a part of Himself. Since all of this *Maya* takes place *in divinis*, the "forfeiting" is not an intrinsic loss or diminishment. Nonetheless, on its own relative plane, that of human existence, it is effectively such. Expressed differently, one could say that perfect omniscience (a necessary tautology if one is to account for gradations in divine knowledge) can only coincide with perfect freedom. But it is precisely this freedom that is limited on the plane of manifestation, as we shall try to explain.

If one can avoid the risks of sophistry as well as that of irreverence, one could formulate it differently by saying

---

6. In Vedantic terms, between God as Brahma and God as Ishvara, which distinction on the level of transcendent reality becomes *mutatis mutandis* on the plane of manifestation that, to speak in Christian terms, between God the Father and God the Son.

7. The whole passionate drama between lover and beloved, depicted in mystical literature the world over, originates from this mystery.

8. Microcosmically, salvation and, especially, realization; macrocosmically, apocatastasis.

figuratively that God in creating man forgets part of Himself,[9] just as in giving him freedom He thereby forfeits—through transference—some of His own freedom. In other words, if God is initially free to make a gift of His freedom and, in so doing, freely renounces it, He is no longer free subsequently to abrogate—on its plane—the very nature of this gift. In this sense, it is not improper to say that God willingly deprives Himself of His unqualified freedom[10] and thereby also, in some relative measure of His omnipotence, all the more so as it is by virtue of His very omnipotence that He is able to limit Himself in some way and to some degree. Or one could say, without attempting to exhaust the near inexpressible, that part of God's unlimited omnipotence (another necessary tautology, this time to account for gradations in divine power) entails the possibility of *self*-limiting Himself, however temporarily, barring which He would not be perfectly omnipotent; the freedom lies in the prefix only, not in the verb. Thus if God, on the one hand, can be seen to be totally free to create *what* He wills and *as* He wills, He is conversely not free to undo—not at the outset, at any rate[11] —

9. Or, as the merry Hindu saint Swami Ramdas put it quaintly: "Man is, in fact, God playing the fool."

10. Cf. the distinction in the Vedanta between *Brahma saguna* and *Brahma nirguna*—qualified and unqualified Godhead, or God with attributes and God without attributes, or between God as Being and God as Beyond-Being or Supreme (Non)-Self. Any level of Godhead is, with respect to creation, absolute and therefore the Absolute as such. But with respect to Himself, there is a hierarchy of levels whereby God can be relatively absolute.

11. God remains of course always free to annul a given possibility—normally by resorption of the lesser by the greater—but never the possibility as such (the Platonic *eidos*, the doctrine of the universals) since it remains a necessary part of His totality, be it only *in potentia*. In other words, He remains unconditionally free to interrupt a given modality—what could just as well be or not be—but He cannot destroy the possi-

what He Himself has freely consented to. He is in effect "bound"[12] to His own freely chosen determinations because, although He is Infinite, He is also Absolute, therefore beholden to the ontological chain of causality necessary to a given possibility lest it never be actualized.[13]

Thus it is the interplay between these two dimensions—that of the Infinite and that of the Absolute, because God's nature is made up of equal parts of freedom and necessity—that lies at the heart of the biblical paradoxes alluded to above. To speak simplistically but nonetheless adequately, God the Creator (Ishvara) surrenders part of His prerogatives when creating His creatures, allowing some form of separation and thereby of nescience—of veiling, or opacity, or even of darkness[14]—to intervene without which the created possibility could never become actualized in its creaturely (heart-mind-object) distinctness, for to know fully *in*

---

the possibility of the possibility without denying Himself, otherwise Totality could not be ascribed to Him. It is God's very illimitation or completeness that "compels" Him to "allow" a possibility to exist. And, of course, we have in mind only positive possibilities, the negative ones being deformations and not integral possibilities in their own right.

12. As this issue is discussed, one is mindful that one does so with a human—all too human—terminology.

13. In a parallel sense, Ananda Coomaraswamy writes, "He is the bird caught in the net, the Ram caught in the thicket, the sacrificial Victim and our Savior, he cannot save *us* except and unless we, by the sacrifice and denial of our self, also save *Him*" ("On the One and Only Transmigrant"). What is clear is that, even though God as "sacrificial victim" is no longer God as such—Brahma, Ishavara, Purusha, Avatara: each is hypostatically different—there is a reciprocity between cause and effect, or Creator and creature, in which the creature mirrors—via the *buddhi* or the universal intellect—something of the nature of the *primum mobile*. This is the meaning of Attar's poem cited at the end of the Chapter on Suffering.

14. In this sense, colors could be said to be shades of darkness in regard to pure light—wherefore Niffari's cry: "I take refuge in the unity of Thy quality against every quality."

divinis is really to become re-absorbed into holy oneness and thus, for the possibility, to become extinguished in undifferentiated totality, whereas to "forget" and thereby to "ignore" is to allow a potentiality the "breathing room" in which to take exclusive form. For God, to create is first to know—actualization—but then also to forget—projection—and finally to remember—redemption.

In this sense, returning to the story of Saul, the dramatic denouement of this king's destiny and the concurrent rise of David could not have taken place had God and his delegate Prophet, Samuel, "known" ahead of time what, on the plane of manifestation, is by definition materially unknowable beforehand, for the dimension of what we have termed "divine nescience" in manifestation is, to repeat, the necessary vital space conceded to a possibility in view of its complete actualization, which is *ipso facto* also an estrangement,[15] the necessary latitude in which its potential constituents can be freely exercised and played out. To foresee, then, on this plane is tantamount to aborting, at least as far as specific possibilities are concerned and, in general, to prevention as far as the creative act itself is concerned.

What God knows immanently and synthetically by essence in the total simultaneity of timeless space He does not know by created actuality. What He knows in Eternity He does not know in time, for on this secondary plane knowledge is bound to the constraints inherent to temporal categories, full knowledge coinciding then only with the temporal fulfillment of the possibility in the sense that its culmination is God's knowledge of it.[16] To formulate

---

15. There is in material actualization an inescapable element of divorce or of estrangement.

16. Ananda Coomaraswamy: "The omnipresent omniscient is 'the only transmigrant,' and that in the last analysis this 'transmigration' is nothing but his knowledge of himself expressed in terms of a duration" (*Op. Cit.*, note # 5).

this in other terms, one could say that God knows in undifferentiated synthesis what He ignores—and must ignore—*a priori* in differentiated analysis.[17] Thus God's "repenting" of having chosen Saul is merely a biblical way of defining God's knowing in time[18] as opposed to His knowing for all of time as the latter passage, in which He declares He knows the heart of His servants, expresses symbolically. And the "repentance" itself is merely an allegorical way of explaining the ultimate prevailing of the Absolute over the relative, or of the Substance's inevitable resorption of the accidents issued from it, which repentance / resorption may operate through wrath, destruction, and purification or, as in the case of Saul, merely through a withdrawal of grace. Again, Saul's self-destruction ultimately coincides with God's knowledge of his heart, which knowledge could be said to begin—or to be operatively effective—on the temporal plane, already with the withdrawal of His favor from him.

Hence, we are in effect dealing with two types of divine knowledge, one immediate and fundamental in view of which God allows Saul to be Saul, at once in the simultaneity of his possibility's total substance glorious and ignominious—the latter aspect being abetted by the former, if one wishes, in the sense of *corruptio optimi pessima* and therefore only fully actualizable in the wake of the for-

---

17. See for this Schuon: "The cyclical process of that being is the sum of the aspects of his manifestation and therefore of his possibility, and that the being, through the exercise of his will, merely manifests in deferred mode his simultaneous cosmic manifestation; in other words, the individual retraces in an analytic way his synthetic and primordial possibility" (*The Transcendent Unity of Religions*, Ch. "Transcendence and Universality of Esoterism").

18. One might also say that God's knowledge in time—or in creation—is sequential as opposed to the instantaneity of His knowledge in eternity.

mer—and another type of knowledge which is sequential in that God first exalts Saul before humbling him. This particularly complex reality brings us to the limits of what can be formulated, it seems to us, in human language—whence the biblical ambiguities and seeming contradictions. However, the key, as we see it, lies in understanding the dimensions of space and time in manifestation which themselves are the reflections of divine prototypes,[19] namely of dimensions in God which, insofar as they can be differentiated, operate according to different and, on the formal plane of creation,[20] mutually exclusive laws, as we have had occasion to point out.

On another level, the biblical phrase wherein God is said to "repent" upon beholding the iniquity of Saul, is the monotheistic way of accounting for the absence of direct causality[21] between the divine and the empirical orders of manifestation which share no symmetrically equatable consubstantiality, either material or "psychological".[22] In

---

19. Space refers more generally to the Infinite and time to the Absolute, although not exclusively so, since the oneness of space can also be said to refer to the Absolute whereas the endlessness of time, and the variety it promotes, refers in its way to the Infinite. But these *yin-yang* nuances would require a lengthy exposition that would lead us too far afield.

20. Although the terms manifestation and creation are often used interchangeably, we use creation in a more separative sense to include all the non-heavenly dimensions of manifestation. And it is on this plane that laws, which on the heavenly plane are melodiously complementary, can become conflictual—e.g. birth and death, both of which, in actuality, foster life.

21. The *creatio ex nihilo* of the theologians.

22. The term "animic" might be preferable to "psychological" were its connotation of primitivism not so prevalent in the modern outlook. The Bible, however, also accounts for the consubstantiality, this time, of *essence* between the two orders when it says in Genesis that "God created man in his own image." At the risk of splitting hairs, we say consubstantiality of *essence* but not of *substance* contrarily to the way pantheism

other words, in keeping with the central biblical premise of a personal God, His seeming "ignorance' is an anthropomorphic mode of expressing the idea of the incommensurability between the two realms.

A further connotation of what we have, from a phenomenological point of view, described as a "divine ignorance" is the idea of God's detachment from His creation, not in the sense of the Deist's indifferent clockmaker divinity who, once he has mechanically assembled the world, leaves it to "tick away" without intervening until its time is run out, but more in the sense of Aristotle's "motionless mover" or in that of the recumbent Shiva. This divine dimension which, in regard to creation, could be characterized as a noble aloofness, wholly sufficient unto itself, impassive with regard to the petty happenings of the world, springs from the majesty of the Absolute. This aspect of the personal God, finding as it does beatific rest in plenitude, is at an ineffable remove from the vicissitudes and chance concerns of earthly creatures whose febrile agitation is premised on the ignorance of their heavenly substance.[23] Or, in metaphysical terms, one might say that this divine remoteness mirrors that of the Infinite from the finite—or of Eternity from time—even though the latter is encompassed by the former.

---

would have it, at least insofar as it becomes a misguided immanentism (instead of—and properly so—a doctrine of theophany) which, by not allowing any real scope for the transcendent ends up, practically speaking, reducing God to a material (or semi-material) order of causality while, parallely, deifying nature—a concept that is anathema to monotheism.

23. In man, dignity of composure and of speech mirrors the wholeness of God. Animals, for their part, especially if they are beautiful, possess this dignity naturally.

THE BIBLE PROCLAIMS the apparent gratuitousness of God's preferences,[24] the seeming inconsequentiality of His favor's bestowal, which can be granted and withdrawn on a whim as it might seem. Again, one is dealing with the typical, almost *koan*-like, ellipses of monotheistic dialectics which, to preserve the idea of God's freedom and omnipotence, do not allow Him ever to appear either bound by His choices or helpless to amend them. However, this anthropomorphic mode of explaining the raising and abasing of His servants implicitly suggests a reality that is deeper than mere arbitrary preference. Notwithstanding the fact that all maintenance of God's grace entails man's scrupulous fidelity to His will[25]—which proviso implies a vast measure of free will on the part of man and, therefore, a corresponding measure of unawareness from the part of God on the plane described earlier—one must bear in mind the impersonal nature of this grace which, like the Spirit "that bloweth where it listeth," is free to come and free to depart.

Yet this grace's freedom, lest it be purely fortuitous and therefore absurd, is drawn to pour itself into a receptacle that is worthy of its nature, namely one that corresponds to its essence in some way. This worthiness is less a question of moral merit (though this is a factor) than an affinity in the sense of like attracting like. It is therefore enough for a substance to have a quality of light—or rather of translucence—for the light to shine through it, if one may speak in metaphors. However, this predisposition constitutes in itself neither a guarantee, nor a predictor of future intrinsic worthiness. To say, as the Bible does,

---

24. The stories, for instance, of Cain and Abel or of Esau and Jacob.

25. In God His will is the same as His nature: being the good, He cannot will anything but what is good. In man, the ambiguity or possible arbitrariness of the will results from the mixture in human nature.

that God's favor was upon Saul[26] is to say that upon his consecration he had the kind of qualities of nature that eminently suited him at that given moment for divine election. And to say that God withdrew His favor from him only to bestow it on David, is another way of saying that nature abhors a vacuum. From another point of view, one could say that Saul's substance is that of a kingly archetype. Thus, in electing him king, God is referring to the substance. At the same time, Saul has an ego—or what with respect to the substance is the accident—which might or might not be in conformity with this substance. Insofar as Saul as accident usurps the prerogatives belonging to Saul as substance, he forfeits the rights of his royal archetype. Therefore in rejecting him, God is referring to the accident. He does not contradict himself because the substance remains what it is in spite of the accident's renegade choice.[27] There is contradiction, if one wills, on the plane of facts, not on that of principles.[28]

---

26. For instance, "For God is with thee" (I Sam. 10:7).

27. The author mentioned the subject of this article to Frithjof Schuon who made the following comments: "To say that 'God repents of' indicates simply a difference—or a change—of planes or of perspective. The Bible does not use metaphysics; it speaks in a language that is strictly human. The divine Intellect, unquestionably, is aware of the opposition between substantiality and accidentality, and this awareness intervenes on the plane of facts. In short, God's 'regret' can mean either that such and such an aspect of substance has played its part or, on the contrary, that such and such an aspect of contingency has done so."

28. This is same as the story of Adam's fall. Though he was created perfect, he had the possibility of wandering and of becoming estranged from his origin. One might ask, would God have created Adam had He known that Adam would fall, or one might ask did God create Adam knowing that he would fall, or why did He create him if He knew that he would fall? If He knew that Adam would fall, then why would He create him? Is this not to condemn someone to suffering, and therefore to do someone wrong? This tangle of questions is typical of a moralistic perspective that cannot see things except from the outside or

In its ebb and flow, grace—just as light or water, ana-logically speaking—can shine or flow wherever there is no obstruction, for the nature of all benefic things is to propa-gate themselves through bountiful effluence where there is a receptacle. Yet its very outpouring can—most paradoxi-cally, perhaps—produce in its wake obstacles by way of a counter-reaction[29] given the intertwining of positives and negatives that constitute the nature of all created things; premature grace can be poison for the untried soul. Moreover, if, on the one hand, the bestowal of grace can be seen as a form of divine election—which it is, all things being equal—it must be seen, on the other hand, also as a promise (not a prediction), as a summons the fulfillment of which lies ultimately in the recipient's power to avail himself.

THIS COMMENT BRINGS us finally to a subsidiary considera-tion in the story of Saul, that of the prophetic credibility of Samuel for, in giving Saul to Israel, he could in retrospect be regarded as having failed his people. Indeed, the very idea of the prophetic nature precludes that of ignorance, precisely; his decisions are meant to serve as the expres-sion of God's own wishes. Does not the Bible declare: "And Samuel said unto all Israel, Behold, I have hear-

---

from the point of view of conflicting levels of reality and which cannot formulate truth except in "either/or" alternatives that can become almost numbingly legalistic or grossly psychological. In creating Adam, God grants him freedom and this freedom—which is meant to choose the good—can be misused to choose what is harmful. The purpose of the gift, from God's "point of view" is to share the good, not the wrong. If the price of the gift is the possibility of evil, that is in no wise its justifi-cation, to say the least.

29. In the way of St. Paul's admonition in reference to the taking of the hosts: "For he that eateth and drinketh unworthily, eateth and drin-keth damnation to himself, not discerning the Lord's body" (I Cor. 11:29).

kened unto your voice in all that ye said unto me, and have made a king over you?" (I Sam. 10:7). But then, in view of Saul's subsequent alienation, could not Israel wonder about Samuel's prophetic qualification? How could he be so grievously wrong as to anoint, in God's holy name, a false king?

Upon reflection, however, the central issue is less Samuel's apparent fallibility than the question of what constitutes the natural limits of prophetic insight for, like all men, a prophet too is bound to judge and decide through the discursivity of time. The providence of his decisions— even those directly God-inspired[30]—lies in their cosmic appropriateness within a given sector of time and a given set of circumstances in view of an outcome that is necessarily imponderable at the outset lest it never be allowed to materialize. In other words, men cannot demand more of a prophet than that he be an instrument of God's will, as well as its interpreter, namely to serve as the most disinterested—that is, objective—intermediary between a cosmic possibility and its fulfillment, be it blessed or, as the case may be, accursed.

Although this ambiguity in the possible results may seem like a contradictory relativization of the prophet's whole raison d'être, what matters is to understand that the prophet's insight is infallible in terms of the moral requirements—not the factual or material ones except insofar as logic can ascertain these—of each moment, not of ultimate outcomes which, given each possibility's freedom, he cannot foresee[31] in that

---

30. Not all of a prophet's pronouncement can be taken as *ex cathedra*, namely as infallible.

31. Except in certain cases, through intuition, but not as a systematic matter of course. A prophet's function—and, in his sphere, a spiritual master's—is not to predict the future in the way of a diviner, but to serve as both a vehicle and a witness to the truth, and, soteriologically, as a psychopomp. Samuel is absolved from any so-called "responsibility" (in

he is bound by the same cosmological restrictions that limit God *qua* Creator; and this entails the impossibility of literally knowing in advance the full play of a possibility's potential modalities without thereby canceling them in the bud. It would therefore be absurd[32] to hold Samuel accountable on a plane where not even God—as Creator—can be held "responsible." The prophet's indefectibility is to be found on the moral plane of his will, which is perfectly non-selfish, as well as on the level of his doctrine, of his spiritual knowledge, not on the level of his temporal knowledge.[33]

And lastly, the "absoluteness" with which Samuel anoints Saul is necessary to set the process—whether ultimately providential or fateful—into motion. It is inconceivable to imagine Samuel anointing Saul with reservations or conditionally in view of the conviction of a future possibility

---

the Catholic sense of a sin of omission—which covers the reproach of a culpable ignorance) for Saul's conduct in that he reproves him. One could say that the anointing and the reproving mark the two boundaries of his spiritual function, the aspects of mercy and of justice. The rest belongs to *Maya*. In no way whatsoever does Saul's fate redound to Samuel's discredit, just as the possibility of evil in creation does not compromise the excellence of the Creator.

32. And a mark of one's own spiritual irresponsibility. Why? Because there is an element of revolt in the soul which awaits the pretext of a spiritual guide's apparent fallibility to shift the responsibility away from itself and to blame him for problems that occur.

33. One will want to add the possibility of a spiritual guide's qualification to speak *ex cathedra* ("from the chair"), namely from the "pulpit" of his God-given function, in which case he is considered infallible—though, the Catholics will specify that only the pope has this infallibility, not the priests. The foundation for this lies in the fact that a human being can be the vessel of divine knowledge. Thus, in John 16:13 one finds: "When . . . the Spirit of truth is come, he will guide you into all truth: for he shall not speak of himself; but whatsoever he shall hear, that shall he speak: and he will shew you things to come."

of transgression,[34] just as God does not create man suppos-
ing his fall. The election is either absolute or it is nothing.[35]
Just as Saul was to be an instrument in the hands of divine
providence, so was Samuel—and so is any man called to
fulfill a possibility, be it that of eventual self-contradiction.
But, in spite of its potential for self-contradiction, a possibility may still serve a positive purpose within a larger
whole;[36] and it is precisely this positiveness of destiny that
corresponds to the positiveness (or absoluteness) of decision—in this case, that of Samuel's anointing of Saul—necessary to its inception. The fulfillment, seen in time, is a
process of discovery. Seen from Eternity, it is a confirmation
of a possibility that could not not be.

To recapitulate, the "divine ignorance" alluded to can
be seen as the intellective counterpart of a possibility's
room for deployment, full knowledge[37] in this instance

---

34. Were the prophet—spiritual master—to sense the outcome of a
situation, he still might have to go along with the *comédie* 1. For the
chance that the fated individual might still amend his ways and 2.
Because of the nature of the play which requires the possibility of betrayal for the plot's fulfillment.

35. Thus Samuel to Saul: "for now would the Lord have established
thy kingdom upon Israel for ever. But now thy kingdom shall not continue" (I Sam. 13:13-4), a passage which reveals the completeness of the
election.

36. For instance , the metaphysical necessity of evil which, ultimately, conspires to work for the victory of the good. Moreover, God can
use a crooked instrument to draw a straight line. Saul's kingship
strengthened Israel militarily and thus paved the way for the future
glory of David and Solomon.

37. A necessary nuance since, with God, we are dealing really with
degrees of knowledge rather than with ignorance as such (the *avidya* of
the Vedanta), but which degrees entail, practically speaking, that the
lesser levels amount to a kind of ignorance when contrasted with the
plenitude of the higher levels. God as *Ishvara* or Creator does not know
all that God as *Atma* or Beyond-Being knows. And, *mutatis mutandis*,
Christ as Jesus does not know what his Father knows, though, as Christ,

amounting to the abolition of its distinctiveness as a unique—and therefore separate—entity. If everything is *Atma*, if *Samsara* is really *Nirvana*, now and forever and totally and literally so, then there would be no creation and no *Samsara*, no subject, no witness, no words, no book. To repeat, if a possibility were perfectly—or, in other terms, exhaustively—knowable in advance, and in all of its details, then it would be deprived of its freedom, hence of its life.

THERE IS ONE more dimension of this question of "divine nescience" that deserves mention, because it is a perspective which works from the very opposite of the premise of this Chapter. God in Himself, as Voidness the Buddhists would say, or as He is in Himself before the creation, the Christians would say, does not know Himself because there is no self-consciousness in the sense of a division between a subject and an object. Thus for Erigena, creation is the act by which God comes to know Himself. And man, being the synthesis of creation, and the one creature capable of knowing the truth consciously, is the instrument by which God comes to know Himself. The Word as *sapientia creatrix* or creative fountainhead produces the *sapientia creata* which is the perfection of creation as summarized by Edenic humanity which was a race of prophets, namely a race in which each man and woman carried the Law (*dharma*) within their heart and was thus a repository of God's wisdom and active communication. The notion of a collectivity of saints may strike men of today as an impossible

---

he is the incarnation of divine wisdom or the Word made flesh. The fact that there is a difference between these hypostases within the one divine being authorizes us to speak about them without thereby incurring the wrath of the religionists who consider it blasphemous to suggest that acknowledging differences in the Godhead is tantamount to assigning some kind of limitations to God. Yet, to describe is to circumscribe.

ideal; however, it is the norm if one understands that the Fall is really an accident and therefore something occurring at the historical periphery of creation and not at its center and something that is unimaginably short in duration when compared to the measureless immensity of the heavenly circles of manifestation.

But to return to the idea of divine nescience as formulated by Erigena, the idea that God is self-ignorant in Himself, or in the peace of his totality (*aseitas*) hinges on the definition of knowledge primarily as a mind-instructed perception of a "what" and a "that," when knowledge can also be a being—the divine inwardness illustrated by the image of the meditating Buddha, eyes closed and blissful countenance—in which duality, while not extinguished, is appeased and reconciled in unity. Or one in which duality is but a potentiality, still blissfully submerged in the sense of oneness. In this case, it would be more appropriate to speak of an ineffable knowledge and not of an ignorance, or of an unconsciousness or unawareness. Yes, if one follows the meaning of the classic image of Vishnu resting while, as the Lord of Sleep, he dreams the universe, yes God might be said then to be unaware of differentiation at the profoundest level of His being, in which all contraries are beatifically reabsorbed. And such an "unawareness" could be said to be—in apophatic terms—a kind of "ignorance." This is the stillness of the essence which is neither augmented or diminished by the creation of the world. However, this unawareness is not unconsciousness in its sense of limitation otherwise there would be no Being. God is *Sat-Chit-Ananda*—Being-Consciousness-Bliss: this triadic definition of the Godhead found in the Vedanta summarizes the indissociability of being and knowledge, whose conjugation produces *ananda* or bliss.

6. THE CROOK AND THE FLAIL

The sultan is the shadow of God on earth.

Turkish Saying

TRUTH HAS A divine face and a human face, or one that looks towards the eternal and on that looks towards time. When the Pharaoh, or the god-man-king, ascended his throne, like the sun rising to its noon-hour pinnacle, he held in his right hand the shepherd's crook and in his left hand the wheat-thrasher's flail—the emblems shown in the depictions of the sovereign god, Amun, whose son the Pharaoh was held to be.

These two instruments were representative of the two necessary attributes of kingship, wisdom or mercy and discrimination or justice,[1] and are seen again in the medieval emblems of the rod of equity and the scepter of power;[2] indeed, equivalents of these are to be found wherever monarchy has existed. And in turn, the attributes these twin emblems symbolize are the reflection each, on the microcosmic plane, of the intellect's polarization into

---

1. To carry on with the metaphor, the sun's rays have both a vivifying warmth and a purifying fieriness.

2. Or it is the orb, surmounted by the cross, held in the right hand and the scepter which is held in the left.

heart and mind, or contemplation and discernment[3] or, by practical extension, action. Now, what are contemplation and action—or wisdom and will—if not the two defining qualities of man and therefore the raison d'être of his existence? In this respect, the figure of the monarch, as validated by the twin emblems of his function, finds its universal justification in the fact that he is meant first of all to embody archetypal man and in so doing, or insofar as he does not betray his vocational duty, to serve as a model for all men.[4]

Of these two attributes, the second, namely will or power, has no scope of its own if sundered from the first, namely intelligence, because will is not free unless guided by consciousness without which it becomes little more than a force of blind instinct or brute power. Thus finally, knowledge, more and above all other attributes, is the cornerstone of authority because the essence of knowledge is certainty or truth, which quality guarantees infallibility. And it is this quality of infallibility—as reflected, if not in the royal agent, at least in the perennial permanence of the kingly function that transcends the factionalism of opinion—which lies at the very heart of the respect granted sovereigns.

Remove knowledge, and authority—inasmuch as it still exists—sooner or later veers inexorably to tyranny because it becomes a matter of might instead of insight. This is not to say, however, that might is not without right, at least insofar as might can accrue from moral superiority or

---

3. Students of symbolism will observe that the crook's rounded top is equatable with union and goodness as that of the flail's right-angled shaft, which sifts the wheat from the chaff, is equatable with separation, severity, and, by abstraction, analysis.

4. "Though royalty hath no superior," the poet Andrew Darklake writes, "It is for this an exemplar / That few, if none, can mirror / But all must emulate far." ("Primeval Matins" in *Twilights*)

simply from natural excellence.[5] In other words, a ruler need not be a sage to be effective, for the rightness of the function itself, rendered operative through proper ritual consecration, in which the powers of heaven are invoked, has a transfigurative genius of its own that can inspire its possessor and so guide him according to the eternal nature of things.[6] But if a ruler need not be a sage *de facto*, he needs must be just if he is not to forfeit the very foundation of his prerogatives, for justice in temporal matters is a form of objectivity that protects against the indulgence of arbitrary preferences or, according to a remark of Alexis de Tocqueville, against "individual and collective egoisms" which, by definition, can only be satisfied at the expense of other people's legitimate needs.

As with everything, authority has its prototype and this prototype is God Who, as Creator, assumed kingship—all non-modern civilizations aver—over His creation from the very beginning.[7] And, in turn, this cosmic kingship is

---

5. Sometimes kingship was granted to the winner in a footrace. However, the function was buttressed by a whole traditional and ritual context that made the victory surely not just an issue of brawn and fleetness, but also one of providence—of "Godspeed" from the goddess. But, more to the point, might is one of the attributes of divine majesty. Thus to the king is given the rod of might, symbol of his sovereign power. In India, Manu and the lawgivers declared that the whole world was governed by the *danda* (the rod) which enjoins holy dread: Agni burns through fear, Surya sends forth his beam through fear; through fear Vayu blows, Mrityu slays, and the stars stay in their courses. And among the precepts of the Mahabharata, we find one which states: "Right leans on might (*danda*) as a creeper on a tree. As smoke follows the wind, so right follows might." Without *danda*, men lose all fear and are tempted to behave heedlessly.

6. In anatomical terms, that the head in man stands cleanly above the shoulders and the rest of the body is not a vagary of blind nature, but has its teleological point.

7. As we shall see, the idea of kingship is inconceivable without that of godship.

234

reflected by divine delegation in the role of the earthly monarch[8] who, notably in the immemorial traditions of Egypt and China (to cite but these two civilizations), is the inheritor of a lineage that blends at the origin with that of the very gods themselves.[9] For those who understand that man is born not of matter but of the spirit, such exalted ancestry will not seem preposterous,[10] despite the near-unfathomable remotion from first principle which characterizes our present-day civilization, a remotion which carries as an effect a real difficulty in remembering how things were "once upon a time," that is to say once and forever according to an eternal archetype.[11]

At the origin, the prototype of the monarch combined the twin perfections of priestly wisdom and secular might such as in the figure of the Pharaoh, who was considered to be a god-man, or a god descended among men. However, history shows that these twin functions became polarized

---

8. Man, according to the Koran and Sufi tradition is *khalifat fil-'ard*, or delegate caliph on earth, or vice-regent. Joan of Arc, addressing the future Charles VII, informed him that: "You will be the lieutenant of the King of the heavens who is King of France."

9. This, incidentally, is the cosmological foundation of ancestor worship which, leaving aside its anthropomorphic excesses, amounts to a reverence for the divine origin of manifestation.

10. Or a "myth" propounded the better to subjugate the credulous masses, as some modern social theorists advance, oblivious as they seem to be to their implicit counter-proposal which assumes that man—any man—is no less "godlike" than his rulers, because if one removes God, then it is man himself who, in the absence of any superior, becomes a *de facto* god, never mind how wretched. This is why all the talk about the "dignity of man," and of the "rights of man," of the Post-Conciliar Church, is so speciously misleading, because it is advocated in the absence of any real standards.

11. Are we to wonder then that, as alluded to earlier, the word "myth" connotes today not the idea of reality but of its opposite, namely fiction? However, as Kathleen Raine so aptly put it: "Fact is not the truth of myth; myth is the truth of fact."

according to the duality that differentiates the spiritual realm from the temporal order so that, in practice, one finds two distinct prototypes of sovereignty which are represented by the prophet or priest on the one hand, and the emperor or monarch on the other.[12] And, more generally, one finds individual prototypes respectively in the saint or the monk/hermit and in the hero/warrior—the nobility of the sword—who can arise from the midst of the commonest of men to assume inspirational roles outside of the official or time-honored lines of consecration.[13] Now, these twin prototypes are the legitimate pinnacles of reference for any authority: remove them, and men are subject to the rule of the blind leading the blind, whatever relative merits their leaders may otherwise possess. The fact that any individual, however menial his predestined station in life may be at the outset, can in principle rise to that level of moral excellence which entitles him to authority—at least

---

12. An argument could be made that the disintegration of civilization over time, to the extent that the secular has taken operative precedence over the spiritual, mirrors the gradual decoupling of these two functions. Thus regicide, as an institutionalized program, became possible only once monarchy had lost its sacerdotal aegis. It is entirely possible that Charles I of England, Louis XVI of France, and Nicholas II of Russia would never have been dethroned, and much less executed, had they not allowed courtly luxury to distort them into glorified puppets, and, above all, had they not allowed the mantle of royalty to eclipse their holy role as defender of the faith. Their otherwise decent and even exemplary character in certain crucial respects—which selected them as sacrificial lambs to the butchering fury of a Cromwell, a Robespierre, and a Lenin—could not offset this fatal weakness. And, of course, one cannot rule a people long when tolerating injustice.

13. Thanks to Confucius' emphasis on noble character, the term *Junzi*—which originally belonged only to hereditary rulers—broadened to include any man of proven virtue. Indeed, virtue—which is synonymous with nobility—is aristocratic by definition, and therefore establishes the only hierarchy that matters essentially, the only one that meets permanent favor in God's eyes.

in a normal civilization, one in which cosmic principles of hierarchy are still socially operative—can compensate whatever potential abuses may accrue from the autocratic concentration of power in the hands of the few. Even in a rigidly and often brutally stratified society such as the feudal order gives instances of, a strong individual could by deeds of arms or strength of prayer escape the possible tyranny of tutelary might and thus aerate, either by his prowess or by his grace, the oppressiveness of the power under which his fellow men might live. In a traditional society, recourse to God was always a viable means evident to everyman.

More generally, individuals normally cannot surpass themselves, and thus realize man's reason for being, if they do not have a model in the person of a saint to venerate, a king to admire, or a hero to emulate. The monarch embodies, in principle by virtue of his superior function if not in fact by virtue of his superior personality, a paragon of a man without which the masses are left to their own fumbling resources. Thus a social order that erects pluralism as a norm succumbs to the invariably demeaning laws of average, for men, when left to themselves, namely deprived of a redeemer or some archetypal model—a role the Old Testament prophets fulfilled—tend by reason of collective gravity to the lowest common denominator. And over time, this law of quantity crushes the very possibility of an elite all the more as it comes with a resentment towards superiority which is finally a self-inflicted death sentence because, when deprived of superior examples, a people will forget who they are, or should have been. Moreover, when moralism confuses the transcending of self with egotistic exclusivism or the oppression of the majority by the few, or when charity interprets "love thy neighbor" to mean "thou shalt be no better than thy neighbor," then society tends by that very fact to forgive what is least forgivable in man, for it excuses moral weakness instead of rewarding moral strength.

It is an established fact of history that a collectivity is only as good as its elite;[14] in other words, a society's worth is to be gauged by the quality of the best individuals it produces and honors.[15] By that token, a society such as the European Middle-Ages, which produced saints and sanctuaries by the hundreds, as well as the flowering of innumerable heroes and storied kingdoms as a matter of natural course—that is, with the effortless abundance of fruit-producing trees—could hardly be as dark as reported.[16]

---

14. In contradistinction to the assertion of a John Stuart Mill (who was one of the first political theorists to argue for universal suffrage) that "the worth of a state . . . is the worth of the individuals composing it" (*On Liberty*), which equation is nothing other than a banal law of averages that dignifies multitudes at the fatal expense of an elite.

15. It is an axiom of social studies that a society's human worth, as well as its collective tendency, can be directly assessed by the types of men it extols and rewards. This criterion affords us a measure whereby to evaluate our own modern society: all one needs ask is, what kind of man or woman is most popular or best remunerated today? Also, by way of ancillary consideration, it was Confucius who said that one could gage the morals of a society by its types of dances, which is revealing when one understands that dance is a direct expression of the heart.

16. Collective terms coined by progressivist historians such as "the Dark Ages" and, conversely (and by way of revenge one might be tempted to remark), "the Enlightenment", mask a whole philosophical program in which their professed objectivity is finally the lesser of their concerns: they are hatched by the modern conceit of a civilization that needs to justify (whether only unconsciously) the desecration of its religious heritage. Moreover, the barbarism imputed to a Genghis Khan, for instance, is a matter of debate, to say the least, for God can use men to scourge men. Be that as it may, it is noteworthy to recall that in the Khan's empire it was reputed that a virgin with a sack of gold could cross it from boundary to boundary and still be a *virgo intacta* at the end, and not dispossessed of a single coin. Who will dispute that morality or ethical grace—rather than material "progress"—is the ultimate measure of a civilization's civility?

The real question that needs to be asked, when establishing criteria by which a civilization may be judged, is: what is the justification for society—security, material well-being, secular power, or moral excellence and wisdom? While moral excellence need not exclude the aforementioned, within certain common-sensical bounds at least, it is certain that a society which places practical priority on any of the former to the disregard of moral virtue—which is the foundation of character—is doomed sooner or later to self-destruct, leaving aside the problem that it has certainly failed in its single most pressing duty, namely to offer its members an operative means to become integral human beings as created in the image of God.[17] And in this respect, all that matters finally is the end, for, in view of the eternity to come, a good death is more important than "the good life," immeasurably so. Unlike animals, who can "justify" their existence just by feeding and breeding, man cannot do so for long: he is defined by truth and by moral excellence. Diminish or banish them, and he is doomed.

No DESCRIPTION OF society is fully intelligible unless one understands what the microcosmic nature of man consists of. Thus, according to an ancient universal ternary, man

---

17. Sociologists may catalogue all of the real or presumed abuses found in pre-modern civilizations. But certain barbaric excesses notwithstanding, such as human sacrifices or the bloody orgies of animal sacrifices whose stench was an abomination to Jehovah (Isa. 1:1), they fail to see the essential, namely that in a traditional society it was impossible to be an atheist: the notions of God and of the Other World permeated everything, from the sights and sounds to the very air men breathed which was laden with what Muslims call *barakah*, or a benefic influence. So all was not lost: men still retained enough of a sense of basic vital proportions not to develop the plague of neuroses afflicting our "advanced" modern society whose combination of egocentrism and transference of moral responsibility to anyone except oneself has reached near psychotic extremes.

can be divided into three recognizably distinct parts: spirit, soul, and body. Or, one could speak respectively of heart, mind, and body—the mind, or mind-stuff, being not just the faculty of reason, but the whole psychic world of thoughts, feelings, and impressions[18] in general which partake both of the formlessness of the spirit realm and of the forms of the bodily realm, but through the common denominator of individual subjectivity.

Following this hierarchical scheme, the heart—as the immanent source of light—is purely active in reference to the mind and body. The mind in turn—as source of reflected light only—is passive in regard to the heart but active with reference to the body. Whereas the body—as congealed or deadened light—is purely passive in regard to both the heart and the mind; thus, it is doubly acted upon though, by rebound, it can act upon the former two faculties—on the heart by petrifying its conscience and on the mind by both dulling its alertness or clouding its receptivity while parallely feeding, absorbing, and ensnaring it in sensorial images that weigh it or suck it down gravitationally. This triad is symbolically recapitulated by the sun, moon, earth stellium, which gives us: a solar heart, a lunar

---

18. The artificial debate pitting rationalists (Descartes, Leibniz, Malebranche—although Leibniz is also a metaphysician) against empiricists (Locke, Hume, and even Kant) would never need to have arisen had men not forgotten the spirit, because the mind partakes of both the inner and outer poles, while belonging in an integrally whole way to neither. In other words, it could be said that both rationalists (innate ideas = knowledge) and empiricists (sense impressions = knowledge) are partially right, while missing the essential point in that each wants to build a noumenological edifice on relative realities (or relative sources of reality). However, the rationalists—in that their point of reference is the mind—are globally closer to the truth than the empiricists whose pole of reference is the physical body; it is all the difference between the kernel and the husk.

mind,[19] and an earthly body. And each of these faculties—
although the body is not a faculty, properly speaking,
unless its sensoriality can be said to act as a medium of
consciousness—can function as a center of gravity in its
own right. Now, it is not in the natural (or immortal) order
of things for either the mind or the body to act as provisorily autonomous centers of gravity, because they can do so
only to the detriment of their real center of reference—the
heart-intellect—which is the only true source of consciousness, hence of knowledge, whereas the other two must
borrow or mirror consciousness. Without entering into too
many details, one can say schematically that mentalism—

---

19. It may not be evident that the mind and the soul can be synonymous, though, on reflection it is easy to see that the mind as faculty of
awareness mirroring the ever-changing flux of sensations, feelings, and
impressions is inherently unstable and passive as well as imbibing. One
might at this point prefer to speak of a higher mind, or the faculty of reason in itself, and a lower mind—or the *mens carnalis*—which would then
simply be the faculty of awareness dependent on the senses or even be
part of the appetitive soul. What complicates the equation is that the
mind can be used by the intellect, whose seat lies in the heart, at which
point the mind becomes a delegate faculty of the spirit and no longer
merely the playmate of the soul. But, traditionally, the mind, along with
the soul, has always been associated with the moon (which only shines
through reflected light and which is cold), whereas the heart is related to
the sun. Depending on the symbolism, however, the mind can also be
equated with reason and reason, while not reducible in its substance to
the soul, partakes nonetheless of the soul's indirectness in that reason
cannot see things in themselves as the intellect does, but only reflect
them through duality. On the other hand, if reason can be said to be
inherently objective and the soul inherently subjective, then it is difficult
to equate them; in that case, reason is more a faculty of the spirit than of
the soul. Yet, in that the soul can appropriate it, in a way that it can never
appropriate the intellect, reason can be situated within the precincts of
the soul's ground. When making these divisions, however, one should
not forget that the human subject is one just as its archetype the *vir perfectus* is one because God is one. Thus, there will always be an overlap-
ping of faculties.

as well as subjectivity by psychic extension—is the result of the mind operating as a center of gravity answerable only to its constructs, and sensuality or grossness when the body does so. And, of course, there are multiple inter-mediary combinations of these two poles giving rise to types such as the passional cerebralist, the calculating materialist, or the sensual skeptic, and so on and so forth—all types characterized by the absence of a com-manding spiritual center and who therefore have no direct celestial archetype.

However, not to dwell overly on the problematical repercussions resulting from this ternary division become schismatic, it must be understood that the polarization between heart and mind exists already *in divinis*—though not in the supra-formal essence, or *Paramatma*, where sub-ject and object are indissociably one—and corresponds then to the difference respectively between the principial poles of immanence and of transcendence, or of being and consciousness, subject and object. No manifestation can be actualized without this initial polarization, be it only pre-figured. As for the body, as fleshly substance, it marks the ultimate boundary of objective outwardness.[20]

If we transpose this ternary onto the macrocosmic order of society, which is the subject of this chapter, the principial division of powers is reflected in the function of the priest, who represents the heart's unitive agency, and that of the king, who represents the mind—or head—with its discriminative agency, the body being then, within this framework, the social corpus at large. From an outward, or social point of view, the king is superior to the priest, just as the head stands above the body. However, from an

---

20. A distinction must be made between the simple fact of physical outwardness and the outwardness of a consciousness prey to the hell of nothingness, the outer limits of which are quasi inconceivable.

inward or spiritual point of view, the priest is superior to the king, just as the heart is situated at the center of the body.[21]

BY ESTABLISHING A principle of hierarchy, the institution of monarchy, in its integral sense, grants the multitudes a means of ascent—both collective and individual—whereof a democracy[22] (or the plurality of the proletarians) deprives them by definition. Hierarchy, through giving man the opportunity to submit to real authority, thereby gives him the means—paradoxically at first sight—to raise himself, for he who does not know how to obey does not know how to rule. One might say, man kneels as a subject to stand up as a prince; or, he need efface himself, insofar as he is base or to the degree that he can be so potentially, in order that his princely substance may arise, for man has no hope of perfection—and thus of immortality—except that he realize an archetype which, inasmuch as it perforce transcends him, requires an initial prosternation and extinction; for man unconverted is a rebel at heart, by way of echoing the Fall: he is always at the edge of revolt and hence of damnation. And the enablement of this twofold process of what in essence amounts to a death and a resurrection, when spiritually understood, is the real meaning of kingship.[23] Without such a sovereign model to guide

----

21. In all of this symbolism, one will want to bear in mind that when we refer to the heart, it is not specifically the organ, but the inmost center of the body or roughly the area that a person spontaneously points to when referring to himself.

22. Not to be confused with its historic model, the Athenian democracy, wherein suffrage was restricted to an elite. And, as such, it was far more similar to many of the nomadic systems of council of tribal elders or to the witenagemot of the Anglo-Saxon nobility than to its bastard modern offspring.

23. It is highly symbolic of man's journey through the *Samsara*, the round of deaths and rebirths, that in the game of chess once a pawn has

him—outwardly by the king's regal bearing and inwardly by the wisdom resulting from his role as judge—man is bereft of any anthropomorphic point of divine reference serving to remind him of what it is to be a man in the most glorious sense of the term and to redeem him from his otherwise fatal ordinariness. Moreover, following the alchemy of correspondences which take their root in the principle of identity or in the unity underlying diversity, subjects love their king inasmuch as he is the mirror image of their own true self.[24] In this sense, only the king is real man; the other men borrow their light from his own reflected excellence. Or, in Platonic terms, one would say that the form, namely the archetype, is everything,[25] whereas matter, or the accidental modality, is nothing, for only the archetype is real, eternal, and thus immortal. And only it can repeat itself: multiplicity, no matter how varied, is but the many-facetted refraction of the One.[26]

---

crossed the board from edge to edge it can be converted into a queen or any other valuable piece.

24. This is the deeper meaning for a whole gestural universe of genuflections, ritual bowing, acclamation, the proskynesis (kissing the earth before the king), the washing of the feet, kissing the bishop's ring, the swearing of allegiance, and also the dubbing of knights, which, very significantly, have all but disappeared from modern social mores. Interesting to note, in a reversal of roles in which a superior now grants subalterns a measure of superiority, it was Jesus who, by washing his disciples' feet before the Last Supper, instituted the tradition whereby a priest, abbot, and even the pope will wash the feet of a select number of people. The footwashing ceremony illustrates the dimension of reciprocity that any true hierarchy must honor if it is to be viable.

25. Whence the geometric impersonality of Egyptian art, for example, which places the emphasis on the profile of the human form and not on its individualizing contents, and groups human forms in repetitive patterns that duplicate each other like the reeds along the Nile.

26. The Sufi idea of the "perfect man" or *Insan al Kamil* and the Christian ideal of the *Vir Perfectus* as incarnated by Christ is based on this prototype which is the goal of creation. Cf. Also Emerson's doctrine of the One Man.

On another level, it must be added that it is rare, if not impossible, for truly superior individuals born in a pluralistic or anti-monarchic society to rise to the public prominence their stamp would normally secure for them because, in a regime where the mass of numbers prevails, they must constantly defer to—and be held accountable—to swarms of inferiors who cannot possibly understand them and who assume that everyone is exactly like them because they have no real understanding of what a being with a *cuor gentil* (or a noble heart, as Dante phrased it) is. Thus democracy[27] by dignifying numbers, sentences the superior "one" to the status of a wandering outcast. Or, by exalting quantity (which is never intelligent) abolishes quality (which can never be "many" according to the cosmic economy of proportions). This much is axiomatic. In Pythagorean terms, numbers can only be multiples of the One refracted through the hall of mirrors of the reign of duality. Remove the unique and the rest is pulverized, because the many can only derive their reality from the One, never the other way round as the proponents of pluralism propose. Democracy is finally less the reflection of a cosmic reality than a philosophical program whereby the many intend to usurp the natural prerogatives of the One. In the most fundamental sense of the term, the concept of authority—which must be sacred in its origin if it is not to be a pastiche—is reduced to a mere term of formal convenience (a bureaucratic ersatz) when cut off from its

---

27. We use this word according to its etymology (demos = "common people"), namely to mean not just majority rule as established by a free electorate—whose ideal is in any case a pure chimera given the ease with which multitudes can be deceived when there is no central and transcendent authority to adjudicate—but the brute fact of the rule of the masses, whether democratic or totalitarian. In the "reign of quantity" that marks the latter phase of the *Kali Yuga*, or any terminal *yuga*, pluralism can never be synonymous with rightness—though it can limit extreme evil in a way that a nation under a false dictatorship cannot.

heavenly roots or, far worse, to a despotism which is an inversion of authority, the social equivalent of unchecked egoism ruled by the principle of arbitrariness.[28] Yet, since hierarchy and order are part of the natural mainstay of the world, there are shell structures of authority which can be legitimate as seen in the corporate culture of the business world and in the army, or even in the domain of sports, none of which could function along purely democratic lines.

However, generally speaking, and to return to earlier remarks, a society which cannot create saints or whose educational priority is no longer to forge sterling virtue and valor stamped by the seal of spirituality has, for all practical purposes, forfeited its right to exist in regard to eschatological finalities, "for what is a man profited, if he shall gain the whole world, and lose his own soul?" (Mat. 16:26)[29] It is in this vital context that the justification for a kingly paragon of a man needs to be understood. In other words, one cannot grasp the necessity of kingship[30] with-

---

28. Far better, then, to have a democracy which could be the lesser of two evils, because *vox populi vox Dei* (the voice of the people is the voice of God), whereby the masses of citizens operate as a counterbalance or a check to the forces of extreme tyranny or any extreme. There is no question but that a democracy, however mediocre, is to be the preferred alternative in the absence of an enlightened autocrat—even though its very numerical weight prevents the emergence of a gifted ruler—because it allows, in its initial stages at least, a real measure of freedom for the individual. However, a democracy cannot but ultimately succumb in that it paves the way to anarchy which results from the very freedom it is meant to protect, because the tolerance embedded in its charter forgives the worm in the apple. Extremes conjure each other.

29. In Aristotelian terms, one would say that such a society has shirked its teleological responsibilities.

30. It should go without saying that we are in no wise advocating the restoration of a pomp and circumstance monarchy, one in which plumed puppets *à la* Versailles would be granted a stage to strut their satined vanity and perfumed idleness. Rather, we are speaking of principles that are ontological mainstays engraved in the very nature of man

out seizing the meaning of man's existence on earth and its dramatic eschatological implications, or without understanding the place terrestrial manifestation holds in the cosmic order which consists in a hierarchy not simply of levels but, properly speaking, of dominions ranging from matter in the "middle," to the heavenly hypostases "above," and then to the increasingly chaotic and ultimately demoniac realms "below."

Empirical experience, when taken alone, suggests that man lives on a purely horizontal plane which would seem to exclude any moral hierarchies or any ranges of spiritual excellence and counter levels of increasing depravity. And for those for whom existence is primarily an affair of the senses, no other reality exists.[31] However, ignorance of

---

as such, that are no less crucial to his existence than his spinal axis. And in so doing, we are not unaware of what is impossible in modern times. However, the fact that the patient is dying should not disallow one to recall what constitutes health. It may be worth mentioning, in this respect, that—to take but one example—shortly before the fall of the Romanovs, there was a brief attempt by conscience-stricken Russian aristocrats, tired of the court's tedious intricacies, "to go to the people" whose daily life had become, in Kropotkin's words, "a struggle for a moldy piece of bread." It was partly the galling contrast between the court's supersaturated luxury—the fruit of privileges sought as an end in themselves—and the bone-rotting squalor of some of the masses that led to the Czar's ruin. How wide the divide that separates a Louis XIVth (preposterously known as the Sun King) from Louis IXth of France, the latter a saint who, to guard against the sin of ostentation, wore shoes without soles when walking in a procession lest the people should notice he was barefoot!

31. The Hindu system of castes—all questions of abuses and excesses aside—is founded on a reality that escapes the narrow bounds of seemingly arbitrary social privileges. Thus the lowest caste, the *Shudras*, correspond to the plebeian element found in all sedentary societies; and this element places priority on the indulgence of the appetites. Without a governing elite to check its coarseness, this caste would debase the whole social order. Ramakrishna said that in the *Kali Yuga*, men are most concerned with the enjoyment of food.

247

supra-formal realms is hardly a criterion of their non-existence.[32] In fact, man, owing to his erect physical stature, is not just a horizontal sense-bound creature bent on survival, but essentially a vertical being ruled by intelligence and consciousness (*homo sapiens*), who, by virtue of his ontological nature, is situated directly on the vertical axis which he incarnates as such, *tal quale*, as we have had to remark several times. And this means that he stands not only under Heaven, but also over an abyss—the solidity of the earth notwithstanding—so long as he remains spiritually unregenerate. Therefore, he must exert himself morally, and with every fiber of his consciousness, lest he plummet to his destruction.[33] Not to know this is not be a man.

And just as man is, microcosmically, the prey of the antagonistic forces of good and evil warring for his soul, so too, macrocosmically, a society is beset with these same contending forces which, while in no way intrinsically equal,[34] practically speaking exert seemingly equal influ-

---

32. When psychologists (such as a William James in *The Varieties of Religious Experience*) wish to ascribe mystical experience to extreme modal varieties of sensory experience, induced—they posit—either by the extreme deprivation (or the extreme stimulation) of one or more of the sense faculties, they are begging the question. Their premise is flawed from the beginning, since they assume that sense experience is an absolute. Of course, they have nothing else on which to pin their measurements.

33. The English anchoress and mystic, Julian of Norwich, perceptively remarked that "Our soul may never have rest in things that are beneath itself."

34. Contrary to a Manichean view of the universe that supposes two separate, or autonomous, principles of good and evil (albeit of unequal spatial scope, the Manicheans held) which is in itself a metaphysical impossibility (cf. the philosophical principle of non-contradiction which, in this case, excludes the possibility of two absolutes) because evil—in that it is nothing other than the absence or the corruption of goodness—can have no substantial or independent reality.

ence, so long as man—while on earth[35]—is situated *entre l'ange et la bête* (betwixt angel and beast); or equal in that it takes a full measure of moral force to counter the ever-present potential for subversion, revolt, and anarchy that relentlessly stalk the social order especially when carelessness or moral slackness are allowed to replace discipline, vigilance, and effort: "The king should always keep the rod of punishment (*danda*) uplifted in his hand" (Mahabharata 12.120.93).

Now, it is true that the forces of economic industriousness offer a certain material safeguard against the forces of moral dissolution[36]—the honesty and conventionality of the dutiful merchant who dreads risks—and can in their way forestall the downward pull in manifestation towards chaos. But to hold in check is hardly the same as to overcome. Nor can simple industry, however meritorious, save man from himself or guarantee his posthumous deliverance from the *Samsara*. Rather, the pursuit of happiness premised exclusively on prosperity masks the fundamental issues at stake by offering men a kind of superficial equilibrium wherein not only the ever-present forces of darkness but also those of light are held in abeyance. And this kind of truce invariably works in favor of evil whose first objective—if one can speak in terms of a cosmic strategy—is to dull consciousness by promoting a forgetful-

---

35. A necessary *distinguo*, for it is not a question here of man as such, namely as *imago Dei*, but only of fallen man.

36. Sublimists, for one, may wonder that materialism—which for them is the root of all evil (*radix malorum*)—could possess any redeeming qualities. But materialism, or rather the dedication to material gain, does provide a stabilizing bulwark of sorts against infra-human tendencies. This is, in part, the justification for the virtues of diligence, thrift, and industriousness emphasized by the Protestants. Moreover, no social order can subsist without its digestive function. If man shall not live by bread alone, neither can he live by Spirit alone, so long while on earth, that is.

ness of final ends. Also, as popular wisdom says it, "where good men do nothing, evil thrives." Such is the nature of the world.

A strictly material *Weltanschauung* would prefer to see in the force which religion defines as evil nothing but a gravitational pull towards inertia, something neutral in itself, the entropy (or loss of formative energy) resulting merely from neglect or remissness. This view, however, in its sense-bound shortsightedness,[37] forgets that manifestation is in substance an affair of consciousness and not of mere matter or a colliding maelstrom of perpetually assembling and disassembling particles, inherently blind and purposeless. The world is ruled not by the more or less accidental interaction of multiple energy centers, but by the confrontation—or *mise en présence*—of different conscious entities.[38] Whether one chooses to call these angels (which are in fact intelligencies)[39] and demons (which would then be passionalities), or *devas* and *asuras*, or Horus and Seth, it should be apparent that

---

37. The Scottish empiricist, David Hume—who embodied this whole current while being one of the watershed mentors for the subsequent drift of modern philosophy away from celestial principles—assumed, in his corpulent conceit, that he was everyman. In other words, because he himself was a jovial, fleshy man, addicted to pleasure, he supposed that all men must be similarly inclined, at least if allowed to be sincere. Hence, in his eyes, the utter uselessness of a notion such as transcendence.

38. This perspective is natural to the spirit worlds of all shamanistic traditions, for instance the Shinto universe of the *kamis*, or the fairy folklore of our forefathers.

39. We are following in this term one of the more intellective of the Desert Fathers, Evagrius Ponticus, who—in the wake of Neoplatonism—posits that creation starts in intelligence or *nous* and descends or thickens into *psyche* and finally congeals into *hyle*. At the summit, the highest entities, among which are the angels, are beings which are totally luminous and intelligent.

man—and, by extension, society[40]—is beset, in a titanic tug-of-war, by forces of light and darkness[41] which, in the nature of things, fiercely vie for supremacy over his heart, the seat of his immortal intelligence. Stated in other terms, manifestation is not simply regulated horizontally by cycles of expansion and contraction, of heat and cold, or of attraction and repulsion, but by the vertically polar cross-currents of an ascensional impetus and a descensional one, the former unitive, separative the latter, the one restorative because theocentric and God-affirming, the other destructive because theofugal and God-denying.

And since nothing can exist as pure unconsciousness[42]—this is this whole book's thesis—these tendencies are animated by the twinly divergent impetuses of homage and revolt, or of adoration and desecration, of love and hate, and, ultimately, of knowledge (truth) and ignorance (error), not to mention all of the modal varieties deriving therefrom such as logic and absurdity, beauty and ugliness, cleanliness and filth, each of which par-

---

40. There was a time, not so long ago, when every town had its patron saint whose influence protected it not only from natural calamities, but above all from evil. A relic of this ancient tradition exists still today in Naples in the veneration paid to St. Januarius (San Gennaro) whose blood, preserved in a vial, has been seen to liquefy on his feast day.

41. We include light along with darkness in the verb "beset" for, unbeknownst to most men, god is actively trying to save man at every instant: "No man ever wanted anything so much as God wants to make the soul aware of him," Eckhart remarked.

42. Hegel, echoing Aristotle, correctly saw Reason as both the substance of the universe and the "Infinite Energy of the Universe" but, incorrectly, assumed it was in a state of evolutive becoming, in the sense of reaching for a supreme alpha pole. Would that he had spoken of transmigration, instead, because, in this case, there is an involutive spiral back to the Spirit.

takes, directly or indirectly, of one or the other of these vertical points of reference.[43]

It is in this context that the nature and necessity of a Heaven-anointed sovereign must be understood. If men were but men, in the strictly humanistic sense of the term, then it would be quite superfluous to conceive of a priestly potentate or of an absolute monarch; the glorious trappings that are the necessary adornment of their cosmic functions[44] would be the most outrageous, and beguiling, of extravagances.[45] But, to continue in this sartorial vein, if dress is the ornament of the soul,[46] then what are we to think of a civilization that has relegated pageantry to the theater? Indeed, it is impossible not to see in clothes—just as in artifacts and dwellings[47]—the unmistakable clues of a collectivity's fundamental aspirations and consequently of its view of Reality. Conversely, one cannot underestimate the powerfully conditioning effects these "trappings" have in molding consciousness, for they are not only the

---

43. This is why everything cannot be just a matter of personal opinion, as libertarians would like, namely an affair of purely horizontal choice. And this is why the truly sincere man understands that all he does cannot not participate in sympathy with one or the other of these poles. If "beauty lies in the eye of the beholder," as it is so often quoted, this is true only for subjectivity, because in reality beauty depends on the truth of the object.

44. The Shah's Peacock Throne, for instance, is meant to mirror the star-studded splendor of the universe in which he, as the sun of his kingdom, is seated.

45. It is crucial to distinguish between glory and luxury or between majestic opulence and pretentious ostentation, because richness need not always be expensive. While true elegance is invisible, as a French saying has it, glory can never be poor.

46. While sacred nudity is the living theophany of the spirit—or of the heart—which is why, in this darkened world of profaning passions, it needs to draped.

47. It has often been observed that one can discern the scale of a civilization's values by the tallest building in its cities.

effect of men's outlook, but their molding cause as well in that they decide upbringing. However, if the garb (or, rather, the garb alone) does not a monk make, it is certain that trivial or slovenly dress renders man unfit to be an interlocutor with the Divine.

To return, once again, to the issue of man's universal status as *pontifex*—or bridge-maker between heaven and earth—namely his position in a world that is cosmically the object of contention between the forces of good and evil, a purely secular ruler is wholly inadequate to the tasks first of representing the light—as solar man—and of leading men back to it, but also of preserving society in any durable way from the inevitable inroads of corruption, disorder, and ultimate moral collapse; one cannot fight poison with legalities or wishfulness.[48] Indeed, the moment absolutes are disavowed, the door is left wide open for all manner of relativisms which, by instinct, bite the hand that feeds them.

Therefore, in the absence of all other justification, it is at least sound logic to conclude that only a supreme authority can have the wisdom, the power, and above all

---

48. This is what a Rousseau, in advocating a civil religion to secure men from the chaos ensuing from unrestricted liberty (or a Kant in advocating a religion of reason—tempting as that might be in an age of fatuous theology), failed to understand, because a virtue or code of ethics that has become a mere civil matter has been eviscerated of its heavenly magic, for there can be no morality without transcendence. In other words, once the underpinnings of absolute principles are removed, civil virtue becomes a matter of sheer expediency—such as that of a John Stuart Mill—or of brute majority consensus, heedless of objective right or wrong. In any case, Rousseau's idea—or lack of it—of religion (just as that of Kant, who admired him), in that it denies the supernatural mandate (or, in the case of Kant, denies man's ability ever to know it with certainty) is completely meaningless for all practical intents. There can be no morality outside of God: "Why callest thou me good? There is none good but one, that is, God" (Mat. 19:17).

253

the supra-human mandate to counter an absolute evil.[49] This argument might best be illustrated with the debate concerning the issue of capital punishment (or of the state's moral right to execute a criminal), one that leads to hopeless ethical entanglements once one removes recourse to a transcendental lawgiver. One could say that, strictly speaking, only God—Who is the giver of life—has the right to take life. Thus, an execution can only be carried out in the Name of God and only under the seal of His delegate authority on earth. All the arguing about the moral right to use capital punishment traces its roots directly to the relativization of authority. Also, the argument that the risk of an unjust execution is an irreparable miscarriage of justice, which can be avoided only by banning this absolute means of punishment, presupposes firstly that this mortal life is of unconditional importance and secondly that there is no celestial tribunal—to say nothing of secondary considerations such as the question of the criminal's *karmic* lot, as also his ability to benefit from the traditional last rites of confession and absolution which are not mere gibberish. Moreover, the argument that it is "hypocritical to punish heinous crimes by means of another heinous crime" establishes a spurious parallel, for not only is the ancient Talmudic talion law grounded in literal fairness, but the moral intention animating both deeds could not be more opposite. Finally, to reject capital punishment on absolute grounds is to deny that there is such a thing as an absolute evil, namely one that cannot be reformed but must be eradicated.

In this respect, the first and paramount duty of the divine ruler or the priestly monarch, as upholder of the "right order," is to protect his subjects, intrinsically from error or heresy and, extrinsically, from the enemies that

---

49. To speak of an absolute evil is not to say that evil is absolute.

THE CROOK AND THE FLAIL

threaten his realm both from outside and from within. Now, to open a parenthesis here, in the *Kali Yuga*, which is the cycle wherein the duality inherent in manifestation's projective aim towards a point of terminal division and chaos achieves its furthermost or widest polarization, the outer enemy serves as the occasional support[50] to rally men to surpass themselves or, at least, not to settle into complacency. Without the stimulus of the ever-present threat of this enemy, men are prone, by collective tendency, to succumb to the temptations of sloth and sensuality which enervate empires.[51] This is why, given the often sordid realities of post-Edenic existence, an absolute peace is neither possible, nor even desirable, because men, when "liberated" from the holy dread that only an absolute authority receiving its mandate from Above can instill,[52] tend to revert to mindless impulse. In the last analysis, it is

---

50 Occasional, because this "enemy" may in fact be noble himself as the feudal tradition of jousting, the samurai duels, or the legendary combats in the time of the *Iliad* or in those of the Mahabharata eloquently attest. In the animal realm, even the cutest little bird or chipmunk goes about his daily rounds with a deadly seriousness threatened as he is not only by his natural predators, but from competition with his own kind. This law of perpetual vigilance and effort lends him a unique alertness to his demeanor, decisiveness to their behavior, and perfection within his form's limits.

51. While it is true that, in the modern world of industrial and commercial prosperity, the threat of penury goads men to achievement, this success at keeping the wolf from the door cannot compare with the glory of exposing one's life to face a valiant foe. Only the threat of death provides the necessary spur to selfless bravery and to total reliance on God. Heroes are heroes because they befriend death on a daily basis. Conversely, modern warfare, with its horrendous weapons of mass destruction, has completely falsified the meaning of traditional combat. And the gun, which allows a coward the safety of distance, has perverted but not, needless to say, abolished the notion of valor.

52. Without Heaven-imposed duties, men can never be expected to "undertake tasks which they would not assume from disinterested motives alone," Montesquieu noted in his *Spirit of the Laws*.

only the imperative of law, preferably anchored in the imperial fiat, that stands between them and beastliness for, as has often been remarked, society is a den of wolves.[53] To assume that men, when left to their own inclinations, are naturally good and moral is either the height of naiveté or of foolishness, when it is not an intentional doctrine of secular manumission, namely a philosophy elaborated to promote, ultimately, emancipation from God, the one true ruler. Thus, advocates of peace forget—or plain deny—the flawed if not corrupt nature of post-Edenic man. In this sense, it should be borne in mind that the necessity of kingship, as well as of hierarchical authority in general, arises in direct proportion to the degeneration of the collectivity[54] while at the same time becoming paradoxically less and less feasible. An ideal society would be a confraternity of kingly and priestly men and hence one with no need for a centrally legislating or autocratic seat of power.[55] And,

---

53. For instance in the Mahabharata: "A king should display severity in making all his subjects observe their respective duties. If this is not done, they will prowl like wolves, devouring one another" (12.142.28).

54. Again, according to the Mahabharata as well as the Puranas, the world at the dawn of time was without a king. This was the *Krita Yuga* or Golden Age, we have alluded to already, when each man was a prophet unto himself and each ruled himself because he understood without external injunction the nature of the sacred *dharma* that governs creation; he carried justice immanently in his heart. The world was without a king when all men were kings.

55. Curiously, but for different reasons, Rousseau intuited this when he said: "Were there a people of gods, their government would be democratic." Now, the several historic attempts at creating such a polity of virtuous men, such as the theocratic communalisms organized by the Jesuits of Paraguay or William Penn's ideal Christian commonwealth, could not but fail given the cyclical juncture in which they were instituted—and this quite apart from considerations of their doctrinal cogency or individual merit. However, one might suppose that it is still possible for a community of saints to exist, at least in the general outlook, and which would then be more or less democratic by the nature of things.

interestingly, this is in fact the ideal that democracy logically assumes, for to be fully effective and not just the tyranny of a generally blind multitude, it presupposes a society of morally upright and therefore sufficiently knowledgeable men.[56]

THE IDEAL RULER would combine the spiritual wisdom of the priest and the secular realism of the monarch. However, as history teaches, these two attributes are so rarely paired as to be normally mutually exclusive, especially in the *Kali Yuga* where the rift between Heaven and earth reaches antagonistic extremes. As a matter of fact, saintly virtues may even prove the ruin of a ruler,[57] because contemplative

---

56. It may be worth recalling that—to take the example of history's most complete democracy (the one De Tocqueville chose as a model case study), that of the United States of America—the Founding Fathers, when articulating the provisions in the Bill of Rights, never envisaged the moral decay that was to supervene and which the Constitution would later have to grapple with. Thus clauses guaranteeing liberties such as the freedom of speech were never remotely meant to grant the absurd, the obscene, or the perverse full license of expression or to countenance indiscriminate liberty, but to ensure that arbitrary taste or that tyranny could never suppress the true, the right, and the good upon which all real freedom is premised. Thus, upon coming out of the Constitutional Convention, John Adams said: "We have not a government armed with sufficient power to tame the animal passions of mankind. This constitutions was made only for a moral and religious people; it is wholly inadequate for any other." It is in any case absurd to claim unconditional rights in an imperfect world, for instance to demand absolute freedom while at the same time wanting to remove the necessary restrictions that are its mainstay. Also, subversions invariably cloak their nefarious designs in the inspiring rhetoric of catchwords such as peace, love, liberty, and equality; the wolf in sheep's clothing is as old as the world. One would be tempted to say that the First Amendment—established to protect men from tyranny—is the devil's personal favorite, because it is the one always invoked by morality abolitionists.

57. A notable example of this is the case of Celestine V who reluctantly gave up his hermit's existence to become pope only to abdicate

detachment or forgiving mercy[58] can disarm the warring impetuousness or simply the active virility and practical decisiveness a leader needs to subjugate and hold in check the savage propensities of men who are generally ill-disposed to listen to reason in the absence of the threat of punishing strength (the ultimate *ratio regis*, if need be). In a world of "ravening wolves," the shepherd's crook is impotent without the flail. If he is to prevail, a ruler can have no artificial compunction about soaking his banner in blood when necessary. In a world of death, peace can only be secured by war, or at least by the readiness for war. Moreover, peace itself, is not always a boon in a world where vice prospers. If it is easy to see why war is an evil— because it can never be an ideal in itself even when beneficial—it is, on the other hand, much less obvious how peace can sometimes be an evil, not ever in itself, but in that it can preserve stagnation and thus prevent necessary renewal.[59]

The greatest of rulers combined the twin perfections of virtue and justice and thus set empires into motion. But, as an Arab saying has it, "power and paradise do not go well together": men like David or Charlemagne, or the pope

---

owing to his lack of experience of the world and his inability (or unwillingness) to confront the machinations of his political sponsors, for which Dante consigned him—quite unjustly it would appear in view of his subsequent canonization—to one of the circles in his Inferno: "I saw and knew the shadow of him who from cowardice made the great refusal" (3: 58–60).

58. Not a tautology, for integral mercy also possesses a dimension of justice which is the guarantor of its goodness.

59. The Swiss historian, Jakob Burckhardt, commented how: "Lasting peace not only leads to enervation; it permits the rise of a mass of precarious, fear-ridden, distressful lives which would not have survived without it and which nevertheless clamor for their right, cling somehow to existence, bar the way to genuine ability, thicken the air and as a whole degrade the nation's blood. War restores real ability to honor" (Reflections on History, Ch. 4).

Gregory the Great, called *Consul Dei,* are the exceptions; for every Mohammed—or Mohammedan type, one in which piety, valor, and political sagacity are combined—there are dozens of Muawiyas who nonetheless, despite their ruthlessness, can serve as instruments of a higher providence, for they are as the sharp edge of a sword wielded finally by a destiny that is far more encompassing than their fierceness or the autocracy their strength of will, power, and wealth enforce.[60] Idealists and moralists, and good men in general, may rue the often murderous cruelty of potentates; but they forget the alternatives, for the "law of the jungle" is a fact of life and therefore has its painful cosmic justification.[61] God's majesty brooks no weakness or relativity; this is death's distant archetype. Even as wise a man as Solomon had, upon his accession to the throne, all rival claimants slain, a measure that the subsequent peace and prosperity of his subjects would seem to have vindicated.[62] If for a priest—whose mandate is "Thy kingdom come"—

---

60. The splendor of the Mogul rulers, "who built like giants and finished like jewelers"—as they boasted—is far more important than their human shortcomings, as the case may be, because at least, while they reigned, men benefited from a human standard of reference that reminded them of God's majesty and power in a way that no society raised on a mercantilist scale of values can be expected to understand. But even the emperor as "son of heaven" can fall and become degenerate to the point if not of justifying a revolution, at least triggering one.

61. As always, a verdict must be premised on the intention of the accused. "Men of my stamp," Napoleon said, "do not commit crimes." In the wake of the Revolution's carnage and mayhem, force—and force alone at first—was the remedy to restore order. The French Emperor's deeds, which catalyzed the European monarchies into a brief wakefulness, most likely contributed to delaying the arrival of Communism by several generations. And, quite evidently, the scope of one man's power is not a criterion of its providence or necessity, because there are men who fulfil a diabolic role, such as a Nero or a Hitler.

62. Some historians will be quick to counter that Solomon's wealth and splendor bled his realm to death. These are the same who object to

the choice must be between good and evil as such, for a monarch this choice, given the worldly diversity of his duties, is often between the lesser of two evils. In an imperfect world, to aim for an absolute ideal—"perfection is the enemy of the good"—can result in forfeiting not only the best, but also the chance for a lesser good,[63] which then amounts to a double failure. At any rate, the monarch's purview is first to preserve the social equilibrium of his kingdom, and not to reform the world. Moreover, where the priest's role is to forgive, crushing the enemy is one of the attributes of sovereignty—for God is also "the Lord of hosts," wherefore warfare's opportune justification in a world that is heir to the original disequilibrium set in motion by the Fall.[64]

---

the cost of the medieval cathedrals while serfs in rags tilled the earth and had to poach for their venison. We must assume they would prefer a dreary world of proletarian egalitarianism where, in the name of the "redistribution of wealth," no one would be entitled to be richer than the most brutish of his neighbors. They do not consider that with the advent of "citadine" civilization, inequality of wealth is first of all a result of inequality of human stature and moral scope, and only derivatively an issue of luxury and abuse. However, the end of any civilization is characterized *grosso modo* by a reversal of poles, whereby not only do men become feminized and women masculinized, but patricians—in the intrinsic sense of the term—become poor and pariahs wealthy.

63. This is partly what happened in the Church when, out of an idealism to establish the supremacy of the spiritual over the temporal, the XIth century pope Gregory VII enforced celibacy on the priesthood, thereby depriving society not only of a priestly caste of men—since they could not longer produce heirs—but also, by emphasizing the absolute superiority of monastic spirituality over any other, inadvertently widened the breach between spirituality and worldliness.

64. The case of the Gupta monarch, Ashoka, is rather unique in the annals of history. Out of remorse from having waged war once, at the beginning of his reign, he renounced it, declaring that the only true conquest was the conquest of men's hearts. With the zeal only a repentant idealist could muster, he also abolished the imperial hunt, imposed a

THAT THE INSTITUTION of monarchy has degenerated over
time to the point of becoming—not undeservedly—an
object held in odium by "progressivists"[65] and democratic
humanists, does not in any wise invalidate the principle of
kingship, just as the measure of man does not lie in the fact
of his corruptibility. An all too common argument against
monarchy, plucked from the very entrails of the "hoi pol-
loi," is that a king is but a mere mortal, a vessel of "paint-
ed clay" subject to the same humbling natural necessities as
all men—as if a man need be made of an ethereal substance
before he is allowed to wear a crown. However tempting
this objection in view of the many frilled monsters of vin-
dictive caprice that have mounted onto thrones "to grind
the faces of the poor," it fails to take account of the essence
of man as *imago Dei*, the stamp of which marks the seat of
his being. In good logic, the assumption of this populist
argument is that man is essentially—not accidentally—corrupt, though this would never be admitted.[66] At the same
time, by a kind of Promethean backlash, this argument's

---

vegetarian diet on his court, and even prohibited the slaughtering of animals for part of the year. Such a utopia was realizable in the context of
this monarch's conversion to Buddhism and in the instrumental role he
was to have in the propagation and institutionalization for this pacific
religion. But, once his role fulfilled, he could hardly expect his succes-
sors to imitate him in every item of his pacifism, even had they so
wished.

65. The French free-thinkers believed it to be a form of government
"hopelessly corrupt, completely arbitrary and rationally indefensible,"
as Will and Ariel Durant describe it in their *Story of Civilization* (Vol. X).

66. In fact, populists want their cake and to eat it too: while denying the possibility of excellence, or that of an elite, they are also the first
to exalt the supposed merits of common man. Thus, on the one hand,
man is declared to be too fallible to be allowed any absolute superiority over his fellow men while, on the other hand, the collectivity is granted some kind of extraordinary superiority that entitles it to every consideration. We can see in this how nothing is more harmful to man than
the cult of man.

veiled intention is to usurp the prerogatives of the higher in the name of the lower. Stated in microcosmic terms, for example those of the Freudian revolt against Moses (or of the son against the father, the creature against the Creator), it is the ego or, to be exact, the unregenerate ego which rejects the spirit's natural right of sovereignty. In other words, to disavow the notion of kingship amounts *ipso facto* to disavow the notion of God—no less!—Who, as Lord the creation and guarantor of its order,[67] is the original king and thus the authority from which all delegate authority derives its legitimacy, failing which society is left to the mercy of parliament fools representing even greater fools, if it is not to become a vassal of hell: when kings go, criminals soon will rule. The king is the only authority capable of damning the devil.

On the other hand, if there is no Supreme Being, or if man is crudely the issue of matter—is but mud's whelp—then authority becomes nothing more than an arrangement of civic convenience or of economic opportunism with no absolute warrant. It is an advantage provisorily secured through superior craft or brute force, and one subjected to the permanent strife of fractional interests verging on chaos. Remove the supernatural and at one fell swoop the very foundation of any man's right to sovereignty over another has been removed. For those, however, who do not believe in the evolutionary hypothesis of a blind and absurdly fortuitous ascent from primal atoms, the Heaven-consecrated bestowal of sovereign power on a singular individual will seem no farther fetched than the apparition on earth of an intelligent being such as man and of the

---

67. Advocates of a kind of "quantum cosmology," which seeks to promote an unholy ecumenism between modern science and ancient tradition, posit a universe "capable of creating itself and running itself, with no outside intervention" (Basarab Nicolescu). They forget that nature exists *gratia Dei.*

262

"miracle of consciousness." The creation of man is a wonder of such extraordinary scope that all other distinctions pale by comparison. Now, kingship is the only human role that accords with the full scope of such a miracle's meaning, just as sanctity is its profoundest moral justification.

THESE COMMENTS BRING us to explore both the implications and ramifications of the principle of paramount authority, the essence of which, as previously stated, is wisdom or knowledge which has truth and adamantine certainty, not murky opinion, as its axial pole of reference. The superior wisdom embodied in the Heaven-chosen ruler, whether implicitly by virtue of ritual anointment[68] or explicitly by virtue of his specific individual gifts,[69] carries with it a

---

68. To this election one might want to add the aura of grace potentially vehicled by hereditary succession, though the anointment itself, which alone actualizes it, takes precedence for it is to monarchy what apostolic succession is to the Church. However, the question of the pre-eminence of hereditary right yields in importance to that of the institution itself, as shown by the example of the Mamluk and Ottoman regimes which recruited many, if not most, of their rulers (trained to become grand viziers) from enslaved prisoners, on the basis of meritocratic selection.

69. Paradoxically, at first sight, a king or priest need not necessarily be wise or even virtuous to be sufficiently effective or deserving of respect, but only true to the duties of his office (the libertine pope Alexander VI was a bulwark of orthodoxy), for it is this function, in the last analysis, that men revere through the human symbol. For example, in the confessional, it is Christ who listens in the person of the priest; and this is why, traditionally, the latter remained hidden behind the grate and why even an immoral priest can validly give the penitent absolution. The grate of the confessional has been removed and now the parishioner (he or she is no longer a penitent) visits face to face with a kind of priest-psychologist which is as much as to say that there is no longer any priest because the whole efficacy of the confession rests not on psychological manipulation but on the idea of absolution which a mere man is utterly impotent to grant. The psychologism which has overtaken thinking since the "Enlightenment" places exorbitant

263

whole existential repercussion or magical aura extending far beyond his words and deeds because what matters is that the archetype shine through the human vessel, or in spite of it.

From the earliest of times, and even up until the beginning of the industrial age, kings were believed to be imbued with a supernatural grace that reflects the assimilation of their being with the sun. According to a symbolism that is naturally self-evident, the king reflects amongst men the centrality the sun holds in creation. The acclaim "the king is dead, long live the king" is directly tied to the perennial phenomenon of the sun's setting and return at dawn as *sol invictus*. Thus the monarch's solar nature, or simply the solar influence of his function—as illustrated and vehicled by the glorious adornments of his office such as the diademed tiara (the "crown of fire"), jeweled scepter, diamond-encrusted throne, or, among certain nomadic peoples, the feathered headdress of chiefs—was believed to carry a magically restorative, quasi-medicinal value that benefited life, much like the sun's rays do, by rendering it fruitful, warding off famine or pestilence, and ensuring well-being among the people and soundness of limb and health for their progeny.[70] In other words, the king's influ-

---

emphasis on the individual to the detriment of the instrumentality of his social function which can compensate any number of personal shortcomings. In fact, these defects, far from being crippling limitations, can, on the contrary, often serve as the necessary goad for this same individual to acquit himself of his duties with distinction.

70. Thus a canon attributed to St. Patrick enumerates among the blessings attendant upon the reign of a just king, "fine weather, calm seas, crops abundant, and trees laden with fruit." Moreover, monarchs as recently as the Restoration practiced a laying on of hands for subjects afflicted with scrofula who believed the king's touch would heal them. For those who see in such beliefs an embarrassing holdover from superstitious times, it may be worth bearing in mind that no heavenly grace is operative without the collaboration of man's faith and therefore one

ence transcends the clamor of politics, which is why, finally, his function cannot be democratically elective.

Upon his accession to the throne, the king was thought to "espouse" his realm, the "lady of the land" which, following the laws of a kind of sympathetic magic, could prosper according to the degree of his virtue and virility.[71] In this regard, the sumptuous harems, and the numerous concubines to which most ancient rulers were entitled,[72] reflect the principle of solar fertilization inherent in the kingly symbol—one that is not unassociated with the idea of the *Logos spermatikos* (the procreative intellect), whose vivifying and disseminative power needs to be fostered so as to forestall the dearth of crops, blight of life, or the general sterility threatening a realm that has forgotten to renew its pact with Heaven. Moreover, the king, as the living symbol of the Absolute, calls for a host of retainers—of which the harem[73] is a particularly eloquent symbol because the

---

could well conjecture that the disappearance of this gift coincides not just with the general decadence of post-Renaissance monarchism but also with the rise of an obtuse, faithless, or even cynical materialism.

71. Virtue and virility carry the same Latin root *vir* ("strength") which makes intellectual sense in that not only does virtue give strength—and indeed is the sole source of strength in that it is already for man a participation in immortality while here-below since it is to participate in God's nature—but virility in its fullest sense is inseparable from goodness, for only the truly good can be truly strong. Incorruptibility and generosity is the essence of real strength. In making this statement, one must distinguish between strength, which is good, and brutality, which is evil and which, despite superficial appearances, is not strength. The brutal know how to kill; only the strong know how to save.

72. It is a question here of essential symbolism, not of the degenerative excesses historians may be fond of relating. The downfall of the Osmanlis began when the sultans ceased conducting the affairs of state from horseback to rule from the latticed privacy of the seraglio in a daze of sensual stupor.

73. Not to be forgotten is the fact that the king had the duty to produce a suitable heir, and the chances of succeeding in this were markedly

multitude of consorts play the role of stars to his sun, or of
the infinite to his absoluteness. And they also lend him the
necessary vital space into which to radiate while arousing
his manhood in the profoundest and most restorative sense
of the word: their beauty, variety, and number both reflect
and inspire his greatness while granting him a heavenly
vastness that conjures his solarity. Also, the flower-field of
wives, consorts, and concubines can be said to serve as the
shakti (or feminine complement) to the monarch's solitary
singleness; in this case, they can be likened to the lovingly
luminous aura of his solar glory. Finally, there is a natural
and providential affinity between the king as embodiment
of truth and woman as a living embodiment of heavenly
wisdom, the Greek *Sophia* or the Hebrew *Shekhinah*: truth
and bounty.

KINGS WERE REVERED by all Aryan races from India to
Ireland, and in the Andean cultures as in African tribes—
indeed in every culture prior to industrialism—as the chosen intercessor between man and God, if not as the very
embodiment of God on earth. It is no more absurd to
believe that God, when addressing man, will assume a
human guise than to believe that He created man. In fact, it
is illogical to think that God would approach man, speak to
him and guide him without an intermediary for who can
behold the countenance of the Lord and live: "thou canst
not see my face" (Ex. 33:20)[74]. And the "normal" corruptibility of man does not of itself preclude the possibility of
an incorruptible man, a saint, or a true god-man such as the

---

enhanced by having numerous offspring, not to mention the stimulating
effect of competition between them. Incidentally, the high number of offspring also greatly lessened the risk of inbreeding which has contributed
so heavily to the *fin-de-race* downfall of Christian monarchy.

74. Whence the protocol, in some royal courts, the Thai notably, forbidding the subjects to look at their ruler.

Pharaoh was supposed to be, however much sheer quantitative numbers militate against this possibility, rendering it difficult if not impossible for most men to believe in a morally spotless paragon.

Likewise, but in a different sense, a king may not himself be morally at the level of the celestial prototype of his function, to say the least. Nonetheless, that human mediocrity has been born to the purple far more often than not in recent times does not necessarily constitute a disqualification, because the function transcends the individual and therefore merits to be preserved in spite of its agent, as the case may be.[75] Furthermore, what constitutes right behavior is to a certain extent open to debate according to the reigning values, or necessities, of a given milieu.[76] Thus, historians, when assessing ancient cultures, must guard against being influenced by a certain bourgeois moralism that arose more specifically with the advent of mercantilism—which is by definition prudent as well as prudish because centered not on heroism, grandeur, and generosity, but on security and calculations as befits the thriftiness of its economic priorities.[77] Hence, when tempted to condemn

---

75. The sickly, diminutive, cunning, doubt-riddled, and near faithless Charles VII of France nonetheless received extraordinary help from Heaven in the person of Joan of Arc to gain rightful access to his throne.

76. Polygamy makes immediate social and economic sense in a warrior society where the male members are subject to a very high rate of mortality, and this quite apart from the providential spiritual symbolism it may otherwise carry. And, inversely, polygamy does not make sense, sociologically, in a society where there is roughly an equal proportion of men and women. And, of course, there is also a direct spiritual symbol in the single man, single wife marriage—the royal couple, prototype of the *hierogamos* or sacred wedding.

77. Civilizationism, anchored in the pursuit of material progress and allied to a Protestant ethic which sanctified industriousness, led to a cult of artificiality, namely to the banishment of nature and consequently

either the massacring of enemies or the apparent sexual profligacy of ancient rulers, one must not lose sight of the symbolism of their duties which, all questions of excess or of decadence notwithstanding, involve no less than the destruction of obsolete or inferior cultures,[78] on the one hand and, on the other, the continuous re-enactment and renewal of the marriage between Heaven—or the solar solitariness of the principle—and earth, as represented by their harems and consorts—or the lunar multiplicity of cosmic All-Possibility. One will want to add, however, that such a symbolism presupposes a traditional context, one in which the ideas of heaven and hell are empirically meaningful.[79] Moreover, sensual men, who place pleasure ahead

---

of naturalness, the effect of which was to estrange man from his primordial heritage. This inevitably fostered a host of complexes and neuroses, for man's vital urge, deprived of a proper outlet, turned in on itself to rend its keeper, whence—to cite but one example—the aberrant hypocrisies and double standards of Victorianism that have been so garishly chronicled. Such strait-jacketing of nature could not but lead to the debacle of modern promiscuity and uncensored license: "*Chassez le naturel, il revient au galop,*" the French say, which could be paraphrased thus, "Starve nature and it will devour you."

78. The savagery of the Assyrians under king Ashurnasirpal II must be situated both in the human context of the utterly ruthless fierceness of their foes as well as in that of a spiritual perspective which emphasized the perennial strife between hordes of demons and gods which, according to their mythology, surrounded them. Furthermore, conquest was the divine mission of kings, as they believed, a statement that is not fraught with the self-serving righteousness one might be tempted to impute to it, because, in a certain cosmic sense, the spoils do indeed belong to the mighty. This warring principle of competing entities is part of the fabric of existence and is not necessarily an evil by itself. In our era, the economist Joseph Schumpeter coined the term "creative destruction" to define the most effective—and wealth producing— *modus operandi* of capitalism.

79. It is reported that Sultan Murad II once asked for a Sufi master to come to his court. Upon entering the court, in which the Sultan was seated in his usual place of spectacular prominence over a host of cowed

of duty, are not temperamentally predisposed to fathom the full scope of the burden that the emperor, as the Son of Heaven, must shoulder. Nor can they imagine the sheer magnitude of character necessary for such a ruler to command the respect of men who, quite naturally, are not inclined to revere another man unless presented with extraordinary proof of his eminence, be it in love or in war, and all that these twin domains entail by way of spiritual and social consequence. One might say that love and war, as the two basic forces in the cosmos, summarize all the concerns and issues worth understanding and living and dying for—the pole love referring to unity and peace—and ultimately to spirituality, because love is heavenly—and that of war to duality and struggle, as well as to justice—and, by extension to discernment and rectitude—for that is meant to be the ultimate result of feuding. And this complementarity brings us back to the twofold obligations of the Heaven-anointed ruler who must embody compassion and vigilance, or mercy and severity, as illustrated by the crook and the flail held in wakeful repose by the Pharaoh over his breast.

OWING TO AN all-too-common reflex, born of an egocentric lack of imagination, the supra-human attributes a king could possess in the case of a genuinely superior man, or the transcendental virtue the throne can instill in its holder, is unintelligible to men who assume that the rest of the world must be as fallible as they are. Instead of wanting to surpass themselves, they wish—without necessarily being aware of it—to drag down to their level anyone whose eminence threatens their own mediocrity or, to be more exact,

---

dignitaries, the Sufi inquired: "Where is the Sultan?" Which question brought a smile to the ruler's face. Such were the times when a king could still be held in check by a man of prayer.

their complacence with their own mediocrity. This attitude has its rational roots in a democratic egalitarianism which is a kind of politicization—or secularization of the religious notion of the equality of all men before their Maker, a notion which, when understood properly, does not exclude the complementary—and equally necessary—notion of hierarchy, for to be equal before God, in the sense of being equally mortal as well as of having equal access to His mercy, does not entail equality between men as such. Hierarchy and equality correspond, by metaphysical analogy, to the complementarity between the poles of transcendence and union: on the one hand, God in His attribute as blinding majesty is unique, as a result nothing can stand before Him, but must bow, surrender, and efface itself; on the other hand, God as goodness, or love, is unity, as a result of which all beings are related and can therefore partake as siblings of His substance.[80] Nonetheless, if these two principles are, in the cosmic order of things, complementary, on earth the pole hierarchy takes operative precedence over that of equality owing to the predominance of imperfection which, to be righted, converted, or purged requires preliminary purification, whence the relative priority of negation and extinction over that of affirmation. In other words, true equality or fraternization cannot be achieved before submission and atonement have been

---

80. However, as Alexander the Great phrased it: "God is the common father of all men, but He makes the best ones peculiarly His own." This emperor's vision of *Homonia* or Concord, namely the brotherhood of all men, presupposed the idea of a common divine paternity, "a truth which," as the remarkable historian Arnold Toynbee observed, "involves the converse proposition that, if the divine father of the human family is ever left out of the reckoning, there is no possibility of forging an alternative bond of purely human texture which will avail by itself to hold Mankind together" *A Study of History*, vol. VI, p. 9 (Oxford University Press, 1951).

taken care of; the way to unity and fulfillment starts with renunciation and abasement. Likewise, as previously mentioned, he who does not know how to obey does not know how to rule. On the other hand, in the reversal of proportions that is typical of spirituality, unity takes precedence—especially in esoterism—over hierarchy in that unity, or the spiritual brotherhood of man, is an anticipation of the heavenly union to come. If in monasteries, the abbot is superior to the monks it is only so as *primus inter pares*; he is otherwise accorded no special favors but partakes of all of the duties of his fellow monks.

Humanism, in transposing to the social order man's earthly equality as dust beneath the feet of the Lord, or heavenly equality in blessedness, robs man of his potential moral eminence as consecrated by God. It levels the natural hierarchical distinctions corresponding to the vertical scale of perfections—*maqamat* in Sufism—and thus removes this ladder without which man finds himself deprived of the means to rise above himself, namely above the animality,[81] passions, ignorance, and the vices inherent to post-Edenic existence. Now, this leveling paradoxically goes hand in hand with a de facto divinization of men *qua* men, entitling them unconditionally to all rights,[82] that is to say irrespective of all considerations of individual merit. The irony of this position is that *homo politicus* cannot become fully what he is meant to be according to the entelechy of his nature as *imago Dei*;[83] what his equalization

81. The animality in man has nothing to do with the saurian antecedents evolution hypothesizes, but only with his bodily functions of assimilation and elimination and those of reproduction and corruption; nothing else.

82. For Robespierre—he, the butcher-architect of the French Revolution's reign of terror!—mankind was the only sovereign of the earth.

83. Hegel, by positing a Teilhardian or evolutionary omega point, to which centuries of history served as the handmaiden, turned

fails to take into account is that man cannot be himself so long as he remains subhuman. And he is subhuman so long as he does not strive towards sanctity, namely so long as he remains an entity subject to a thousand theofugal impulses that plunder his vital substance until he slinks into death, a vacated husk.

In this sense, the kingly paragon, by virtue of his human superiority, whether effective or merely symbolic, offers society not only a role model enabling men to understand what being a man entails, but it could well be said that he is the only real man, the lodestar of human reality. Thus, in Egypt, to worship the Pharaoh as the bodily manifestation of Atum (meaning "whole") or, in China, the Emperor as the Son of Heaven amounts, for his subjects, to worshipping what is realest in themselves inasmuch as he is a living mirror of their innermost self, a flesh-and-blood representation of the *imago Dei* resting in their heart.[84] Hence, the ascendancy of the king over his subjects is not, in the normal order of things, a tyranny, destructively repressive, but very much on the contrary a relationship which establishes for each man his function and place in the world. To remove the king is tantamount to self-

---

Aristotelian entelechy on its head, because he reversed the process to serve man and not God. Instead of seeing in history a flight away from the origin, he saw in it, rather, a preparation leading to sublimation. Incidentally, we assume that Hegel, forgetting the Fall, might have borrowed some his ideas from a misreading of Erigena who saw Christ redeeming mankind but not society. He did use the notion of Christ, as the *vir perfectus* who is the goal of history (cf. Bernard McGinn, *The Growth of Mysticism*), but in an apotheosis of the return to God occurring only in the next world.

84. This relationship is also complementary: "The king represents God for the people; however, in turn, the people represent God for the king" (Mahabharata 10:8). An illustration of this is found in the tradition, mentioned earlier, the English sovereigns observed of washing and kissing the feet of the poor.

beheading. It is to remove the polestar and consequently to reject the whole axis of principial reference—a point of vertical contrast for a play of forces leading man up or down the ladder of existence—around which an order is to be articulated. Society soon disintegrates.[85] If the erection of a sacred temple can be said to correspond microcosmically to the building of the cosmos, then the king functions as the keystone in the society's arch without which the whole edifice crumbles. To continue with this analogy, men without a king are as the chaotic rubble of stones, all semi-useless debris until they receive a role in the edification of the society's sanctuary which the king crystallizes, as it were, into a perfectly articulated whole.

To condemn hierarchy in the name of a false egalitarianism is also to abolish the crucial notion of merit—not to mention those of discernment and judgment—which is both the indispensable goad to excellence,[86] humanly speaking, as well as the cosmogonic "vindication" of the diversity in unity.[87] The paradox of royalty is that its very uniqueness, or eminence, is its claim to universality—or universality of example for all to model themselves on. Thus, in a certain way, nothing is more democratic, that is to say suitable for all people, than royalty. Democracy, meanwhile, in its negation of the elite, ends up hurting all people because it robs them of the notion of absolute superiority.

---

85. For the ancients, the institution of kingship constituted the very foundation of civilization since it hailed back to the creation of the world.

86. Thus the Koran: "And for all there will be ranks according to their deeds" (Ch. "The Wind-curved Sandhills" v. 19).

87. In metaphysical or scholastic terms, the accident (the fragment) has no right to exist except insofar as it worships the Substance; and it worships the Substance by testifying to a dimension of its richness: the relative is meant to proclaim the Absolute. Thus, qualities, such as a diamond's luminescence reflecting incorruptibility, have, strictly speaking, no "merit" of their own.

273

The proletarian hatred of kings stems from a confusion of who or what is the object of the veneration. It does not see, in its regicidal impulse—born really of a megalomaniac revolt—not only that the king is not a private individual and therefore cannot be judged as such (as Joseph de Maistre points out), but that individuals as such are but fragments of the one universal man,[88] and, as with all fragments, have therefore no hope of enduring and consequently no hope for lasting happiness because, if such a schematization is allowed, happiness of the part cannot be achieved outside—and certainly not at—the expense of the One. In other words, individuals, when mindful of their normal role, can be likened to planetary satellites that need borrow their light from the central personage of the monarch[89] just as planets take theirs from the sun. And, incidentally, therein lies the deeper justification for the gold ornaments of the monarch, for gold is said to be the flesh of the gods, which is immediately understandable when one thinks of this metal's warm luminosity.[90]

---

88. The word "individual" means "undivided" and therefore can only belong properly first to God and, by extension, to the earthly individual insofar as he reflects the qualities of his Maker; otherwise, he is no more unique than a fragment is.

89. "I have made bright *Maat* (right order) which he (Re) loves. I know that he lives by it. It is my bread; I eat of its brightness; I am likeness from his limbs, one with him (Queen Hatsheput in *Ancient Records*, Breasted, vol. II, par. 299). It goes without saying that—notwithstanding her effacement in this example— the queen fulfills for her subjects the same role as the king if she is the sovereign. It is for the sake of verbal economy that we speak in this chapter only of the king.

90. The golden sarcophagus of Tuthankhamon, as well as his golden likeness, comes to mind here, or the golden funerary mask, attributed to Agamemnon, found in the ruins of Mycenae. One also thinks of the legend of Eldorado commemorating the custom of a Colombian Indian chief who plastered his body with gold dust before plunging into a lake into which were then tossed all manner of gold ornaments.

The emphasis placed on the individual as such in all republicanisms obscures the fact of his expendability, metaphysically speaking, as accident, not, of course, as substance. Humanism assumes that the man's right to life—any man's—is sacred and absolute unconditionally so, that is without placing any qualifications on what this right entails. It assumes furthermore that this right is free—in short, that the mere fact of an individual's existence entitles him to live, irrespective or whether he be morally good or bad, or whether he deserves to exist. It does not occur to humanists that the right to human existence carries with it certain preconditions that can be forfeited by the individual, most notably by the criminally minded, but also by the hypocrite, the opportunist, the atheistic free-thinker, and any number of spiritually indifferent human types. Nor do humanists wish to see that the license to exist as such, that is to say unconditionally, is an open invitation for men to indulge their most subhuman instincts under the cover of a charter of arbitrary rights in which freedom has become, practically speaking, synonymous with permissiveness if not outright perversity—never mind how many innocents must put up with the depravity of a minority. One must show kindness, humanists say, never severity because that is unkind.

Now, it is one thing for a ruler to pledge protection to the poor and the ailing or to the oppressed—which is a sacred duty incumbent on his function—from the unscrupulous predation of the powerful over the weak, but quite another for a social order to protect the iniquitous simply because they exist or simply because the moral boundaries that normally separate evil from good have been blurred by irreligion,[91] and this, as always, in favor of

---

91. "Reason and experience forbid us to expect public morality in the absence of religious principle," George Washington felt compelled to remark.

275

perversion and of evil which, of course, has everything to gain from such intellectual vagueness and civic sentimentality. Modern democratic societies, founded on the notion of humanity's progress, pride themselves on having relegated the summary feudal justice of their ancestors to the dustbin of history, of which the only surviving vestige is the death-penalty.[92] Without elaborating on this point, which has been addressed elsewhere in these pages, suffice it to say that in traditional societies the right to life was something entirely conditional on proper moral behavior on the one hand, and on divine providence on the other.[93] In other words, this right normally had to be earned or secured by religion, otherwise an individual forfeited it and no one, in a society still decisively tilted towards Heaven, thought more about it.[94]

---

92. Capital punishment should simply be an impersonal lever which the criminal himself triggers by his misdeed. And for those who insist that such justice offers no deterrent to the criminally minded and that it is therefore useless, we will respond that the first objective of capital punishment is not deterrence but purging. Moreover, the fact that capital punishment is no deterrent to an inveterately evil person—which, incidentally, is another of its justifications because those inured to punishment would, logically, be inured to reform—does not mean it is without deterrence to the lukewarm, to borderline murderers, to say nothing of the influence its existence instills into the social body at large. And there are no statistics on would-be murderers. If we have insisted on this question it is because it is a touchstone of a person's understanding of what the human possibility is all about and its *post-mortem* continuation. What is ultimately real is not the life of a person, but the person himself. To confuse the two is not to understand the nature of the soul.

93. Attila's swathe of carnage and terror across the Italian peninsula was halted by Pope Leo I, who went out to meet him on muleback armed with but a crucifix. The shepherd's crook, when in the right hands, is mightier than the conqueror's rod.

94. Needless to say, we are not advocating a return to medieval times or even a wholesale reform of modern society. That would be impossible; and if not, it certainly could not be achieved by man alone. We are simply pointing out that non-modern man had a different scale

But more importantly, the whole focus in theocentric civilizations, namely those structured along the lines of "Thy Kingdom come," was, as stated previously, to ensure a good death or a safe passage to the next world. In the last analysis, a good death, as guaranteed by the civilization's Church, was all that really mattered and, indeed, might explain and could redeem all the human miseries suffered. It may be difficult to understand the point of so much of men's suffering unless one understand with what stubbornness men cling to the here-below and must, therefore, be forced to relinquish it by dint of conquering adversity: "I came not to send peace, but a sword" (Mat. 10:34).

Now, the king, as defender of the faith,[95] had not only the role of ensuring the well-being of his subjects, but also and above all, the duty of ensuring their successful entry into the next world where, in many traditions, he was believed to rule or where his intercession "with the gods" could ensure his subjects' posthumous felicity. It is this vertical dimension of a ruler's obligations that pluralism forgets.[96] And this is why it is finally difficult to divorce the priestly mandate from the kingly.

One of the paradoxical consequences of republicanism's emphasis on the collective individual—as opposed to feudalism's glorification of the single individual, the hero for instance—is that by dint of its demographic principle, which fosters quantity at the expense of quality, men have multiplied locust-like so that instead of having a small society of outstanding individuals[97] led by a chief—or a coun-

---

of values, one that took a full account of man's total cosmic situation with regard to posthumous realities.

95. The Pharaoh, as mentioned, is upholder of *Maat*, right order.

96. Pluralism is by definition anti-heroic.

97. One of the positive effects of both nomadic and feudal warfare, or the once perennial see-saw between civilization and barbarians, is that it weeds out human parasites—no one could afford to be weak (cf.

cil of chiefs—we have termite collectivities composed of less and less significant individuals led by committees. Pluralism—which can easily veer into populism—by its very structure,[98] denies the possibility of the divine man as well as the idea that one man can be the preeminent depositary of sapience. And this denial engenders the very evil collective suffrage is meant to remedy, namely ignorance, because pluralism, all told, is nothing other than an avowal that absolute wisdom does not exist, or at least that no one man can know absolutely. In other terms, democracy is premised on ignorance and, if allowed to run its logical course,[99] cannot but end up in the anarchy accruing from the confusion of too many contending voices, as well as from the unleashing of pent-up instincts thwarted from their transcendental fulfillment in certainty, namely in Truth which alone gives peace. Moreover, mediocrity, which has a stability of sorts, is the consolation prize for consensus rule.[100]

---

the earlier quote from the Swiss historian Jacob Burckhardt). And this is ultimately of more social moment than the fact that innocents may also be victims in the process. That said, one will want to bear in mind that life on earth can be an antechamber to both purgatory and to hell; in other words, in transmigrationist terms, a soul's destiny may bring it to pass through a historical epoch of terrible suffering.

98. "The majority . . . is the opinion of the least able," as Pascal noted.

99. As it happens, democracy is often far from "running its course out" in the sense that a plurality can be cornered by special interest groups which can be superiorily intelligent and efficient. But this "intelligence" is no substitute for real authority and is not sustainable on a long term basis, all the more so as it usually is nothing more than pragmatic and thus not doctrinal, except perhaps in the most superficial of senses such as the charters that exist in certain membership-only groups or business associations.

100. "Democracy," Plato cautioned, in the *Statesman*, "is the worst of all lawful governments and the best of all lawless ones." Indeed, pluralism can provide a safeguard of sorts against tyranny in an age where the

One cannot forget, when assessing the meaning and role of aristocracy, the impersonality—or transpersonality—of the kingly function which, in its essence, is assimilable to that of the divine intellect itself. In starkest terms, the king can be said to be the only real man, as mentioned above, the *chen jen* (universal man) of Taoism, the *Sapa Inca* (unique Inca), *the Insan al Kamil* of Sufism, the *vir perfectus* of Christianity, of which his subjects—as stated above—are like the morselled pieces.[101] In the same vein of analogy, the caste system of Hinduism is thought to issue from the division of Prajapati's cosmic body. It is in this sense that each pharaoh or each king was thought to be the perennial remanifestation of the Creator Himself.[102]

---

possibility of legitimate authority, in the fullest or regal sense of the word, is no longer practicable or where knowledge of the true nature of things is lost. However, this safeguard can only be of the most provisory sort, because it cannot offer a permanent solution but only an expedient.

101. In Africa, many Hamitic people cast the corpses of ordinary men into the bush but give their chiefs an elaborate ritual burial since they alone are thought to survive death. This otherwise barbaric custom is symbolic in that it indicates that the king is really the only one who does not transmigrate whereas the others are still caught in the wheel of the *Samsara*. Also symbolically noteworthy, and correcting the possible over-simplification of the first point mentioned, James Frazer remarks in *The Golden Bough* on the fact that some African tribes, notably the Yaos, call *mulungu*, the king, not only the ghost of a dead man but also "the aggregate of the spirits of the dead," which is full of significance for those who understand the human implications of the principle of unity. And this is why, *mutatis mutandis*, in a context now of spiritual alchemy, Christ can tell St. Catherine of Sienna: "I am He that is, thou art she who is not."

102. As Henri Frankfort remarks with great pertinence, "The essential quality of kingship could not be the *praesens*, 'this king rules;' it had to be the *perfectum*, 'this king has ascended the throne,' or, in mythological terms, 'Horus has succeeded Osiris'" (*Kingship and the Gods*, The University of Chicago Press).

279

In fine, if a ruler does not represent "the gods," then he is either representing himself, in the case of tyranny, or else, in the case of a republic, the will of the people or, more probably, that of a powerful clique. In either case, he cannot be worthy of any fundamental respect except insofar as he may have some individual merit of his own or uphold some values worth defending. Even so, the cornerstone upon which absolute authority rests, has been taken away and this leaves the floodgates of quarrelling disunity opened wide.

LEST THE CONSIDERATIONS above suggest that the best form of government would be the fusing of Church and State into a single theocratic rulership, it may be worth specifying that while the priestly and kingly functions overlap[103] and, indeed, are often interchangeable, they nonetheless have mutually exclusive purviews, especially in societies where Mammon vies with God for supremacy. Thus the duties of warfare and of justice, as those of finance, and by extension all temporal or political issues entailing the allocation of power, wealth, and property, and their administration, involve duties that logically concern the king as temporal ruler, or the State. On the other hand, the duties of mercy and redemption, as all otherworldly matters, specifically doctrine and by extension education—in its ethical foundation at least—to say nothing of the performance and preservation of ritual, naturally fall to the priest or to the Church's lot. It is not for nothing that in nomadic tribes and in most civilizations, the function of priest and warrior were kept separate so much so that the priest or the

---

103. For example, Pharaoh leading his armies, the Old Testament prophet Ehud killing the king of Moab, David slaying his enemies, the military pope Julius II as well as Gregory the Great known as *Consul Dei*, or Joan of Arc repulsing the English from the soil of France.

holy man was not allowed to engage in any of the activities of war, nor to engage in politics.

As Dante expounds in his *De Monarchia*, the emperor should not be subordinate to the pontiff in affairs temporal—whence Christ's injunction to render unto Caesar's what is Caesar's. Simple common sense should demonstrate this because if and insofar as the Church engages in worldly matters, it exposes itself to the *cupiditas* that fuels them and is consequently vulnerable to losing the necessary detachment or unifying transcendence of perspective that protects it from favoritism and corruption. Not forgetting also: "For all they that take the sword. . . ."

Moreover, this division of powers is necessary to the extent that it reflects a de facto division existing between the spiritual and secular dimensions of manifestation which mirror the rift between Heaven and earth—at least in the measure that earth cannot be Heaven. This is also the distinction between contemplation and action or that between inwardness ("My kingdom is not of this world"), and outwardness. In this respect, earth, or the horizontal axis, has certain rights and attendant prerogatives—relative though they may be when assessed from the perspective of the Eternal—that allows it some practical independence from Heaven, or the vertical axis.[104] But, quite obviously, these rights—born from the fact that material existence in order to exist must of necessity repudiate in a certain sense its origin—cannot exceed the boundaries of

---

104. Hence Joseph de Maistre's plea for the temporal ruler to defer unconditionally to the supreme pontiff is too idealistic because it does not allow sufficient room for certain mundane as well as material contingencies which are of decisive practical import. For instance, it is really no business of the Church to get involved in territorial disputes concerning political boundary lines. When the Renaissance Church proposed to divide the terrestrial globe between Spain and Portugal, it set itself up to be pilloried by sovereigns.

earth's limited scope.[105] For example, it is not wealth, or possessions in general, that is the evil obstructing man's spiritual ascent, but attachment to it to the exclusion of both his otherworldly obligations and of his charitable obligations. Those who, out of zealous idealism for the House of the Lord, would abolish wealth or all property rights[106] would, according to this fundamentalist logic, and to be absolutely consistent in their sublimist intention, want to abolish all distinctions, material or other. They forget, however, that to speak of creation is, by the same token, to admit to differentiation, multiplicity inequality, and separateness. What is needed is an equilibrium between the two

---

105. Science, for instance, errs when it presumes to philosophize.

106. Property is the inalienable bastion of the individual who himself, along with the family cell, is the foundation of civilization. Thus property is a citadel protecting both the individual and the family from the plundering chaos of mob rule: "Thou shalt not remove thy neighbor's landmark, which they of old time have set in thine inheritance, which thou shalt inherit in the land that the Lord thy God giveth thee to possess it" (Deut. 19:14). Even monasticism cannot do without an enclosure, and the idea of Church property is almost as old as civilization. Assuredly, property needs to be shared, not on terms set by the state but on those of the individual, to avoid the sclerosis of selfishness or the diseased surfeit of monopolistic excess. "All that is not shared is lost," says a Hindu proverb. Still, property, in its principle, is nothing other than the material token of the individual much in the same way as his bodily parts or character traits or temperamental dispositions, merits and faults, are his private province and responsibility. Therefore, possessions cannot be legislated away without in the same stroke doing away with the constitutive parts that make an individual unique or that guarantee his rightful pride as a distinct person. If the hunter cannot claim his kill as his own, the shepherd his flock, the husbandman his field, the vassal or citizen his dwelling, or likewise the king his realm, then society ceases to exist or men might as well be ants. The right to ownership is the safeguard of freedom and of value just as surely as despoliation is a breeder of poverty and ensuing slavery, is morally demeaning and destroys character which is the bedrock of a sound society.

poles, such as leavening wealth with charity. However, in a world of radical duality,[107] this can only be achieved by the complementary allocation of the separate purviews of Church and State, between spiritual pontiff and secular potentate.

In the conflict that has historically pitted Church against State, or pope against king, suffice it to say that, from the point of view of secular independence, the king stands for the freedom of the part, just as the pope stands for the transcendent unity of the whole. Diversity in unity, unity in diversity: these are the warp and weft of all social orders.

Now, if the roles of king and priest can overlap,[108] more normally, in civilizations ruled by cities, they are mutually

---

107. When civilization anchored itself in stone by erecting permanent buildings, it sought to preserve or crystallize the origin—most eminently in the form of the temple, sacred symbol of the cosmos and of the heart. But while so doing, it confirmed the principle of temporal division and precipitated the difference between an outside and an inside, an above and a below, as well as indirectly promoting a division between "haves" and "have-nots."

108. The worst interference occurs not when popes compete with princes, but when sovereigns intrude in the Church's domain. A notoriously infamous example of this was the Czar Peter the Great's utterly arbitrary "reform" of the Russian Church when he created a synod whereby he not only took it upon himself to name ecclesiastical officials, or usurped the pulpit by turning it into a tribune for political propaganda, but also personally—and sacrilegiously—altered the canons of the religious services. Such a precedent paved the way for the later Bolshevist suppression of the Church. But this example must be contrasted with the epic struggle that pitted the Holy Roman Emperor Henry IV against Pope Gregory VI, a conflict that resulted from the complicated and finally improper intertwining of the temporal and ecclesiastical prerogatives of the pontiff—leaving aside the thorny issue of the subordination of German Christianity to Latin rule. This struggle for hegemony over temporal affairs ended with a Pyrrhic victory for the Roman pontiff, because the unfortunate, and unnecessary, humiliation of the monarch sowed the seeds for the future schism that marked the

283

exclusive. Thus Christ did not accede to the zealots' wishes that he become king and Prince Gautama—the future Buddha—forsook all his royal privileges to become a monk in the midst of men. Among the founders of religion, the case of Muhammad is unique in that his *maqam* or spiritual station required that he be an example of perfect man— not perfect god-man—in a world of imperfection, the only role that accords with the Islamic emphasis on God's absolute and incomparable eminence over men who, in this respect, cannot be kings but only servants (the *ubudyah*), this so as to forestall the temptation of associationism (*shirk*) and concurrent pride. Yet, the corollary of submission is authority and this could not be excluded in a complete civilization such as that of Islam. Thus Sufism recognizes the idea of man as *khalifat fil 'ard*, or caliph on the earth, delegate authority of God who created man in His own image.

"LIVE FREE OR die" is a glorious motto which, however, is rendered meaningless without a powerful authority to uphold it. Authority, to be even minimally effective, has to be absolute *de jure* if not *de facto* lest it be nibbled to death by the chicanery of a myriad petty individual restrictions and exceptions. At the same time—and this is the grief egalitarianists nurse—absolute authority, when in the hands of a mere man or a single party, becomes a license for abuse, if not tyranny. As the saying goes, power corrupts and absolute power corrupts absolutely, though one must remember that the grandeur of the office can also transfig-

---

birth of Teutonic evangelicalism. That said, one cannot forget the prototype of the Holy Roman Emperor or the example of a Constantine convoking at Nicea the first Church Council over which he presided. In the absence of a supreme pontiff, the Church needed the intercession of a man of Constantine's stature to secure its nascent unity, to say nothing of the fact that it is one of the duties of a monarch to protect the church.

ure its holder into a superior person. There is, indeed, no moral reason or justification for a collectivity, or even a single individual, to have to grovel before an arbitrary power, for man is not meant to be a slave—"Ye are the salt of the earth"—though, terrestrially speaking, he is but dust beneath the feet of the Lord.

Nonetheless, man, insofar, as he has not transcended himself, is nothing but a slave, whether it be in regard to a moral superior, or whether it be in regard to himself insofar as he is controlled by his passions—the unimpeded indulgence of which can hardly be said to constitute freedom[109]—or again insofar as he is the plaything of the tides of marauding fate, whether she come in the guise of hunger, disease, plague, war, poverty, injustice, or whatever of an endless series of possible tribulations that man's perishable flesh is heir to.

In this respect, that is to say inasmuch as man cannot avoid the thousand importunities that infest the very fabric of earthly existence—imperfect by cosmological necessity—freedom is won more often through a negation or privation (the Vedantic *neti neti* or the apophatic Christian's *via negativa*) freely consented to—this is the key[110]—than through an affirmation of self or through immediate gratification. In other words, he alone is truly free who has succeeded in detaching himself by an act of noble will from ambition's contentious battles; he alone is truly free who grasps the futility of worldly glory. Now, one might contend that the freedom of the intelligence to consent to the evidence of necessity is not freedom

---

109. Wherefore the absurdity of John Stuart Mill's assertion that "Liberty consists in doing what one desires," an opinion which Hegel was to qualify (not necessarily in reference to the social theorist) as one of "utter immaturity." Intemperance is not liberty but bondage.

110. "Whosoever he be of you that forsaketh not all that he hath, he cannot be my disciple" (Lu. 14:33).

because there is no real choice. However, man has the choice—absurd as it is—to reject the truth; that is what defines him. The freedom, of course, is finally less in the choice than in the object: to chose the truth is to chose life, freedom, and happiness because these cannot be defined outside of it. In so doing, man trades a lesser liberty for an immeasurably greater one.

Now, without the uplifting exemplar of a kingly paragon or of a priestly ideal, it must be reiterated, both of whom set the tone for an entire social order according to the "sacred politics" their roles command, man is left to flounder hopelessly in a race that here below he cannot but lose, whether to others in life or finally to death which has no favorites, for the king—or the hero—teaches man to overcome the world and himself, and the priest—or saint—teaches man to give up the world and himself: "Whosoever shall seek to save his life shall lose it" (Lu. 17:33).

And just as there is no freedom without authority, so there is no freedom without knowledge, because if one does not know who one is and, more broadly, what man is, then there is no way to know what one truly wants and needs. Consequently, one is an easy prey to desires and aspirations which instead of dismantling karma, perpetuate it in the endless round of existences the Eastern religions mention. In this sense, doing exactly as one pleases is the most fatal of illusions because that amounts, by dint of inertia, to doing exactly as the ego (the *nafs al-ammarah* the Sufis describe, or the naturally egotistical and passional soul) wants and not as the spirit would do if allowed to rule as it should when restored to its throne in man's heart. It is meaningless to speak of freedom when there is no urge, or understanding, to overcome oneself. Indeed, before the soul can say "yes" to itself, it must first say "no"—"He that hateth his life in this world shall keep it unto life eternal" (John 12:25)—for, in Christian terms there

286

is something in every man born of the Fall that must be either exterminated, transcended, or converted.[111] It is quite useless to speak of freedom where the notion of redemption, and all that this entails eschatologically, has become a dead letter.[112]

There cannot logically be any "sacred" right to liberty—that leaves out the super-natural—for a godless humanity,[113] because the very notion of liberty cannot be divorced from that of God Who, metaphysically speaking, is the only One that is free, or the only One that is completely free if one allows for the fact of man's relative liberty. In other words, man can only be free inside of God, not outside of Him. Paradoxically, however, man is free to reject God, as alluded to above, which is tantamount to saying that he is free to renounce freedom; but he cannot then expect to be free in the results of what is an initially free choice.

---

111. One of the results of the Fall—which Shakespeare has eloquently described in a number of his plays (for example, *The Tempest, The Winter's Tale, Cymbeline*)—is the banishment of the kingly—or queenly—intellect, namely the spirit, while a jealous usurper, namely the unreformed and passional individual will, rules. This is why, in the absence of proper spiritual renunciation and conversion, the popular adage of a Joseph Campbell—"Follow your bliss"—is so perniciously seductive. No bliss without sacrifice; this is man's lot.

112. The religion of Humanity, promoted by a John Stuart Mill for instance, whose premises were laid already in the anthropocentrism—and parallel egocentrism—of the Renaissance and actively propounded in the spiritual benightedness of the so-called "Enlightenment," has been codified into dogma by no less an authority then the Post-Conciliar Roman Catholic Church (intellectually open to all the "breakthroughs" of science and secular progress), negating thereby the "Thy Kingdom come" of the "Our Father."

113. Some might counter that religion and the modern world are not incompatible. However, nominal belief in God—that is to say belief unsupported by a sacred framework—does not automatically entail practical or concrete belief, because modernism knows well how to arrogate the notion of God for its own Promethean ends.

IN THE LIGHT of the foregoing, it would not be overbold to conclude that a society without kings is a moribund society that has forsaken its bond with its origin, or severed its link to Heaven, and cannot therefore be long in perishing. It will have no posterity in centuries, for the rejection of kingship ultimately amounts to the rejection of God. No less. A regicidal social order, once all the sham justifications of authority and justice have been discredited by either the anarchy or tyranny that are bound to arise, is nothing other in its essence than a parricidal one, for the king is the father of a society in the same way that God is the Father of creation.

At the risk of belaboring the point, but only because modernism is so averse to this fact, we will say again that royalty is founded on the nature of things, namely on the natural order of the cosmos. Just as the galaxies circle around a center, and cannot not do so without disintegrating, so must society revolve around a center without which it is doomed to collapse. To each body its heart, a sacred center.[114] To imagine a being, or a social order—which is a macrocosmic being—without both a heart or center or without an origin or a progenitor, is to imagine something that does not exist. This is why authority, in the purest sense, can never be elective,[115] for to be all that it needs to

---

114. In his opening lines of *Light on the Ancient Worlds*, Schuon writes that "the whole existence of the peoples of antiquity is dominated by two presiding ideas, the idea of Center and the idea of Origin." The king—or queen—as heart, is the human personification of both ideas.

115. It could never be elective in the full pluralistic sense of collective suffrage. When the Conclave elects a pope, who is meant to be *primus inter pares*, it is a body of his peers, not of commoners, that exercise this privilege. Having said this, one cannot exclude that an elected leader may be so providentially. Yet, one cannot assume that *vox populi* is automatically *vox Dei* unless one were to jettison all notions of the right order of things. As it is, the majority usually elects the least unqualified, not the most qualified person. It takes a national crisis to select a great leader.

be requires an investiture from Above, a consecration that renews the bond between man and God.[116]

Far more essential than the fact of the opportune necessity of the king as a figure of unity saving society from being rent by internecine factionalism,[117] is the role of the king as spiritual heart. Thus, in the case of the emperor of Japan, the Mikado, his person is considered to be no less than the dynamical center of the universe, its beating heart, from whose vital nucleus lines of force radiate in solar fashion to all quarters of the earth. As such, he is the fulcrum[118] on which hangs the balance of the world. And, consequently, it is thought that the slightest irregularity on his part may upset the delicate equipoise of opposites governing the play of existence. This play of opposites is symbolically entrusted to his care in order that a harmonious equilibrium be maintained in the realm, itself a reflection of the galaxied cosmos.[119]

In the mythical tale of the origin of the Japanese emperor (who is *Aki-tsu-kami*, a "god manifest"),[120] the sun

116. Wherefore Christ says to Pontius Pilate: "Thou couldest have no power at all against me, except it were given thee from above" (John 19:11).

117. This is Hobbes' vindication of monarchy, lame though it be.

118. Likewise, in Hinduism, the Universal Monarch or *Chakravartin* is considered to be the hub of the universe: all things tend towards him like the spokes of a wheel.

119. The Pharaoh was also known as "The Two Lords" in that he embodied the perennial antagonists Horus (light) and Seth (strife). "The king was identified with both of these gods, but not in the sense that he was considered the incarnation of the one and also the incarnation of the other. He embodied them as a pair, as opposites in equilibrium," as Henry Frankfort makes clear in his *Kingship and the Gods*. As for a material illustration of this equipoise, we know that the balance between heat and cold depends on the exact and dependable orbit of the earth around the sun; were this orbit to veer slightly askew, life, as we know it, would disappear, either scorched or frozen.

120. This is a question of primordial symbolism, not of the falsification for political ends of the Emperor's function in the Meiji period.

289

goddess Amaterasu bequeathed three treasures to Prince Ninigi, the royal ancestor of all emperors: a mirror, a jewelled necklace, and a sword.[121] The necklace and the sword correspond to the polarization of the functions of mercy or benevolence and justice or bravery, as seen earlier. But it is the first treasure, the sacred mirror, which must now hold our attention, for it is the non-formal synthesis (or, in Buddhist terms, the form of the void, *shunyamurti*) of the other two which are, as it were, the formal and therefore dualistic exteriorization of its essence. As such, this mirror— the sacrosanct object of Shintoism—is the symbol of wisdom or knowledge, as yet undifferentiated, and corresponds macrocosmically to the sun itself which is the king of the universe: "Consider this mirror," Amaterasu is said to have told the Prince, "exactly as if it were Our august spirit and revere it as if it were Ourself thou didst revere. Illuminate the whole world with the brilliance of this mirror."

It will not be difficult for those conversant with the laws of symbolism to see how the polarization of mercy and justice—or love and strength—find their common origin in the limpid substance of the mirror: its spotless purity welcomes everything without distortion just as its keen clarity reflects the truth, or the true nature of everything reflected in it. Like pure intelligence, which coincides with the transpersonality of the divine void, or complete detachment, the mirror is able on the one hand to receive everything while remaining absolutely untouched and, on the other, again like pure intelligence, to reflect all light without diminishment.

These gifts,[122] which symbolically recapitulate the divine monarch's faculties and corresponding duties as

---

121. These treasures recall the gifts the Magi brought Christ the child: gold, frankincense, and myrrh—namely wisdom, beauty (or goodness), and the capacity for heroic self-sacrifice.

122. "Every good gift and every perfect gift is from above, and cometh down from the Father of lights, with Whom is no variableness, neither shadow of turning" (James 1:17).

principal upholder of *dharma*,[123] recall in turn the Sufi ternary of, in ascending order, fear or action, love or being, and knowledge or intellective identity with the Principle.

Thus the king, upon his coronation—which corresponds cosmologically to sunrise (or to the sun's accession to its zenith) just as his reign corresponds to a solar cycle—comes to men, who still "sit in darkness and in the shadow of death, fast bound in misery and iron" (Ps. 107:10), like "the day-spring from on high," to teach them to live in a clear intellectual daylight. His eagle's eye view of the world, born from the fact that he belongs neither to himself nor to any factional interest, allows him to re-establish the earthly reflection of the *civitas Dei*, or Augustine's City of God.

To recapitulate what was said in the opening of this chapter, the institution of sacred monarchy reflects the fact that God is the Lord of creation, "to him be glory and dominion for ever and ever" (Rev. 1:6). The king, upon anointing by the Church, inherits this feudal paternity joining Creator to His creatures who, in this perspective, are the vassals in His realm that owe Him obeisance and eternal fidelity. Thus a king is meant to remind men of God's cosmic suzerainty without which they are shorn of both their sense of center and their sense of origin. And, microcosmically, the descent of the god-king among men—reenacted and commemorated in the ceremony of the coronation—can be likened to the descent of the Name of God into the believer's heart: it restores order in the soul/society, quells passions/anarchy, and transfigures by restoring man to his own kingly and priestly essence. The king,

---

123. In Hindu terms, the king's *shakti* (or regal radiance) consisted of the three elements of *prabhava* or "majesty," *utshaha* or "energy," and *mantra* or "wisdom".

embodying the sun, renders light intelligible to man; as such he is the human actualization of the Absolute in the relative and as Logos he is the *imago Dei*. In Christian terms, his prototype is Christ who is the prince of the kings of the earth and who "hath made us kings and priests unto God" (Rev. 1:5,6).

7. THY CENTER IS EVERYWHERE

*God's center is everywhere. His circumference is
nowhere.*

St. Bonaventura

MAN ON EARTH is situated at the junction of two dimensions, that of space and that of time.[1] But without the
notion of the center, these two dimensions lead to his alienation and, ultimately, to his annihilation. If an individual
can pause long enough from his habitual routine or self-
absorption, he is confronted on the one hand by the sheer
immensity of space whose boundaries exist nowhere
because an absolute frontier, were this to exist, presupposes an absolute emptiness against which it could be measured and this is a material impossibility. And on the other
hand, he is confronted by the sheer endlessness of time
whereby things—not in their individual specificity but in
their generic, or at least archetypal, possibility—are fixed[2]
to continue forever since an absolute end is just as inconceivable as an absolute limit. The Night of Brahma or the

---

1. These dimensions have also their equivalences in non-terrestrial
realms.

2. Relativists will of course argue that in the horizontal space-time
continuum the notion of a center can have no absolute significance. On
the face of it, this would not be entirely incorrect if the vertical dimension could be disposed of somehow.

293

Christian apocatastasis do not refute this since, from the point of view of Brahma, there are innumerable "nights" each followed by a new "day."[3]

And even from an individual standpoint it is fairly evident that something as practically absolute as death or a terminal destruction is finally but a metamorphosis that sustains a new possibility. Though the former one may be irretrievable in its individual distinctness, perhaps even tragically so within the balance of a cycle,[4] new equivalents spring afresh in its wake that celebrate the perenniality of the creative principle, just as life surges anew at each dawn reminding us afresh of the ancient rhythm of being.

Without the notion of the center, space and time lead to man's downfall—space by scattering man's vital substance into a thousandfold variety of individual pursuits and time by implacably dismantling everything he undertakes. In itself, the endlessness of both space and time is, in the mode appropriate to each, a refraction of God's dimension

---

3. One the most vehement of the disputes in the Middle Ages centered on the idea of the eternity of creation which was proposed by the Neoplatonists, including some of the Arab philosophers, but explicitly rejected by Christian theologians on the basis that to assume a perennial creation detracted from the omnipotence of God as well as that of His supreme antecedence to anything other than Himself. However, to state that God is unique does not exclude the fact that He is also total. And it is in virtue of that totality—the pleroma—that one can speak of an eternal creation which, with regard to a specific cosmos, is nonetheless periodically reabsorbed into and reissued from a primordial divine substance. Some of the problem results from Christian eschatology's emphasis on a single creation, a single redeemer, and a single opportunity for man to be saved or lost, whereas in a perspective such as Hinduism, in which the idea of multitudes of creations and multitudes of rebirth is taken for granted, this is not an issue.

4. The death of a civilization, like that of an individual, carries with it an irreversible finality which can nourish the mournful reveries of a romantic or the ruminations of a pessimist. But it can also free a contemplative from the snare of accidentality.

of infinitude and thereby of grandeur.[5] Microcosmically, St. Bernard speaks of the soul's reflecting the Word's *magnitudo* or greatness and dignity. However, when seen without the stabilizing and redemptive notion of the center—that is when seen only from the perspective of man's individual measure—they loom as a terrifying and ultimately alienating, all-engulfing vastness wherein man's destiny, deeds, and delusions are discarded or pulverized into meaninglessness: "And how many a generation," the Koran asks, "before them We have destroyed? Canst thou see a single man of them, or hear from them the slightest sound?" (Ch. "Mary", v. 98).

Man without a center faces the immensity of the starry void,[6] at once condemned to be and condemned to disappear, neither able not to be[7] nor unable not to die. A paradoxical temptation for the individual confronted with the impassive face of eternity is to believe that his subjectivity is the only reality—"Only human beings really exist" (Sartre)[8]—which marks the nadir of alienation from objective reality[9] and the consummation of inversion: "Existence

---

5. This dimension of endlessness is compensated by the formal reality of things, or by the reality they borrow, which is a reflection of God as Absolute. This is why things seem so real or rather, to borrow from Augustine, "are not altogether unreal."

6. Theodore Roszak quotes, in *Where the Wasteland Ends*, what he terms Pascal's "cry of sheer existential terror:" "Cast into the infinite immensity of spaces of which I am ignorant and which know me not, I am frightened!"

7. Suicide does not resolve this; it only recasts the issue posthumously.

8. Cf. Sartre's essay, "La transcendance de l'égo," which is as extreme a contradiction in terms (an oxymoron) as can be found because it "canonizes" the most unequivocally Promethean—if not Luciferian—in man in an act of terminal solipsism.

9. The term "objective reality" is used advisedly, although this is a tautology, simply because from an empirical point of view one is entitled to speak also, quite provisorily, of a subjective reality.

precedes essence" (Sartre). How far we are from St. Augustine's declaration in his *Confessions*: "I would more easily have doubted my own existence than the existence of truth itself."

Now, be it said in passing, the fact that absolute notions such as those of the truth and the center—which is its spatial coordinate—have become for most people abstractions or empty terms is a testimony to the primacy the pole matter has insidiously assumed in today's social consciousness. What is habitually concrete or real for man now is no longer the principle or the essence, but the materiality of the world which provides him with a dense or even an inverted sense of objectivity. And therefore, by a kind of vengefully compensatory reflex against the suffocation resulting from this opacity of reference points, subjectivity has parallely assumed an omnipotence whereby individual opinion becomes the de facto authority in all issues.

WHEN SEEKING TO trace the origin of life, of the vital principle, the question naturally arises whether consciousness is born of matter, as evolutionism alleges, or on the contrary whether matter is a condensate of ethereal energy or even of consciousness. From the point of view of Plotinian emanationism, matter is a projection—a coagulation or a downward crystallization—of life, and life is a projection—cosmogonic and downward—of consciousness, namely of intelligence or spirit. Thus, the "gross state" proceeds from the "subtle state," and "downward," somewhat in the manner of a precipitate.

From a purely empirical point of view, it might seem plausible to subordinate consciousness to matter not only because, as Aristotelian inquiry suggests, the mind cannot a priori think outside of sense categories, but because, again as the Stagirite proposes, the soul does not seem to be able to exist without the body, to say nothing of the fact that consciousness, as earthly man understands it, is encased—Plato would have said entombed—in a material container which would seem to set very restrictive boundaries to what it can naturally perceive. In Aristotle's defense, however, it is worth remarking that owing to the direction of his inquiry—which is almost exclusively inductive and not intuitive—he proceeds always from the outside to the inside; in other words, his point of departure is invariably the visible, namely man's corporeal existence, contrary to Plato whose starting point is the invisible, namely the archetypal "ideas" or essences. Nonetheless, Aristotle is eventually led to affirm that there is a motionless mover whose substance is pure consciousness or intelligence (reason or *nous*) that "thinks" the world into being.

An individual's vision, which is the most extensive of his sense faculties, cannot overleap the nearest hill or curtain of trees, and much less so the four walls of a room. In short, this subjugation to material form makes it difficult for man to conceive of a disincarnate conscious entity, be it the soul or God. And this limitation appears to support the hypothesis of a purely sense-dependent consciousness, all the more so as, again empirically, consciousness emerges from within and, therefore, seems to be wholly circumscribed by bodily confinement without which it would not only be non-operative, practically speaking, but vanish into thin air. In short, for the sensorialist, and even for the sensualist, reality recedes in direct measure that it becomes incorporeal. But such a viewpoint, which can be specifically egocentric, does not begin to explain essential or fundamentally selfless modalities of consciousness such as idealism and heroism, or notions such as that of the sense of truth, justice, and the sovereign good, nor that of love when freed from passion, except insofar as these have some material incidence. Thus bliss, for instance, is materially ascertainable only in its bodily incidence as pleasure.

But bliss is not, in its essence, physical pleasure. Nor does the strictly materialist point of view account for the fact why, when pleasure is experienced, the sense of physical boundaries appears to dissolve, leading perhaps to a near beatific merging of the individual's consciousness with a far greater whole which it intuits. Nor does it explain why, when a plenitude of love is experienced, as in mystical ecstasy or simply poetic love, the bodily senses are ascentionally transfigured, reabsorbed, or extinguished into a higher, trans-individual state of consciousness whereby distinct faculties such as sight, hearing, and sensation can become perhaps not only blissfully interchangeable ("seeing" sound or "hearing" colors, for example, or resonating forms),[10] but often lose their material sensitivity to the point of becoming extinct since the physical body—and, by extension, the individual ego—ceases to be the locus or prism of awareness.[11]

In the inversion of poles accompanying the process of manifestation, the pole matter becomes operatively predominant over that of the spirit, so that what in the Absolute is the greatest, namely the spiritual, becomes, in the relative, the least; and conversely, the least in the Absolute, namely material density, becomes the greatest— or rather the most extensive—in the relative.[12]

---

10. The technical term for this is synesthesia. Cf. St. Bernard's rich use of the permutability of the five senses to describe mystical insight.

11. Thus, in a higher respect, Schuon explains that "a spiritual vision of things is distinguished by a concrete perception of universal relationships and not by some special sensorial characteristic" (*Light on the Ancient Worlds*, Ch. "Man in the Universe").

12. One might object that there is no trace of matter in the Absolute which, strictly speaking, would seem to be true. However, there must nonetheless be some prototype in the Absolute for the possibility of density, and this prototype is the quality of concreteness of which matter is the terrestrial issue. Moreover, there must also be some kind of sacred matter in the Absolute—"this is my body" (Mark 14:22). One might also

In its extreme mode, the pole matter is characterized by two culminating degrees: near absolute density the one, which corresponds to the mirroring in manifestation of the static principle and chaos the other, which corresponds to the mirroring in manifestation of the dynamic principle. Thus matter, when divorced from the spirit—or rather in the measure that it can be[13]—reflects principial unity, but in inverse mode, by a tendency towards petrification, and it reflects principial infinity, likewise in inverse mode, by a concurrent tendency towards fragmentation—or a principle of division which, at its outermost point, becomes fragmentation. In virtue of these twin tendencies, the center—in matter—becomes multiple, being at once nowhere per se, because always outside of any particular "that" and yet able to appear everywhere insofar as any particular "that" carries, immanently, something of the universal Thatness without which it would be void of any reality, hence non-existent.[14]

---

want to remember that the notion of matter itself is rather generalistic since it would be more exact to speak of our sense of matter as translated by our five senses, or by our position on what is in fact an endless continuum of reality. Moreover, the visible portion of matter is, according to physicists, but a fraction of the whole realm of mass. That is to say that the rest of what we cannot see or touch is enigmatically termed to be "dark" matter; we can perceive it only via the clues of the circumstantial evidence offered by the pull it exerts on galaxies or the manner in which it bends light.

13. This point of "absolute density" is never reached because matter, by its very nature, cannot be absolute. Physicists know of the near infinite porosity of matter and of its near infinite compressibility. Absolute spirit, however, is the very essence of reality—and of every reality.

14. In Thomist metaphysics, one would say that accidents exist in some substance but never, in the natural course of things, exist by themselves. Nietzsche formulated the idea of Thatness thus: "Every moment beginneth existence, around every 'Here' rolleth the ball 'There'. The middle is everywhere."

The error of nihilism derives from the virtual nothing-ness inherent to accidentality, whereas the error of idolatry derives from the trace of absoluteness inherent to any acci-dent insofar as it exists. The mistake, in each case, is to exaggerate one aspect to the detriment of the other. In other words, the illusion of reality in existence is the cornerstone of all associationisms (*shirk* in Islamic terms) or the Pentateuch's sin of idolatry, whereas the illusion of noth-ingness is that of all nihilisms. Magic, such as in the use of spells, the blowing on knots, or the use of effigies, derives its operative power from the fact that a fragment can serve as a symbolical substitute for the whole. But the limits of magic—providentially—come in parallel manner from the fact that the fragment can never be the whole, whence the impotence of these same spells which, to be even minimal-ly effective, require a corollary "passivity," so to speak, on the part of the object, namely a lack of homogeneity or an inability to be fully what it is. In nature, things are meant to be mutually exclusive, for this is what guarantees their uniqueness and preserves them from being reabsorbed into other things—silk is not steel. At the same time, no single thing can be hermetically unique; each thing in creation has, in virtue of its inescapable relativity, a porosity that renders it permeable to other things. And it is these fis-sures, at least insofar as they can become critical, that magic can also exploit.

To conclude this series of remarks, if one can say that the center can both transcend any particular thing[15] while

---

15. When Spinoza denies God that attribute of transcendence, argu-ing that He is infinite and therefore cannot be outside of anything, he overlooks the fact that God, Who is also totality, cannot be totally in every thing otherwise that thing would be the Absolute as such. That one can say that the drop of sea spray is nothing other than the ocean does not allow one to say that the ocean is sea spray. When the Vedanta designates the universe as *Shivaswarupa* (i.e. as the true form of Shiva), it

appearing immanently in it (however remotely or dimly), one must also take into account two more facts: first, that some things and some creatures are more central than others, owing to the hierarchical deployment in manifestation which retraces celestial hypostases—both directly and indirectly—and, secondly, that one thing can be central with respect to another, not necessarily on all accounts, but at least in virtue of one or more decisive aspects whose excellence does not impugn the superiority of the other. For instance, if flight were everything, any bird would be superior to a cat. However, with respect to flight, it is so, although very partially so unless one is talking of the greatest of birds in which case there is global equality. Moreover, one thing or creature may have a dual symbolism. Thus, to take a central example, woman as Eve is the temptress but as Mary is an agent of redemption. Indeed nothing, in the realm of manifestation, which is by definition dualistic, can claim absoluteness in all respects.

Some extreme examples of what one might want to term the opportuneness of symbolism are illustrated by the figuratively central role that otherwise peripheral creatures can assume in traditional symbolism. Thus the wild boar, the spider, the scarab—even creatures that belong properly to quasi-infernal circles of manifestation such as the bat, the snake, the scorpion—or simply any number of normally peripheral creatures, can provisorily take on a central meaning that belongs by right only to those creatures which are most central by the beauty and nobility of their form allied, normally, to the scope of their size. In this respect—and this

---

is not saying that universe is Shiva as such, *tale quale*, but that the universe has no intrinsic reality save as a form assumed by Shiva. That is altogether different from the pantheistic assumption which, in its terminal point, amounts to a denial of God since to reduce the divine to perishable matter amounts effectively to eliminating it. And this is why idolatry is a sin and not just a mistake.

time on an eminently qualitative plane—the dove, as a vehicle of the Holy Ghost, plays a role in Christianity which, in
other traditions such as that of the American Indians or in
medieval chivalry belongs more directly—and naturally—to
the eagle by virtue of its sheer size and majesty. More paradoxically, it is enough that a creature evidence one decisive
aspect for it to eclipse, in the economy of a traditional symbolism, other apparently more suitable candidates. Thus the
crocodile in Ancient Egypt, owing to the Kali-like function of
its all-devouring jaws (cf. also the Vedic *makara*) which
makes it a fit guardian of the gates separating the two
worlds, is elevated to an object of reverence that this creature
in its literal hideousness could hardly deserve. The same
could be said for the shark in the Polynesian culture—and
one might want to add that the choice may be dictated
more by the lack of alternatives than by the eminence of the
creature so designated: not every culture has lions or tigers
or jaguars that it can enroll into its cosmology. But the evidence of a creature's formal ugliness, or fearfulness, should
not offer ammunition to the relativists who, in wanting to
salvage the merits of the periphery, discredit by that fact
those of the center in an operation that is finally satanic
because its ultimate goal is to divinize macrocosmically
what microcosmically in man—St. George's dragon—
needs to be conquered, destroyed, or transfigured, and not
coddled. The way we look at creation, finally, is the way we
look at ourselves.

WHEN ARISTOTLE OBSERVES in his Physics the principle of
autonomy in things "which exist by nature"[16] and comments on their "inherent impulse to change," he is touching on one of the greatest of philosophical inquiries, the
origin of causation, a question which short of the beatific

---

16. As opposed to things manufactured: "What exists by nature
appears to have the principle of movement or rest within itself."

vision of first causes, can be answered only by rational induction or by intellective intuition.

One of the marvels of creation is the apparently autonomous movement of creatures or what is in essence the gift of freedom which, properly speaking, can in fact only belong in its totality to the One Being and not to the many. If one watches a butterfly fluttering happily about or a fish slipping through the stream, it would seem that creatures[17]—or ourselves—when seen from the outside, can move freely at will and would possess the automotive sufficiency to exist and operate in the absence of any distinctively separate principle of motoric sustenance, that they are intrinsically active and only acted upon extrinsically or coincidentally.

However, upon closer examination, this autonomy of creatures, while real enough as far as volition is concerned and relatively absolute within the narrow confines of their possibility, is, strictly speaking, a metaphysical impossibility. The fact that they can have no permanent self-sufficiency, namely that they must derive the entire sum of their material sustenance from outside the limits of their respective forms, is but the first clue of their intrinsic dependence on a center that perforce transcends their bodily entity and without which they would cease to exist.[18]

Leaving aside the dependence creatures have on obtaining nourishment outside of themselves, which in

---

17. The vegetative and mineral realms also possess an inherent capacity for change or for variety in form; but what distinguishes them absolutely from creatures is the fact of their rootedness in earth. In other words, they possess none of the autonomy of creatures because their capacity for change ceases the very moment they are cut off from their "umbilical" substratum. Cut a flower, and it wilts; chip out an emerald and it remains forever crystallized. Nor do they possess in any way the locomotive capacity of creatures, a capacity that corresponds to the faculty of will because involving the capacity for choice.

18. Ironically, and perversely, of all creatures, human beings can ape the absoluteness of divine autonomy, not on a positive plane of course,

itself is but the most external proof of their lack of fundamental autonomy, can we say, speaking now of their consciousness, that despite the semblance of intellective self-
sufficiency they are no more independent psychically than
materially? Indeed, the issue of consciousness is the be-all
and end-all of philosophy. The material sciences of biology
and physics, no matter how far they push back the limits of
their respective inquiries, are impotent to answer this most
essential of mysteries and that because of the very episte-
mological grounds of their inquiry which, owing to its
material or mechanistic premises, cannot step above the
plane of things physical which is by definition relative.

To answer the question concerning the origin of causation, one could posit that creatures are invisibly bound to a
higher, or transcendent, existential ground by some kind of
ethereal, luminous,[19] or reverberant filament imperceptible
to the senses, but this would be missing the point—leaving
aside the possible quaintness of such an assumption which
does not, in the last analysis, escape from the conundrum of

---

but on a negative one in virtue of the principle of the inversion of poles
whereby the lesser can analogically retrace through its voidness the fullness of the greater; for example, death mimics the absoluteness of what
it denies: life. Thus when a Sartre says that "freedom is the capacity to
say 'no'," he is touching on the one point where man can achieve a
degree of individualistic absoluteness, never mind its nothingness or
absurdity. In other words, only the individualist—not animals, nor man
when normal—can be fundamentally in error and that is a distinction of
sorts, but a meaningless one. In this sense, man's unique capacity for
suicide is the inverted equivalent (insofar as there can be any kind of
geometric parallel here) of God's capacity to bestow life.

19. The Christian idea of a guardian angel would be close to this
imagery in that it is said that a ray of light connects it to the individual
soul. We recall reading somewhere that one of the reasons for the ton-
sure used by certain monastic orders was to symbolically reopen the
fontanel (from the French word for "fountain") which functioned as a
kind of gate between the soul and the higher orders of manifestation.

physical causation. In its defense, one could cite the Koran where God speaks of holding man by his forelock. The validity of this imagery, however, is not so much in its literal verisimilitude, but in its symbolism. Thus to speak of a ray of light connecting the soul to its guardian angel is to transcribe into spatial terms a reality that would otherwise elude all categorizations familiar to man on earth. An analogy need not be a literal adequation to be correct or effective.

To understand causation proper requires understanding the law of inverse analogy ruling manifestation, namely to reverse the approach which has it that for something to exist it must originate from something lying outside of itself; this is one of the legacies of what Sufis might term the sin of outwardness. While this sequence of causation is real enough as regards purely physical entities, it begs the crucial question: wherefore being or, rather in this case, wherefore "beings"? Why not assume instead that all beings are not moving *outside* of their common ground of existence but rather *inside* a continuum of consciousness whereby they acquire individuality, and especially individual distinctness, through remotion from the Principle? This view of reality or that of what in Sufism is known as the *wahdat al wujud* (the principle of the "unicity of existence")—a close parallel of Shankara's *Advaita Vedanta* (or school of non-duality)—posits that beings can be but transient coagulations of an in-itself fully unified substratum of being/consciousness whereby they exist no longer as outcasts from some heavenly Eden, but as ideas in the mind of God or as pleasurable modalities[20] of His Being, surfacing for awhile before subsiding thereinto like waves of the ocean. Their apparent autonomy is then wholly derived from a boundless center which, although immanent when seen from the outside, is in reality all-encompassing when seized from the inside because what for man lies "outside" in the form of

---

20. Thus a dolphin could be one expression of Brahma's joy in being.

created separations—as cut-outs—is in reality "inside" for God. And this brings us back again to the law of inverse analogy: whereas in the created order, the center is inside, in the universal order this relationship is reversed so that the center is greater than the periphery.[21] One could recast this to say that while on earth if the innermost core of our being is a wellspring of bliss encompassed by seemingly endless stratas of separateness, coldness, emptiness, and loneliness, as evinced by the galactic night, in the heavenly order, there is a point— really only a seed—of separateness and of potential solitude and emptiness[22] encompassed by endless vistas of bliss.

Likewise, for the man who realizes his center in God, the world and things are no longer outside, but are included inside as possible extensions of himself while dwindling in proportion to the wonder of otherworldliness. The same can be said about his ego which, instead of surrounding him in its passionate grip, has now become just an objective part of him and, indeed, the lesser in importance as befits the true scale of proportions of which the pinnacle is the Divine Self. For the profane man, however, the one caught in the clutches of his ego contraction, the world, and by distant extension its Creator, is experienced as outside to the degree that this contraction acts to separate him from totality—wherefore the silent despair, to paraphrase Thoreau, of men unable to release the bait of egocentrism.[23]

---

21. Koran: "Whithersoever ye turn, there is God's Countenance. Lo! God is All-Embracing, All-Knowing" (Surat "The Cow":115).

22. Of course, solitude also has its positive symbolism, i.e. the transcendent purity of the one principle, void of duality's corruption.

23. Madness is the ultimate degree of this alienation, because sanity can be operative only so long as a sense of one's universal identity is not overcome by a sense of individualistic singularity which, when absolute, duplicates a kind of nothingness since nothing can be unique save the One. Hence the importance in Buddhism, notably, of the Third Jewel, the *Sangha* or "community," for relating with others restores a measure of proportion and completeness that compensates the tendency towards self-centeredness; it is a vicarious way of regaining our own wholeness.

306

It is then not really God Who is in the universe, but the universe which is in God.

THE NOTION OF the center, as has been mentioned, becomes, in a secular or quantitative culture, a term of convenience devoid of symbolism. It is operatively meaningless except in the most technical or geometric of senses. Thus if it is still possible today to speak of a point being spatially central with respect to other points that are, practically speaking, peripheral to it, it has become near impossible—certainly since the advent of the theory of relativity[24]—to maintain that any one point can be absolutely central with respect to another. To take but one "central" example, if a person says that the sun is the center of the our galaxy and therefore can stand as a dazzling symbol of the center as such, another person is sure to come to refute this, proposing that there are millions of suns and that ours, therefore, cannot be central except in the most relative of respects. This point of view, when carried to its logical extreme, becomes properly alienating because, were the empirical universe to be the only one that exists, man would then be fully entitled to feel that he was but a particle, ultimately meaningless, lost in the unchartable voids of space. What this reasoning fails to take into account, however, is the laws of symbolism—for which quantitative measures are irrelevant[25]—and also the simple existential fact that for

---

24. The currency this theory enjoys in the modern *Weltanschauung* extends well beyond the realm of mere physics. Thus, for instance, the populist theories of democracy and socialism, although at feuding variance, paradoxically agree in relativizing man to the lowest common denominator, because both succumb to the tyranny of demographics that effectively crush the notion of the elite discussed in the Chapter "The Crook and the Flail".

25. The closest the science of symbolism could come to corroborating material equations would be through the laws of proportions which

man the sun is a spectacular absolute with respect to which the other "suns" are but stars and do not shine until the sun sets. In fact, even a single ray is not only the sun as such, but light as such: it is the Light. It is thus not false to see in one isolated thing the archetype itself, in one man, man as such, because the One can multiply Itself a thousand times over and still be the One each time. Not to see this, but to dwell instead on the fact that the accident is nothing but an accident, to dwell on the imperfect or the limited, to overemphasize in a given human being, were he or she the most perfect, their possible limitation or their fallibility[26] is to miss the point and to miss life, to say nothing of the potential for sacrilege, because to scorn the creature for the sake of the principle, or simply because it is "just" a creature, is also to spurn their essence. In superior creatures, especially, their form directly manifests an archetype—the *splendor veritatis*—and therefore there is something manifestly divine—or godlike[27]—in them that merits respect if not worship even if they themselves are not individually at the level of their formal quality. One cannot tire of repeating this. And wherever there is beauty or nobility, there is a manifestation of the center, an echo of immortality. To perceive this is to be momentarily freed

---

work according to similar patterns in both the material realm and that of analogies. Pythagorean numbers would be one example of this. Modern man's obsession with statistics masks his understanding of natural ratios and distracts him from appreciating values—because a minority, for instance, is not necessarily synonymous with paucity. Of course, mass production can only be monitored via statistics, but then the problem is mass production itself.

26. Ananda Coomaraswamy summarized the dilemma perfectly in his essay "Literary Symbolism": "From one point of view, embodiment is a humiliation, and from another a royal procession." It is, of course, the aspect of royalty that vindicates our fascination.

27. To say "god-*like*" is to allow for a distinction between the creature and the Creator.

from the snare of the periphery and to be redeemed, at least for a golden moment, for to experience wonderment is to taste of paradise.

The dilemma posed for philosophy that a physical entity such as the sun[28] can be both dazzlingly central and at the same time an inconsequential speck of light when taken in the total context of a measureless universe[29] is unresolvable unless a distinction first be allowed between the material and spiritual planes of reference. Therefore what is true on the material plane of physics, which is quantitative and thus indifferent to qualitative hierarchies, is not necessarily so on the plane of symbolism. On this latter plane, each sun is as it were a spark off the one supernal sun—one not visible to the naked eye[30]—and therefore, according to the Hermetic law of analogies of "like above, like below" can serve as an effectively absolute manifestation or support of the center[31] as such which can be

---

28. It is interesting to note that in astrology the position of the sun in an individual horoscope is, generally speaking, the most central reference point, at least where forecasting is concerned. In fact, in astrology, the individual is considered to be a miniature sun in his own right which, when one understands the principle of reciprocities ruling manifestation, is not at all surprising: "God became man, that man might become God," as a famous Patristic formula enunciates it.

29. This fact alone should give pause to scientist obsessed with calibrating reality. But then, they would dispute that this could be a "fact" since it presupposes an act of faith, even if supported by the laws of inductive logic.

30. "'When the sun has set, and the moon has set, and the fire has gone out, and speech has stopped, what light does a person here have?' 'The Self, indeed, is his light,' said he, 'for with the Self, indeed, as the light, one sits, moves about, does one's work, and returns'" (*Brhadaranyaka Upanishad*, IV, 3:6).

31. It is not for nothing that the Upanishads speak of the *Deva Yana*, the path of the Gods or of immortal rebirth, as passing through the sun. The Upanishads equate the sun with the *Janua Coeli* (the "gate of the sky") by calling it *moksha-dvara* or the "gateway of liberation". Or they speak of

309

refracted a thousandfold to the very ends of creation while suffering no inherent division or depletion. This image is illustrated in the Temple of the Thousand Kwan Yins in Kyoto where row upon row of golden statues, each representing a goddess resting in luminous peace. We find this image also in Tibetan *tangka* paintings depicting whole assemblies of saints or throngs of *bodhisattvas* as manifold as the leaves on a tree. In connection with this, it is worth remarking that heaven holds fields of saints, numerous like infinite meadows of poppies and daisies, who, in the balance of reality, are measurelessly more numerous than the mortal multitudes winding through the *Samsara*'s eons.

Likewise, microcosmically, each human being has a heart which functions as his effective center, not just physically, but above all intellectually in the form of a kernel of pure and boundless consciousness. However, more to the point, we wish to address not simply the technical incidence of the presence of a center, but the existential concreteness of this principle. In other words, what would be the attributes, the perceptible qualities whose manifestation indicates the living presence of the center?

To answer this, one must first say that to speak of the supernatural in natural terms risks reducing what are qualitative notions to quantitative measures. With this proviso in mind, one could say that the center combines the dimensions of depth, height, and breadth,[32] namely of imma-

---

passing "through the midst of the Sun" (*Jaiminiya Upanishad Brahmana* I.6.1), of going through the "Sundoor" (*Maitri Upanishad* VI.30).

32. "That ye, being rooted and grounded in love, may be able to comprehend with all saints what is the breadth, and length, and depth, and height . . . that ye might be filled with all the fullness of God" (Eph. 3:17-19). St. Paul's quaternary is reducible to a vertical trinity if one allows that the dimension of length can be subsumed under that of breadth.

nence, transcendence, and dilation, or of being, consciousness, and beatitude, the Vedantine *Sat-Chit-Ananda*. The
center, which from the profane[33] point of view appears as a
constrictively exclusive point, the "narrow gate" of the
Gospels through which the endless, conflictive diversity of
the world is reduced or mortified back into original singleness, becomes "inside" a liberating breadth where what
was before multiplying fragmentation or a disjointed babble of voices and sounds, is transfigured into the sparkling
infinitude of one substance now become a tapestry of unified threads or the chorus hosanna of bliss rising from creation. Language cannot do justice to this reality.

In this way, what at the threshold was sacrifice
becomes, once inside, consummation, for what was
renounced was multiplicity, not substance, because this can
never be renounced by being; self-negation is not self-abol-
ishment when operated in view of Self-affirmation—which
explains the deeper meaning of "one-self". "In God," says
Angelus Silesius, "no thing is glimpsed: He is a single
Whole. What we perceive in him, indeed, must be ourselves." Or, in other terms, as Guénon wrote, in the center,
time is turned into space or into that everlasting now. This
is why Thoreau could write that "God himself culminates
in the present moment."

To say that the center—insofar as it lends itself to spatial configurations—is characterized by the dimensions of
height, depth, and breadth may be meaningless in practical
terms for man when he is not naturally predisposed to contemplation. If a demonstration of first principles can in theory be adequate in itself, it nonetheless always presupposes a sufficient capacity for understanding on the part of the
audience for whom it is intended. And since not all demon-
strations are evident to all men, it goes without saying that

---

33. From the Latin *pro-fanum*, "outside the temple."

some proofs will remain a dead letter to many all the more so as understanding far from requiring simply intelligence, presupposes good will or at least openness. Where skepticism, or especially cynicism, is erected as a principle, no demonstration will ever be conclusive.[34]

Still, even the most hard-bitten of skeptics may allow us to a lay a preliminary ground for the intelligibility of essences if we adopt a "technical" line of reasoning. Thus, to return to the notion of the center, one could propose—in the wake of Augustine—that the center can be grasped, at least intuitively, through the notion of the changeless; this is the proof, of last resort perhaps, of the nature of God. Indeed, even if one were blind to the argument of God's majesty or insensitive to that of His goodness, one could still approach the evidence of His existence through that "technical" basis. Thus, in the absence of all other evidence, or of all sensible proofs such as those of beauty, of light, of joy, and so forth, one could starkly define the nature of God by asserting that He is the Changeless.[35]

Conversely, all that is not God would logically be characterized by change which, on earth, amounts to corruption. Now it might be objected that nothing is permanent, all is change. However, if this assertion is fully true materially or empirically speaking, for nothing earthly eludes death, to make of change an absolute involves a degree of shortsightedness or a certain lack of imagination because this premise overlooks the simple fact that all change can occur only against—or within—a fundamentally immovable background or substratum. Of this, nature itself offers

---

34. For example the obscure doctrine of malism posits that the world is an evil one. For such as believe this, no argument of the good will be convincing.

35. "For that which exists remains unchangeable" (St. Augustine). Also, God is designated in the Old Testament as the Rock—an analogy full of meaning.

312

innumerable examples: the waves surfacing on the ocean or life emerging on the plane of earth—individual waves surge and recede, individual beings arise and then are laid low, but the original substance endures,[36] notwithstanding the apocatastasis though, in turn, it itself is only one night in the innumerable "days and nights" of Brahma. Were this not so, that is to say were change able to occur without an unalterable foundation to sustain it, the world would instantly volatilize. This is axiomatic.[37]

In other words, change, like all motion, cannot occur outside of or except in relation to a fixed base which is the trace of the sacred permanent in the impermanent: mountains rest on planes, Kali dances on Shiva. This law can be banally demonstrated: man could not move his arm were it not connected to a trunk which, in relation to it, is fixed. Likewise, he could not walk or move about did he not have a foothold on a solid plane. Even birds could not take wing were the air not there to offer the indispensable support to their flight. All thrust, in manifestation, is premised on a base. And this argument can be pushed back all the way to

---

36. To avoid the accusation of pantheism, one will add that the laws governing the essence ripple out into all of nature; thus it is permissible to base oneself on patterns in creation to infer something of the nature of principles. And we stand fast with Averroës when he affirms the eternity of the world though one would want to specify that it is a co-eternity—which he would concede—and also one that does not entail the permanence of our specific galaxy.

37. Change can in fact, within the context of the Fall or in virtue of the ultimately descensional tendency in manifestation, be defined as a betrayal of the changeless. This is why, for instance, all the talk in the Post-Conciliar Catholic Church of adapting to changing times is illegitimate—a program, moreover that cleverly masks its humanist relativism under the guise of returning to the original church, something they know nothing of since they have destroyed the sense of the sacred, replacing it with a kind of pietistic psychologism mixed with an ambitious agenda of social activism which, in its fraudulent sublimism, denies the unreformable nature of the world.

first principles. Consequently, one can infer with logical certainty that the universe itself, in its base, is necessarily fixed, unalterable, and everlasting even if this cannot be apprehended through animal senses. The very laws of divergence themselves exist only in reference to an underlying unity which, though temporarily refuted by the appearance of division, transcends the common ground which holds their opposition. It is hence just as absurd to imagine the possibility of change outside of changelessness as it is to posit duality without unity, or motion without immobility. The fundamental assumption of Aristotle's *Physics* was that the natural state of an object was to be at rest. This assumption was echoed by philosophers for over two millennia, even by a "profane" one such as Descartes, until Newton counter-argued that motion, not rest, was the natural state of an object. This revolutionary thesis, an early forerunner of relativism, was to turn man's view of reality upside down. Its premise, by inescapable implication, suggests that the universe is inherently dualistic whereas its converse, namely the assumption of rest, logically posits unity as its *Urgrund*. Indeed, the idea of the center cannot be divorced from the ideas of rest and of unity. And unity is wholeness. In man, serenity would be the fruit of this understanding. The "illusion" of motion as an absolute derives from the nature of Being which is forever creative and, being alive, is joyously free. Perhaps, one might prefer to say, echoing Buddhist dialectics, that the essence is neither still nor not still. However, what is at issue here is motion as an absolute divorced from wholeness; and that is a metaphysical impossibility.

IN A SENSE, man is all past and all future, because he cannot abide in the present or hold on to it. He is at once forever leaving and forever (be)coming: on the one hand, everything that he thinks says, and does is no sooner engendered

314

than already past; on the other hand, he is forever on the verge of thinking, saying, and doing something that has not yet happened. "You cannot step twice into the same stream," Heraclitus remarked.

The changeless is that which has neither beginning nor end; it simply is—forever, supremely, and beautifully. However, even things temporary bear the imprint of the changeless; and this quality of changelessness is mirrored in the fact that they, above and beyond the fact of their impermanence, simply are: they exist in virtue of God's *esse*. In other words, Reality is and therefore existence happens. If things were nothing in an absolute sense, then there would be nothing about which something could thought, said, or done. Hence, to posit nothingness as the substratum of things would be meaningless were one not to say at once that things can be "nothing" only in reference to something—that is to say, something that transcend either in reality, power, goodness, or light[38] their relative lack of these attributes. The mutable can be understood only in reference to the immutable, the temporal only in function of the eternal, "for that which truly exists remains unchangeable" (St. Augustine). It follows, therefore, that the eternal or the changeless must be interwoven in the very fabric of manifestation on pain of the latter's nonexistence. Furthermore, man as such cannot be said to be in the present except through God, for to be truly present is in reality to be immortal and thus already to participate in eternity.

The paradox for the man prey to the snare of appearances is the seeming absence of God. He that is the Changeless and therefore the Ubiquitous is nowhere to be

---

38. The reference to light, which may seem quaintly poetic, is to recognize the fact that all creatures have an inner fire or spark visible, to the eye of the soul, as an aura.

seen and nowhere to be found for the man who casually seeks Him here or there, to localize Him in this or that, or to identify Him as such or such to the equal of any other object whose "hard" concreteness dominates human perception. Here one would be tempted to say that it is the superabundance of the evidence of God's being that blinds man to His presence were this not to open the door, once again, to the reproach of pantheism or to the temptation of materializing Him à la Spinoza. However, to say that God is not material is not to say that He is immaterial.

In the last analysis, the issue of the localization of the Divine—and thus of the Center—depends, practically speaking, on who is the center. In other words, so long as the individual ego believes itself to be concrete—or more concrete than anything else—everything outside of itself recedes *ipso facto* in importance while correlatively increasing in abstraction. Then God, Who is objective totality in the most absolute of senses—as opposed to the ego which, from the point of view of the intellect, is objective part— becomes the farthermost entity empirically conceivable. Thus for the individual who materially, emotionally, and habitually considers himself real—whether overtly, as in the case of the arrogant, or naively out of subconscious habit, as in the case of the heedless—the world becomes a fragmented puzzle of separate realities that will mirror his own fragmentariness and distance from wholeness. In this manner one sees how the notion of the center can, for man, shift according to the sense of unity and therefore according to the sense of identity. In contrast, for the holy man, or simply for the man of God, his sense of self is effaced before that of God. Thus, his first reflex is always to think of God first, to safeguard the Lord's interest.

WORLDLY MAN DOES not—and cannot—have a proper sense of proportions. He sees only emptiness and destitution where the contemplative finds liberating peace. He does

316

not see that spatial distance is a measure of God's grace or munificence as time could be said to be measure of His majesty or depth. Thus what for man, when taken in his physical puniness, can loom as ultimately terrifying dimensions of reality, may become transfigured by his virtue into extensions of his inner nobility of substance. For the superior man, namely the one who understands the necessity of sacrifice or who foregoes the gratification of egoic impulse, divine eternity can be understood as the metacosmic archetype of his own adamantine fidelity which steadfastly endures against the vicissitudes of "faithless" time.

In connection with the above, but on another level, when one speaks of a boundless distance, one must immediately ask: boundless relative to what? Thus a distance that is boundless relative to man's physical limitations is not necessarily so relative to his knowledge—or to his love.[39] Moreover, there are moral equivalents to these dimensions that could be brought into play here. In this sense, what will prove boundless for greed or ambition, where insatiability is surpassed only by the ridiculous narrowness of their scope, need not be so for generosity whose scope blends with God's own ever-renewed abundance— as seen, for instance, in the miracle of the fish and the loaves.[40] This is why to give is to receive, and why the

---

39. A French proverb says "far from the eyes, far from the heart," namely that absence is the best solvent for lovesickness. While practically true, for minor love, it is not so for deeper love. The same could be said for time: it dissolves attachments or cures lovesickness. However, in a superior man, distance and time are gauges of the sincerity of his sentiments. Thus, a Nietzsche could say that "it is not the strength but the duration of great sentiments that makes great men" (*Beyond Good and Evil*).

40. Cf. Gregory of Nyssa's famous doctrine of *epektasis*, or, as Bernard McGinn comments, the "endless pursuit of the inexhaustible God," (*The Growth of Mysticism*) or the depthless desire for the divine which is forever satiated in drinking from the fountain of the Godhead.

generous are never poor which is another way of discovering what Nicholas of Cusa terms "the infinite center."

Man's sense of alienation can change in direct measure to his capacity for virtue which blends with God's own infinite generosity. And likewise, loneliness, which is a concomitant of alienation, can grow or dwindle in proportion to an individual's sense of universality as well as in his capacity for disinterested generosity. In other words, he who takes his repose in the universal plenitude of being or who finds a reward in the happiness of others—though he may suffer from the estrangement natural to the spiritual man exiled on earth—cannot suffer the same absolute degree of deprivation as that of the fundamentally selfish man jealous of his possessions of which all of time and space appear threatening to dispossess him.[41]

In connection with the above, one would like to say that profane man thinks he can get away with a fault or that he can commit a misdeed and then assume, with an impunity born from lack of imagination, that he can just walk away from it, leaving it somehow forgotten in the past. This man, insofar as he even cares to think, sees his

---

41. Whence the American Indian "giveaways" meant to foster tribal generosity as well as to blend the sense of individuality with that of the whole tribe. Also, as Thoreau said, "A man is rich in proportion to the number of things which he can afford to let alone." Since we find that we are fond of quoting the *sannyasin* pilgrim of Concord, we would like to specify that Thoreau combined a contemplatively universal soul in a somewhat rustic or unvarnished guise. His Platonic intellectiveness was also hobbled by some rude, no-nonsense, puritanisms and a backwoodsman's scorn for civilization—whence some anomalous inconsistencies in his nature bordering on the crank. Yet, much like Socrates, he was a gadfly, puncturing men's pretensions and pricking them to think about the most meaningful of things. We will also want to remember that he had no tutors because he had no superiors except probably Emerson. However it is a matter of record that the latter held a special admiration for him.

life as an aimless line or, worse, as a line segmented into a series of disparate acts, not realizing that it is in fact a circle. Thus damage on what he assumes is a disjointed line is in actuality damage to this circle which, unbeknownst to him, constitutes his whole possibility—only illusorily broken into past, present, and future—and from which he cannot actually dissociate himself. His only link to the "perpetual" immediacy of this circle ("perpetual" insofar as his individual possibility can be said to exist) is his conscience which is polarized, on the one hand, into memory which, if he eschews full personal responsibility, he will attempt to suppress and, on the other, into intuition of the future which, again if he wants to live recklessly or unaccountably, he does little or nothing to anticipate. In this respect, death marks a return to the center which is first a return to the center of one's human possibility and secondly, and far more essentially, a return to the possibility of one's genus which for man is to be created in the image of God. This return is as transitory for the impious as it is permanent for the sanctified man. Dissimilarity with his immortal essence propels man back out into the *Samsara* just as similarity releases him from it.

THE REASON FOR this return to the Center stems from the simple fact that no man is an island: each person is part of a greater whole. And this brings us to the Platonic doctrine of participation. The very heart of this doctrine involves the insight of integral consciousness—namely omniscience. Plotinus, in the wake of Plato, advises us firstly that the omnipresent is not to be thought of as necessarily coextensive with the universe or with any part of the universe; secondly that it lies clean outside of the quantitative;[42] and

---

42. Thus, history reports that Plotinus seemed ashamed of being locked in the body—what Shakespeare referred to as "this muddy

ON AWAKENING AND REMEMBERING

thirdly that extension is a bodily property whereas omnipresence, the essence of which is spiritual, can have no such measurable extension. These qualifications have direct bearing on the idea of the infinite center. This is not to say, however, that the Divine cannot be identified with any number of different sacred centers which, though geographically specific and therefore mutually exclusive, operate as a heart in relation to a surrounding social body. Creation, inasmuch as it entails separation, involves duality and therefore will give rise to multiple centers, just as the sun can be reflected in more than one lake.

Omnipresence coincides with omniscience because it is only consciousness—being the finest of substances—that cannot be held by a substance grosser than itself and is therefore free. In a parallel way, the notion of the center itself coincides with that of the intellect which, owing to its divine nature, is uncreated. As Eckhart says: *aliquid est in anima quod est increatum* ("there is something in the soul which is uncreate") *et hoc est intellectus* ("and that is the intellect"). This is why Christ can say that "the spirit bloweth where it listeth" for, being formless, it knows no boundaries and is therefore everywhere present; it is immanent in the very air creatures breathe. It is non-compressible, nor expandable, because it lacks nothing. Because it is formless, it gives birth to forms. In this role it can be likened to light which though indivisible in itself can, through the means of a prism, be refracted into different colors while suffering neither loss nor division in its substance. Thus one might say the center is wherever material condensation is superseded by spiritual dilation. In keeping with this logic, bodies in their material mass—not

---

vesture of decay." Because of this, he could never suffer to talk about his parents, his race, his native country, and refused to have an image made of himself.

320

in their form which is essentially intellectual[43]—are, in the last analysis, nothing other than the spirit's falling off point, namely the stage where the spirit's energy[44] is least operative or moves slowest or is the most obstructed in its natural freeplay. By that (rather limited) standard, the denser the mass, the remoter the center, figuratively speaking—whence the alchemical symbolism of lead which, being the densest of the metals, is the one that symbolizes man's fallen nature and ignorance.[45] Yet there can also be a compensatory relationship between mass and centrality, as seen by the possibility of mountains or between hardness and truth as seen by the possibility of crystals and the idea of crystallization.[46]

To extrapolate this notion of what one could term cosmological physics, the individual is farthest from the center the more he clings to—or identifies himself with—an

---

43. We have read somewhere that Boehme explained that one could know the heart, or the nature, of a creature by the form of its body. And in the ancient Egyptian text of the "Memphite Theology," we read that "He (Ptah) made their bodies (those of the Gods which assumed both human and animal guises—yes, both) resemble that which pleased their hearts."

44. The term "spiritual energy" does not mean that the spirit is either reducible to or apprehensible through the energy (or particle) waves physics describes. While it is impossible to conceive of matter without spirit, to speak of spirit without matter is not only conceivable, it is the norm.

45. Likewise, there is a relationship between the idea of density as physical mass and density as ignorance.

46. The steel swords of the Samurais combined both characteristics in that they could cut through iron and yet required wiping off a fingerprint which otherwise would start to rust it. The process of forging a sword involved hundreds upon hundreds of flattening out and re-folding until the blade was a compressed amalgam of a near endless number of fine sheathes, each one hammered by and infused with the iron of the sword-maker's spirit.

object's materiality as opposed to its essence.[47] And this essence, by dint of its subtlety, can be refracted in any of a theoretically unlimited number of separate objects because it is not bound by limitations inherent to solids, which are mutually exclusive. To borrow from Taoist terminology, one would say that every creature or every created thing is a particular expression of the one principle of *Chi* (vital force or spirit). Thus marble would be one possible expression of its unalterable quality, water of its fluidity, freshness, or humility, fire of its warmth or of its fierceness, fruits of its sweetness, earth of its fertility, and so on and so forth. The distinction in qualities manifested by each thing results from the impossibility of any one thing englobing all of the qualities of the spirit. This is why it is wrong to divinize any one manifestation of the spirit; but this is also why it is wrong to deny it the immanence of the spirit and hence respect, if not veneration. Each quality can serve as a reminder of the center without, self-evidently, being able to replace it. Metaphysics is, among other things, the art of making proper allowance for different levels of reality.

THE POINT CONCERNING God's purported remoteness brings us to an ancillary consideration, that of the apparent inaccessibility or distance between different dimensions of manifestation—for example, those of paradise and hell,

---

47. We know that nominalists will object here that essences are purely mental constructs that have no being of their own. But from where then, according to them, do things originate—out of thin air? When the shaman hunter slays an animal, he makes a token offering back to its archetype or gives it a sip of water to help it on its journey back to the celestial herd from whence it came and from which he has only "borrowed" it. Such ritual propitiation, the hunter believes, ensures the possibility of the "grateful prey" and favors the possibility that the bounty of Heaven will never dry up for him and his tribe. He understands the nature of archetypes which are an aspect of the essence, of the essence's objective being of which even he himself is but a passing projection.

and also of the beings who sojourn there. Both time and spatial distance, and the apparent remoteness of beings bound to different zones of the cosmos is eminently relative because this remoteness is less a factor of the extensiveness of space per se—empirically measureless though this may be—than of the state of consciousness that fixes or dictates the degree of apartness.

Given that time is really nothing other than a dimension of space,[48] temporal remoteness is a factor that is directly governed by the extent to which consciousness subordinates itself to, or is tributary of, a given set of material reference points that determine a given creature's sense of identity. Hence Takuan can say that "when mind is nowhere it is everywhere. When it occupies one tenth, it is absent in the other nine tenths." And likewise Schuon: "If we were 'pure consciousness' like the Self, we would be 'always' and 'everywhere'."[49] This is not to say that distance, be it either temporal or spatial, is purely a "state of mind;" what we are saying is that through consciousness of the center, or of the divine as it is reflected in a sanctuary or sacred art or in a sacred being, man can escape—if not in fact at least in principle—the determinism governing psycho-physical realms but, of course, without being able to abolish their seeming endlessness of variety (form and space) and extensiveness (being and time) which, for those who reject or simply ignore the vertical dimension, take on a practical absoluteness that lies at the core of all philosophies advocating the hopelessness, the apparent gratuitousness and insignificance of human destiny.

---

48. When one speaks of transcending time and space what one is really saying is that one is transcending the *limitations* of time and space, because one cannot transcend space proper insofar as space is representative of the principle of infinity, nor time insofar as it is representative of that of eternity. To transcend time is to live in the moment and to transcend space is to dwell in the center.

49. *Gnosis, Divine Wisdom,* Ch. "To Behold God Everywhere".

However, if man, while in the flesh—or in any other equivalent formal bondage—cannot outwardly avoid the servitude of such a limitation, this does not mean that he is inwardly severed from supra-terrestrial realms because nothing can exist outside of unity in an absolute degree. The countless testimonies of mystics across the centuries prove that man can commune with God anywhere, and he does so through the heart, namely through his own center which in itself is immortal therefore timeless, hence essentially free from all determinations. And, he can also rejoin, by a kind of sympathetic nobility, the company of other mystics: his prayer places him in a kind of blessed proximity to them, for prayer, when it is profound, rejoins the heart of all communion. At all events, freedom to be here or there is above all a question of consciousness. And this is seen in that if an individual is not free to be bodily in two different places at once, he can be so in consciousness, and even in no place at all. This said, one cannot avoid the fact that to be born at a given time, in a given place, and to be a given individual carries with it a finality that has to be endured throughout one's lifetime. This is destiny and because of this, one is not able to be effectively elsewhere or free to be someone else or free to be with someone who is elsewhere. However, none of this need be absolutely so in the heart. Through the heart, one can commune with at least the archetype of a possibility. And to love someone who is no longer with us, is not to love in vain even if destiny obliges us to endure separation, because once we have paid our dues to time's separation, one may hope that one's love will bear the fruit of a reunion.[50] Moreover, to be

---

50. Apparently souls in paradise, and even those in purgatory, can help those still on earth which proves that the disconnection is more an affair of situation than "distance." In other words, it is the physical body that is an impediment to the soul and not the soul's essence as spirit.

324

born in a given place at a given moment does not prevent a link to the center. This is why Thoreau could say that he had been born "into the most estimable place in the world, and in the very nick of time, too" (*Walden*).[51] If separation is inevitable outside, it is not so inside for one cannot be fully and permanently united to anything or anyone outside, only inside. Thus, seek ye not fulfillment outside, away from the center, but in an inside of which the outside then becomes the support or the overflow.

And this brings us to one last point, of no mean relevance to man's happiness. We have said that man can already participate in the timeless while here on earth and this he does through the practice of virtue. When Emerson says that "the hero is he who is immovably centered," he is alluding to the practice of the virtues whose assimilation by man connotes a corresponding degree of sacrifice as well as of imperviousness to the tireless solicitations of his baser nature that forever would induce him to dilapidate his immortal birthright in trivial pursuits. When transposed to man, the Changeless manifests itself in virtues such as truthfulness, incorruptibility, and loyalty. And virtues such as generosity and charity are implicitly connected to this same principle in that to share is to receive, because one of the magical qualities of the Changeless is its inexhaustible abundance. Thus to give in a spirit of complete disinterest is to tap this abundance which cannot be depleted and which renews itself the more vigorously the more it is solicited. Also to give and to share—but not at the expense of discernment[52]—is to live in terms of the Center

---

51. Because of this sense of center and infinity, and being ever consequent as he was, he could declare both that "I have traveled a good deal in Concord," and that he had "a real genius for staying at home."

52. In giving and sharing, one cannot forget that our first duty is to give oneself to God and not to men—something which will be explored in the last chapter of this book, "Intellective Compassion". There are

and not of the periphery, for it is to live in terms of the One Self and not of one-self. Likewise, the essence of charity is to recognize that one's fellow man is but another myself, or to recognize that a common identity of selfhood between the two is realer than the differences, which is another proof of the Changeless, otherwise the principle of differ-ence would be realer than that of identity—an identity which, when life's feverish course is over, rediscovers its common wellspring in God. The Stoics ascribed autonomy (*autarkeia*) to the virtuous man, a quality which likens him to the Immovable Center, the *primum mobile*, namely to the trace of the Logos everywhere inwoven in creation.

EVERYTHING IN CREATION moves around a center, simply because all things have an origin that they cannot elude. And this origin is also their end for, in the manner of trees, all creatures have roots, even if these are invisible; thus a creature can stray only so far from its base. Much as appearances would tell us otherwise, a straight line course is conspicuous only when origin and end are either veiled, forgotten, or rejected. The forward flight of beings and events seems to suggest a linear trajectory cast along an ever-receding axis. These strands of existences, seemingly free to converge or diverge from other parallel existences, appear as if flung along lines where the end is completely foreign to the origin, thus giving one the impression that the line and not the circle is the operative principle of man-ifestation. This illusion of perspective is further reinforced by our modern-day culture which obliges people to adjust to ever-faster change. We live in times of a dizzying obso-lescence, where the exhilaration of novelty masks the

---

priests who claim that they are too busy helping men to set a time aside for prayer. Such charity is no longer mindful of the fact that, in Christian terms, it is not we who can help but Christ in us.

destruction of tradition, where the frenzy for change trivializes achievement, where the infatuation with progress demeans the value of heritage. What history and culture may gain in nostalgic appeal by this trashing, they never really regain in intellectual prestige. What characterized the first age of mankind, the *Krita Yuga* of the Hindu scriptures, is the notion of the Center and the myth of the Eternal Return[53] where the idea of repetition—not of change—around a perennial principle ruled. This is due partly to the fact that the first age is so close to the origin as to being wholly identified with it. However, by a motion of expansion, which resembles an ever-widening spiral, manifestation grows/falls away from this divine origin and, without being able to escape the circling around the center, nonetheless moves farther and farther away from it while, at the same time, gaining in speed. If one can characterize ancient man as being static, in conformity with a view of existence centered in space and not in time, one can then characterize modern man, or man in the *Kali Yuga*, as being dynamic in conformity with a view of existence that is centered on time and on change, and therefore, by extension, on destruction. Preservation of tradition was the essential value of ancient man who, through the seasonal rites celebrated, was ever-mindful of renewing and guaranteeing the bond with the original center. But in a civilization which is addicted to progress, and which proceeds on the assumption of man's former ignorance, when not inferiority, breaking out from the "deadening" mold of tradition becomes imperative. What is forgotten is that—to return to the image of the spiral—the tendency is to spin out farther and farther until everything spins out of control; this has become more and more apparent as we live in a world where speed has been accelerating in direct proportion

---

53. Cf. Mircea Eliade, *The Myth of the Eternal Return.*

with the abolishing and transformation of the past. This, despite the lure of its excitement, is inherently aberrant and destabilizing: men cannot live at a more and more frantic pace without becoming alienated from themselves. Yet, it is a necessary component of a cycle that cannot end otherwise than in disintegration. To believe this is not pessimism, it is cosmological realism.[54]

If man's vantage point were sufficiently elevated, he would be released from the illusion of linearity and would remember origins and foresee conclusions; he would understand consequences. Examples of the circular principle nonetheless abound, whether from the Hindu doctrine of the millenary cycles (*manvantaras*), which we have just mentioned, or the *periodos* of the Stoics, whether in the carrousel of the seasons to the concentric ripples of raindrops in a pond, whether from the orbs of the great galaxies to the gyrations of a hawk, the circle of the day or the circle of the year, nothing takes exception to this law[55] whose loving immanence—Dante's force that moves the sun and the other luminaries—rescues manifestation at every moment from disintegrating into the nothingness that is forever drawing it out. The circle is perfect *dharma*, and perfect *dharma* is truth.[56]

---

54. Cf. René Guénon's *Crisis of the Modern World*.

55. This is why the earth is round. A square or a triangular universe is a cosmological impossibility.

56. This principle puts into proper perspective the fallacy of the notion of social progress. Obviously, however, one cannot deny that medical knowledge—to take but one example—has facts today not available (or necessary. . .?) in Galen's time. But disease is still here—and new diseases, at that. Indeed, modern knowledge seems always to come at the price of a parallel amnesia whereby an important piece of ancient wisdom is lost. It has also been remarked that man today knows more and more about less and less. And what avails it to place a man on the moon when he is trashing his environment or allows his urban centers to deteriorate into a moral hellground? Progress can only be a very relative thing: the universe is immeasurable, it laughs at progress.

The dynamic principle of the circle, celebrated by the hoop dances of all "primitive" cultures,[57] possesses its static counterpart in the principle of the sphere whose roundness[58] is to form what circularity of course is to motion. Our earthly globe is a sphere and belongs in turn to a galaxy which spirals around—and away—from an invisible center of which it is the spherical projection.

Of more immediate import, man stands beneath the vault of the heavens and can behold, from wherever he may be, everywhere, the same rising and setting of the sun, the ceaseless circling of the moon, and the processional round of the starry constellations. He is witness to the timely return of the seasons while his very flesh is heir to their reflection in the cycles of youth and age that mark the processional stages of his mortal sojourn in which ends meet, because old age can be, spiritually, a second youth. Is it then not true that all man sees and all that he experiences follows fundamentally changeless perennial rhythms? And to speak of rhythm is to admit of repetition. And what is repetition if not return and if not circularity?

---

57. In fact, all dances, in that they replicate the divine *lila* or cosmic play, follow circular patterns because they commemorate, however indirectly, perennial rhythm patterns of ever renewed beginnings and ends, or the regeneration of time. It is only modern dances which, by rebelling against the laws of rhythm, break this principle of circular continuity. However, it is arguable whether one can still speak of dance in this case: the flailing spasms of a stricken creature testify less to life than to death, or to madness. Once the magical wholeness of the circle is ruptured, dance is no longer restorative. In normal dancing, namely one in which the human being's centrality is honored, the poise of the head is never compromised, and this applies even to the dynamic genius of African dancing when it is not excessively animistic.

58. The ancient doctrine of cosmic signatures would remark that it is no coincidence that the eye, which is the organ of intelligence that beholds reality, is itself a sphere.

Such evidence is full of meaning would man but pause to ponder their implications. To see that Reality can be geometrically understood as a circle, or a sphere, proves, moreover, the goodness of the universal substance for, as Plato recognized, roundness is the concrete form of the good, the kind, and the loving. Despair encroaches not the serenity of he who understands this in his heart.[59]

So too the pageantry of the annual migration of different creatures are witnesses to the pulse of one great being pervading nature's silent majesty. Hummingbirds, monarch butterflies, salmon, which all return to their nesting sites or spawning grounds, need no "radar system" for they are the emissaries of heart-centers: they travel with the flux and reflux, projection and return of these centers of which their journeys trace the arterial configurations along radii unseen but immanently alive. And for the contemplative, the breath and pulse of Heaven is wheresoever the breeze rustles in leafy boughs or water splashes in running streams, or crickets chirp. And the divine center is anywhere a mountain rests, a flower blooms, or a maiden laughs. And it is especially so where a man prays.

To say that the center is everywhere is to say that God is in all things, because if any one thing can be posited of the Supreme Being it is that He is pure being and therefore present everywhere, otherwise nothing could be.[60] As a matter of fact, it is never God Who is not present, it is man

---

59. Thus it occurred to Thoreau, when watching the sun set one evening that if he stood in the same place, the sun would only be leaving to return, an observation that prompted him to remark: "All things come to the good for he that standeth still," (we quote from memory), an insight that belongs to the category of metaphysical intuition.

60. "You must understand," Eckhart says, "that all creatures are by nature endeavoring to be like God . . . . If God were not in all things, nature would stop dead."

who is absent. And it might also be said, by way of an audacious ellipsis and paraphrasing Eckhart, that the best proof of God's presence on earth is man—the *imago Dei*.

The attribute of "presentness" is an attribute that only God can possess to an absolute degree because He alone is absolutely real. To imagine that He could be absent—to any degree or for even an instant—is tantamount to declaring that He is only relatively real. Thus, to be absolutely real is to be totally actual, namely to be everywhere and without any lack whatsoever.[70] The whole objective of prayer, when it is remembrance of God and not just petition, is the actualizing of the Divine Presence (what the Sufis term *istihdarah*) for God is mysteriously present in His Name. Thus, he who loves God is everywhere in the center for he sees nothing, nor does he will anything outside of God Who is the All-Encompassing. Likewise, the creature itself receives its very being by participating in God's continuing presence: "'Heart' is Thy name, O Lord!" Ramana Maharshi declared.

The center—or the manifestation of the center in creation—coincides with the sacred. It is the consecrated altar of a sanctuary, but it can also be, according to the laws of sacred geography, a mountain, a cave, a waterfall, a fountain, a glade or a forest, or sacred hunting grounds. Or it can be the manifestation of any noble creature seen in its archetypal symbolism which, for the contemplative, recalls heaven. For man, the center lies in his heart/intellect, that core point in his being of pure immortality which coincides with Truth and which belongs to God and without which he could not know anything, without which he would not know the True, the Beautiful, and the Good.

---

70. Of the ninety-nine names Islamic tradition attributes to God, names such as the All-Hearing (*As-Sami*), the All-Seeing (*Al-Basir*), the Aware (*Al-Khabir*), the Preserver (*Al-Hafiz*), the All-Embracing (*Al-Wasi*), the Alive (*al-Hayy*), the Self-Subsisting (*Al-Qayyum*), or the Patient (*As-Sabur*) describe God's abiding realness of presence and consciousness or, in Scholastic terms, His divine *esse* or act of being.

8. INTELLECTIVE COMPASSION

Follow me; and let the dead bury their dead.
Mat. 8:22

THE PERFECT SAGE is the perfect misanthrope. One might say, paradox permitting, that he hates men for the love of man. Because he carries men as stars in his bosom, he rues the day they have become stones.[1] His love is the alchemy that despises the dross for the sake of the precious stone enclosed within; for the sake of the butterfly, he spurns the grub. But his love, whose possible outward harshness is but the converse of its inner sweetness,[2] is misunderstood by men who, to follow in this metaphorical vein, are obdurate in believing they are stones and not stars, grubs and not butterflies.[3]

---

1. In the Bible, Lot's wife, for turning away from grace out of curiosity for the things of this world, is transformed into a pillar of salt which, in this case, loses its positive symbolism and becomes synonymous with hardness. The Koran speaks of man's heart being even harder than a stone.

2. Similarly, the sun both burns and heals. Again, in the Koran, one finds the allusion to a gate one side of which is mercy, the other doom (*Surat* "Iron", v. 13).

3. Emerson formulated it thus: "The state of society is one in which the members have suffered amputation from the trunk, and strut about so many walking monsters—a good finger, a neck, a stomach, an elbow, but never a man" (*The American Scholar*)—an essay which, among other things, is an appeal to men to be restored to their intellective essence.

This relationship is to be reversed, however, when pretension is in play, because if man is willing to abase himself with regard to his ontological vocation, conveniently eschewing the kingship of his original stamp *in divinis*, he is, with regard now to vanity, more than willing to believe that he is better than he actually is. This combination of a false humility, which spares him—quite illusorily, of course—from transcending himself and vanity—the stepchild of his failed greatness—is a defining characteristic of the fallen ego.

Whether from lack of imagination, myopia, or arrogance, most men want to be loved for what they are, not for what they should or can be; whence the temptation to an overly easy familiarity with their fellow men that cultivates superficiality or celebrates triteness. As a matter of fact, a characteristic of a degenerate society is one in which men wish to enroll others into supporting their idiosyncrasies with little or no sense for exemplary—one would like to say "archetypal"—norms of behavior which, as part of humanism's legacy,[4] have either been forgotten or discarded. Concretely, what has happened is that the traditional ideal of the saint and of the hero has been replaced with a bourgeois caricature of what passes for propriety and decency—where being nice, for example, exempts one somehow from being right;[5] never mind how mediocre the results, or never mind how wrong. Is the sage's contempt for such men's delusions blamable? And is not the acuteness of this contempt the first mark of

---

4. Humanism, one will remember, is to replace God with man. In such a scenario, divine norms have no place since the divine, when not denied, is gravely misunderstood or subverted by the all-too human.

5. According to this scale of values, which cultivates appearance at the expense of fundamentals, the way in which one says something becomes more important than the content of one's speech.

his intelligence? "I will spue thee out of my mouth" (Rev. 3: 16). And who could rescue them from their cave[6] if no one knew they were in a cave? Nothing is more radically false, more radically destructive for man's salvation than a certain modern Christian charity which gratuitously proclaims that "God loves you just the way you are." This idea destroys the whole meaning of bettering oneself, nullifies the keen goad of the eschatological wager, voids the notion of judgment—and therefore of responsibility—and, ultimately, is an open door for all manner and form of moral waywardness.

To say that love which cannot scold is not love but sentimentality, indulgence, or flattery, is the same as to say that perfect charity coincides with perfect discernment—which is also perfect justice. The true sage displays severity, or at least impassivity, in order not to gratify an averageness—that is really sub-human—with cheap kindness. Or he is sternly impassive to disarm the temptation of social superficiality which, shunning the divine, saps man's character of its lofty substance and thus denies its root of immortality. By the aloof dignity of his attitude, the sage makes an instant distinction against the dross in favor of the gem. And, more generally, in a world of corruption—or one in which human weakness invites it unless censured—there can be no love without preliminary justice. If it is more than plausible to assume that in paradise, fruits need no bitter rind to protect their sweetness, nor men severity to protect their love, on earth, love lavished without discernment is worse than wasted: it can be poison for the intended beneficiary, sealing his doom. Man's propensity for ingratitude is something difficult to exaggerate in a realm where a measure of ease is enough to appease his anguish; the incident of the ten lepers, narrated in the Gospels, is instructive

---

6. Cf. Plato's metaphor of the cave in *The Republic*.

in this respect.[7] In other words, to know what man is—man as created in the image of God (*Atmaswarupa*)—requires (following Plato's cave as a metaphor of earthly existence) as a preliminary condition a coolness that freezes wanton familiarity, namely that urge in most men, no matter how unwitting, to drag others down to their own level of trivial comfort or mindless dissipation, "for he flattereth himself in his own eyes, until his iniquity be found to be hateful" (Ps. 36:2).

Contrary to a certain humanistic idealism which seeks heaven on earth, realism obliges one to take stock of the fact that all collectivities are liable to inertia and complacency; as a consequence, and out of a kind of plural reflex, they reject any spur to self-transcendence. One might say, however, that if the urge to transcendence is innate to man's psychological make-up, then it cannot be suppressed—much less rejected—even on the collective level. This is very true. In that case, even though the imperative of self-transcendence can be said to be rejected as such, namely in its form of effacement or of self-naughting before the Divine, it becomes—strangely, given its root in Godhead and its pre-condition of humility—diverted into an urge for self-aggrandizement, self-expansion, and self-perpetuation which, needless to say, borrows its power from an original grace: "I will multiply thy seed as the stars of the heaven, and as the sand which is upon the sea shore" (Gen. 22:17). Societies, as individuals, vie with one another in material ambition and political supremacy because of life's unwritten mandate that requires all entities, single and collective, to prevail or perish—Nietzsche's "will to power". This is the basis of excellence.[8] Hence society is justified, to a temporal extent, in resisting the mystic's *contemptus mundi* provided, of course, that it

---

7. Cf. Luke 17:12-19.

8. And this is why Nietzsche abhorred humilitarianism. One would like to think that he could have made a distinction between humility and humilitarianism, which should be opposites, but we do not know this.

preserves a balance between this world and the next, and provided also that it honors its spiritual duties—for even the most naked of ambition knows that it cannot compete with death and no human endeavor can hope to outlast the pulverizing action of time. Now, if ethics and idealism stand poles apart from practical politics and material expediency, they need not annul one another; Spain destroyed the Inca civilization but, in so doing, created a Christian empire that produced saints and shrines. Certainly this is no justification for the carnage, but it does indicate that Heaven can look beyond the possible horror of the means.[9]

The shackled denizens of Plato's cave, who can only know of reality by the lurid shadows projected on the wall in front of them, instinctively loathe the philosopher king come from the realm of light. If freed from their chains, they would quite likely condemn him to death, Plato tells us, for disturbing their "peace."[10] Or perchance it will be that they will mask their resentment with conviviality, inviting him to break bread with them and toast forgetfulness; with such as these, he will not make himself comfortable. Yet, and herein lies the greatness of his sacrifice, he comes to them notwithstanding; contemptible as they may be—covetous, lusting, intemperate, or swaddled in luxury[11]—they are still men if by nothing more than their form and, as such, are susceptible to recalling their origin *in divinis*. His abhorrence of them—where applicable of course—is salvational because it is

---

9. In the case of the Aztec empire, the situation is different enough from the Inca that one can suppose that the blood-drunk degeneracy of the Yucatan civilization was bound to invite some kind of cosmic retribution.

10. "But first must he [the Son of man] suffer many things, and be rejected of this generation" (Luke 17:25).

11. A quick note on material possessions: one of the paradoxes of citadine civilization, and especially with the modern society of affluence, is that men of little virtue may disguise their moral poverty with wealthy trappings. This phenomenon is not encountered so readily in

impersonal, objective, and thus wholly dispassionate. Also, it stems spontaneously from the contrast of his very being which, in its regal self-mastery, constitutes a direct reproof to their pettiness, passion, and blindness that compels them to help themselves to torpid surfeit of creation's bounty while squabbling for leftovers. His contempt (if this be the word) becomes then the only hope for their atonement, for folly merits rebuke before love, otherwise it will rob love of its gift.

It is imperative, at this point, to distinguish between a hate that is the fruit of passion, or of an envious egotism or a frustrated self-interest, or one that despises the holy and the beautiful out of resentment or revolt, and a "hate" that is only the outer face of a profound love of the Sovereign Good and that therefore hates what is contrary to it. This hate—and the word is used advisedly—becomes then the proof of the sincerity of this love. As folk wisdom reminds us, he who does not know how to scorn does not know how to worship, because the true, the divine, and the beautiful can never be lightly esteemed. The "lukewarm will be spued out," because the most incurable of vices is indifference or a hardening of the heart and a deadening of conscience, which, when its nature is not falsified, is all radiant light. Moreover, this "hate" is not an affair of personal emotion, but rather the instinctive recoil of a soul when confronted with the swamp of human delusion.

To follow in this vein of paradox, if, as Meister Eckhart affirms, "the kingdom of Heaven is for the thoroughly dead," then it is not outlandish to conclude that God's mercy is not for the living but for the dead, metaphorically speaking, in the same way that Christ warned that he who seeks to save his life shall lose it. In keeping with this kind

---

semi-nomadic peoples, or at all among pure nomads, where possessions, such as many horses, are normally the measure of an individual's moral superiority because force in those people goes with courage and integrity, and cannot last without generosity.

of reductive logic, which prepares the *vacare Deo* (vacating the soul of the world for God), one might be tempted to say that the first duty of man is to "hate" his neighbor just as he must despise his own life[12]—at least insofar as it is clouding passion or dense indifference ("turn back, dull earth, and find thy center out," as Shakespeare's Romeo exclaimed when pierced by love)—if he is to embark on the journey leading to self-recollection; this is the foundation of monastic life.[13] This reflex, the horror of a luminous nature fleeing the wasteland of humanity, is the foundation of all spiritual ascent. Now, it could be readily averred that monastic life can never be the rule for society,[14] but only an exception that confirms the rule; for the world must exist, including its baser functions, just as a physical body cannot be merely a projection of the mind and heart as it is when transfigured *in divinis* and therefore dematerialized but not deformalized. Thus to baser men[15] are assigned duties—as

---

12. In the famous words of the Gospels: "If any man come to me, and hate not his father, and mother. . .yea, and his own life also, he cannot be my disciple" (Luke 14:26). But, one would hasten to add, this stipulation is but the pre-condition for a second and sovereign duty—because rooted in eternity—to love one's neighbor. The proper understanding of the first duty ensures that love will not be an affair of self-interest. And the proof of disinterest is the refusal to prefer a creature to God, namely to prefer it to the demands of both truth and virtue.

13. Thus Eckhart affirms that he is beloved of the Lord who "hath riddance of three things: love of possessions, love of friends, and love of self."

14. Contrary to Joachim of Fiore's disconcerting vision of the monastery as the penitent antechamber of paradise that would be, not just for a spiritual elite, but for all of mankind. This is an instance where an excess of spiritual logic, born of a mystical sincerity that wishes to leave nothing outside of God, runs square up against the prerogatives of Caesar which, finally, are also God-given.

15. We read in Hermes, the sacerdotal wisdom of Egyptian antiquity: "To some men then, but to very few men who are endowed with mind uncontaminate, has fallen the high task of raising reverent eyes to heaven. But to all who, through the intermingling of the diverse parts of

dharma—which, however, if performed correctly, that is to say according to the proper nature of each task, carry a redeeming virtue of their own. Such men as these are certainly not to be disparaged unless they fail in their *dharma*, precisely. This hardly needs to be said.[16]

Although one might counter that the issue at stake here is redemption, not worldly success, it is nonetheless possible to realize the extinctive virtues, which have self-effacement and objectivity for premise, while actively engaged in the world. And, as a matter of fact, worldly enterprise may actually derive strength from these in the sense—as it is propounded throughout the Bhagavad Gita—of renouncing the fruits of one's labor by offering it as a sacrifice to God, in effect doing everything for God alone by the scrupulous performance of one's assigned duty as dictated by one's natural caste,[17] and thus by one's destiny. Success

---

their twofold being, are weighed down by the burden of the body, and have sunk to a lower grade of intelligence—to all such men is assigned the charge of tending the elements, and the things of this lower world" (in *Hermetica, Ascl.* 1:9, compiled by Walter Scott, Oxford, Clarendon Press, 1924-36).

16. Class envy and class warfare are metaphorically equivalent to the stomach or entrails revolting against the head. The problem presented by dialectical materialism (i.e. Communism) is, metaphorically speaking, to foment envy of the stomach against the head and the heart. Pharaoh's crook and flail guard against this.

17. By "natural" caste is meant not the social caste structure in India, but the universal caste system which corresponds to the hierarchical nature of reality and from which individuals derive according to their karma. Thus it is entirely possible—especially in today's heterogeneous mix of origins—that an individual born to a family of merchants, which in India would correspond to the *vaisha* caste, could by essential temperament be a contemplative or, in Hindu terms, have the nature of a *brahman*. And, of course, the reverse is also possible, namely for an individual to be born in an upper caste milieu but exhibit lower caste tendencies. These anomalies become more and more the rule with the moral breakdown of a social order, contributing a random quality to

in such an endeavor entails a preponderant measure of self-renunciation. And it is here that worldly duty and monastic idealism converge, as much as they can.

Why should the sage love his fellow men—as a sentimentalists might demand—when, instead of self-renunciation, these men contend in worldly increase? Or should the sage love these whose love of one another is premised on the unavowed commandment "Thou shalt be as fallible as I am," and therefore reject the superior man as a threat to their sleep?[18] Why should he, who is awake, cast his lot with a race of sleepwalkers bound for the cliff-edge of death? And could they but lift their heads,[19] they would not recognize his brand of ethics as theirs, based as his are on absolute nobility and not on self-interest. Or, in the measure that they are compelled to behave ethically, they will adopt, in Nietzsche's term, a "herd morality" where staying blindly within the bounds of certain collective norms overrides all other considerations, be they lower or higher. In this sense, heeding consecrated tradition can become an excuse for not thinking.[20] For such as these, the sage is a threat not only to their sin, but also to their

what normally would be a mostly homogeneous pattern of heredity. Civilizations usually terminate in some form of confusion, whether genetic, cultural, moral, or other.

18. Not to belabor the point, but it is sometimes necessary to highlight a problem so as to emphasize its relevance. The modern-age Hindu saint, Ramakrishna, who knew whereof he spoke, said: "The worldly men are like flies. At times they get a momentary taste of divine sweetness, but their natural tendency for filth soon brings them back to the dunghill of the world."

19. "We have set a bar before them and a bar behind them, and (thus) have covered them so that they see not. / Whether thou warn them or thou warn them not, it is alike for them, for they believe not" (Koran, *Surat Ya-Sin*: 9-10).

20. Thus the Sufis could say that the good deeds of the believers are the bad deeds of the gnostics.

virtue,[21] at least insofar as it becomes an affair of mere moralism or of sentimental convention and not of intellective communion with the Real.

ALL OF THE above considerations concern only the sage's outward function as reprover or ethical conscience of men, not his inner nature as vivifier and redeemer. The sage's (the *avatara, bodhisattva,* or saint)[22] great message for mankind is that of inwardness—"the kingdom of God is within you"— in respect to which, outwardness becomes the pre-eminent sin. Hence, his ultimate purpose is to draw men inward or, at least Heavenward. This latter distinction, where there might be none, is made in order to take account of the fact that most men do not see Heaven as being accessible while here on earth, but instead see it as temporally as well as spatially remote, something to be attained only posthumously. Be it said in passing, this is a fundamental distinction between esoterism and exoterism: while esoterism is founded on the divinely eternal *here* and *now*, exoterism is anchored in the quasi unbridgeable division of the here-below and the here-after, as well as in that of a penitent present paving the way for a redeeming tomorrow set far off in some yonder future, unattainable in this life.

---

21. As Nietzsche, crazed individualist though he was, phrased it: "Know that the noble man stands in everybody's way. The noble man stands in the way of the good too" (*Thus Spoke Zarathustra*). This philosopher, his sacrilegious excesses and Promethean evolutionism notwithstanding, had the merit of unmasking the husk morality of a religion become bourgeois Pharisee convention and the rule of the mediocre by the mediocre, when not the unscrupulous.

22. It may be worth specifying that not all saints are sages—at least as regards understanding the nature of men or of the world. Likewise, the term of sage may, by convention, be too vague as regards the possibility of full spiritual realization in God. However, the term is used here to connote a man, or a woman, who is fully awake, namely who has realization or full knowledge of God as well as of the world.

In virtue of this primacy of inwardness, the sage allows the world to be what it is, knowing that to enter into contention with it is not only folly but would be to forfeit his mission. The only permanent succor he can bring men is to attract them inward—or upward—so as to escape the entire plane of contingency itself, namely that of the phenomenal world—perennial and incurable cause of all suffering and frustration—which is granted de facto legitimacy or concrete reality by man's sense-animated desires. He does not interfere with its course, nor with the destinies of individuals unless they, of their own accord, choose to follow him.[23] Whence his apparent indifference, his surface inaccessibility, or even hostility.[24] Now it is true there is a

---

23. The Modern Roman Catholic Church lost its mystical aura when, after Vatican II, it sought to promote social justice—its militant advocacy, for instance, of the "rights of man," a pursuit which, in open contempt of Christ's admonition to leave unto Caesar what is Caesar's and of the fact that "My Kingdom is not of this world," carries with it the inevitable consequence of obscuring the real purpose of human life. How far this new church has veered from the missionarism of a St. Francis Xavier, for instance, which was catechizing and not socializing, can be seen in its message of socialism and psychologism and, as a result, in the prevalent theological disregard for the traditional concepts of hell and purgatory and the attendant concepts of sin and virtue. It has forfeited, out of excessive worldly concern and a radical loss of the sense of the sacred, this mystical aura which alone can cow tyrants and compel exploiters of all stripes to at least hesitate in the pursuit of their greed.

24. Stories abound of saintly hermits who throw rocks at would-be visitors, of monastery gate-keepers who cudgel would-be postulants. But the fact that these practices have near vanished, and have completely disappeared in the Christian West, tells us more about the loss of what one might term "salvational severity." And, for that matter, the Modern Church should not be singled out in this indictment of philosophical sentimentalism which divinizes man: no religious tradition, it seems, is immune today from this creeping paralysis of discernment. Thus present-day spiritual authorities, very unfortunately, are not averse to bowing and scraping before almost anyone—the question of their potential "Buddha nature" notwithstanding, which, in the case of sub-human

prototype of mercy, that of the Bodhisattva, most notably, that wishes to save all beings. More prosaically, there are millenary customs of courtesy—Bedouin hospitality, to mention but one—that treat any stranger as a potential delegate of God. However, this *adab* (traditional Islamic etiquette) has its rules and, above all, presupposes a normal world, namely one where God holds court and where all courtesy is but a modality of respect which takes the fear of God as a lodestar for its behavior. And even the boundless mercy of the Bodhisattva cannot be unconditional, otherwise it would sanction evil. Moreover, love combines with aloofness so as not to cast pearls because the sage does not—to paraphrase the Upanishads—love the creature for the creature's sake but for the love of *Atma*. This is why a false charity carries its end within itself and is, therefore, not exempt from self-interest, or from ambition, be it in disguise, or even harbors a secret desire for power over others. Consequently, it has no real patience because it does not sow with eternity, nor does it defer to Heaven for the results: it seeks to achieve its ends while here on earth and as soon as possible.[25] Real charity, on the other hand, effaces itself before the supreme Benefactor and may therefore operate in complete silence and anonymity—"Why callest thou me good?"—insofar as it is compelled to do anything at all for, when all is said and done, God alone is the real agent of any blessed assistance.

----

people especially, does not apply—treating all human creatures as "wonderful beings." The immediate result of such incautious praise—to say nothing about the casting of pearls entailed—is that swine begin to believe that they are gods.

25. One trait which strikes one upon meeting American Indians is a kind of quiet immovableness about them. It is a trait, which we suspect is shared by other nomads. It is bound to the sense of the eternal which frees one from agitation. We have heard them say that a prayer that is offered to the Great Spirit today is always answered but it may not be answered to the petitioner in his lifetime, but perhaps only several generations later. But it is answered.

Thus, human mercy for creatures, according to the rules of spiritual courtesy, comes only in third place after, firstly homage to God alone—and to Whom all good deed belongs—and, secondly, homage to the Logos and its human embodiment as a prophet or holy sage. In other words, only a proper recognition of God and of His envoys, or a proper sense of man's role in creation, can guide the practice of mercy. Without that preliminary effacement, man risks doing more harm than good, to say nothing of the fact that he can never be a net creditor, only a borrower. As Schuon has remarked, "Man is so poor that God has to lend him even virtue."

TO BE FAIR with the whole problem of divine compassion, what it is and what it is not, one ought to differentiate between two levels of hypostases without which the whole issue becomes unintelligible, at least from the point of view of sentimental piety whose reference point is specifically human[26] and dualistic as opposed to metaphysical or intellective. Roughly speaking, one might say there are two aspects of mercy: one is, in operative terms, anthropocen-

---

26. The irony is that sentimental piety, which over-emphasizes morality or man's sinfulness by stressing the negative virtues such as penitence, sacrifice, renunciation, effort, and quantitative prayer in view of placating and seducing a "punishing" God, thereby humanizing Him, is at the same time the first to emphasize God's absolute non-comparability to man by downplaying or condemning anything human that, for a contemplative, could become a spiritual support and not a cause of egotistical temptation. Such a contradiction is typical of voluntarism which is not interested in the nature of things as much as in provoking a spiritually opportune reaction. And it sees in the metaphysical perspective, whose profound inclusiveness it does not comprehend, a kind of inhuman or coldly abstract vision of reality, while conveniently overlooking the exclusivism and unfairness of its own dogmatic positions which are often rife with prejudice and have instigated much bloodshed in the name of religion.

tric in that it seeks to alleviate man's misery or needs primarily through acts of kindness and material succor; this
kind of *philanthropia* is the point of view of a spirituality
whose focus—to speak now in terms of karma—is the
accumulation of merit through the performance of good
deeds. The other face of mercy is, operatively speaking,
theocentric and therefore non-committal, silent, impassive
in regard to the world, apparently indifferent, for all practical purposes, to its plight. Its foundation is not man in
need of reform and capable of regeneration but the
Absolute which is changeless and everlasting with respect
to which man is considered, not in his fallibility, but in his
immortal essence as *Atmaswarupa* (whose true nature is
Atma)[27] or as the *adipurusha*, the "Primordial Man" before
the Fall.

One might, at this point, suppose that the very notion
of mercy or of compassion becomes meaningless if
deprived of all practical—or terrestrially human—outlet.
From a *bhaktic* point of view, which derives its energy
from the interaction between two distinct poles of consciousness—and which depends on the idea of the quasi
absolute separateness between the Divine Object and the
human subject—this objection makes complete sense; and
it is a point that will be accounted for further on. In the
meantime, one could refer to the example of Prince
Siddharta who, when leaving the palace, abandoning his
wife and family, thus apparently deserting everyone and
all his duties, to seek enlightenment as the future Buddha,
declares paradoxically: "I do this for the good of all
men."[28] For the humanist, such behavior is absurd. And

---

27. This is why, in Sanskrit, the soul is called *atman* ("self") which is
derived from *Atma*.

28. As a matter of fact, there are numerous examples of this kind
"merciful withdrawal" from society. Young Ramana Maharshi's

yet, the results are there for all to behold: the Buddha, like Christ, changed the world for the benefit of countless people.

While it is undeniable that perfection of knowledge is verified by perfection of deeds—or purity of heart by probity of behavior—it is just as undeniable that deeds alone cannot be the measure of knowledge, otherwise hypocrites and Pharisees would be saints. On another level, if sublimists can take spurious refuge in metaphysical speculation, staking a claim to knowledge by virtue of their erudition while scorning human society and social deeds, this anomaly does not, quite obviously, invalidate the hermit's vocation; the whole difference lies in the quality of the motive, precisely. To retire from the world does not presuppose elitist pretensions. However, the hermit cannot escape from the censure of those who, according to a kind of Protestant ethic[29] of social assistance, believe that a man is not good unless he is actively involved in bettering his fellow men's lot on earth and that, conversely, to ignore their plight, for whatever reason, can only result from selfishness. This same prejudice dismisses the contemplative as useless because it does not understand the intense nature of the activity prayer entails.[30] And, indeed, when it is all that it is meant to be—an act of white-hot fire of veridical awareness/concentration—it is nothing less than the pure activity

---

absolute silence towards his mother in the face of her tearful entreaties to return home yielded in time as its fruit her own renunciation of the world to come and live by his side. An example of the reverse is Marpa's wife's inopportune compassion for a suffering Milarepa, her husband's disciple, which deprived him of the illumination he was about to achieve—or, rather, receive.

29. One finds the same criticism leveled in Buddhism against the *arhat*, or solitary saint.

30. "Know that the greatest things which are done on earth are done within, in the hearts of faithful souls" (St. Louis de Montfort).

of the Spirit and thus merges with the primordial act of God. To misunderstand this most essential of activities is the same as to ignore the inner spark of light that animates all things: it is not less potent for being invisible; all to the contrary. Intensity of contemplation calls, of course, for a gentle counterpart, and this is to be found in the blissful repose of loving faith in the divine presence.

Apart from the risk of wallowing in a kind of victim psychology where love of man may be but a disguise for indicting God, what the proponents of social welfare forget is that if relief of human misery is the criteria by which perfection of love is to be measured, then what is one to think of a God Who, despite His attribute of All-loving Omnipotence, allows disasters to befall without apparent regard for human merits: "He destroyeth the perfect and the wicked" (Job 9:22–23). Seen from the outside or from man's point of view, how great can this love be if God allows an earthquake to level a city, a famine or a plague to decimate a people, wars to whelp hordes of widows and orphans? Both "the perfect and the wicked" are spared not. Taken from a purely material standpoint, the idea of such a divinity stands at cruel variance with a world of often ghastly suffering, oppression, and lingering death. And, unless one conclude (quite cynically)[31] to the inexistence of God simply on the basis of the world's imperfection, or on that of the Church's failings—or rather, to be exact, those of its prelates—one is constrained to concede that divine love must operate according to measures that transcend the plane of material causality and escape mere rational inquiry. By the same token, to propose that it is unforgivably tragic that men suffer can mask a more probing question, namely what is the worth of individual men or, for that matter, of an entire collectivity? The fact that

---

31. For instance, in the shallow spirit of Voltaire's *Candide*, eulogized by scoffers at religion.

nature can produce an endless number of individual beings—shapen and misshapen—to replace any number of those that die suggests that the value of the individual does not lie in the simple fact of his material existence. Thus, it is the individual's very expendability as accident—not as substance!—that does not brand a Genghis Khan a ghastly murderer, inasmuch as he can function by stellar destiny as a scourge of God or simply as a hurricane force. However, such a statement absolutely requires a corollary, namely that it is the individual's value as a child of God that damns a capricious monster such as a Nero. It is this very duality of the individual—mortal but endowed with an immortal soul—that renders him either irrelevant or uniquely precious. However, this preciousness cannot be fairly assessed if one denies the opposite premise because, as stated above, "God alone is good."

One will note, furthermore, that there are domains in manifestation where mercy does not reach, at least not outwardly, for were mercy to intervene directly it would abolish that plane.[32] This is as much as to say that humanism, which seeks to wipe out misery, is bound to run up against cosmic laws that are unskirtable. Because of this, divine mercy will not intervene to abolish suffering on a plane where suffering is unavoidable. Animals continue to kill other animals, and men will slay men. Thus spins the world. Where is mercy to be found? It will be immanent, which is to say that one will not find it in its plenitude except in the depths of the heart. What is pain outwardly, can be consolation and love inwardly. Understanding this, the sage remains serene.

---

32. It is true that Christ descended into hell, but this is in reference to the non-eternal (perpetual but non-eternal) nature of this domain, on the one hand, and, on the other, on the fact that there can be no domain which lies wholly outside of God's purview. However, Christ's visit to hell did nothing to abolish it.

In practical terms, this means that a charity that is all that it must be cannot unilaterally favor one point of view at the expense of the other. These twin modalities of the human condition determine each other's specific limits. The individual is valuable—namely, deserving of respect, love, and immunity—only in that he accedes in some measure to his archetype, not insofar as he betrays it. In a certain absolute sense, only the saint or the hero is unique for, having realized the blessed center of his celestial archetype, he alone is one and therefore irreplaceable, *Deo gratias*. This is something Dante well understood: "For no created being is the final goal in the intention of the Creator, as Creator; but rather is the proper function of that being the goal. Wherefore it comes to pass that the proper function does not come into existence for the sake of the being, but the latter for the sake of the former" (*De Monarchia*, I.iii.22). This is a rephrasing of the doctrine of archetypes as well as that of the Hindu doctrine of *dharma* or the specific spiritual function of an individual and his social destiny. As such the individual can only find protection and help—yea, immortality—insofar as he first understands what the nature of his archetype is and then how to be true to it. It is his archetype that is the enabling cause of his lasting success because it is the teleological cause of his being. To help him otherwise risks pampering his mortality.

TAKING HIS REST in divine unity, the sage does not rush to remedy the world's ills. He shuns involvement in the world for he does not, in Hindu terms, wish to engage in the never-ending and solutionless play of karmic cause and effect. From this point of view, to engage in action is to engage in a vicious circle from which it is impossible to extricate oneself because each attempt to move produces a new circle of ripples and knots. Rather, his prayerful silence and noble aloofness from the world's incurable

349

turmoil offers a message of healing peace for those able to perceive it. Being a witness to the Immutable, the sage shuns outwardness although he also has the virtue, through his sense of the metaphysical transparency of phenomena, of transfiguring outwardness into inwardness. However, to intervene on the plane of outwardness itself, where no permanent good can be achieved, is tantamount to missing the whole point: "But one thing is needful: and Mary hath chosen that good part, which shall not be taken away from her" (Luke 10:42).

According to this perspective, suffering can only be permanently allayed by stepping inside, as mentioned earlier; and this is achieved through detachment—the quality Eckhart considered placed man closest to Godhead.[33] Such was the essential meaning of the life of Buddha who found "that knowledge that should release all beings from sorrow." From this point of view, silence—and its corollary non-action—is the only remedy, whence the Buddhist doctrine of voidness, *shunyata*. Seen from this perspective, to speak or to act is only to engender duality and duality is sorrow.[34] Thus, very paradoxically perhaps for the proponents of action, supreme charity would be to ignore the world for the greater glory of God, *ad majorem Dei gloriam*. Once there is detachment,

---

33. The Dutch woman mystic, Hadewijch, in the wake of Eckhart, wrote that "the soul which is most impassive, is most like God" (*Mengeldicht* 126).

34. This is the *pratitya-samutpada* doctrine (the twelve-linked, and mortally wounding, chain of causation) of Buddhism: from 1. Ignorance, follow in unavoidable consequence 2. Action 3. Consciousness (the sense that "I am") 4. Name and form (*nama rupa*) 5. The senses 6. Contact 7. Sensation 8. Craving 9. Attachment 10. Becoming 11. Birth 12. Old age, disease, and death. Of course, these can be transfigured by virtue, in which case they become salvational and not limitative. The sense of selfhood is a problem only in that it is accompanied by selfishness, because intrinsically, God willed creation and "saw that it was good."

however, then there is the possibility of worldly engagement—if only to introduce the possibility of detachment in the midst of the world's hubbub—because there is then no longer the risk that it will be tainted by self-interest or forgetfulness.[35] Moreover, the sage, as the embodiment of truth, of the center, and of permanent God-consciousness, has a role to manifest the divine in the secular. Thus he is both emptiness and fullness, detachment and union, sleep and wakefulness. These twin realities are synthesized in Buddha's Earth-touching Posture where he holds his left hand (that of the heart) in his lap, cupped in receptivity to Heaven, while letting his right hand (that of action) come over his folded knee to touch the earth in a gesture of contact with creation. When one gazes at this iconography, it is at once evident that concern for the world is entirely dependent upon a preliminary and total receptivity to Heaven.[36]

WE HAVE CHOSEN to call the sage's compassion intellective so as to differentiate it from an empathy that is operatively sentimental or directed by social concerns even if framed

---

35. In a way, the authentic sage is like a temple in the midst of a city, a sanctuary where time melts. Anyone who has visited a traditional sanctuary, not usurped by secular activities, will know what is meant here.

36. It is significant that this posture was adopted in response to the assault of Mara—the seductive personification of evil—who assumed the form of the god of duty, or *dharma*, in specific reproof to the Buddha's indifference to the world, blaming him for shirking his social obligations. In response, the Blessed One simply moved his right hand to his knee, letting the fingertips touch the earth. It may be worth noting that the hand, even while in contact with the outer world, remains turned away from it thus indicating that there can be no action without detachment, no awareness without renunciation, no mercy without impassivity to the results. In this gesture, there is no asking, only an impersonal act of presence.

by religion. Whereas the latter operates on the basis that man is fallen and is therefore determined by sin to a quasi absolute degree, intellective compassion starts from the premise of man as a theophany—the most perfect object of God's creation—and therefore starts from an immortal norm which is in principle accessible here and now and not just in some remote hereafter. Thus, while it certainly does not minimize the gravity of error and corruption—quite to the contrary—it does not make of it a kind of practical absolute that requires a permanent emphasis on repentance by shrouding the soul in zealous mortification and erecting a barrier between it and all earthly manifestations of beauty, for instance, in an attempt to protect it from the temptation of sensual deviation. Moralism, on the contrary, by defining man as sin and not as intelligence, seeks to save by depriving rather than fulfilling, by eliminating rather than restoring, by scourging rather than deifying. For such a perspective, pleasure is seen to be dangerous, if not as a poison, because it can be an occasion for sin. Never mind that it can also be a foretaste of divine union or hold, when nobly experienced, a dimension of spiritual communion. And never mind that all beauty, as all pleasure, has a celestial origin and that its heavenly essence is not altered to any degree by the abuse of libertines. In fact, given this essence, stigmatizing beauty entails the very real possibility of sacrilege which is in fact the graver fault, because temptation and dissipation of the flesh is, to a certain extent, natural to the animal in man ("the spirit is willing but the flesh is weak"). Rather than dealing with such precarious nuances, religious moralism crudely simplifies the issue by reducing beauty to its effect as temptation and thus creates an irresolvable dichotomy between beauty and sin. Attraction and desire, or even lust, are not seen as energies that can be converted heavenward or transubstantiated,[37] but that must be mercilessly purged.[38] The net result is that beauty—and especially fleshly beauty—is sentenced to religious exile and, as an outcast, is then left for libertines to appropriate with all the abuses that a Sodom and Gomorrah civilization can invent.[39] The reason for what may seem like a digression on the nature of pleasure—which in itself is a divine mercy—is that the whole domain of the erotic is as a touchstone of a perspective's view of man and therefore serves to highlight the difference between the two basic poles discussed—that of exclusion and that of inclusion, of separation and of union, or that of difference and that of identity.

To return, now, to our earlier thoughts, sentimental compassion—heroic as it may otherwise be—is founded upon a solidarity of misery with other men in which the acuteness of the suffering becomes the fundamental catalyst for this perspective's vocation of charity in penitence. Intellective compassion, for its part, while sympathetic to

---

37. To transubstantiate desire does not mean that desire ceases to be desire, but simply that it becomes theocentric instead of being merely dissipating, that it becomes illuminating and not obscuring, generous and not just possessive.

38. There are religious sectors where women are taught to "dress to please the Lord," in other words to cover as much of their feminine charms as possible, sometimes in a mummification of the human body. Modesty has become confused with prudery. This outlook has reached inhuman extremes in certain Islamic countries where the idea of the veil—in itself something positive and mystery-enhancing—becomes transmogrified into the walking horror of a black shroud equipped with a kind of grate-like opening for the face. One cannot imagine a more torturously uncomfortable mode of dress for a woman, to say nothing of the grimly lugubrious castigation of her possibility as beauty.

39. This problem is the same as the anathematization of reason by the Church, which was then appropriated by profane rationalists, as was discussed in the first Chapter, "The Eighth Cardinal Sin". (Cf. "freethinker" in this book's *Index*.)

the plight of suffering, on pains of being inhuman, nonetheless does not make of suffering the determinant factor of its outlook, just as it does not make of sin the defining characteristic of man. It starts from the idea of the original holiness of man which is masked by men's individuality, or accidentality. Therefore, this individuality, as all of its suffering and error, can never be of decisive import. In fact, to overrate that would inevitably be at the price of man's deathless nature as heavenly prince. On the contrary, with sentimental charity—or moralism—man's accidentality as suffering and sin can assume a near pathetic importance. Now, this importance does not become excessively disproportionate so long as it is framed by religion which, because it keeps final ends in mind, can use it as a lever for faith and spiritual improvement. Nonetheless, at the core of this perspective, there is an element of mistaken identity which finally cannot but aggravate the impact of the suffering. Even if moralism allows for the supremacy of God, by defining man as sin and suffering, it grants pain and deprivation a practically absolute status that makes it almost a crime to minimize. In that respect, it becomes paradoxically anthropocentric, not so much theoretically—because God is still God—as practically. Though still dependent on God, it is nonetheless the "dupe" of the illusion of the multiplicity of individual selves. Intellective compassion, on the other hand, beholding God everywhere and in everything, is less interested in such or such a man than in man as such. It is less interested in man as mortal than in man as immortal. If one dare use an ellipsis rife with potential misunderstanding, what is important for it is man, not men. In fact, since it defines man primarily in function of God, or in terms of the great archetypal virtues—intelligence, love, courage, magnanimity, nobility, compassion, and even beauty—it may be practically disinterested in men, even to the point of antagonism if the latter make of their

354

accidentality a practical absolute somehow deserving of special consideration and interest. Where these men feel themselves to be important, in some degree or another, the sage will see a noisy ripple or a pure naught—whence his aloofness or impassivity.

Having said this, and in a way that may arouse controversy, one will want to emphasize that the difference between the two kinds of charity is more one of style or of point of departure than one of fundamental content, unless one is dealing with purely humanistic charity[40] which in any case does not count since it seeks to create the kingdom of heaven on earth which is as vain as it is heretic. It is only too obvious that a proper charity exercised within the framework of religion seeks to help the individual because of "the martyred Christ within him." However there is a complementary problem that, once again, differentiates sentimental from intellective compassion. As if to compensate for its over-emphasis on man as fallible, sentimental charity will then go overboard in the other direction, this time by assuming that any man is a bearer of the divine seed. In other words, the idea of the "Christ within" can easily invite abuse when insufficient allowance is made for the fact that a given individual may be, by fundamental and ineradicable substance, a miscreant or perverse, or simply "flat," that is to say incurably "horizontal;" in other words, he will have no capacity for self-transcendence. Perhaps, from a moral point of view, it is better to overrate an individual than to misprize him; however this does not make it less of an abuse objectively speaking, to say nothing of the fact that it can cheapen the whole notion of Christ itself and this, then, affects an entire society. The key, to continue in this Christian vein, is to raise man to Christ, not

---

40. The term "humanistic charity," is, in fact, an oxymoron because a charity that excludes the divine is a counterfeit as well as a cruel snare.

to lower Christ to man.[41] Intellective compassion, because its premise is the substance and not the accident, avoids these kinds of dilemmas altogether.

LEST THE ABOVE considerations suggest that intellective compassion is an ideal to be sought, one should now hasten to add that men as such—or man, in the singular, as "accident"—are not entitled to it and this for the reason that it is, by its very nature, supra-individual. Thus, it is an attitude, a vision of Reality that cannot be adopted as if by choice. It simply ensues as a result of the sage's inner spiritual realization. One might say that only the perfect man has the right to "hate" men; or only he who has a heart to forgive can criticize; or only he that loves God perfectly has the right to become a recluse and thus to shun men. We say "the individual as such" and not intelligence as such, for intelligence cannot be other than it is by its nature which is pure objectivity and which thus sees things for what they are, namely by placing itself above the usually deforming bias of individual feelings.[42] The privilege of spiritual solitude belongs to he who has quieted and overcome the inner mob dwelling in his soul. However, it is also true that one becomes a hermit so as to learn to love God perfectly. Finally, this is a question of destiny, namely one that allows for different degrees of preparedness.

----

41. It is this second tendency that has given rise to blue-jean and tee-shirt prelates, so mindful of cavorting with the sheep that they forget what the shepherd is supposed to be.

42. This is not to say that intelligence and feelings need oppose each other, but simply that when intelligence is free to operate without fetters, then the feelings—as the other faculties—will conform themselves logically to its vision which must be that of truth. Thus love, for instance, will accrue in intensity where intelligence perceives nobility or vice-versa. Sentiments unguided by intelligence are inherently unfair.

Normally, for almost all men, the way to God is non-operative outside of a spiritual community because, in this consecrated context, one's fellow man serves as a practical support for the presence of God and for His "opinion" about us, and not, as is the case with purely worldly people, as a source of distraction and a threat to inwardness. In other words, it is, so to speak, easy to attempt humility and patience and to be high-minded in the silence of one's cell where, unchallenged by men, one can assume almost anything about one's degree of spirituality and of virtue. However, virtue requires concrete verification that only the frequentation of other like-minded men can bring—to say nothing of the fact that most virtues are meaningless without the practical support other men offer us: it is not possible to be fully forgiving or loving in solitude. Thus charity, for example, may remain nothing more than a pious concept or a flattering self-delusion in the absence of a human outlet which obliges us to give up something of oneself not just in theory but in actual fact, and thus to act on terms not set exclusively by oneself, whence the sacrifice. There is no virtue without sacrifice—at all events, not on earth. From this standpoint, no mortification can be said to be real so long as one lives according to parameters and notions controlled entirely by oneself, for the essence of mortification lies precisely in giving up one's very self. And, it is not for nothing that community or "*sangha*" is listed as one of the Three Jewels (*Triratna*) of the Buddhist tradition; without it, the human norm is eliminated, which is as much as to say that the spiritual path becomes operatively meaningless for anyone except the pure pneumatic.

Without the objective verification offered by the person of "thy neighbor," the risks of egocentrism, pretension, narcissism, or sublimism grow exponentially, at least for the passional man who is, by definition, partly the dupe of himself, that is to say, the dupe of the illusory concreteness of his individuality and thus of its impulses and desires which he has trouble relativizing. But, far more essentially, "thy neighbor" serves as an alchemical support for the presence of God in that he serves as a means whereby the soul can demonstrate the fullness and sincerity of its love of God via another creature[43] become the providential— though perhaps accidental—delegate of His Will toward that soul. In this manner, virtues which might otherwise remain dormant in man's heart can be actualized and thus developed through the alchemy of human communion. Above and beyond all this, however, is the fact that the neighbor is another "myself"[44] who also carries the image of God in himself and therefore to help him is to help not only oneself but to welcome God.[45] In Titus Burckhardt's felicitous definition of the term, "charity is to recognize the eternal Word in creatures."[46] The indispensable practice of *satsanga* (the frequentation of holy men) in Hinduism applies by extension to the frequentation of all spiritually-

---

43. Nonetheless, love of God may also require a parallel hate of men—as explained in this chapter—to become fully all that it is meant to be. In a world of duality—or rather of divisive duality—no one attitude is applicable all of the time or in all circumstances. Thus, strange to say, the rightness of an attitude is usually verified by the ability an individual has of demonstrating its opposite when called for. Of course, there are different individual temperaments or human archetypes: thus kindness or friendliness is more natural for certain human types than severity or aloofness; and these fundamental tendencies come, Hindus might say, with different *dharmas*. Thus, it is not a question here of adopting a perfect balance between compensatory opposites so much as avoiding inappropriate extremes.

44. "Thou shalt love thy neighbor as thyself."

45. "I was an hungred, and ye gave me meat: I was thirsty, and ye gave me drink: I was a stranger, and ye took me in: / Naked, and ye clothed me: I was sick, and ye visited me: I was in prison, and ye came unto me" (Mat. 25:35-36).

46. *Etudes Traditionelles* 1953, p. 74.

minded men. Without *satsanga*, no sincerity in front of God. The vocation of the hermit is the exception that confirms the rule.

Because it is difficult to judge another man beforehand, the practice of charity requires holding a favorable prejudice towards all men first in virtue of their potential redemption and, secondly, in virtue of the spark of divinity resting in them. Also, and to paraphrase scripture, we must not recoil from helping strangers lest we shun angels unawares. Lastly, one's fellow man offers the individual self a unique means of objectifying his own nature, granting him that indispensable mirror whereby he can see himself, first by the other's reaction towards him, which compels him to make necessary adjustments and, secondly, by the other's mode of being which can serve as a model, either to emulate or to avoid, and also as a proving ground for his own moral capacities.

Though the foremost duty of the monastic ideal—and this concerns all sincere layman as well, according to the means at their disposal—is to devote oneself to prayer and, if possible, the prayer of the heart along with the scrupulous performance of the prescribed rites, it is traditionally understood that prayer alone is not, curiously enough, sufficient a guarantor for the efficacy of that prayer. If prayer were all that it is meant to be, namely the supreme activity of contemplative wakefulness centered on the truth combined with devotional abandonment to the divine presence, there would then be no problem. However, in still unregenerate man, prayer can be performed without the prerequisite humility. Therefore, it is contact with other men that, as surprising as this may seem, helps anchor prayer in God. The reason for this is that other men are normally the only touchstone God vouchsafes us for our spiritual sincerity, while offering us a healthy sense of our own relativity without which humility is difficult to realize. And

359

this sense of relativity—which is none other than a sense of the right proportions of things—is the cornerstone for a man's approach to the Absolute. In other words, the Absolute remains hidden from him who, even though in principle humble, assumes for all practical purposes a kind of literal absoluteness whereby he continues, at one level or another, perhaps only sensory, to believe that he is realer than other men and therefore, by ontological extension, realer than the very Absolute Itself. This loss of the right sense of proportions, innate to original man, is the psychological legacy of the Fall.

The man who is spiritually awake is immediately aware that other men are, in their essence, nothing other than his own self illusorily segmented into distinctly separate others. This is why it is said in the Tao-Te Ching that "The sage has no self to call his own; he makes the self of the people his self." Whence, be it said in passing, the ridiculousness of a fault such as envy, for if the other is "myself" than we ought not to worry about his success or perceived advantages, but rather rejoice in our good fortune in knowing him since his success will redound to us if we do not sever our communitarian bond with him. But whence, also, the real gravity of envy for, like animosity, it perpetuates the scission between Heaven and earth; this is why it can be ranked as a sin against the Holy Ghost— those which are impardonable. This said, it is interesting to note that a feeling such as rivalry is a kind of legitimate envy provided, of course, it is a rivalry serving as a spur in developing a quality or in attaining a good. Such would be the example of the struggle between noble foes, in medieval jousts for instance, each inciting the other to surpass himself. What makes rivalry different from envy is the element of admiration which neutralizes the acid of the former. Admiration is the crown of humility.

360

AT THE RISK of belaboring what may now be all too obvious, it is worth restating that nothing can challenge the primacy of prayer, not charity, not effort. Prayer entails, as its preliminary condition, withdrawal, effacement, and extinction of the self before the Supreme, for it is a law of nature that the *mortificatio* and the *nigrido*—namely what in the art of alchemy corresponds to the preliminary phases of pulverization and calcination or putrefactive entombment—are the prerequisite basis for all spiritual maturation: there can be no wine if the grapes are not crushed and the juice stored in darkness if its hidden light is to be kindled. Sunlight, which had once been its friend, now becomes the enemy. On the other hand, to follow in this analogy, the wine must be shared before it turn to vinegar, for light was not meant to be hidden under a bushel. As with everything in this world of duality, a balance must be sought between two seemingly antithetical poles. Still, in spiritual matters, unlike mundane matters, this is not an equal balance or a balanced parallelism, for the infinite cannot be compared to the finite. Therefore, care for one's fellow man can never be the paramount among a believer's concerns for, as Lao Tzu explains, "annihilation of Tao in order to practice charity and duty to one's neighbor—this is the error of the sage." And just what is "annihilation of Tao?" It is to forget the primacy of the inward for, as Taoism might say, because it is invisible, silent, and still they hold it in low esteem.

To approach this issue from another viewpoint, one might say that charity and love must be leavened with detachment so as to allow the necessary void in which God as sole doer is allowed to manifest. Hence, Schuon can say, "a saint is a void made clear for the passage of God."[47] Otherwise this love can be tainted with a hidden self-interest and, if the Truth be not placed first in the oratory of the

---

47. *Stations of Wisdom*, Ch. "Complexity of the Idea of Charity".

heart, and the best of one's energies spent in realizing It, then charity will be no more than another case of the blind leading the blind.[48] It is not that the importance of alms-giving, the feeding of the hungry, the visiting of the sick, the rescuing of the destitute, or the comforting of the desperate is to be minimized—indeed St. Basil, to name but one authority, considered that *philanthropia* was inseparable from the monastic vocation—but that this charity must be offered as a beatific overflow of one's love for God[49] in imitation of His loving-kindness that leaves no prayer or legitimate need unanswered. And it must be offered in God's name with a full catechistic intent, if possible, because the purpose is not merely to relieve the flesh but to save souls.[50] The hospital or orphanage or shelter becomes then the antechamber to the Church where dispensing the great *Misericordia*—which "sendeth rain on the just and on the unjust" (Mat. 5:45)—serves as a basis for evangelization. However, it is fruitless to stake one's faith in such accomplishments,[51] for men as a collectivity cannot be

---

48. Even cenobitic orders which, traditionally, have been the most active in the world, have always considered that the foundation of their mission began in prayer and retirement—for instance the *Filles de la Charité*, founded by St. Vincent de Paul and Louise de Marillac.

49. "I do not want that creatures have a single atom of my love," St. Theresa of Lisieux writes; "I want to give everything to Jesus, since he makes me understand that he alone is perfect happiness." However, she also will say that "Above all I learned that charity is not meant to remain locked in the depths of the heart." And she who made the vow "That creatures be nothing for me, and I nothing for them!" also said that "I am ready to give my life for them [the novices in her charge] and my affection is so pure that I desire even that they never divine it."

50. Microcosmically stated, "It is better to restore one dead heart to eternal life," Pir Murad, the Sindhi saint, tells us, not without hyperbole, "than life to a thousand dead bodies." (Quoted in Shah Abdul Latif of Bhit by H. T. Sorley , Oxford, 1940, p. 248.)

51. As one of the illustrious Persian Sufis, Bayazid al-Bistami, aptly remarked: "Whoever puts his confidence in acts of piety is more

saved, only individuals; it would be idolatrous to pretend otherwise.

To open a brief parenthesis, the division of the two ways, that of contemplation and that of action, has often been referred to, in Christianity, as the difference between Rachel and Leah or of that between Mary and Martha, or even John and Peter, which, in the glossing of commentators such as Augustine, Gregory, and others, are seen as saintly prototypes of these twin aspects of devotion to God. Now despite the fact that no less an authority than Gregory the Great vouches for the superiority of contemplation over action, because in Heaven action is no longer needed, there has historically been a tendency to treat both as practically equal which, finally, goes to the benefit of action— which, however, is thereby prejudiced because action that is not sufficiently informed by prayer, namely by a truly virtuous attitude, is, as we have seen, more or less blind. This is a dilemma the Neoplatonists, in the priority they placed on the contemplation of archetypes, never had to contend with. For a more passional mentality, however, one which places merit on the heroism of the deed, there often is a quartering of the conscience. In favor of those who follow the way of good deeds, one will want to quote the advice of an Augustine when he says that the *vita contemplativa* can never dispense with the *via activa*:[52] so long as man remains on earth, he is not wrong although he seems to

---

culpable than he who sins," a caution echoed by Eckhart: "As for those who see their salvation in outward practices, I do not say they will be lost, but they will get to God only through hot cleansing fires; for they follow not God who quit not themselves."

52. In the *City of God*, Augustine writes: "No one should be so contemplative that in his contemplation he does not think of his neighbor's need; no one so active that he does not seek the contemplation of God." For an insightful account on all this, cf. Bernard McGinn's *The Foundations of Mysticism*.

363

place contemplation on perilously equal footing with action. The error—which is less in the practical need than in the theoretical parallel—is that contemplation has for fundamental object the Divine Presence, whereas action normally has man as its object—that is to say, when considered in the absence of contemplation or when given priority over contemplation.[53] This is why Christ can say that "Mary has the better part." What is forgotten, when action is lauded equal to contemplation, is that contemplation, by its nature, is intellective and self-sufficient because, in its apprehension of the divine object, it entails the perfect fulfillment of all of man's faculties including, of course, love. This is why a Gregory the Great can say that "Holy men work harder in their sleep than they do when awake."

It may be a preposterous leap of logic to say that valuing the Way of Martha equally with that of Mary, and sometimes even above that of Mary, opened the way for Christianity's subsequent solidarity with civilizationism and finally with the machine age. However to value action equally with contemplation does amount to misunderstanding the nature of contemplation which, in its essence, is none other than a sense of the sacred, of the *mysterium magnum*. As a result, we think it is no accident that the apogee of contemplative Christianity was reached during the 12th Century's Cistercian[54] explosion of abbeys, with a gradually steady decline of monasticism/contemplation thereafter which followed in parallel a growing secularization of society, albeit with periodic redresses. Also—and

---

53. Action presupposes duality and contemplation unity. That being said, it is true that contemplation contains a dynamic dimension of activity.

54. It may be interesting to note that the charter for the Cistercian order was called the *Carta caritatis* or "Charter of Charity".

this is an observation fraught with controversy—the near absolute emphasis of love's superiority over knowledge in Christianity has quite paradoxically over-emphasized the duality first between subject and object or man and God, and secondly between earth and Heaven thereby granting the abyss between the two a *de facto* importance that the way of knowledge or of identity precludes. This cosmic abyss, which in man becomes separation and alienation, could not but widen over time. More critically, however, the emphasis on faith is premised on the certitude of man's ignorance before the great mystery of the Godhead, which carries the risk of depriving man of any practical outlet for his intelligence other than secular pursuits. We have spoken of this: by emphasizing the impossibility for man to know God, intelligence is deprived of an integral spiritual outlet. Debarred from the normal fulfillment of his intelligence in gnosis, man's capacity for knowledge becomes a vagrant faculty,[55] left to wander in the world, and all the more as he is told that to think of a God that is relentlessly defined in apophatic terms (via negation) is not only futile but morally presumptuous. In these circumstances, faith can be heroic but it cannot replace the "unfulfillment"—or disuse—of a crippled faculty. And the history of the West, of the modern world, could be said to be the spectacle of an intelligence gone awry, of an intelligence become mechanically, artistically, and psychologically brilliant—even

---

55. One of the consequences of the Church's derogation of intelligence was the farce of Galileo's trial. Unfortunately, in order to avoid such ridicule, the Church—especially since Vatican II—has now gone too far in the opposite direction, claiming, for instance, that one needs to interpret the Gospel in the light of modern science which is patently ridiculous when one considers the difference between the two orders, one heavenly and the other earthly. On the other hand, the advances of science, such as birth control and the medical sciences in general, confront the Church with the thorniest of moral dilemmas.

demonically so—but ignorant of its divine essence. Having said this, one cannot forget that each divine revelation not only introduces something new and unique into the world, but is also meant to correct a past excess. In the case of Christianity, the emphasis on love is meant to correct the Greco-Roman abuse of rationalism as well as the excess of Judaic legalism, of the letter that kills the spirit—namely of a mind unmindful of the heart's prerogatives.

There is an analogy between the soul and the universe whereby the soul is, mysteriously and symbolically, an image of the whole cosmos in virtue of the laws of reciprocity governing the macrocosm and the microcosm. This analogy says that whatever is of spiritual benefit to the soul is of equal benefit to the whole universe, including all of mankind. Thus, a kind of "holy egoism" requires that charity begin at home, with oneself—whence the paradoxical advice of a St. Isaac the Syrian that it is better to "build one's own soul" than to "convert whole multitudes. . . ." In this way, a hermit like St. Anthony of Egypt could, from the solitary retreat of his cell become, as St. Athanasius put it, "a physician to all Egypt." Holiness, and nothing else—not feeding, not clothing, not consoling—is the only permanent cure for all worldly affliction. To forget that is to forget God.

AT FIRST SIGHT, the expression intellective compassion may seem to be a contradiction in terms—the coupling of a term connoting a maximum of abstraction, mathematical in its logic, with a term connoting a maximum of empathy. However, the term intellect is used here in its essential meaning of heart or *cordis*—the latter term connoting, according to its etymology,[56] the dual meaning of heart and

---

56. The Latin *"cor"* is used interchangeably to mean "heart" and "mind"—which proves that the scission was not yet completed. In *King*

mind, whence its total meaning as the vital seat of consciousness (*buddhi*).

The metaphysical basis for intellective compassion is
the idea, enunciated by Shankara in his philosophy of
Advaita Vedanta (non-dualism), that the world is essentially
unreal (*jagan mythya*) because the Self alone is Real (*Brahma
satyam*)—or alone completely Real. This is analogous to
saying, if one were to borrow a material analogy, that all
terrestrial forms are reducible to a common substratum of
primal matter, "dust unto dust." Thus a creature, a tree, or
merely a vessel of clay are but transitory manifestations of
one earthly substance which is neither increased, nor
decreased, nor even essentially modified by the endless
permutation of possibilities that are derived from it.
However, this analogy, even if instructive, is not perfect
since it does not take account of the archetypes *in divinis* of
the creatures who, finally, are not just earth—or, in their
spiritual substance, ether —but manifestations of active
attributes of the Divinity.

Thus, in the gaze of the sage, all of the phenomenal
world is reduced to ashes by the fire sacrifice of his burning insight which sees everything *sub specie aeternitatis* and
which seizes the motionless mover behind the dance of
beings. Analogically speaking, the basis of his impassivity
results, one might say, from his human manifestation of
the void—Nagarjuna's *Shunyavada*—in that there is nothing in him, no arbitrary desire or opinion, that interrupts
the unceasing flow of Divine Totality, the pleroma, of
which his nature is a blessed embodiment. To meet him is
to meet the sky.

Lear, Shakespeare gives his heroine the symbolically evocative name of
Cordelia for she plays the part of both reason and love to her father's
temporary madness. In rejecting her, King Lear has taken leave from his
senses and rejected his own heart.

His impersonal detachment transcribes, on the human plane the metacosmic principle which has it that the Essence is not "interested" in the accident qua accident, because the Real is unaware of the unreal: for It the dream never was. If Vishnu sleeps and dreams the universe into being, Brahma sits above him in an eternal wakefulness limited by nothing; the sleeping and the dreaming are essentially unreal to Him Who is Totality and never part. And, *mutatis mutandis*, the true sage replicates in his nature this metacosmic reality whereby the Absolute ignores the relative as relative while—and this cannot be omitted— containing a dimension of mercy towards that which in the relative belongs to the Absolute,[57] namely of Vishnu, and his avatars.

To repeat, in practical human terms, there results from this perspective of detachment founded on *Advaita*, that to concern oneself with the fate of souls struggling in the mesh of Maya is not only to grant some kind of formal reality to what is ultimately but a dream, but it is also to thereby risk forgetting God, to say nothing of the risk of getting enmeshed in the illusion oneself. This is why the Bhagavad Gita can state: "For the living and for the dead the wise grieve not" (2:11), or why Christ can say, "Let the dead bury the dead."

It is natural for mercy to want to succor distress wherever it occurs, and to do so without making what is called a "moral judgment," namely without pausing to consider whether or not the distress incurred is fair or unfair, that is to say, merited or unmerited. And it is also natural for a spiritual perspective founded on love, mercy, and charity to see the world as a kind of sinking ship in which souls need to be rescued, even those which seem merrily

---

57. For an illuminating examination of this complex relationship, cf. Frithjof Schuon's "Dharmakara's Vow" in *Logic and Transcendence*.

indifferent to their plight. To minimize the quality of such mercy, which has been the unstinting way of so many saints, would be monstrous. Yet there is another kind of mercy which entails discernment and which is no less mercy, that of the sage whose essence is knowledge. The sage cannot be blamed if his knowledge grants him a lofty vantage point from which he sees the rows of struggling men, many of whom are only accidentally in the human state because unable, by intrinsic temperament, to take advantage of the divine prerogatives this state entails. For the sage who knows that crows will be crows,[58] there is absolutely no point in seeking to delude himself that they could be doves. He sees the tides of creatures proceeding from birth to death and to rebirth as they flow back and forth through the *Samsara* and does not interfere much as one does not expect weeds to be flowers. Thus, he does not waste his time with men in the plural sense unless they are worthy of some merit. However, it is precisely this assessment that shocks the inveterate humanist and leads him to misunderstand the quality of the sage's

---

58. This comment touches on the doctrine of predestination (Augustine, Ashari) which, in its most summary expression, presupposes that different people are what they are, once for all, and, as a result, cannot change their posthumous fate. In its substance, predestinationism is a close cousin of the Hindu doctrine of the *Samsara* which accounts for the fact of why the majority of men continue on in the round of existence without obtaining freedom—or the Christian idea of salvation which, according to Augustine, is reserved for a small elect. For us, predestination is to say that an individual's life on earth corresponds to an arrow that was drawn and released in a previous existence. If nothing is done, this arrow's flight is predetermined. However, one will add that the definition of the human state entails the possibility also of being the bowman and not just the arrow, so that it is possible to start over, so to speak. Of course, depending on a given arrow/man's flight/nature, the chances of taking renewed aim can be anything between excellent or nill.

mercy.[59] Sentimentalists do not see things as they are but as they wish them to be, which may be all to their credit if they are true idealists, but not if they are humanists because the latter have a social agenda which is incompatible with true spirituality which, by definition, can never put the world first.

IF SHANKARA'S PERSPECTIVE of *Advaita* or strict non-dualism can be said to correspond to Reality as such while serving as a transcendent bearing for men to steer their ship by on the sea of the *Samsara*, one might be forced to conclude, this time with Nagarjuna, that it is futile to even attempt to conceptualize the Absolute or to verbalize Truth—for instance in the form of this book—since all that one might want to say about It is a priori false or, at least, contradictory and therefore misleading because, as such, It transcends all thought. But then the question arises: from whence does thought originate if not from the Absolute? And, if originating from the Absolute, then it must be able to apprehend, on its mental plane, something of the Absolute's nature since in ultimate analysis—and inasmuch as the laws of logic are not violated—the whole process of thought is none other than the Absolute thinking Itself via

---

59. A Sufi tale tells the story of two saints in a town that are both potters. A young man comes to this town with the intent of verifying if they are really saints. First he comes to the shop of one and has him show him one pot after another, tediously rejecting each one, making the saint unstack pile after pile of plates which the potter does with unwearying patience. Satisfied, the young man goes to the other potter saint and starts again. But after showing him the first bowl, the potter stops him short and says curtly: "Don't try this with me!" Who is the greater of the two saints, the Sufi narrator asks? The answer, one might surmise, is that both may be saints, but the kindness and patience of the one is not morally superior to the insight of the other. Or, conversely, the impatience of the second is not morally inferior to the patience of the first.

the prism of duality, to say nothing of the fact that the faculty capable of conceiving of the Absolute proves (teologicallly) its capacity to know it. The mind has often been likened to a mirror: if indeed the image is not the object itself, it nonetheless is an adequation.

Correlatively, if the Absolute is everything and the world nothing, one might be tempted to cease not only carrying on a relationship with other men, but to cease even taking care of oneself out of a sense of the utter futility of this endeavor which must be constantly renewed. One could become suicidally desperate at the thought that all sense of difference between things was but a bitter illusion serving only to seduce or to confuse the better to destroy. If the Absolute is everything, the one and only thing with naught else, then wherefore the world, or its appearance? For the world, and its myriad creatures does de facto exist, however provisorily or however illusorily; and does so precisely because the Absolute is the Absolute, whence the brief reality of its droplets.[60] Beings exist, be it only within the cosmic parameters of this alleged illusion, as separate entities in witness to a principle of differentiation inherent to the *Shakti* of the Absolute, namely to the Infinite, the divine feminine with whom the Absolute consorts: she appears as the manifestation of the Absolute's wealth of possibility—Its richness, beauty, and bounty, whence the

---

60. Some will say that the apparent reality of the world is due only to the subject's viewpoint but that it is completely different in itself. However, what then is it that determines the difference of the subject's viewpoint, assuming that the subject is objective about what he perceives? A mountain, after all—especially when verified by more than one person—is not just a mirage or a figment of a person's imagination. One might want to say that, from the point of view of the substance, there is no absolute difference since both viewer and mountain are derived from the same earth; but formally and practically speaking there is an absolute difference.

multiplicity of phenomena. Therefore, one is entitled, at least insofar as one is a participating member of this cosmic dream, to introduce—in the footsteps of an Eckhart or a Schuon—a distinction first between Being and Non-Being (or Supra-Being) or between Ishvara and Brahma, and then, within Being, between God and the world. These differentiations are so many echoing hypostases of the Supreme in His form as cosmic manifestation.

Thus, creatures, while still being in some essential way identical with God or inasmuch as they are the projections of divine attributes, can nonetheless be seen to be efficiently distinct, separate, and relatively autonomous with respect both to each other and to the Principle[61] and therefore, from the perspective of *Boddhisattvic* compassion, ultimately in need of rescue. Proof that the diversity of beings is not pure illusion lies in their mutual antagonisms, though the unity underlying even the most extreme of antagonists always resurfaces such as in the case of a predator and its prey—for in assimilating its prey, the predator testifies, in this harsh way, to the principle of non-difference: he could derive no sustenance from something totally alien to him. If, on that basis, one wants to say that diversity is a pure illusion, so be it. But we would prefer to say that unity overrules diversity or that unity precedes diversity or, again, that unity is realer—far realer—than diversity or that diversity has no meaning except in reference to unity.

Formulated differently, one might say that the reciprocal alienation between creatures, and all the diversity of earthly things, is more a question of form or of corresponding *dharma*, if one wishes, than a question of substance. If

---

61. Of course, the ontological cause for their efficient autonomy is that they borrow this from the Absolute itself which is always One in the many.

fire and water oppose each other, they can still meet in air. Thus, any doctrine of existence must account for duality as a polarity within one underlying substance without which no polarization could occur in the first instance. This polarity, however, and its thousands of ramifications is nonetheless real—or real enough—in that it manifests the richness of the original substance and, as such, cannot not be: the totality of the One requires it. As previously mentioned, this is the principle of infinity from which the manifold splendor of the universe is produced.

IN STRICT METAPHYSICAL terms, and with respect to Shankara's doctrine of *Advaita*, this perspective of duality within unity—that of Ramanuja's *Vishistadvaita* or qualified non-dualism—can only be secondary and therefore non-essential. In the classic Hindu doctrine of *Bhedabhedavada*—the theory of difference / non-difference—the problem lies in admitting first the possibility of difference itself and, secondly as a result, conceding some measure of reality to this difference; and this allowance is a real Pandora's box. Ramanuja's disagreement with Shankara, on the surface, is less in the denial of the idea that the individual self is ultimately different from the Self, but in granting some practical importance to the (temporary) difference between the two. In other words, Ramanuja's dialectics presupposes a break between the Creator and the creature whereby the creature assumes an autonomous concreteness or phenomenological distinctness. A host of possible consequences issues from this, not the least of which the possibility of producing an unbridgeable gap between God and man, of which atheism and a parallel divinization of man is the ultimate consequence—a problem which, quite evidently, has nothing to do anymore with Ramanuja's viewpoint which, in spite of its philosophical risks, is religiously legitimate. Nonetheless, in

373

contrast with the perfection of Shankara's perspective, one is entitled to mention what some of the possible or ultimate consequences of dualism are.[62]

It is this problem, the festering gap between God and man—the pestilential breeding ground for philosophical disputes—that the sage's indifference to phenomena, and his refusal to intervene to help man as man, addresses implicitly—whence the use of the term intellective compassion to connote a form of consciousness that saves man ontologically rather than eschatologically, that is to say via his root identity with the One Self, and not through moral judgment. As a result, the salvational efficacy of this consciousness is rendered more or less inoperative so long as man refuses, or is unable, to recognize that basis of identity which manifests itself not just through truthfulness, but also through nobility, dignity, and beauty in imitation of the Edenic norm when man was not a fearful creature of cringing obedience, or even a forlornly wandering love-stricken mystic, but was both priest and king.

These considerations invite another brief, and final, parenthesis. Having established a difference between God and man while preserving the notion of some kind of rela-

---

62. If Ramanuja, in qualifying unity, had kept the emphasis on unity, there would be no problem. But, in fact, once he proposes the idea of multiplicity as a necessary dimension of Reality, he undermines his premise as is demonstrated by his de facto dualism and the practical exclusivism of his devotionalism as well as by his misunderstanding of those who follow the path of identity whom he assumes will spend their eternity in solitude—which is properly absurd if he were consequent with his assertion about the supremacy of unity because then these *jna-nis* would not be solitary but enjoying the bliss of union. Instead of attacking Shankara with polemics, he could have expanded Shankara's non-dualism much in the way that Schuon speaks of a relative absolute. Nonetheless, he is revered as a saint and one must concede that his way of devotion has its providential necessity in the economy of spiritual means God grants men.

374

tionship between the two, religious devotionalism—which in principle should promote an attitude of holiness before the presence of the sacred—must find a formula whereby God's supremacy is not somehow diminished by His contact with man. This has led to all kinds of pious exaggerations and dialectical contortionism. Thus, in its zeal for reverence, devotionalism might be tempted to compare God's relationship with man with something like that, *mutatis mutandis*, between man and, let us say, an ant—though that analogy, from the standpoint of a fanatical humilitarianism, may still be granting man for too exalted a station before God. But that such a parallelism would be wrong, aside from the fact that it is unnecessary, results from this: either the relationship between God and man is incommensurable, in which case no analogy can do justice to it without establishing some kind of potentially idolatrous standard of comparability and in which case it becomes superfluous to speak of any possible relationship. Or else, there is a standard, perhaps not of comparability in the strict sense of the term, but of consimilarity along the lines of the theological notion of *homoiousia* which emphasizes a likeness of substance in contradistinction to a likeness of identity,[63] in which case the analogy of the ant becomes ridiculous. According to the perspective of *homoiousia*, if God is sound then man would be echo; if God is fire, man is spark; if God is the ocean, man would be a wave or a ripple; and so on and so forth.

The point is that if man is created in the image of God (*Atmaswarupa*), then it is not false to say that God takes an interest in man who is, in Hinduism, *rajaputravat*, "like the king's son," whence, in Christianity, the image of God as the Father, an image whose richness of symbolism serves

---

63. From the Greek *homoiousios* (of like substance) and not *homoousios* (of the same substance).

as a model for the relationship between God and His creation. However, this bond between Heaven and earth is hardly unconditional; the key here lies in the possibility of likeness because creation is also *anomoios* or unlike the Principle in every practical respect, which entails a rupture of this original bond at some level or to some degree or another. Now love, and its concomitant of compassion and charity, can only operate on the basis of this underlying principle of unity, for to love is properly to make whole again. At the same time, it must be discerning because no love, however strong, can pretend to repair the breach between Heaven and earth outwardly; it can do so only inwardly.

THE SAGE CARRIES the whole universe and all its creatures in his bosom. Within his body "wander the sun and the moon, the cause of creation and destruction," we read in the *Shiva Samhita* (2:3). Thus he is silent and unapproachable from the profane outside. The world is redeemed through his perfect act of detachment—proof of his selflessness. And it is this selflessness that is the leaven whereby the world is renewed daily and at all hours. Hence, it is not he who does not love but the creatures, insofar as they are congealed in their egoity, that forfeit the boundlessness of his invisible love. Far from being divergent, these two tendencies—that of inwardness and of withdrawal and that of the gift of oneself—are complementary because there can be no communication, or communion for that matter, without integrity (or integrality) which derives from the capacity to be true to oneself. And to be true to oneself, one cannot stoop to a common average. It is through the depth of inwardness, whose root joins being as such, that one finds one's fellow man in his trans-personal or theomorphic substance. It should be clear that, finally, one cannot meet another person fully, that is to say in depth, outside oneself. Whence

376

the generosity of the sage's inwardness, not an easy paradox to explain, whose outward sign is an impassiveness which engages others to step over their shadow selves.

Moreover, as the embodiment of truth and the center, the sage must remain impassive with regard to the world because to compromise would be to deny his nature or to stray outside of it. Detached, he rests in his own substance and this substance and the world's are finally one in virtue of the metaphysical principle of unity which holds all reality together—a unity that has been broken by man's fall from grace and which is perpetuated by his outwardness, the penalty ensuing upon this fall. In Hindu terms, a stream of virtue pours forth from his heart like a life-giving rain of graces: *dharma megha samadhi* or rain-cloud of virtue and justice, love and discernment. Though the sage remains unaffected by the vicissitudes of man's *samsaric* travails and does not therefore intervene, as an embodiment of light he, by the force of his total existence or by his "dragon power" and "thunder voice,"[64] burns the dross off the souls of men who, mistakenly believing they are dross and not gold, suffer.

More essentially, the sage, whose entire being opens out onto the blessed Infinite surrounding manifestation as a halo of grace, draws the world in the wake of his contemplation back into the blessed substance with which he is united. To recognize him is to love him and to welcome him; and to follow him is to love, welcome, and follow God, it is to remember who we are and to enter into that blessed land of light and warmth, our celestial homeland, where all winter snows melt and where the heart blooms once again and forever in fullness of knowledge and in fullness of being, in the height of truth and in the depth of holiness.

---

64. Cf. Chuang Tsu.

INDEX

consciousness (*Continued*)
    continuum of, 197, 305
    degeneration of, 18
    divine, 16, 112
    dulling of, 92, 140, 250
    immortal, 213
    in lower species, 100
    in non-human realms, 100
    in *prakriti*, 176
    integral, 319
    lack of, 77
    loss of, 201–202
    metaphysical, 173
    miracle of, 16, 263
    molding of, 252
    molecular dimension of, 98
    negative attributes of, 100
    of God, 16, 173
    of the heart, 181, 201
    outwardness of, 242
    overwhelmed by sentiment or passion, 126
    perfect, 202
    restoration of, 86
    scission of, 192
    selfless modalities of, 297
    sense-bound, 298
    separative, 144
    social, 296
    stream of, 115
    subjective, 200
    supra-, 203
    surrender of, 183
    universal, 98
    waking state of, 185
conservative, 12
Consolata, Sister, 164
consolation, 119, 141, 161, 164, 213, 278, 348
    earthly, 194
Constantine, Emperor, 284
Constitution, the
    of the United States of America, 257
contemplation, 19, 52–53, 95, 149, 158, 180, 207, 233, 281, 311, 347, 363–364, 377

"uselessness" of, 347
    and action, 233, 281
    and mortification, 158
    original state of Adamic man, 53
    sacred, 53
contemptus mundi, 116, 156, 336
contingency, 31, 225, 342
contraries
    resolution of, 35
conversion, 74, 160, 162, 261, 287
Coomaraswamy, Ananda, 35, 45, 212, 219–220, 308
coronation, 291
corruption, 140, 248, 253, 271, 281, 306, 312, 334, 352
cosmology, 39, 144, 262, 302
    quantum, 262
cosmos, 17, 27, 45, 59–60, 68, 81, 100, 104, 136, 193, 269, 273, 283, 288–289, 294, 323, 366
    soul as image of the, 366
couple
    the royal, 267
courage, 75, 128, 354
cowardice, 116, 258
craftsmanship, 29
    and machine age, 29
creatio ex nihilo (creation out of nothingness), 222
creation, 16, 23, 27, 29, 32–35, 47, 62, 66, 76, 81, 83, 86, 95, 97, 100, 123, 130–131, 135, 138, 141–143, 145, 152–153, 155, 162, 168, 176–177, 190, 204, 206–207, 210–212, 215–218, 221–223, 228, 230–231, 234, 244, 250, 256, 262–264, 273, 282, 288, 291, 294, 300, 302–303, 310–311, 313, 320, 326, 331, 337, 344, 350–352, 376
    act of, 141, 153
    agony of, 176
    anathematization of, 32, 95
    and God, relationship between, 376
    and joy, 143
    and paradise, 35

good, the (*Continued*)
  roundness of, 328
  victory of, 229
goodness, 26, 48, 57, 82, 102, 121, 132,
    141, 206–207, 233, 248, 258, 265,
    270, 290, 312, 315, 330
  and virility, 265
  as "godness", 26
  corruption of, 248
government, 114, 256–257, 261, 280
  by monarchy, 261
grace, 31, 36–37, 39, 41–42, 47, 50, 53,
    73, 88, 102, 125, 148, 150–151,
    156, 161, 168–169, 196, 205,
    215–216, 221, 224, 226, 237–238,
    263–264, 317, 332, 335, 377
  and collaboration of man, 264
  and misery, 168
  as a poison, 226
  bestowal of, 226
  impersonal nature of, 224
  investiture of divine, 215
  seed of, 151
  turning away from, 332
  withdrawal of, 221
grammar, 145, 209
grandeur, 87, 193–194, 210, 267, 295
  sense of, 193
gratitude, 5, 101, 124, 128
gravity, 52, 86, 140, 143, 146, 149, 172,
    189, 195, 237, 241–242, 352, 360
  body as center of, 241
  celestial, 140
  center of, 86, 189, 195, 241–242
  center of egoic, 86
  collective, 237
Great Spirit, the, 122, 124, 343
greater, the, 80, 87, 106, 123–124, 149,
    152, 218, 350, 370
  notion of, 123
greed, 317, 342
Gregory IX, Pope, 105
Gregory of Nyssa, 317
Gregory the Great, 42, 49–50, 53, 147,
    259, 280, 363–364
Gregory VI, Pope, 283

Gregory VII, Pope, 260
grief, 124, 135, 138, 151, 284
  of separation, 138
guardian angel, 304
Guénon, René, 311, 328
guide
  spiritual, 228
guilt, 44, 134
gunas (in the Sankhya philosophy, the
    three primal tendencies or states
    of existence), 66, 68

Hadewijch, 198, 350
Hallaj, Al, 42
Hamlet, 186
happiness, 44, 104, 132, 135, 138, 140,
    146–147, 249, 274, 286, 318, 325,
    362
  and character, 104
  as essence of man, 135
  of others, 318
  pursuit of, 249
hardship, 131, 150
  as law of existence, 131
harem, 268
harmony, 85, 198
hate, 100, 251, 337–338, 356, 358
  of men, 358
Hatsheput, Queen, 274
hawk, 100, 183, 328
head
  in anatomy, 234
health, 61, 72, 135, 191, 247
  and truth, 72
heart, 8, 13, 22, 27–28, 41, 48, 55, 58,
    60, 62, 64, 66, 69, 72–74, 77–78,
    86, 94, 96, 99, 112, 130, 139, 145,
    148, 150–152, 154, 164–165, 172,
    180–183, 189, 201, 203–205, 211,
    213, 216, 219, 221, 230, 232–233,
    238, 240–243, 245, 251–252, 256,
    272, 283, 286, 288–289, 291, 310,
    317, 319–321, 324, 330–332,
    337–339, 346, 348, 351, 356,
    358–359, 362, 366–367, 377
  and body, 240

and mind, 48, 60, 73, 181, 201,
    240, 242, 338, 366
and mind, polarization of, 27, 58,
    73, 241
and mouth, relationship
    between, 204
and sacred nudity, 252
as center, 310
as container of truth, 48
as jewel, 77
as seat of intellective conscious-
    ness, 181
as seat of will and desire, 182
broken, 164
cleansing of, 204
divine heart and hearth ritual, 96
hardening of, 78, 337
king as spiritual, 289
nature of seen in bodily form,
    321
of man and influx of grace, 148
of man as battlefield, 145
oratory of the, 362
prayer of the, 201, 359
purity of, 346
the noble, 243
unregenerate, 211
wakefulness of, 203
warring desires in, 165
hearth ritual, 96
heat, 102, 148, 216, 251, 289
heaven, 21, 35, 42, 48, 62, 68, 88, 96,
    98, 101, 107–108, 134, 137, 145,
    154, 157, 160, 164, 168, 170, 175,
    178, 192, 198, 207, 234, 248, 253,
    257, 259, 265, 267–269, 272, 276,
    281, 288, 310, 322, 330–331,
    335–338, 341, 343, 351, 355, 360,
    363, 365, 376
accessibility of, 343
and earth, division between, 281,
    360, 365
and earth, healing of scission
    between, 376
marriage between earth and, 268
receptivity to, 351
society's pact with, 266

Hegel, 251, 271–272, 285
hell, 87, 107, 128, 134, 139, 152, 168,
    242, 262, 268, 278, 322, 342, 348
descent of Christ into, 348
non-eternity of, 348
Henry IV, Holy Roman Emperor, 283
Heraclitus, 315
heredity, 340
heresy, 33, 38, 42, 107, 110, 254
hermaphroditism. See androgyny
hermeneutics, 37
Hermes, 54, 62, 338
hermit, 236, 257, 346, 356, 359, 366
hero, 93, 162, 210, 236–237, 277, 286,
    325, 333, 349
heroism, 106, 123, 152, 154, 158, 200,
    267, 297, 363
hierarchy, 119, 121, 218, 236–237,
    243–244, 246–247, 270–271, 273
and equality, 270
moral, 119
rejected by relativist, 121
hierogamos (sacred wedding), 267
Hilton, Walter, 150
Hinduism, 45, 77, 132, 155, 187, 209,
    212, 279, 289, 294, 358, 375
history, 270–272
Hobbes, 204, 289
holiness, 50, 67, 83, 87, 152, 166, 354,
    366, 375, 377
as wholeness, 50, 166
wager of, 152
Holy Ghost, the, 41, 67, 77–78, 302,
    360. See also Spirit, nous, logos
sin against, 67, 77, 360
Holy Spirit, See Holy Ghost
homeostasis, 45, 127
of the soul, 45
Homer, 215
homo carnalis, 53. See also flesh, the
homo politicus, 271
homo sapiens, 49, 180, 248
homoiousia (of like substance), 375
homonia (concord),270. See also broth-
    erhood of man

homoousios (of the same substance), 375
honesty, 128, 174, 249
  forged by pain, 174
honor, 93, 244, 258
hope, 13, 23, 75, 135, 145, 243, 274, 324, 336–337
horizontal, the, 92, 102, 169, 183, 281, 293
horizontality
  of animals, 150
horoscope, 309
Horus (Egyptian sun-god depicted with falcon head. analogous with the Logos), 250, 279, 289
hubris, 134
Hujwiri, 158
human
  infra-, the, 193
human state, the, 88, 130, 140, 162, 369
humanism, 72, 76, 108, 117, 119, 128, 271, 275, 333, 348
humanity
  Edenic, 230
  religion of, 287
Hume, 20, 58, 184, 240, 250
humiliation, 157, 161, 283, 308
humilitarianism, 43, 95, 335, 375
humility, 43, 57, 65, 67, 75, 79, 91, 98, 100, 116, 123, 158, 161, 168, 207, 322, 333, 335, 357, 359–360
  and the rabbit, 100
  crown of, 360
  false, 333
  self-righteous, 91
hummingbird, 330
hunger, 157–158, 285
hunting, 99, 123–124, 331
  nomadic hunting cultures, 99, 123–124
Huxley, Aldous, 193
hyena, 121
hyle (corporeal body), 250
hylic, the, 68
Hypatia, 41

hypocrisy, 106, 123, 132, 151, 158, 165, 208
hypostasis, 217

Ibn Ata illah, 55
ice, 216
iconoclasm, 108
ideal
  absolute, 260
  secular, 158
idealism, 21, 23, 25, 32–33, 35, 67, 81, 116, 118, 126, 151, 260, 282, 297, 335–336, 340
  humanistic, 118, 335
  monastic, 340
  of the relativist, 118
  rejection of, 81
ideas, 15, 30, 46, 61, 65, 82, 187, 196–197, 199, 210, 240, 268, 272, 288, 297, 305, 314
  in the mind of God, 305
  innate, 61, 65, 84, 136, 240, 335, 360
Ideas, the divine, 30. *See also* archetypes
ideé fixe, 127
identity, 18, 49, 51–52, 60–61, 77, 86, 88, 95, 100, 104, 135, 168, 187, 192, 196, 210, 244, 291, 306, 316, 323, 326, 353–354, 365, 374–375
  and difference, 326
  and formal shape, 104
  as basis of knowledge, 51–52
  consciousness of, 187
  mistaken, 49, 354
  principle of, 61, 244
  root, 49, 61, 88, 374
  sense of, 316, 323
  spiritual path of, 374
  theomorphic, 135, 168
  universal, 306
  with ignorance, 77
  with the One Self, 374
  with the vertical, 196
idolatry, 34, 125, 300–301
Ignatius of Antioch, St., 97

Manu (in Vedic Hinduism, original
    man as lawgiver), 234
manvantara (in Hinduism, cycle of
    four ages), 146
maqam (in Sufism, spiritual station),
    284
Mara (personnification of evil in
    Buddhism/Hinduism), 351
Marcus Aurelius, 159
Marduk (chief god of the Babylonean
    pantheon), 143
marga (spiritual path), 156, 158, 161
Marillac, Louise de, 362
Maritain, Jacques, 192
Marpa, 346
marriage
    between heaven and earth,
        267–268
    sacred, 267
martyr, 52
marvelous, the, 32
Mary, *See* Virgin, Blessed
Mary and Martha, 363–364
masculine, 92, 192
masochism, 159
mass, 42, 162, 245, 255, 258, 299, 308,
    320–321
    and centrality, 321
    realm of, 299
masses, the, 114, 237, 245–47
    rule of, 114, 245
    vulgar, 37, 81
master, spiritual, 166, 227, 229
materialism, 33, 249, 265, 339
    dialectical (Communism), 339
mathematics, 12, 86
    Pythagorean, 86, 245, 308
matter, 12, 17, 22, 28–32, 35, 41–42, 48,
    61, 67–71, 78, 81, 83, 94, 96, 98,
    107, 109, 112–114, 116, 118, 133,
    148–149, 163, 174, 182, 189, 192,
    197, 203, 206, 227, 233, 235, 238,
    244, 247, 250, 252–253, 257, 262,
    296, 298–299, 301, 304, 318, 321,
    330, 333, 335, 339, 342, 345, 347,
    367, 376
    and notion of reality, 30

and spirit, 28, 149, 174
as born from the spirit, 29
as eternal, 30
as evil, 107
as projection of the pole sub-
    stance, 192
corruptibility of, 192
dark, 299
divorced from spirit, 299
indestructibility of, 36
origin of, 299
primal, 367
sacred, 298
static and dynamic dimensions
    of, 300
supra-natural essence of, 31
totalitarian thralldom of, 17
Maya (the cosmic illusion), 64, 68,
    125, 145, 166, 197–198, 212, 217,
    228, 368
McGinn, Bernard, 50, 139, 205, 272,
    317, 363
meditation
    as the activity of the Gods, 82
megalomania, 274
Meiji period, the, 289
memory, 5, 18, 58, 64, 319, 330
Mencius, 151
mens carnalis (the sensual or lower
    mind), 241
mentalism, 127, 241
mercantilism, 267
mercy, 27, 92, 102, 105, 126, 133, 137,
    141, 144, 151, 153, 157, 176–177,
    192, 228, 232, 258, 262, 269–270,
    280, 290, 332, 337, 343–345, 348,
    351, 353, 368–370
    and justice, 102, 228, 290
    as knowledge and discernment,
        370
    external and intrinsic, 345
    immanence of, 348
    limits of, 348
merit, 39, 44–45, 76, 91, 112, 122–123,
    125, 130, 133, 136, 158–159, 187,
    210, 224, 256, 271, 273, 280, 341,
    345, 363, 369

pantheism, 222, 313, 316
papacy, 42
Parabrahma (God as Supra-Being),
133, 176. *See also* Brahma
paradise, 35, 44, 62, 97, 105, 138, 141,
153, 176, 206, 258, 309, 322, 334
exile from, 136
souls in, 322
paragon, 21, 161, 237, 246, 267, 272,
286
Paramatma, 242. *See Parabrahma*
Parmenides of Elea, 72
parricide, 142
part, the
as opposed to the whole, 17, 59,
77–78, 84, 101, 110, 224, 249,
274, 283, 300, 311, 367
parthogenesis (lit. "virgin" birth), 20
Pascal, 278, 295
passion, 36, 74, 79, 106, 109, 125–127,
134, 149, 156, 172, 188, 207, 297,
337–338
age of, 207
and egotism, 127
and emotion, 127
displacing intelligence, 125
passivity, 137, 205, 300
Patanjali, 183
paternity
divine, 270. *See also* God as
Father
of Creator and man, 291
path
spiritual, the, 49, 162, 166, 205,
357
Path of Light, 84
Path of Smoke, 84
path, spiritual, 166
patience, 148, 167–169, 343, 357, 370
Patrick, St., 264
Paul, St., 226, 310
peace, 42, 85, 101, 113, 124, 146, 148,
152, 231, 255–259, 269, 277–278,
310, 316, 336, 350
absolute, 255
of disbeliever, 148
secular, 258
secured by the sword, 257

Pedro Claver, San, 158
penitence, 157, 344, 353
Penn, William, 256
people, the, 43, 88, 140, 215, 217, 244,
246–247, 264, 272, 280, 360
as God, 272. *See also* vox populi
perfection, 21, 95, 106, 119, 121, 150,
191, 199, 215, 230, 243, 255, 260,
346–347, 374
degrees of, 215
of God, 95
rejection of, 119, 121
universal, 95
periphery, the, 86, 95, 124, 141, 164,
190, 302, 306, 309, 326
Perry, Clara Ines, 95
Perry, Whitall N., 162, 206
persecution, 105, 110
personal, the, 87, 185, 223
perversion, 276
Peter the Great, Czar, 283
pharaoh, 102, 232, 235, 267, 269, 272,
277, 279–280, 289, 339
phenomena, 13, 57, 64, 84, 96–97,
102–103, 111, 140, 143, 166–167,
184–185, 187–188, 197, 207, 214,
350, 372, 374
as coagulated modes of consciousness, 64
cosmic, 143
imperfection of, 140
metaphysical transparency of,
207, 214, 350
nothingness of, 166
privative, 96
sacred, 111
trace of archetype in earthly, 84
voidness of, 103
philanthropia (love of man), 345, 362
philosopher king, 336
philosopher's stone, the, 148
philosophers, 30, 36, 58, 169, 294, 314
materialist, 58
nominalist, 30
philosophy, 12, 20, 25, 27, 29–30,
36–40, 50, 66, 68, 103, 118, 138,
174, 250, 256, 304, 309, 367

and man, 22–23, 70, 230
and man, difference between, 22,
    167
and spiritual realization, 167
as embodiment of wisdom, 266
as Eve and as Mary, 301
debasement of, 22
shrouding of, 353
wonderment, 29, 101, 309
    as the beginning of philosophy,
        29
word, 19, 22, 183–184, 188–189, 201,
    204–206, 208, 210–211
    conjurative magic of, 183, 188
    conjurative power of, 208
    derivation from reality of a, 210
    idle, 186
    integrity of, 208
    keeping one's word, 189
    original, the, 19, 208, 210
Word, the, 19, 22, 26, 36, 64, 80, 93,
    145, 184, 188, 201, 204, 230, 235,
    266, 274, 279, 295, 337
    as *sapientia creatrix* and as *sapien-
        tia creata*, 230
    God as, 204
    made flesh, 230
    original, 19, 208, 210
word-being
    complex, the, 184
words, 19, 20, 22, 55, 76, 88, 144–145,
    188, 204, 208, 210
    and mouth, 204
    as engendering a reality, 210
    coining of, 144, 210
    emasculation of, 208
    etymology of, 145
    from the mouth of God, 76
    midwifery of, 22
    molding influence of, 188
    slang, 210
Wordsworth, 17, 29
world, the, 11, 15, 30–31, 34, 84, 93,
    100, 110, 119, 124, 127, 129–130,
    132, 135, 139–140, 142, 146–148,

151, 160–161, 163, 172, 182–185,
189, 195, 198, 201–202, 211–212,
217, 223, 231, 246, 250, 256–258,
260, 269, 272–273, 286, 289, 291,
296–297, 306, 311–313, 316, 325,
338–342, 345–351, 362, 365–368,
370–372, 376–377
    apparent reality of, 371
    appetitive, 205
    as actualization of Platonic *ideos*,
        182
    as evil, 313
    as outwardness, 132
    balance of, 289
    center of, 100
    concern for, 351
    consciousness of, 202
    creation of, 231, 273
    degeneration of, 84
    Deist notion of, 223
    detachment from, 351
    difference between creation and
        the, 132
    divine agency of, 30
    engagement in, 338, 351
    eternity of, 313
    false divinization of, 119
    fruit of urge to multiplicity, 142
    history of the modern, 365
    imperfection of, 284
    issued from divine thought, 297
    materiality of, 296
    modern, 255, 287, 328, 365
    and religion, 287
    negation of, 148
    nothingness of, 371
    overcoming, 286
    psychic, 240
    redemption of, 376–377
    reformation of, 260
    renewing of, 376
    renunciation of, 346
    restoration of, 129
    shaped on the form of God, 201
    sustained by God's awareness,
        142

433